PENGUIN BOOKS

The Bus Stop Killer

The Bus Stop Killer

GEOFFREY WANSELL

PENGUIN BOOKS

PENGUIN BOOKS

Published by the Penguin Group
Penguin Books Ltd, 80 Strand, London WC2R ORL, England
Penguin Group (USA) Inc., 375 Hudson Street, New York, New York 10014, USA
Penguin Group (Canada), 90 Eglinton Avenue East, Suite 700, Toronto, Ontario, Canada M4P 2Y3
(a division of Pearson Penguin Canada Inc.)
Penguin Ireland, 25 St Stephen's Green, Dublin 2, Ireland (a division of Penguin Books Ltd)
Penguin Group (Australia), 250 Camberwell Road, Camberwell, Victoria 3124, Australia
(a division of Pearson Australia Group Pty Ltd)
Penguin Books India Pvt Ltd, 11 Community Centre, Panchsheel Park, New Delhi – 110 017, India
Penguin Group (NZ), 67 Apollo Drive, Rosedale, Auckland 0632, New Zealand
(a division of Pearson New Zealand Ltd)
Penguin Books (South Africa) (Pty) Ltd, 24 Sturdee Avenue,
Rosebank, Johannesburg 2196, South Africa

Penguin Books Ltd, Registered Offices: 80 Strand, London WC2R ORL, England

www.penguin.com

First published 2011
1

Copyright © Geoffrey Wansell, 2011

Set in 12.5/14.75 pt Garamond MT
Typeset by Jouve (UK), Milton Keynes
Printed in Great Britain by Clays Ltd, St Ives plc

A CIP catalogue record for this book is available from the British Library

ISBN: 978–0–241–95281–8

www.greenpenguin.co.uk

MIX
Paper from
responsible sources
FSC™ C018179

Penguin Books is committed to a sustainable
future for our business, our readers and our
planet. This book is made from paper certified
by the Forest Stewardship Council.

For Tom and Veronica,
Leaf, Michael and Andrew
who believed in me

Contents

Illustrations

Amélie's parents, Jean-François and Dominique Delagrange (Peter Macdiarmid/Getty Images)

Amélie's parents lay floral tributes (Alessandro Abbonizio/Getty Images)

Milly Dowler had her whole life ahead of her

Milly got off the train one stop early

Leaving school the day she was kidnapped

A nationwide search followed Milly's disappearance (Oli Scarff/Getty Images)

It was six months after Milly went missing that her body was found (Barry Phillips/*Evening Standard*/Rex Features)

Milly's father, sister and mother walk behind her coffin (Michael Dunlea/Rex Features)

A court drawing of Levi Bellfield in the dock (Elizabeth Cook)

Milly's father Bob Dowler reads a statement outside the Old Bailey (Carl Court/AFP/Getty Images)

Prologue: Death's Shadow

'The soul of a murderer is blind.'
Albert Camus, *The Outsider*

The scene is a warm Thursday evening in August 2004, and dusk is falling gently across the shops and bars of Twickenham's London Road, just half a mile south of the famous rugby stadium. The bright lights from the pubs and clubs on both sides of the busy street are gradually beginning to illuminate the pavements outside the Waitrose supermarket and the railway station that lie at the heart of this comfortable, leafy west London suburb.

On the patio outside Crystalz wine bar, just beside the police station, sits an attractive twenty-two-year-old French girl, just 5 feet 4 inches in height, 9 stone in weight, and with collar-length blonde hair, who is drinking a glass of white wine with three of her girlfriends. Her name is Amélie Delagrange, and she's wearing white linen trousers, a low-cut red vest and a white cardigan. There is a broad smile on Amélie's face, for she's enjoying being back in London after some time in France and working in a café and patisserie in the eminently respectable middle-class suburb of nearby Richmond. The group of girls are laughing and telling each other how this part of west London is a 'very safe' place to live.

What they do not know, however, is that it is to prove exactly the opposite for this vivacious, charming young French girl – for within an hour she will be killed by a complete stranger.

Amélie was born on the outskirts of Paris in February 1982. Her parents, Jean-François and Dominique, named her after her grandmother. Amélie's father was an architect who had built the family a house in the Picardy countryside in northern France when she was a girl, where she had been brought her up alongside her elder sister, Virginie. Balanced, enthusiastic and eminently sensible, she had decided to come back to England to improve her English still further and she had even recently found a new boyfriend, Olivier, who worked with her in the patisserie.

Just after 9.30, with the light finally fading, and a chill starting to make the patio feel a little less welcoming, Amélie Delagrange starts to leave. She throws her handbag over her shoulder, collects the Next carrier bag that she's brought with her, containing a new top she had bought that day, and gets up. She's had three, perhaps four, glasses of white wine, she can't quite remember, and is just a little unsteady on her feet, but that doesn't worry her for a moment. With a grin she tells one of her French girlfriends, Floriane, that she's 'a little bit drunk', and asks another of the group, Vanessa, if she would mind walking her across the road to the bus stop to wait for the R267 red double-decker that will take her the short distance home to the room that she's been renting for the past few months in a street just north of Twickenham Green. Her bus duly arrives at 9.39, and from across the street her friends watch her get on and wave goodbye. It is the last time that they will see her alive.

Amélie's good mood, helped a little by the white wine, means that she overshoots the right bus stop for her home – perhaps she dozed off for a moment or two – but, undismayed, she gets to her feet to speak to the driver, to check if she has indeed missed it. He tells her she has, but then explains that if she waits for a moment she'll be at the end of the bus's route and she can walk the half mile or so back towards Twickenham Green and home.

Hardly any time has passed – barely five minutes since she waved goodbye to her friends outside Crystalz – when the double-decker's CCTV security cameras show her getting off outside the Fulwell Bus Garage on Hampton Road. For a moment, she isn't quite sure which way to go and stops to look at the map on the bus stop to get her bearings. That only takes a moment, and within seconds Amélie starts to walk towards the Green.

The walk takes Amélie just a quarter of an hour, and lots of people see the young French girl making her way northwards. She passes the Prince of Wales pub, where one drinker sitting alone at the bar notices her looking 'a little unsteady on her feet', while a lady parking outside her home sees her checking her route at another bus stop to make sure she's still going the right way. She is even captured on the in-car video system of a police car that drives past her.

Finally, just after 10 o'clock on that warm August evening, Amélie crosses Hampton Road and walks on to the south-western tip of the triangular Twickenham Green, which boasts a handsome white cricket pavilion and a cricket pitch, and slips into the dark shadows of the trees that shelter the Green on its edge. There are no cricketers at this time of night, no sounds of white-flannelled players congratulating one another after an evening game as they prepare to walk across to the pub to celebrate or drown sorrows. There is just a cloying darkness – the street lights don't reach far on to the Green itself. Unconcerned, Amélie walks quickly past the rope that protects the cricket square towards the lights of the shops and wine bars on the far side and home.

It could hardly be a more English scene: a cricket pavilion surrounded by leafy suburban roads and comfortable middle-class villas on the western outskirts of London. Twickenham doesn't boast the alleyways and runnels of Dickens's east London, haunt of Jack the Ripper; nor the red lights of the backstreet terraces of Leeds, where the Ripper's Yorkshire namesake took his victims. This is affluent, unthreatening, comfortable suburbia. That makes not a jot of difference. Amélie could just as well have been in Whitechapel on those terrible nights in the summer and autumn of 1888 when Jack eviscerated his five victims, because just moments after she starts to walk around the cricket pitch and across the Green a family in a nearby street hear a plaintive scream in the stillness of that evening – 'a ten-second shout rather than a cry for help', they remember later.

Amélie was not alone on Twickenham Green that evening. Men were walking their dogs, stubbing out their cigarettes behind the white cricket sightscreens, hurrying towards the Indian restaurant and the wine bar on the north side to join friends, but no one stopped when that scream went up, no one turned a hair, or called a police-man. No one spotted a threatening man in the shadows, no one saw a hooded figure bent on violence, or a tramp begging for money for food, drink, or drugs. No one saw anything. It was simply an ordinary summer's evening in west London – and yet into that utterly commonplace set-ting someone injected a brutal murder.

Amélie Delagrange never reached the far side of the Green and home. She died, alone, in the shadow of the cricket pavilion, murdered for no apparent reason.

Shortly after 10.15, with the shadows now deep and dark, student Tristram Beasley-Suffolk was walking across the Green, 'taking a breath of air from his studies', when he saw what he thought was some white plastic sheet-ing lying on the ground on the edge of the cricket square. But as he got closer he realized, to his horror, it was a person.

Amélie was face-down on the grass with her right arm underneath her and her legs bent up towards her chest in what was almost the foetal position. She was breathing, but only just: she had been hit viciously on the head with a heavy blunt instrument – not once but several times. Tristram did what he could to make her comfortable and ran across the Green to ask the local wine bar to call an ambulance.

The paramedics arrived at 10.31 and rushed the severely injured young woman to the local west London hospital, but Amélie's life couldn't be saved. She was pronounced dead at two minutes after midnight on that same August night, in the first hour of Friday, 20 August 2004.

Amélie's handbag and mobile phone weren't there when

she was found, which made it difficult for the first police officers on the scene to identify her – until in the end they did so by calling two mobile numbers they found on a piece of paper in her Next shopping bag, one of which was her boyfriend's.

For a moment the police considered that Amélie's death might have been a mugging that had gone tragically wrong, but within a few hours they realized that this was no robbery. There was no motive for the attack. This pretty, unassuming French girl had no enemies. No scorned lover stalked her every move, no crazed maniac had targeted her, no threats had ever been made towards her. It was that rarest of all modern murders – a blitz attack on a complete stranger by someone who has no relationship whatever with the victim. She had been battered ruthlessly on the head from behind without the slightest warning. It was murder most foul – by someone who killed for pleasure.

The scene changes, to a chill night in February 2003, just eighteen months earlier. And once again there is a young blonde woman – this time just nineteen years of age – getting off a bus in the leafy west London suburb of Hampton, not far from Twickenham Green.

Marsha McDonnell is just over 5 feet 5 inches and a little over 9 stone, and she's working during her gap year between school and university at a gift shop in the Bentall Centre in Kingston. One of four children, she lives with her parents, Philip and Ute, in a neat semi-detached house in Hampton, about five minutes walk from the local railway station.

It is just after five o'clock on this particular Monday evening, 3 February 2003, and after work Marsha is going to meet two girlfriends in a local bar to discuss what they are going to do that evening. In the end they decide to go a late showing of Steven Spielberg's new film, *Catch Me If You Can*, starring Leonardo DiCaprio and Tom Hanks, which tells the story of con-man Frank Abagnale, Jr, who conned millions' worth of cheques out of unsuspecting victims before he reached the age of nineteen by posing as an airline pilot, a doctor and a lawyer.

The movie ends at about 11.45, and Marsha and her friends walk to the bus stops in central Kingston to catch their buses home. Her friends are going in the opposite direction and say goodbye, while Marsha waits for the red double-decker number 111 to take her back to her parents' house in Priory Road. She is wearing a pair of black trousers, black V-neck top and white trainers underneath a full-length black coat with a hood that has fur trimming, and her shoulder bag is slung over her left shoulder. The bus arrives at 12.07, and Marsha goes to sit at the back of the lower deck. What she doesn't realize is that this makes her all too visible to anyone who might be passing the bus and surveying the passengers. It's a dark night, and the bright lights on the double-decker make the eight passengers clear to anyone in the world outside. But Marsha isn't thinking about that as the number 111 makes its way through the gentle suburbs of west London.

It's a short journey, and it's just seventeen minutes after midnight on that February evening when Marsha gets off at the stop in Percy Road, just round the corner from her parents' house. She's made the journey hundreds of times,

7

and she thinks nothing of it as she turns left as she gets off the bus and then right into Priory Road towards her home at number 88.

But Marsha McDonnell never gets there. Shortly before 12.20 she is attacked without warning outside number 60 Priory Road, barely a hundred yards from her own front door. She is battered repeatedly on the head from behind by a blunt instrument and left for dead on the pavement of this leafy respectable little road, just yards from a local primary school.

Number 60 is the home of David and Bernadette Fuller, and it was Mr Fuller who called the police at 12.23 that morning after he had been woken up by what he thought was a 'loud thud' and the sound of a car door closing. Originally he had got up and looked out of the window to see what had made the noise, but, as he couldn't see anything, he had climbed back into bed. Moments later, however, Mr Fuller heard what sounded like a 'long continuous moan' from outside his house, and when he looked out again from his first-floor bedroom window he saw what he thought was blood on the pavement. Now very worried indeed, he woke up his wife, and they both went outside to investigate.

The Fullers found Marsha McDonnell lying face-down close to the gate to their front garden in a pool of blood that was seeping from a deep wound in her head. Her right arm was slightly above her head, and her left arm was bent underneath her body, with her shoulder bag caught in the crease of her elbow. Her blue eyes were shut, and she was groaning quietly, but she wasn't moving.

David Fuller rushed inside to call an ambulance, and

the paramedics arrived in minutes, just after 12.30 on what was now a distinctly cold Tuesday morning in February. But by now Marsha was demonstrating all the symptoms of a severe head injury – her breathing was growing noisier and noisier by the second. The paramedics didn't delay. They rushed her to the Accident and Emergency department of the nearby Kingston hospital, but – in spite of the doctors' efforts and intensive care over the next forty hours – Marsha McDonnell died at 4.41 p.m. the following day, Wednesday, 5 February 2003.

The pathologist later reported that Marsha's death was the result of no fewer than three heavy impacts to the skull caused by a blunt weapon – possibly a 'lump' hammer. The blows almost certainly took her completely by surprise, for there were no defensive wounds on her hands. She had been killed by someone who had hit her over the head three times in quick succession, not allowing her any chance whatever to protect herself.

Once again it was a blitz attack on an unsuspecting victim by a total stranger. Marsha had no enemies, no angry boyfriend or outraged stalker, no outstanding arguments about anything with anyone at all. She was a well-adjusted happy young woman, with a job she liked and a future she was looking forward to. Marsha wasn't a drug addict living on the edge of society, prey to other addicts out of their minds on heroin or crack cocaine; she hadn't even had a drink that evening – no alcohol or drugs were found in her bloodstream. And this was no robbery. She was still clinging to her handbag when David Fuller and his wife found her.

Like Amélie Delagrange, Marsha was the victim of a

brutal, violent motiveless crime, a murder committed by someone who was most definitely killing for pleasure.

The scene changes for a third time, this time to a busy road outside the railway station in Walton-on-Thames, another leafy area of suburban south-west London, only a few miles from Hampton and Twickenham Green. It is just after 4 o'clock on the sunny afternoon of 21 March 2002, and thirteen-year-old Amanda Dowler, known to her friends as Milly, is walking back from the station to her parents' home in Hersham about half a mile away. Milly is a bright, vivacious girl, with a cheeky smile, who likes pop concerts and playing the saxophone. Her mother, Sally, teaches at her school, while her father, Bob, is a computer consultant. Milly's elder sister, Gemma, who is sixteen, goes to the same school as she does, Heathside, in Weybridge. In fact, Milly always goes to school in the morning with her sister and mother, but they like to stay on after the school day, while Milly prefers to get home.

On this particular damp March afternoon she has caught the 15.26 train from Weybridge, but decides to stop off at Walton-on-Thames station with a group of friends for chips in the station café. It will mean she'll have to walk the 800 yards or so home, rather than staying on the train to her own station, but she doesn't mind a bit. It's not something she does very often, but it is perfectly normal, and Milly doesn't give it a second thought.

She's wearing the familiar dark-blue blazer and grey skirt that make up her school uniform, though she's taken her pullover off because the drizzly rain has made it feel a bit warmer than she expected when she set off for school that morning.

Not long after 3.45 Milly borrows one of her friends' mobile phones to call her father to tell him she'll be home in about fifteen minutes. She then stays just a little longer than she plans to, but at about five minutes past four she sets off to walk home down Station Road. A few minutes later, at 4.08, she passes a bus stop, where one of her school friends is waiting. The girls acknowledge one another, and Milly continues her walk down Station Road, past the Bird's Eye factory.

Once again, it's a perfectly ordinary day in a respectable suburb of south-west London. Mothers are bringing their children back from school; businessmen are coming home a little early after meetings in the City; the television in the pub opposite the station is showing a repeat of a football match; and the taxi firm which works out of the station building is busy, with cars parked outside waiting for work.

But, as Milly's friend turns to get on to a single-decker blue bus to take her home, the fresh-faced thirteen-year-old blonde schoolgirl walking away from her on the opposite side of the road disappears into thin air.

In the days and weeks that follow Surrey police mount the biggest missing persons' inquiry in their history – codenamed Operation Ruby – in a desperate attempt to find this home-loving schoolgirl with a winning smile, but they fail, conspicuously. The police find no sign of her Nokia mobile phone – she had run out of credit, which is why she had used a friend's to call her father – no sign of her dark-blue Marks and Spencer blazer or her short grey skirt, no sign of her clumpy black shoes with their thick high heels, no sign of her blouse or her light blue jumper, no sign of her black-and-white Jansport rucksack or her purse with its Ace of Hearts design. No trace of her whatever.

What remains of Milly Dowler will not be discovered for six whole months, and even then there is only a skeleton that has to be identified from dental records. There are no clothes, no rucksack, no purse, nothing whatever when she is finally discovered again – except her bones.

The question that baffles the police, her distressed parents and the rest of the world is simply: why? Who on earth would want to harm a vivacious, well-liked schoolgirl innocently making her way home from school on an ordinary afternoon in suburban Surrey?

The answer would shock the world.

The scene changes for the final time, and brings us to the central character in this contemporary tragedy.

Once again it is dark, but this time we are under the flashing neon lights of a brash nightclub called Royales on Uxbridge High Street, another upright suburb west of London at the end of the Piccadilly and Metropolitan Underground lines and about four miles north of Heathrow airport. Indeed, it's not all that far from Twickenham and Hampton, providing you have a car.

It's a cold February night in 2001, and a crowd of young people are waiting in a line outside to get in to the club. Barring their entry is a vast man – more than 20 stone in weight, a little over 6 feet 1 inch tall, and sporting a gold ear-ring in each ear. His hair is cropped close, which makes it look as though his head is too small for the vast body beneath – as if it's been added as an afterthought.

His dark-brown eyes are as dead and cold as a landed trout's, but there's a glacial smirk on his face as he eyes the young women dressed in the shortest of skirts and skimpiest of tops shivering in front of him. For the bouncer knows full well that most of the girls waiting to get into the club just round the corner from the RAF base at Uxbridge are there to meet a man – if not for life then certainly for the night. This certainly isn't Mahiki in London's Mayfair, haunt of young royals and the offspring of the super-rich. This is a local nightclub which trades on being local, and non-judgemental. The boys are dressed in Ben Sherman shirts to match the girl's Primark dresses. It may not be every parent's dream, but it's a place where girls go to dance, meet boys and let their hair down. Drugs may be available, and fights can break out from time to time, but it's the prospect of sex that draws the crowd. 'Any muppet can pull there,' one regular told a local website not long ago. 'It's got sticky carpet, smells of cheesy feet, and you're guaranteed to get three fights a night, especially if any of the boys in uniform are in.' The truth is that there is always the scent of imminent sex in the air, and the doorman knows it. In fact he relishes it. To the muscular man on the door, Royales is paradise.

'You're all here to get laid,' he tells the girls in the queue in front of him, his high-pitched voice with its London accent squeaking in the night air. 'You should give me a try,' he murmurs. 'You don't know what you're missing.'

The girls standing in front of him in their low-cut tops and scanty dresses giggle on cue. As they do so the doorman's eyes gleam like an urban fox's caught in the headlights of a car.

The doorman's name is Levi Bellfield, a thirty-three-year-old who has spent his life in west London and who is known to almost every girl in front of him as a 'bit of a Jack the Lad'. Rumour has it in the queue in front of Royales that he's also been known to provide drugs for anyone who might be interested, be it a tablet or two of ecstasy, cannabis – always known in the club as 'puff' – or even cocaine. Those are only rumours. What is not in doubt is Bellfield's appetite for sex. 'He used to hit on some girl every single night,' one of his conquests from the queue explained later. 'I used to watch him. They were young girls, some of them probably fifteen, sixteen. There used to be a room at the top of Royales, and he used to boast about it. There was a grotty sofa in this room, and he used to take them all up there.'

Not that his reputation put her off. She became one of his many sexual partners after encountering him in the queue, just like the other girls she saw being ushered upstairs to the room with its grubby sofa.

But the doorman with the easy line in chat and the lascivious grin doesn't restrict his sexual appetite to young women he encounters outside the nightclub. Even though he's living with his partner and their two children, Levi Bellfield uses a number of cars to trawl the neighbourhood at night, looking for possible targets for his sexual appetites: willing young women whom he would later describe as 'slags that were begging for it'.

One of his vehicles is a white Toyota Previa people-carrier that he calls his 'shagging wagon', equipped with blacked-out windows, purple neon lights, a mattress with an orange quilt and – perhaps most significantly of all – handcuffs. In this car Bellfield tours the streets of Hounslow and Hillingdon, West Drayton and Twickenham, Isleworth and Feltham, searching out young women alone at bus stops, or catching a glimpse of them alone on the bus on their way home, intent on stopping them to engage them in a suggestive conversation that might persuade them to join him in his shagging wagon.

To this day no one can say for certain how many girls actually did so, for most of them can't even remember the experience. The reason is clear enough, this giant, pasty-faced man would offer them a can of Red Bull or a Malibu, 'just to get us started', and before they knew it the effects of the date-rape drug GHB would render them defence-less. Some would allege later that he would then rape these poor, unknowing girls, many of them under fifteen, and then offer them as sexual favours to his friends, while others would tell stories that he would even dress his prey up as schoolgirls while they were under the influence of his drugs for the amusement of his mates. But no one ever proved it.

What is not in doubt is that Levi Bellfield was capable of horrific violence towards the young women he stalked at bus stops across west London. Indeed, the police became convinced that he had murdered both Amélie Delagrange and Marsha McDonnell, and may even have abducted and killed the Surrey schoolgirl Milly Dowler. That is why in the early hours of a November morning in 2004 officers from a Metropolitan Police murder squad arrived at his front door to arrest him on suspicion of the murder of

Amélie. It was then that the central character in the tragedy of the lives of these young women took centre stage.

But to understand why we need to travel to a tiny brick built house on the edge of London: the home of Levi Bellfield.

1. Arrest on the Attic Stage

'Cowards die many times before their deaths.'
William Shakespeare, *Julius Caesar*

Little Benty is a tiny, nondescript cul-de-sac of houses in the shadow of the M4 motorway as it passes London's Heathrow airport, a row of brick-built semi-detacheds, with cramped gardens, and a set of garages hidden around the corner. If you are driving east into London, with the airport on your right and just before the spur that takes you to three of the main terminals, you simply wouldn't spot it. It's hidden behind a lush green wedge of trees and overgrown bushes. Negotiating your way there, if you don't know the area, takes concentration and a good map. It seems to exist in the midst of a maze of identical roads on a housing estate that even the locals admit that they find confusing. Even when you find it, you notice that means of escape are everywhere. There's a pedestrian bridge over the motorway right in front of the houses, and a set of lanes to each side that lead in every direction. If you were to choose a place to conceal yourself, Little Benty would be an excellent option. It's a fox's lair – concealed and yet still accessible to the world.

Life in the small group of squat villas that make up Little Benty is all but drowned by the incessant roar of the motorway that sweeps past them twenty-four hours a day, leaving it a downtrodden, unhappy-looking street, a place of broken dreams and rusted cars, with back gardens submerged in old sinks, broken flower pots and cracked glass.

It is here in the early morning hours of Monday, 22 November 2004 that we find Levi Bellfield, the by now thirty-six-year-old muscle-bound nightclub doorman, asleep in a small double bed alongside his current partner, Emma Jane Mills, in the upstairs front room of their cramped three-bedroom house at number 11. The couple's three children, Lucy, who is almost seven, William, five, and baby Georgina, who is just four months, are asleep in the two other bedrooms.

On the surface it is a commonplace scene – a man, his partner and their children, asleep in their home at 3.30 in the morning of a perfectly ordinary night not long before Christmas. But Levi Bellfield is no ordinary man, and this will not turn out to be an ordinary night.

Three miles away in a grey, steel Portakabin in the yard of Hounslow police station more than eighty officers from a double-sized murder squad are being briefed by the senior investigating officer, Detective Chief Inspector Colin Sutton, in the hunt for the murderer of Amélie Delagrange. They are about to launch a series of raids in search of the occupant of 11, Little Benty.

The officers are being told by Sutton, a bluff, smart north Londoner, that the Metropolitan Police's expert surveillance teams – who have been tracking Bellfield's movements night and day for the past twelve days – have identified seven houses and flats across west London where he could be staying that night, but they are pretty convinced that he is actually at Little Benty. That was where the surveillance team had 'put him to bed' just a few hours before.

The teams can't be too careful, however, and so they are going to raid all seven addresses simultaneously, just in case Bellfield has slipped away from Little Benty in the early hours of the morning without the surveillance team noticing. There are, after all, as Sutton explains, 'an awful lot of ways out of Little Benty'.

A mild-looking man in his mid forties with thinning hair and a confident manner, Sutton explains that he wants his seven teams of twelve officers to go to all the addresses to be absolutely sure of getting their man. But he's also decided that the arrest does not demand the presence of armed officers.

'We don't believe he is a danger to the arresting officers,' he tells his squad, 'but you should be careful.'

Sutton became the SIO in charge of the double squad only in the wake of Amélie's murder in August, but after hours of painstaking police work he is absolutely convinced that there is a good reason to believe that Bellfield is the killer.

'It wasn't forensic evidence,' he explains later. 'We didn't have any DNA, or the stuff that makes television shows like *CSI*. We just had masses of CCTV images of Amélie walking up Hampton Road from the bus stop and pictures of this small white van that always seemed to be there.'

It was that white Ford Courier van and the knowledge that it was almost certainly being driven along Hampton Road, and then parked beside Twickenham Green, on the evening of Amélie's death, that persuaded Sutton to organize the surveillance of Bellfield. For it was Levi Bell-field who owned the van and drove it regularly around London as part of the wheel-clamping business that he had started as a sideline to his job as a nightclub bouncer.

After months of detailed work, Sutton's squad had tracked down more than 128,000 white Ford Courier vans, like the one that the CCTV images from the buses travelling past Amélie showed, until they had found that the one in question was almost certainly being driven by Bellfield on that warm August evening earlier that year.

That white Ford Courier van, with the number plate of P610 XCN, was distinctive in many ways. There was its 'sporty' wheel trim, the fact that it appeared to have once had a 'beacon' light on its roof – suggesting it may have been used at an airport – and the fact that its distinct-ive blacked-out rear windows had a small gap at the top which meant someone inside could peer out without being seen. The assembled CCTV footage also revealed that it was being driven that evening by a large, round-faced man who sat forward over the steering wheel in an unusual posture, a man who bore a striking resemblance to their target in the early hours of that Monday morning in November.

DCI Sutton didn't believe Bellfield knew that he had been followed for the past twelve days. He had every faith in the expertise of his surveillance teams – which usually consisted of five cars containing two plain-clothed detec-tives and one officer on a motorcycle.

The surveillance had given the officers on Sutton's squad an insight into the character of the man they were targeting that morning. They had watched Bellfield driving around west London after dark, looking for very young girls. On one occasion he had stopped at a bus stop and talked to two schoolgirls waiting for the bus on the way home. On seeing this, the surveillance team had decided to split up – one group staying with Bellfield and another tracking the two girls – to discover what their target had been saying to them. When the girls got off their bus they were interviewed by members of the surveillance team. The two girls, aged twelve and thirteen, had explained to the team that Bellfield had made a string of sexually suggestive remarks to them.

'I bet you're both virgins,' he had had told them with a grin. 'You certainly look like virgins.' He had then invited them both to get into his car, so they could 'go and have a good time'. 'I bet you're nice and tight,' he had added. 'I like nice tight young girls.' It was a conversation that had convinced the schoolgirls that the last thing they wanted to do was to get into Bellfield's car. But when they had refused, he had called them 'slags' before driving away.

The officers reported the conversations to the murder squad and took formal statements from the two teenagers. It only served to heighten the squad's conviction that they were looking at a particularly unpleasant individual with an unhealthy interest in sex – but they had no idea just how significant that insight was to become.

At that moment the squad were simply trying to arrest a man they believed had attacked and killed a young woman without the slightest hint of provocation.

It was just after 4.30 a.m. when the seven teams of detectives climbed into their cars and vans and left Hounslow police station for the addresses that Bellfield was known to use across west London. They had been carefully instructed to wait for a clear signal from Sutton to go into the houses – he wanted each team to burst in at exactly the same time, 5 o'clock that morning. The SIO himself went with the team to Little Benty.

And so, in the dark hours before dawn, Sutton's team of cars pulled up silently in front of Bellfield's cramped little house. For a moment it seemed as though every officer was holding his breath, until, on the single command of 'Go', they leaped out and rushed at the frail front door with a ram that could break it down in a matter of seconds.

Uniformed officers wearing stab-proof vests and blue helmets with their identification numbers painted in yellow swarmed into the house's narrow hallway, shouting 'Police' at the top of their voices. One group pushed into the sitting room on the left, while another rushed up the stairs in search of the 20-stone nightclub bouncer with a high-pitched voice.

Inevitably, the officers' shouts woke the children, and baby Georgina started crying as they poured into the house. Her mother scooped her youngest up in her arms and appeared at the top of the stairs to ask, 'What on earth is going on?' She then rushed to look after her other two children, who had begun to shout in fear as the officers went from room to room in search of Bellfield, while Emma held her four-month-old in her arms.

'Where is he?' DCI Sutton asked Emma Mills.

'Who?' the twenty-seven-year-old brunette with a pale open face replied angrily.

'You know who – Levi Bellfield.'

The young woman shook her head and said simply, 'He's not here.'

Sutton didn't believe her and told his officers to search every nook and cranny of the house, before turning their attentions to the garden, which one of them later described as 'looking like the yard in the BBC television comedy *Steptoe and Son*'. The search took five minutes and yielded absolutely nothing. In spite of the surveillance, the well-laid plans, the briefing, Bellfield simply wasn't there.

Sutton was furious. 'It was a question of which one of the surveillance team was going to find himself driving a Panda car the next day,' he was to say later. Even more annoyingly, he also discovered that the other six teams had also drawn a blank. None of them had located Bellfield. Their suspect was nowhere to be found.

Exasperated, Sutton decided to launch a search of one or two of the hotels that he knew Bellfield sometimes frequented on the edge of Heathrow airport. There had been reports that he had sometimes taken young women to the Premier Inn and the Ibis hotels that overlooked the runways for sex. It was a long shot, but it was worth a try. Sutton called one of the other teams back from their search and started for the airport perimeter road, leaving one of his most experienced sergeants at Little Benty with the angry Emma Mills and her upset children.

But by nine o'clock that morning, even that extra search had drawn a blank. Bellfield wasn't at any of the airport hotels, and the discovery left Sutton and his team anxious that they had let a man they thought capable of murder slip through their fingers.

'We had lost him and we couldn't understand why,' he

was to say later. 'It was an absolute mystery. The surveillance had been right, he couldn't have known that we were coming, and still we couldn't track him down.'

It was then that old-fashioned police work kicked in again, just as it had done in tracing the suspect white Ford Courier. As Sutton was driving past Heathrow after the futile search for Bellfield, his mobile phone rang. It was the experienced sergeant he had left at Little Benty.

'You won't believe it, guv'nor,' his sergeant told him. 'Bellfield's here. Emma's just told me that he's hiding in the attic.'

Sutton was amazed. 'How did he manage that?'

'Apparently as soon as he heard us at the door he jumped out of bed stark naked, ran out into the hallway, jumped on to a chest of drawers pushed open the trapdoor to the attic, lifted himself up and then shut the trapdoor behind him. It's why we couldn't find him.'

The other reason, of course, was that his partner Emma Mills had told DCI Sutton that Bellfield wasn't there, when he was all the time. The sergeant was a wise old officer, however, and hadn't taken her denial at face value. After his colleagues had left for their futile search of airport hotels, he had had a cup of tea with the young woman and her children in their kitchen and explained to her exactly why they were so anxious to interview the man she had been with for the past nine years.

'When I told her we were looking at him for the death of the young French girl on Twickenham Green she sort of changed her mind,' he told Sutton, 'and whispered that he was hiding in the attic.'

'Whatever you do, don't try to go up there,' Sutton told

his sergeant, mindful of the fact that they were searching for a man they suspected of hitting a woman on the head with a hammer without a moment's compunction, and only too aware that the only way into the attic for his officer was through the trapdoor. 'If you go up there you'll have to stick your head through first,' Sutton told him, 'and I can't take that risk.'

No matter how anxious he may have been to get Bellfield into custody, Sutton wasn't willing to jeopardize the safety of one of his officers. He decided that he was going to get hold of one of the police dog teams that had been allocated to the raids and ask one of the handlers to push open the hatch with his hands and throw his police dog up into the attic to flush Bellfield out. Turning his own car round to go back to Little Benty, Sutton called his dog team and explained what he needed, but no sooner had he done so than his mobile rang again. It was his sergeant.

'Don't worry, guv,' he told him. 'I've got him. He's in custody.'

'How did you manage that?' Sutton asked.

'I got bored with waiting, guv'nor, so I got on to the chest of drawers myself and pushed open the trapdoor and hauled myself up there.'

There was no blow to the head. Indeed, when the sergeant climbed up into the attic, Bellfield was nowhere to be seen. It took the sergeant some time to find him. The giant bouncer had hidden himself underneath the yellow fibreglass roof insulation that was laid between the attic beams and across the ceilings of the bedrooms below. He had completely covered his 20-stone frame with the 2-inch thick material, in a desperate attempt to make sure the police didn't see him even if one of them did take the trouble to poke his head through the trapdoor and look into the attic. After a few minute's searching, however, Sutton's sergeant spotted a large lump in the roof insulation and peeled it back to reveal a distinctly embarrassed Bellfield – naked and noticeably scratching himself after spending four hours under fibreglass.

After reminding him of his rights, the sergeant then accompanied his prisoner back down through the trapdoor. 'You don't know what you're talking about,' Bellfield shouted him in his squeaky, strangely unthreatening voice. 'This is all some kind of terrible mistake. I don't know anything about this woman Amélie, whatever her name is, and I want a lawyer.'

Bellfield's protestations made no difference; he was under arrest in connection with the murder of Amélie Delagrange, and there was no wriggling out of it. But it was only after the officer was confident that the arrest had been correctly carried out under the strict terms of the Police and Criminal Evidence Act that the sergeant allowed Bellfield to find a pair of blue tracksuit bottoms, a white T-shirt and a pair of trainers to wear. Emma Mills had already told him that her partner never wore underwear.

By the time a smiling DCI Sutton arrived back to Little Benty shortly after 9 on what was now a clear, bright November morning, Bellfield was sitting at the kitchen table in handcuffs. Not that he was altogether repentant: almost the first words he uttered to Sutton were: 'I want a lawyer.' Bellfield even named a solicitor in Woking he had in mind. It was someone he had dealt with in the past, and the detective had no alternative but to agree immediately to the request. It was to be the first of a string of delays, obfuscations and refusals to collaborate that Bellfield would inflict on Sutton and his squad in the weeks and months to come. 'I don't know what you're talking about,' he would tell them time after time. It was a barefaced lie, but never once would the truth come from the mouth of the suspect himself.

2. Innumerable Questions

'Hence with denial vain, and coy excuse.'
John Milton, *Lycidas*

In spite of his muscle-bound 20-stone frame; his 19½-inch neck and hands the size of dinner plates, Levi Bellfield didn't look in the least intimidating as he was led from his home at number 11, Little Benty to the waiting police car outside. In place of his customary belligerence there was a look of embarrassed, meek self-pity on his face as a uniformed officer put his hand on the suspect's head and bent him forward into the rear of the red-and-white car with its flashing blue lights.

To the watching neighbours, Bellfield looked pale and drawn as the police car accelerated out of the tangled streets of the estate and down towards the massive roundabouts that make up the spur of the M4 motorway that leads to Heathrow and its terminals. Followed by a second unmarked police car, he was swept down towards the airport at full speed, while in the back Bellfield rocked back and forth on the spot, as he did so often when he was anxious.

Bellfield was not being driven back to Hounslow police station, where the double murder squad had gathered in the morning chill more than six hours earlier; instead he was being taken to the newly constructed fortress of Heathrow police station on the airport's northern perimeter with its view of the departing jet airliners. Heathrow police station is one of the few within the Metropolitan Police area with sufficient security to contain a Category A suspect like Bellfield – that is, someone who is suspected of a major crime like murder. DCI Colin Sutton had arranged with the custody officers at Heathrow that he would bring his prisoner there before he had even set out on the raids to locate him.

White-faced and clearly frightened, the handcuffed Bellfield was helped out of the police car in the Heathrow station's yard and ushered into the custody suite, where he was officially entered as a remand prisoner who had been arrested for, but not charged with, the murder of Amélie Delagrange. At that stage neither Colin Sutton nor any of his fellow officers had any certain knowledge whatever that their prisoner might well have committed more equally heinous crimes.

'To be honest he looked rather cowed,' one of the officers was to confess to his colleagues later, 'certainly not the big man he thought he was.' Bellfield's handcuffs were removed, and he was ushered into a clean, new cell, complete with its own aluminium toilet, and the custody sergeant was instructed to keep a close eye on the prisoner. He was to wait while the murder squad decided on its interrogation team for their new prisoner, and which officers would be responsible for his interviews.

It was just as well that the custody officers had been told to keep a close watch on their new charge, for it was only a matter of minutes after he was first placed in a cell that they caught Bellfield in a crude attempt to commit suicide by wrapping the laces of his trainers around his neck and then thrusting his head into the toilet bowl. The custody officers intervened before he could do himself any harm, but the bungled suicide attempt convinced DCI Sutton that the safest thing would be for the police to take him to the nearby Hillingdon hospital for a complete medical check-up. It would delay his interrogation, but better safe than sorry, and besides it would also allow time for Bellfield's solicitor to arrive at the Heathrow station to be present at the first interviews.

It was well into the afternoon on that clear blue November day in 2004 before Bellfield returned to the Heathrow station with the officers who had accompanied him to the hospital. The doctors at Hillingdon had declared him fit enough to be questioned, although they had cautioned that he should be supervised carefully because of what they described as a 'comparatively fragile state of mind'.

Not that Bellfield was made to feel entirely comfortable on his return to Heathrow. He was still suffering from the fact that he had spent several hours naked under the fibreglass in his attic, with the result that his body had become itchy all over. In fact it wasn't until the following day that he was finally allowed a shower by the custody team, some twenty-seven hours after he had emerged from beneath the scratchy yellow fibreglass.

So it was that, on the afternoon of 22 November 2004, Bellfield began the first of what would be a long series of interviews by officers in the interrogation suite at Heathrow, accompanied by his solicitor. Not once did he admit a thing. He firmly denied any knowledge whatever of the killing of the French student Amélie Delagrange, or owning the white Ford Courier van P610 XCN that was seen on CCTV in the area on the night of 19 August that year. Indeed he fiercely denied ever owning any van at all. At turns both wheedling and arrogant, Bellfield deflected every question about Amélie's murder on that August evening just three months earlier.

'I don't own a white van.'

'I wasn't there.'

'You've made a mistake.'

As time passed, however, Bellfield became increasingly belligerent.

'This is ridiculous,' he shouted at his police interrogators across the table in the interview room at Heathrow police station. Time after time, throughout that day and the next, he firmly insisted, 'It must have been someone else.' No matter how politely they asked, 'Were you in the pub that night, Lee? Which pub was it? You can tell us that surely?' their suspect became ever angrier. As DCI Colin Sutton was to remember afterwards, 'He just denied everything, every single thing.'

But the police weren't just interested in Bellfield. They were also about to question his partner, Emma Mills, the young woman who had originally covered for him when he had climbed up into the attic at Little Benty. Her interviews were to form the first turning point in the case against the nightclub bouncer with a taste for teenage girls. Before they could begin, however, the police hit a legal problem. By coincidence, Emma Mills asked if she could be joined at her formal interviews by exactly the same solicitor that Bellfield had already chosen. The reason she gave was simple. She felt confidence in the woman, whom she'd met two years before when she had taken refuge from Bellfield in a hostel for battered women in Woking and taken out a restraining order to prevent him seeing her. Under the law, the same solicitor couldn't represent both Bellfield and the woman who had born him three children, and so it was decided that Mills should have the right to her first choice, while Bellfield would, instead, be represented by the firm of solicitors on call to Heathrow police station that day.

The change was made, and the interviews with Bellfield resumed, but now – on the advice of his new solicitors – he suddenly resorted to announcing, 'No comment' in answer to every question the police put to him, no matter how commonplace.

'Do you own any cars, Lee?'

'No comment.'

'Do you sometimes live at 39, Crosby Close on the Oriel Esate in Hanworth?'

'No comment.'

'Have you ever worked as a wheel-clamper?'

'No comment.'

As the questioning went on, Bellfield's refusal even to look at the detectives who were sitting across the interrogation table from him became ever more marked. He would turn to face his solicitor, then turn his chair around completely so that the officers were addressing his back. It was a display of arrogance that was eventually to find its way on to YouTube, by way of Romanian television, where his flat refusal to say anything but 'No comment' become an unlikely hit.

In stark contrast, his partner Emma Mills was telling the police everything they wanted to know – and more, far more. She was to reveal the truth about the man she had spent the past nine years of her life with. In particular she was to tell them that Bellfield's crimes were not restricted to murder.With tears in her eyes the young brunette told the police that the man she had shared her adult life with was, in fact, a sexual sadist and predator, who had violently raped her on a number of occasions. She also told them that he had an appetite for videotaping sex and dealing in drugs. It was the first time that the double murder squad realized that the man sitting in the custody suite of Heathrow police station was a great deal more dangerous than they even they had first imagined, a man not simply capable of cold-blooded murder but also rape.

As the hours slowly passed the detectives gently peeled back the layers of deception and deceit that Bellfield had wrapped so carefully around his adult life for more than fifteen years. The process revealed the ugly reality of the man beneath. Indeed, as Emma Mills talked to them in the days after her partner's arrest they realized that they could well be dealing with someone capable of serial murder.

'At first we really didn't know about the other crimes,' DCI Sutton was to admit later. 'It was only after we started interviewing Emma that the full extent of what Bellfield was capable of became clear.'

The brutal reality began to dawn as officers from the murder squad began to interview the white-faced mother of three, who had first encountered Bellfield as a night-club bouncer at a club called Rocky's in Cobham, Surrey, when she was an impressionable seventeen-year-old. The slight, shy teenager who had attended Trinity School in Esher and 'wouldn't say "boo" to a goose' grew into a headstrong young woman who would follow Bellfield to the ends of the earth – no matter how badly he treated her. Shortly after they had met, Bellfield had brought Emma home to her mother's house in the early hours of the morning after she had had too much to drink and stayed the night. And so started their relationship together.

Emma's revelations in those last days of November 2004 would come to transform the police's attitude to the burly nightclub bouncer. 'We began to think we had something else on our hands altogether,' DCI Sutton said later.

The grim reality was that the murder squad was confronting a man who could well be both a serial killer, a serial rapist and a kidnapper – for Emma Mills was to tell them in great detail about the day that Surrey schoolgirl Milly Dowler had disappeared just yards from the flat that she was then sharing with Bellfield.

The suspicion that had been lingering at the back of DCI Sutton's mind since he had initiated the round-the-clock surveillance on Bellfield back on 10 November – that his suspect might also have had something to do with Milly's disappearance – began to harden into reality as the police's conversations with Emma Mills continued, even though at that stage they were only investigating the murder of Amélie Delagrange.

What was not in doubt to the police was that they were dealing with a violent, sexually aggressive, domineering man with a voracious appetite for sex with young women as well as a desire to maintain multiple female partners at the same time – and to have children with each and every one of them. But an even more terrifying portrait also began to emerge – of a man who could control the women in his life to such an extraordinary extent that they would seldom complain about his brutal behaviour, never condemn his blatant womanizing, never run from his persistent violence or even report him to the police for raping them repeatedly, sometimes at knifepoint. Bellfield was a sexual predator, the detectives discovered, who kept woman after woman in his thrall, almost no matter how he treated them. Almost impossible though it might be for the police to conceive, he turned his female partners into virtual slaves, prepared to do anything that he suggested, to accept whatever depravity he loaded upon them, who never, ever, complained to the police or social services about his repeated violent domestic abuse. His was a reign of terror that a string of women had allowed themselves to put up with for decades, a habit of violence that none of them would ever fully recover from.

Emma Mills made clear throughout her many conversations with the police after Bellfield's arrest that, although he had been charming at first, he had rapidly become brutally controlling. Colin Sutton had a similar impression: 'When we started dealing with him he came across as very jokey, like he's your best mate. But he's a cunning individual, violent. He can switch from being nice to being nasty, instantly.' It was that capacity to transform himself from gentleman to monster in the blink of an eye that Emma Mills confirmed.

The twenty-seven-year-old told the police that Bellfield was the boss in their relationship. She described him as domineering, possessive, threatening and violent, especially in the bedroom. As she was later to repeat to the press, he had hit her, strangled her and raped her.

She had met Bellfield at the age of seventeen, when she was working as a nanny. She and a group of friends had become regulars at Rocky's, and she had quickly became infatuated with the muscular man who started buying her 'buckets' of red roses. They started having sex together, even though he was living with another of his female partners at the time, a girl called Jo Collings. By the time of her nineteenth birthday, in August 1996, Emma's relationship with Bellfield was so consuming that she decided to leave her mother's house and move in with him. The headstrong teenager turned her back on her mother and went to live with Bellfield in a room in his 'uncle' Charlie Brazil's house in Feltham, Middlesex, before they got a bedsitting room in a tall Victorian house in Manor Road in Twickenham, barely 400 yards from where Amélie Delagrange was later to be found murdered on Twickenham Green.

By the spring of 1997 Emma was pregnant with her first child by Bellfield; Lucy was born just two days before Christmas that year. What Emma didn't know at the time was that it was Bellfield's seventh child. He already had four children with a woman called Becky Wilkinson and two with Jo Collings – the second of whom, a son, Henry, had been born while Emma Mills was pregnant with Lucy.

But it wasn't only Bellfield's serial promiscuity that cast a shadow over their relationship, it was also his appetite for domestic violence – a violence that could, and often did, turn into forced sexual intercourse.

The first time was just six months after their relationship began. It was December 1995, and Emma had gone to a party given by some of her friends without telling Bellfield. But as soon as he heard about it the bouncer became furious, telling her on her mobile phone to 'get back' to Rocky's nightclub within half an hour – 'or there'll be trouble'. She did, and everything appeared normal, until a couple of days later. At the time Bellfield owned a white Ford Escort convertible and the next afternoon he asked Emma to drive him in it, proceeding to direct her down a series of small roads, until they reached Walton Bridge. When they got there, he grabbed her by her hair and said, 'You think you're going to get away with the other night?' Undoing her belt and pulling her jeans down, he told her, 'Next time I tell you not to do something, don't do it.' After the attack was over, Bellfield pulled up his trousers and told her to drive on. It was all the teenager could do to meekly comply.

The next day Bellfield rang her and acted as though nothing whatever had happened, leaving the young woman confused. As she later told the press, she questioned whether it could have been rape at all, given that he was her boyfriend, and began blaming herself for being 'dramatic'.

Bellfield's attack on Emma Mills underneath Walton Bridge was to take its toll on the young woman from Surrey; it was to become part of a violent pattern that she learned to live with as the nine years they spent together went by, a pattern that would colour their entire life together. Yet in spite of the physical abuse, in spite of the sexual attacks, Emma still had feelings for the man who was abusing her so relentlessly. As she explained, it wasn't every time that he forced her and afterwards he would cry and say that he was sorry.

Not long after their daughter Lucy was born in December 1996 the couple moved to a bigger flat in Hounslow, but the move didn't protect Mills from her partner – not for one moment. It had become commonplace for Bellfield to call Emma a 'bitch' and a 'slag' during sex, to slap her about and pull her hair, but some times he would go further, and the violence would spill out of the bedroom. On one wintry evening Bellfield forced her outside of their flat to have sex, naked, in the garden, leaving the young woman 'humiliated'. Afterwards Bellfield locked his naked girlfriend out of the flat for half an hour. On another occasion Bellfield pulled her outside the building to rape her in the stairwell of the building where they lived. Using a Stanley knife, he traced lines across her back during sex, leaving her terrified that he would kill her.

The truth was that Mills lived in abject fear of the man who was the father of her first child, yet, no matter the abuse she suffered, no matter how many other women he might see, no matter how many times he forced himself upon her, she was still prepared to love him unconditionally. Indeed by the beginning of 1999 she was pregnant again.

It was during this pregnancy that the couple moved to the house in Little Benty, and it was there that she brought her first son, William, home when he was born in October 1999. But even that did nothing to reduce the torment she suffered at the hands of her lover. Bellfield was now, according to Mills, regularly raping her once a fortnight.

She was later to describe how on one occasion Bellfield

raped her 'all night' before producing a video camera. He instructed her to perform for him in front of the camera – and to smile while she was doing so. He then proceeded to try to strangle her with her own cardigan. Afterwards he destroyed the tape and told her to have a bath 'to wash it all away', forcing her into hot water that she later described as being 'boiling' and telling her, 'Get rid of the all the evidence. You know it's my word against yours.'

Bellfield's attack with her cardigan was to be the last she would tolerate for a time. In despair Emma Mills decided to ring her mother, Gilly, who had naturally been worried about her daughter and who had promised to help her find a place in a women's refuge near Woking if ever she plucked up the courage to leave Bellfield. So it was that, on the morning after the cardigan attack, Emma's next-door neighbour at Little Benty gave her and her two children a lift to her mother's house in Hersham after she had packed some things. The teenager slipped out of the semi-detached brick house she had shared with Bellfield without a word to anyone while he was out.

It was to be almost four months before she would see Bellfield again, by which time she had spent some weeks in the refuge and then found a flat in Walton-on-Thames for herself and her children. But gradually Bellfield began to wheedle his way back into her life and affections, claiming that it was 'only fair' that he be allowed to see Lucy and William – 'after all they are my kids'.

Emma finally agreed to allow Bellfield to see their children, but only at the refuge. That didn't satisfy him. Without her knowing it, the nightclub bouncer started to stalk her. He tracked her down to her new flat and launched a series of intimidating telephone calls to her – and to her mother – which provoked Mills finally to make a statement to a local solicitor in an effort to make him stop. Significantly, however, when she made her statement to the solicitor she did not go into the full details of the sexual abuse she had suffered. 'All I really wanted was for him to love me,' she said by way of explanation, still blaming herself for the attacks she had suffered.

The full details of Emma's suffering at Bellfield's hands were to wait for the murder squad detectives two years later.

But the most single most terrifying revelation during the police interviews with Emma Mills conducted by the detectives in the last days of 2004 came when she revealed exactly where she had been living with her children in the last months of 2001, after she had left the refuge in Woking. It was the flat that Bellfield had tracked her down to, and one into which he was to move back into with her in November that year. That two-bedroom flat was 24, Collingwood Place in Walton-on-Thames, and Bellfield and Mills had been living there with their children for five months when Milly Dowler had disappeared on the way home from Heathside School in Weybridge on 21 March 2002, a day that had started grey and gloomy. The pedestrian entrance to Collingwood Place lay right beside the bus stop where Milly's friend had last seen the schoolgirl on that fateful day, and only yards from the point in Station Road in Walton where she had disappeared.

But, at that point, Colin Sutton's double murder squad weren't investigating the abduction and murder of thirteen-year-old Milly Dowler. That was a matter for Surrey Police.

They were only interested in exactly who Levi Bellfield was, and what crimes he had committed in their area.

It was to be Mills allegations against Bellfield that would eventually allow the police to keep him in custody as they began to piece together the precise details of the murder of Amélie Delagrange on Twickenham Green. After his first court appearance on charges of rape and buggery – not of murder – Bellfield was moved from Heathrow police station to the confines of Her Majesty's Prison at Belmarsh in south London, home to Category A prisoners from terrorists to murderers. He was to spend almost three years there, waiting to face a jury.

3. Twilight Citizens

'Soon as she was gone from me,
A traveller came by,
Silently, invisibly:
He took her with a sigh.'

William Blake, *Notebooks*

Before the opening of London's Heathrow as a civilian airport in 1946 – in the wake of the ending of the Second World War, when it had been used principally for military aircraft – the vast acres of heath and common land that it and the surrounding suburbs now occupy to the west of London were home to thousands of gypsy and travelling families. This western section of London was ingrained into gypsy and travelling culture; it was a place that they had come to call home. In the early part of the twentieth century, for example, gypsy families regularly camped near Walton Bridge over the Thames, just as they did at Chertsey Bridge and on the gravel flats that were to become Kempton Park racecourse, not far from the village of Hampton. These families roamed across the western outskirts of London for large parts of the year, attending the Derby race meeting every June on the downs of Epsom just a little to the south, where many of them worked on the fairground that formed an essential part of the fun on the centre of the course, before disappearing to Kent for the summer's hop-picking.

Gypsies and travellers had been a part of British life and culture for 400 years. First called 'Egyptians', they had arrived from northern India in the sixteenth century. Nevertheless, they were often regarded as social pariahs by local populations, outcasts to be treated with care, even disdain. This is turn bred a sense of 'differentness' among them, and they almost revelled in their place outside mainstream culture by taking on jobs that the ordinary population might see as beneath them. That too was traditional: after all gypsies had served as tinkers in India, undertakers in Romania and even hangmen in Brazil. In the nineteenth century their traditional occupations in Britain had been as horse-dealers, basket-makers, knife-grinders, tinkers, peg-makers, blacksmiths and entertainers, although as the twentieth century progressed that gradually evolved into more general 'dealing' – in anything from scrap metal to cars – as well as to the seasonal work of picking hops. But as farming grew ever more mechanized, they started to remain in London throughout the year in pursuit of work, and the opportunity to make money.

But whatever their trade, Britain's gypsies and travellers, like their counterparts in Europe, forever retained this feeling of being apart, a people subject to persecution – a view confirmed by the fact that no fewer than 400,000 were exterminated in the concentration camps by the Nazis during the Second World War.

One academic expert, Dr Becky Taylor, describes them now as 'Britain's twilight citizens', a people only too aware of their place on the fringes of conventional society, and it is an entirely apt description. The distinguished commentator Brian Belton, a gypsy himself, has named his people 'Outsider, Insiders' in British society, arguing in his 2005 book *Questioning Gypsy Identity* that the very nature of their tradition sets them apart from other racial or ethnic groups in the country. In his view it is a 'differentness' that seeps into every area of their lives. Vividly describing his own upbringing, for example, Belton remembers: 'While many of my school-age peers were hanging round street corners or playing table tennis ... my gypsy contacts introduced me to stalking pheasant, and they took me into the brutal, fearsome, yet exciting worlds of cursing, dog fighting and cockfighting.'

Belton was also exposed to bareback horse riding, poaching, gambling and bare-knuckle boxing – experiences that were also to form part of the upbringing of the man that Colin Sutton's murder squad found in the attic in Little Benty on that bright November morning in 2004, a boy born Levi Rabetts but who came to be called Levi Bellfield. The life of the gypsy and the traveller was his heritage.

But Belton draws a distinction between what he calls real Romany gypsies – 'I'm a true Didikois,' he says of himself – and the less traditional 'travelling families' who may demonstrate some of the characteristics of the gypsy life but don't necessarily share the same ancestry or grasp of gypsy traditions of behaviour. Belton believes, for example, that the boy born Levi Rabetts is more of a traveller than a gypsy, as he insists that gypsy culture does not condone breaking the law, nor acting outside it.

That may be true, but what is not in doubt is that one of the best-known gypsy families in south-west London in the 1950s and 1960s were the Brazils, whose reputation as one of the original gypsy families guaranteed them influence and respect. Significantly, the boy born Levi Rabetts was the nephew of a Brazil, and as such was steeped from childhood in the traditions and culture of a people who saw themselves as outside the normal confines of British society. Encouraged by the tradition, the boy who grew up to become Levi Bellfield came to see himself as an outsider to whom the law did not apply, a man who need only answer to his own conscience and not the conscience of any other: it was in his blood.

Charlie Brazil, a senior surviving member of the Brazil gypsy family, told the police after Bellfield's arrest that Levi was his brother's nephew and very much a part of the family. Indeed it was Bellfield's 'uncle' Charlie – as he was known to Bellfield and his mother – who had first started working as a bouncer at Rocky's nightclub in Cobham in Surrey. It was he who first helped his brother's nephew to get a job there.

The closeness between Brazil and Bellfield is clear enough. It was to his 'uncle' Charlie Brazil's home in Walton-on-Thames that Bellfield first took the impressionable teenager Emma Mills to live after he whisked her away from her mother's home in Hersham. At the time Brazil was living with his partner, Vern, and the young Emma Mills was astonished by their lifestyle, which appeared to her to involve drinking for most of the day, sleeping in chairs in the sitting room and ignoring every single one of the social conventions that her mother had brought her up to respect. What Emma did not understand when she first met the Brazils was that they played an enormously significant role in Bellfield's life, so significant that he would for ever remain supremely conscious of what his 'uncle' and Brazil cousins thought of him. Gradually Emma came to realize that they were the yardstick by which he measured himself: their attitudes were his attitudes.

But if the Brazils were a signal part of Bellfield's life, his mother, Jean, was even more important. If there is a single person who could be said to have been the dominant force in his childhood and adolescence it was his forceful, domineering mother, who steadfastly maintained his innocence against any criticism from anyone over many years. A traveller herself, Jean Bellfield had married a fellow traveller, a motor mechanic named Joseph Rabetts, in the mid 1950s, and born him a son, Richard, in 1961, and then two daughters, Lindy – also known as Lindy Loo – and Cheryl. The couple's last and youngest child, whom they named Levi, who was born in Isleworth, Middlesex, barely half a mile from his later stamping grounds in Twickenham, came into the world on 17 May 1968.

From the very beginning of his life – he was a sickly baby – Jean Rabetts doted on her youngest son. When he first went to Crane Junior School in Hampton she made sure the other boys there never got a chance to bully him, a habit she maintained even after he had progressed to what was then the nearby Feltham Comprehensive. Bellfield would tell his female partners later in his life that 'my mother wiped my bum until I was twelve' – a habit he encouraged them to adopt. Everyone of them rapidly came to realize that it was not a joke.

Throughout his childhood Bellfield lived with his mother in a cramped semi-detached brick villa on the edge of the reservoir in Hanworth, Middlesex, no distance at all from Hampton and the polite, suburban road that was to see Marsha McDonnell's life come to a sudden and brutal end. Interestingly, the Bellfield family home looked remarkably similar to the house that would later witness Bellfield's arrest for murder at Little Benty. Both were hidden in hard-to-find cul-de-sacs protected from the public gaze by undergrowth and with a myriad of local alleys which afforded a quick escape from unwelcome visitors. Both houses seemed to represent the Bellfield need for a lair, a warren to escape the prying eyes of the world.

Not that life was without its dramas for the man who seemed to like to hide from the world. In 1976 tragedy struck the family when Bellfield's father died suddenly of a heart attack at the age of only thirty-seven. It left his children in the charge of his ferocious wife, but that was a challenge she didn't shirk. She became the 'materfamilias' of the Bellfield family, a formidable defender of their every action. In fact, gypsy tradition has it that the strong woman in any group, called the *phuri dai* in Romany, always has a particular influence over her own family – not least because of her place as the matriarch and also the simply fact that in many gypsy families the woman had the greatest earning capacity.

In the wake of her husband's death Jean Rabetts reverted to her maiden name of Bellfield and never married again, although when her youngest son Levi was still only ten years old she moved another male partner, Johnny Lee, into her house on the edge of the Hanworth Reservoir, and he has remained there ever since.

The death of his father seemed only to have increased

Bellfield's reliance on his mother and reinforced his closeness to her. His friends at the time remember him as a 'spoilt mummy's boy' who found it difficult to relate to his contemporaries.

One childhood friend, Richard Hughes, always known as 'Yosser' after a character in Alan Bleasdale's seminal 1982 television drama *Boys from the Blackstuff*, remembers that as a child Bellfield was 'very skinny and short', yet a boy, he recalled, 'with no appetite for violence whatever'. That was not to last, for the puny boy was to be transformed as he became a teenager. Bellfield later admitted to Hughes that he had taken steroids regularly to build up his muscles.

Bellfield was well aware that he was something of a runt at school. Years later, when he was well into his thirties, he would reveal the extent of the private insecurities of his schooldays by confiding to the Friends Reunited website that he 'was short at school – now over six feet Ha Ha', before adding: 'I haven't grown up still think I'm 18 out clubbing, Ibiza, Tenerife'. He even went on to admit that he was 'a bit flash', adding, 'Am I sounding a prat????' before concluding, chillingly: 'Don't look my age have seen a few people from school they look 45 sad . . . any single girls out there e mail me'.

After he had reached puberty Bellfield not only built up his muscular physique but also developed a lascivious attitude towards young girls. In particular he was fascinated by the pupils that attended the nearby Gumley House Convent School for Girls in Isleworth, just half a mile from his birthplace. It was a fascination that would eventually see him attempt to abduct one of them. Even as a teenager he would haunt his local area, prowling for girls that he fancied, like a dog marking out his territory, trying to engage them in suggestive conversations that always turned to sex. It was a habit that was to saturate his life.

There was a perception in his family that a traveller has to make his own way in the world, and fight for what he believes is his by right – especially when it comes to women. This led to Bellfield becoming ever more possessive of his female conquests – determined that they should never leave him. Once his partner, they could be no one else's. Any suggestion that they might choose another man was impossible to accept and would only lead to violence. That paranoia too was to shape his life, and there may have been a chilling early example of what it meant.

When Bellfield was twelve years old one of his first serious girlfriends was a blonde local schoolgirl named Patsy Morris, who was two years older than he was. Patsy's father, George, a retired army chef, and her mother, Marjorie, had only recently moved to Isleworth from Birmingham and sent their daughter to Feltham Comprehensive, along with her sister and two brothers. It was there, shortly after the start of her first term in the autumn of 1979, that she met and befriended Bellfield.

Barely nine months later, on the sunny afternoon of 16 June 1980, Patsy Morris disappeared from her school at lunchtime, never to be seen alive again. Her lifeless body was discovered two days later in undergrowth on Hounslow Heath, and a post-mortem discovered that she had been strangled with some kind of ligature, but there were no signs of any sexual assault. Had she angered the young

Bellfield by telling him that she didn't want to continue their adolescent romance? Had she refused to agree to his demands that she do whatever it was he told her? Had she refused to have sex with him? We may never know. All that we do know is that the fourteen-year-old who had been his first serious girlfriend was murdered.

The Morris family never fully recovered from the loss of their daughter, and to this day suspect that Bellfield may have had something to do with her death. Patsy's sister Nicola, who is now in her forties, said recently, 'It was a shock when we found out they knew each other.'

George Morris, who has spent thirty years grieving for the loss of daughter, remembers that he received a phone call shortly after her body was discovered from what he thought was 'a young teenage boy'. 'The phone rang,' Morris said recently, 'and someone said, "I'm going to kill you." It was a local male voice and it was very strange.' To this day Morris is convinced in his own mind that the anonymous voice on the end of the phone in July 1980 belonged to Bellfield. 'He's a local man, which is why it could be him,' he's maintained. 'And it's terrifying to think that someone of twelve or thirteen could have done it.'

George Morris has no proof whatever that his daughter's relationship with the young Bellfield resulted in her death, and the Metropolitan Police have certainly not charged Bellfield with the offence. But the suspicion that the spoilt 'mummy's boy' who lusted after 'tight young virgins, young schoolgirls' might have had something to do with her death is difficult to avoid completely – not least because no one else has ever been convicted of the crime in the three decades since it was committed.

Whatever the truth, Bellfield quickly put the death of his first girlfriend behind him and grew into a burly, tall young man weighing more than 17 stone. But what he could not change was the timbre of his voice. No matter how large and intimidating he became, no matter how many steroids he took, his voice was to remain the high-pitched squeak it had been during his childhood. Yet his Chipmunk-like, cartoon voice brought its advantages, for it meant that he somehow seemed less intimidating to the young women he met than he might have done. It meant the girls who might have been wary of his muscular frame were lulled into a false sense of security by the unthreatening sound of his voice and the slick charm of his patter.

Never exactly a committed student – there were too many other more exciting things to do – Bellfield left school in 1984 with no formal qualifications whatever. He had always preferred 'ducking and diving', as one of his contemporaries was to put it years later, picking up pocket money where he could by providing what he later called 'personal services' to his friends. Those services might include helping them to find a source of cannabis, ecstasy or cocaine, a little 'protection' from bullying friends if they were under threat or buying and selling cars of all shapes and sizes. Bellfield quickly became what many a traveller had been before him, 'a dealer' in everything – but one with no fear of violence, and prepared to use it if the occasion demanded it. This is not to suggest for one moment that every Romany gypsy or traveller has an appetite for violence, it is simply to point out that the tradition, when added to Bellfield's sense of his being an outsider during his adolescence, reinforced his belief that he could operate outside the law as society defined it, and when it suited him.

The first time that Bellfield's disdain for the law showed itself came when he was just thirteen. He was convicted on two counts of burglary and theft in April 1982. One friend at the time remembers: 'He always believed the law didn't apply to people like him, or his family.' It was a belief that led to long string of criminal convictions.

The young man who was often called Lee by his friends started to spend almost all his time on the fringe of the law, a place where he felt comfortable, whether it was the exotic worlds of illegal cock fighting and dog fighting, or illegal gambling and bare-knuckle boxing. Bellfield increasingly developed the habit of dealing in drugs for his friends, as well as seizing the opportunity to indulge his appetite for cars, and dealing in those as well. By the time he had learned to drive at seventeen he had amply demonstrated his disdain for other people's property by taking no fewer than three cars without their owners' permission, which saw him convicted on three counts of taking a conveyance in December 1985.

Less than a year later, in November 1986, he was in trouble with the law again, this time for failing to surrender to the court when he was bailed for another driving offence, and in March 1987 he was convicted on three further counts of taking a conveyance.

In an effort to escape the attention of the police, the teenage Bellfield then took to the habit of using a string of aliases to confuse anyone who might take an interest in exactly what he was doing. If no one knew his real name it made it all the easier to get away with something. It was a desire to disguise his true identity that Bellfield would never lose – just as he would always take particular care not to be directly connected with any single car or van if he could avoid it. That way no one could be certain that he was the owner or the driver. If he called himself by a different name he could flee back to the lair of the family home in Hanworth with no one any the wiser.

Over the next two decades Bellfield would come to use no fewer than seventeen different aliases, ranging from some close to his own name – Liam Rabetts, Leroy Bellfry and Levi Smith – to David Bennett, Gavin Mercer, David Smith, Lee John, Liam James and Troy Nugent. The reasons for the subterfuge became clear just after his twentieth birthday, when he was convicted of possession of an offensive weapon in June 1988. The young man who had also started to dabble in a little small-scale benefit fraud – including claiming unemployment benefit when he had a part-time job – was growing far bolder and more dangerous by the day.

Nowhere did that display itself more clearly than in Bellfield's relationships with women and in particular his first long-term partner, barmaid Rebecca Wilkinson. No one would come to see the strain of violent brutality that was burgeoning in his soul more clearly than this cheery blonde, whom he met in September 1989, when he was twenty-one and she was just seventeen. She was to become the first true victim of his fascination with young women and his disdain for the law.

4. A Dark World of Abuse

'At worst, is this not an unjust world, full of
nothing but beasts of prey, four-footed or two-
footed?'

Thomas Carlyle

When Levi Bellfield first met the cheery, blonde and slightly
chubby Rebecca Wilkinson in the autumn of 1989 she was
working behind the bar of the Oxford Arms pub in Twickenham Road, Hanworth. Her elder sister Lucy was already
working there, and it had seemed a natural place for the
young woman to get a part-time job to help her make ends
meet. With its polished brass rail and etched mirrors, the
Oxford Arms was one of Bellfield's regular drinking
haunts; now that his body mass had expanded to a steroid-
packed 18 stone, his appetite for alcohol had grown
dramatically. Now twenty-one, he liked to start the mornings with a can or two of Tennent's Super Strength lager
and progress from there, with more lagers at regular inter-
vals throughout the day, topped up with a little Malibu or
vodka.

If Bellfield was 'Jack the Lad', then Becky – as she was
known to her friends – was certainly no saint. When she
first encountered him she already had a six-month-old
daughter, Hayley. She had become pregnant at sixteen by

her first proper boyfriend. Her relationship with him wasn't destined to last, and he moved out of the area during her pregnancy, leaving Becky to cope with motherhood alone. In fact she had only seen him twice since Hayley's birth in March 1989. But that hadn't dismayed her in the least. Calling on a natural supply of pluck, and her mother's help, she had just about managed to look after her new daughter 'after a fashion', as she told her friends.

Money was tight, and Becky needed all the financial support she could get to buy baby clothes for her daughter and put food on the table. That was why she was working at the Oxford Arms, while her mother looked after her daughter. It was to be those needs that made her a perfect target for a natural predator like Bellfield. Vulnerable to the charm of a man with money in his pocket, Becky was flattered by the attentions of this older man with a ready smile when they first met, even though she knew very well that he had a steady girlfriend called Cherie. That was no secret – everyone in the pub knew it – but she was young and, besides, she wanted to believe that her life could be better. Perhaps he could be the one to make it so. What could be more tempting than the attentions of a man who wasn't slow to flash his wad of banknotes? For a teenager struggling to bring up her baby daughter it was nothing short of intoxicating.

Like a fox that senses a rabbit across a cornfield on a winter's morning, Bellfield saw this cheerful young woman as prey. Encouraged by his mother, he had grown into a man who believed he could have whichever woman he wanted, and what's more could persuade her to do anything he chose. He certainly sensed that opportunity with the impressionable Becky Wilkinson and, before she had really understood it, he had pounced.

'He was a real charmer when we first met,' the young barmaid would say fifteen years after their first meeting. 'I thought he was a nice bloke.' What she didn't know was that her life with him would rapidly turn into a seven-year nightmare.

At first everything seemed fine. Becky bathed in the glow of being wanted by a man older than she was who seemed to 'know his way around'. The only trouble was that, after Bellfield's initial charm offensive, he suddenly became hard to contact. Within months she discovered that she was pregnant with his child. Uncertain what to do, Becky tried to make contact with Bellfield. Finally she discovered that he was in Great Yarmouth in Norfolk and would be back soon. He didn't explain why he was there, didn't apologize for the silence, didn't ask if she was all right, just assumed she would be pleased to hear from him. Though Becky Wilkinson didn't know it at the time, it was to be the shape of things to come. Things were to get worse, much worse.

Bellfield's problems with his girlfriends weren't the only things preying on his mind at that moment, however. One reason for his trip to Great Yarmouth was a desire to 'make himself scarce' to the police, as he was about to add to his criminal record with another conviction in July 1990. This time it was for using a fraudulent tax disc on one of the many cars he had access to as well as, once again, failing to surrender to the court while on bail for the offence. The habits he had grown into as a teenager were now ingrained.

Becky Wilkinson knew nothing of that as her pregnancy developed. The local authority understood her predicament and in August 1990, when she was five months pregnant and with an eighteen-month-old to look after as well, she was offered a three-bedroom house in Hounslow for her and her growing family. In the meantime the father of her unborn child would arrive from time to time to pay attention to her, before disappearing again for days at a time, without telling Becky where he was going.

As she later revealed, during her pregnancy Bellfield's lack of concern was clear: 'The night I went into labour, it was snowing, and we didn't have phone, but he would not take me to hospital. I had to walk to a phone box and call my mum to take me.' Worse was to come, as two days after she returned home, Bellfield kicked the young mother down a set of stairs, demonstrating a pattern of violence that was to become a regular feature of their relationship. As their family life together began, Bellfield was soon hitting Wilkinson and 'bringing other women back to the house' when she was out.

Tragically, the abusive relationship between the young barmaid and Bellfield was to be exacerbated once again by her partner's latest brush with the law. Once again he had been knowingly avoiding the police – this time aware of a charge of causing actual bodily harm. But at 5 o'clock in the morning of Monday, 21 January 1991, just four weeks after the birth of his daughter, the law caught up with him. Police officers broke into Becky's house in Hounslow and arrested him. He was immediately taken to Isleworth Crown Court, where he was sentenced to three months' imprisonment.

Even from his prison cell, however, Bellfield continued to control the young mother of his child. He insisted that Becky should go to live with his sister, rather than move into another new flat she had been offered in nearby Feltham. The reason he gave was that if she did so it would mean he could 'keep an eye on her' – from his prison cell. It was an outrageous demand, but Bellfield's possessive, jealous nature when it came to his girlfriend knew no limits.

Nevertheless, still hypnotized by his charms and in spite of his violence, she agreed to stay with his sister Cheryl, just as she agreed to visit him every two weeks while he was in jail. By the middle of June 1991, however, the young barmaid was growing ever more uncomfortable with the company of Bellfield's sister – not to mention his mother Jean – so much so that she decided to move into the new flat she had been offered in Feltham. But she didn't escape.

On 4 July 1991 Bellfield was released from jail and immediately returned to haunt her, though not to live with her every day, as that would have constrained his right to do 'whatever I want'. For his part Bellfield simply resumed his habit of drinking heavily and disappearing from her flat for hours, or even days, at a time. But the more she questioned him, the angrier he became, leading him to beat her on many occasions. Even more dramatically, however, Bellfield also turned his young partner into a prisoner in her own home. He decided that he would not allow her to go out of the flat without him, paranoid that she might meet another man.

Bellfield's appetite for violence, which could appear at a moment's notice, and disappear just as quickly, was not fuelled by Becky Wilkinson, however, there was also the question of his relationship with the police, who had become an ever present part of his life.

Even though he had served his latest sentence, Bellfield's brushes with the law certainly didn't come to an end in the months after his release, not least because of his repeated attacks on his young partner. Police officers from the local station often visited Becky's flat – called by neighbours who had realized that he was assaulting her with ever-increasing regularity. But the charm he had used trap his young partner hadn't deserted him. A smiling Bellfield would answer the door to the officers when they arrived as a result of the neighbours' complaints and protest his innocence.

Bellfield's belief that he was free to treat any woman in his life in any way he chose was gathering its own terrifying momentum. Bellfield would demand sex whenever he was in the mood: if Becky refused him he would simply hold her down and rape her. Yet at no point did Becky Wilkinson consider leaving her brutal and sexually aggressive partner, explaining to her friends that she was still 'petrified' of him. No matter how bad things might get, she felt powerless, because her belief was that he would only find her again and make her pay.

And so, in spite of the violence and the repeated sexual demands, in spite of the fact that she found herself pregnant again, Becky Wilkinson didn't finally leave Bellfield until a brutal fight broke out in June 1992. That night Bellfield raped Wilkinson at knifepoint.

A breaking point had been reached, and Wilkinson reported the rape to the police in a thirty-six-page statement; yet tragically she was to withdraw the charges. Meanwhile, although she moved herself and the children out of the flat, the trauma was far from over. It wasn't long before Bellfield had tracked her down. Breaking into the new home where she was staying, he waited for her return. Once more, Bellfield raped her, explaining it was 'to teach her a lesson'.

The couple struggled along together – on and off, although rather more off than on – over the ensuing years, and Bellfield's uncanny ability to hypnotize her into obeying his every demand remained, but he began to spread his net ever wider in his search for women to control.

A decade later, when Colin Sutton's double murder squad were investigating the murder of Amélie Delagrange, they asked Becky if she would be prepared to go to court to repeat her version of her relationship with Bellfield between 1989 and that June evening in 1992. Despite admitting that the thought of him made her shake with fear, Wilkinson bravely decided to help the police. It was her accusations of rape against Bellfield, alongside those of Emma Mills, that were to help the police keep their suspect in jail at the end of 2004, as they investigated the murder of Amélie Delagrange.

Becky Wilkinson may have been one of Levi Bellfield's first victims, and one whose abuse was committed under the very noses of the local police. She was not to be his last.

5. The Master and His Slaves

There are some solitary wretches who seem to
have left the rest of mankind, only, as Eve left
Adam, to meet the devil in private.
Alexander Pope, *Thoughts on Various Subjects*

No matter how terrified and alone the women in Levi Bellfield's life may have felt when he beat them, abused them, locked them in their houses, kept them without money and controlled every aspect of their waking lives; they still continued to do everything in their power to remain his partner.

Becky Wilkinson put up with fifteen years of relentless abuse, bearing Bellfield no fewer than four children and accepting the violence that he rained down on her with barely a flicker of anger. For his part Bellfield kept the willing young barmaid who had become the mother of his children on a string – charming at one moment, monster the next, keeping her off balance so that she could not decide what she truly felt about him from one moment to the next. This was a man who was capable of beating her to within an inch of consciousness at one moment, but who also went out and had the word 'Becky' tattooed on the lower part of his left leg.

Bellfield's mind games with women were to become

the signature of his adult life – a brutal, heartless and deliberate process to make sure that they obeyed his every command and were never not under his control. He insisted that they should not see other men, but that was only the excuse, a cover for his determination that each and every one of them should be his creature. He was to be their master, they were his slaves.

Though Bellfield kept the women in his life separate and usually alone with their children, he himself was nothing if not gregarious. He was no hooded loner stalking the streets of west London – quite the opposite. He liked nothing more than the company of his fellow bouncers at whatever nightclub he happened to be working at, as well as the men he worked with laying tarmac, building fences or cementing crazy paving. He was not a man who shut himself away from ordinary society, harbouring dark fantasies in the privacy of a solitary room. When he felt like it – which was often – Bellfield also took pleasure in being a cheerful family man who enjoyed the company of his children and who liked to take them to Toys 'R' Us to buy them presents. This was a man who knew only too well how to fit in and preserve his place as a member of the local community.

After all, that was what travellers had always done. They were loyal to fellow travellers, sought out their company, did their best to protect each other from what they saw as the criticisms of 'ordinary' society and felt themselves to be a part of a distinct community, one with its own traditions, rules and behaviour. It was attitude that each and every traveller accepted without question. Bellfield was no exception.

Whether it was drinking in one of his favourite pubs, of which there were many across west London, working together or even committing crimes together, Bellfield perpetually felt himself to be one of a group. 'Lee was always one of us,' one of his fellow bouncers would remember later. 'He liked to be liked, and he was. There was a smile, and the odd rude comment, and he liked the company of men. He didn't have much time for women – except to shag them.'

It was that sense of belonging to an all-male 'community' that he commemorated by covering himself with a set of tattoos, as if to prove his membership but also to underline his power. Two of his tattoos hinted at the devil in him. On the upper part of his right arm, Bellfield had a tattoo of a devil wearing a pair of boxing gloves and another of a similar devil wearing boxer's shorts with the name 'Levi' embroidered across the waistband. For good measure he also had a tattoo on the same right arm commemorating his favourite football club, Tottenham Hotspur. Not unlike some of the more extreme football hooligans, Bellfield liked nothing more than to belong to an exclusively male society and bathed contentedly in the testosterone-driven machismo and potential violence that it offered. It reinforced his feeling that all men were superior to women – except when it came to their mothers. He was always in awe of his mother, Jean.

But Bellfield's delight in the company of men who weren't afraid of violence meant that he usually associated with men whose attitude to women could be both exploitative and abusive. They confirmed and accepted his desires, and that, in turn, fuelled his escalating habit of stalking young women. His stalking provided his friends with sexual conquests too. If young girls were 'begging for it' then there could be nothing wrong in satisfying their desires, even if they didn't know he and his friends were doing so. In Bellfield's mind the provision of young women for the sexual gratification of his male friends was simply an extension of his providing them with drugs – which had become one of his sidelines during his years with Becky Wilkinson.

Bellfield's interest in drugs did not end with cannabis, cocaine or heroin, however, for he was also well aware that the 'date-rape' drugs GHB and Rohypnol (always known as 'roofies') were also readily available and had their uses, especially when it came to sexually abusing naive and innocent young women.

What could be more natural for a bouncer at a west London nightclub than to know that drugs of all kinds were available and could easily be provided? For Bellfield it was just another opportunity for a 'deal' in the twilight, illegal world that made up his life, another opportunity to tie his male friends ever closer to him and to manipulate any young woman who came across his bows.

The more Bellfield succeeded in making himself 'indispensable' to his male friends, the more secure he became. But the 'services' he provided to some of his friends didn't stop at providing them with sex, cannabis, cocaine, GHB or 'roofies'. There was also the offer of violence. If ever any of his friends were intimidated they knew only too well that Bellfield would be only too happy to provide a little muscle to fight back against anyone who tried to frighten them. 'Lee was a terrific enforcer,' one fellow bouncer admitted later. 'He could terrify the wits out of almost anyone, and wasn't afraid to use violence to make a point. He loved a fight.'

Bellfield also had an appetite for weapons. He liked to brag about a brass knuckle-duster that he kept in the glove box of whatever car or van he happened to be driving that day, just as he always kept a baseball bat in the boot. That wasn't all. There were also guns, notably a shotgun, as well as a machete and a samurai sword. Bellfield's appetite for weapons almost matched his enthusiasm for drugs – for they both contributed to ensuring that he remained the alpha male within his group of friends, the man who could 'sort things out' or 'get things done' when the going got a little rowdy or violent.

Throughout his twenties, Bellfield was establishing his reputation as a local 'Jack the Lad'. As one of the girls he came across was to say, 'Levi had this reputation for being a drug-dealer and a gangster,' and he loved the image he had created – even to the extent of getting his own personalized number plate, LEV 135V, which had been attached to a white Ford Escort van, but which he transferred to a black and then a white BMW.

Bellfield's sense of being an 'outsider' was then overlaid by his mother's intense interest in him. The closeness between mother and son lead to private speculation among some police officers that their relationship may have bordered on the incestuous – but that was an allegation that could never be substantiated. What is not in doubt, however, is that, during Bellfield's adolescence, his rapidly developing sexuality was almost certainly encouraged by his mother Jean's proud nurturing of him and his ego.

This, in turn, fanned his self-belief into a form of narcissism. Bellfield came to believe that women – other than his mother – were no more than playthings, to be taken for granted, used and abused, but never to be treated as human beings. Many years later he memorably told a fellow prison inmate that they were no more than 'pet dogs', adding: 'You feed them, you keep them, you can do what you want with them.' It was the response of a man whose psyche was still rooted in his narcissistic adolescence: a man who would go on to attack young schoolgirls.

One young woman who witnessed that at first hand was Johanna Collings, a keen young horsewoman from Strawberry Hill, west London – barely half a mile from Twickenham Green – who first encountered him when he was working as a bouncer at Rocky's nightclub in Cobham in the spring of 1995.

Collings was twenty-three and living with her mother in a comfortable suburban house, while Bellfield was twenty-six and flitting between addresses – including his mother's house, the flat he still, notionally, shared with Becky Wilkinson and their children, and the flats and houses of his other friends. Collings had known Becky as one of the local girls since she was eighteen. They had met at a local nightclub in Twickenham then known as Cellars, where Bellfield worked as a bouncer. She was also well aware of his reputation with women – and his appetite for violence. However, none of that knowledge put Collings off embarking on a relationship with Levi Bellfield.

Small for her age, at just 5 feet 3 inches, with muscular arms and dirty dyed blonde hair, Collings fitted Bellfield's

preferred sexual stereotype – blonde, a little naive, still lived at home. She even looked a little like a schoolgirl.

Inevitably, Bellfield ensnared his latest victim as he did so many others – by flattering her while she waited in line to get into the nightclub he happened to be doorman for at the time. In fact this time he acted as her 'Prince Charming' – in her words – comforting her when she was crying in the car park outside the club after being dumped by a current boy-friend. In her heart she may have known it was a line, but her vulnerability trumped the suspicion.

Whatever Bellfield's motive, the two hit it off, and he moved in with her almost straightaway. The prospect of living in a comfortable suburban villa in Strawberry Hill rather than a cramped flat clearly must have appealed to the peripatetic bouncer, even if it did mean sharing it with her recently widowed mother, Sheila, who was then fifty-nine.

Within a short time of Bellfield's moving into her mother's house Collings realized that she was pregnant with a child, but as soon as that happened his attitude towards her changed dramatically. Just as it had done with Wilkinson, her pregnancy and the thought of fatherhood seemed to enrage him.

Bellfield would kick and punch her on a very frequent basis, Collings was to explain, regardless of whether he was drunk or sober, and without any provocation. It was a pattern that was to repeat itself time after time, yet out of fear for her life Collings did not report the assaults to the police. Despite the degradation, humiliation and pain she could not bring herself to tell anyone.

The pattern of their relationship and Bellfield's power over the young woman who was to bear a daughter, in

February 1996, was fixed in stone, and it would never change. He made sure the surname was Bellfield on the birth certificate.

Sheila Collings watched her daughter's ordeal at Bellfield's hands from close quarters, and it horrified her, yet there was nothing that she could do. Her daughter was in thrall to the mountainous nightclub bouncer who could seduce a woman without apparent difficulty, even if he was then revealed as a violent abuser almost before they could blink. As so many women were to confirm after Bellfield's arrest, he could 'charm the birds from the trees when it suited him'.

That was Bellfield's good side. In the months after their daughter's birth Collings saw the bad, as he would hit her for absolutely no reason. As with his other partners, sometimes Bellfield could display remorse. He could be apologetic and possibly buy Collings flowers but on other occasions he would hit the bruises he had given her.

Bellfield conducted a systematic, sustained campaign to intimidate and control the young horsewoman who had become the mother of a daughter. Like Becky Wilkinson before her, Collings was raped repeatedly by Bellfield. She was even to tell the *Sun* newspaper that he had effectively made her his 'sex slave' for two and a half years of their relationship. As she later revealed to the press, 'Usually he would wrap his belt round my throat and choke me and rape me. He would make me do whatever he wanted. I'd be told to "be a good little slut". Levi used lit cigarettes on me, beat me with pool cues and ashtrays, threw me down the stairs and even once took a claw hammer to my body.' Johanna said she became so terrified of Bellfield

that just hearing his key in the front door made her wet herself. She added: 'Until you've known that sort of fear, you can't understand what I went through.'

Though she didn't recognize it at the time, these outbursts of domestic rape and violence were a clear sign that Bellfield's desire to harm women was escalating rapidly. He was becoming ever more prepared to ignore the law, or the conventions of society, in his desire to take his form of revenge on the female sex.

Yet, remarkably, both Collings and Becky Wilkinson were aware of his reputation before they even embarked on their relationships with him, and both tried repeatedly to sustain those relationships even when they knew he had moved on to a new partner. Throughout her time with Bellfield, for example, Collings repeatedly put up with Wilkinson coming to her mother's house in Strawberry Hill, searching for Bellfield. On one occasion Bellfield even started giving Wilkinson a 'battering' when she came to find him at Collings's house. The spell Bellfield cast over both women saw them unable to shake free of his grasp – even though both knew – from bitter experience – exactly the violence he was capable of.

The truth remains that Jo Collings and Becky Wilkinson put up with the fact that they knew of each other's existence, and that Bellfield was having a sexual relationship with both of them at the same time, as well as relationships with other women. Both were trying desperately to cling to a man whose only apparent interest for large periods of the time was to abuse them – and the means they used to hang on to Bellfield was to bear him more children.

Becky Wilkinson's second daughter, Levi-Jane, was born shortly before Bellfield started a relationship with Collings, but while he was having an affair with one of her friends. Wilkinson's third daughter, Hannah, was born after Bellfield started his relationship with Collings, and her fourth, Jacqui, while he was still in the relationship with Collings. Meanwhile Collings's first daughter was born before the birth of Wilkinson's fourth daughter with Bellfield, while her son, Henry, was born after Bellfield had embarked on a relationship with Emma Mills, who was pregnant at the same time by him.

The bleak reality is that both Collings and Wilkinson were prepared to pay almost any price to cling on to the 20-stone nightclub bouncer – and they were only too prepared to bear his children. And the reason Bellfield made sure to keep in touch with both women was straightforward – to sustain his sense of control over them, but, even more importantly, to make sure that they didn't tell the police exactly how vicious and abusive he'd been towards them.

When Collings's son Henry was born in July 1997, Bellfield was present at the birth, but – as usual – paid little or no attention, beyond ensuring once again that his name was on the birth certificate. He was proud of his parentage, even if he despised the mothers of his children.

As Jo Collings was finally to admit years later, 'Levi kept on saying, "I hate blondes, I hate women. You're all cunts. You're not worth a bolt."' They were words that she was to remember all too clearly in the light of the other things Bellfield confessed to her in months to come at the house they shared in Strawberry Hill.

6. The Alleyway Stalker

'The only shame is to have none.'

Pascal, *Pensées*

At the bottom of the garden of the house that Johanna Collings shared with her mother and Levi Bellfield in the mid 1990s in Strawberry Hill, west London, runs a secluded footpath that stretches from the local railway station down beside the tracks towards a set of railway sidings and the next station at Teddington. It's an ordinary enough alleyway, covered in dark tarmac, with a mesh wire fence on one side – to prevent its pedestrian users from risking the dangers of the tracks – and wooden fences on the other, protecting the gardens of the houses on Strawberry Hill Road. It runs for about 600 yards, wriggling both left and right. Bright, light and harmless enough during the day – with boys on bicycles using it as a short-cut and mothers walking their dogs – it nevertheless becomes distinctly more threatening as darkness falls. For the few street lights are sometimes as much as 40 yards apart and do little to illuminate its spectral shadows, enclosed as the alleyway is by the trees and shrubs of the gardens and the undergrowth that lines the tracks. If you walk down it at dusk there is no denying that it brings a faint shiver to your spine, for there is something unsettling about its verdant secrecy, hiding as it does at the end of the gardens of a row of supremely respectable Victorian villas.

The girls on their way to the station who use the alley every morning and afternoon on their way to and from school might never think so, but it is a perfect place for a stalker to seek his prey, the ideal spot to watch from the shadows and pounce on an innocent victim. And it was in this alleyway that Levi Bellfield practised doing exactly that.

The reason was clear enough. No matter how many women might fling themselves at him, Bellfield was never satisfied. He might have had a harem of partners, but he wanted fresh blood, young women he could use and discard, women who would not answer back, not tell their parents, or the police – in short women who would become his victims. And none were more desirable than school-girls. To Bellfield they were all 'begging for it'.

Perhaps it can all be traced back to his adolescent infatuation with the girl who had become his first fantasy, Patsy Morris. Did she perhaps reject this once spindly, uncertain traveller's son with the domineering mother and refuse to accept his immature fumblings? Did he then lose his temper with her so dramatically that he couldn't control himself? And did that cost her her life? Did she become what the behavioural psychologists now describe as the 'trigger' to his violent, obsessive behaviour towards schoolgirls and young blonde women? No one can be certain, but what is without doubt is that Bellfield rapidly developed an obsession with very young women that was to remain a central part of his character throughout his adult life, a part that would shock his female partners – not least Jo Collings.

After Bellfield's arrest on suspicion of murder in November 2004, Collings told the police how horrified she had been when she had first encountered his appetite for schoolgirls. She explained that he took a particular interest in the girls from Gumley House Convent School in Worton Road in Twickenham.

'He would look at them as we were driving along when the schools would turn out and he'd be really dirty,' Collings would explain. 'He used to call them dirty little whores and slags and they all needed fucking because they had little skirts on.' Then he would demand that she dress up as one herself. When she said no, 'I'd get a really good hiding because I refused point blank to do it,' she added. 'I said, "You're sick," and he went mad, the usual stuff: screaming, shouting, kicking and punching.'

That wasn't all. Bellfield also wanted her to walk up and down their bedroom in school uniform carrying a vibrator and then use it on herself as he watched so that he could videotape her doing it.

Girls from a number of the local schools regularly used the alleyway at the back of the Collingses' house as a short-cut to the railway station at Strawberry Hill, and it was there that Bellfield would lie in wait for them. Originally, it may only have been as a voyeur, a stalker who wanted to stoke up the fantasies he carried from his own schooldays in Isleworth – and the image of Patsy Morris – but as time passed so his desires grew darker and more dangerous.

Jo Collings certainly noticed the change in him, so much so that, towards the end of 1996, she tackled him about his habit of 'going out for a walk' after dark in the winter, when the alley behind the house was cloaked in shadows.

'It would normally be 7 o'clock or so,' Collings would remember, 'and he would be wearing dark clothing – the dark jacket that my dad owned and dark top, black nylon bomber jacket, black Reebok jogging trousers, trainers and maybe dealer boots.' Bellfield always went out through the garage at the side of the house, where he kept the dark jacket. Sheila Collings had given him his own set of keys. 'I thought he was out seeing another woman,' Jo Collings was to explain, 'so I confronted him.'

Sobbing like a child, Bellfield sat on the end of their bed and told her, 'I've got a problem.'

'What is it?' she asked.

'I'll take you and show you.'

Bellfield led her to the alleyway at the bottom of the garden, and together they walked along it until it veered slightly to the left, where there was a gap by a tree.

'That's where I wait for girls – victims,' he told her.

'What the fuck are you talking about?' she screamed.

Bellfield told her that he had nearly caught one girl, but that he had been disturbed by someone appearing out of the gloom further down the alley. Collings told him bluntly that he was 'sick and needed help'. But she didn't tell anyone else about the conversation. She didn't even tell her mother, or the police, though she knew in her heart, as she was to admit later, that he was 'waiting to attack a girl'.

That wasn't the only confession that Bellfield made to Collings. At one point during their four-year relationship he also bragged to her that he had raped a disabled girl on a car bonnet in the car park of the nightclub he was work-ing at as a bouncer: 'I lifted her out of the wheelchair,' he told her with pride in his voice. On another occasion he told her that he had given a girl a lift home when he was a doorman at Rocky's in Cobham and that he had ripped her tights and her clothes.

'What do you mean?' she asked.

'I wanted it so I took it,' he replied. 'I raped her.'

Again Collings meekly accepted Bellfield's explanation that he 'felt guilty' about it.

Perhaps she thought he was exaggerating about his sexual conquests – though that is a little hard to believe, as she later admitted to the police that she thought he was 'shagging' one of his cousins when his former partner Becky Wilkinson was in hospital having his daughter. Even when Collings was confronted by the clearest evi-dence of his violent sexual attitude towards women she did nothing to stop him. For it wasn't just Bellfield's appe-tite for the alleyway behind her house that pointed to his desires, there was also the three-quarter-length jacket that she discovered in the family garage towards the end of 1997.

'The pocket was cut away from the inside,' she explained later, 'and in it was a nine-and-a-half-inch bladed kitchen knife and a full-faced balaclava with only eye and mouth holes.' It would have concealed Bellfield's face completely.

That wasn't all Collings discovered in what she was later to describe as his 'rape kit'. There were also a number of issues of *Cosmopolitan* and other women's magazine in a black bin liner. The face of each and every one of the blonde models in the magazines had been slashed with a knife. 'Not the dark-haired ones,' she was to remember: 'Only the blondes.'

When she challenged Bellfield, he confirmed without a moment's hesitation that he would go out into the alleyway behind their house wearing the dark coat and balaclava to wait for women. He calmly told Collings that he 'wanted to hurt them, kill them or stab them or rape them'.

But Collings didn't tell the police. One reason was that, after she had discovered the mutilated photographs, Bellfield had beaten her with exceptional ferocity. 'He forced my face over the pictures of the blondes shouting, "I fucking hate blondes, they should all fucking die,"' she said. Collings also confessed later that he had told her: 'I hate women.'

But even that extreme reaction from the man who was sharing her house didn't convince her to take any official action. She made no anonymous call to Crimestoppers, no furtive call to the local police – nothing at all. 'I was still sort of with him at this time,' she was to say years later. 'Even though he was with Emma by then, he was still controlling me; you weren't allowed to have a life.'

Time and again Collings forgave Bellfield – in spite of the beatings, the cigarette burns and the relentless abuse, in spite of the fact that he took cocaine and smoked heroin when he was with her, and in spite of the distinctly strange fact that he would repeatedly burn brand new clothes that he had only worn once without explaining why. Nothing provoked her to blow the whistle on this violent, sadistic and abusive man.

It was only after Bellfield's arrest that Collings was able to tell the *Sun* newspaper that she believed he had attacked more than 100 women, sometime two in one evening, and had described blonde girls as 'evil fucking bitches who must die'. She also admitted that he would regularly boast to her when he got home in the early hours of the morning about having 'another little slut' in the back of his car that night, and would force her to get out of bed when they were together and go and 'scrub out' the car he had been using so that 'there was no trace of what he had done'.

Despite this, Collings was reluctant to give evidence against Bellfield in court for fear of the reaction of his family. 'They will think that the fact I am prepared to give evidence is disloyal,' she explained, 'and I will feel very uncomfortable with all of them watching me.' However, she would also admit that having to stand up in a court and 'tell people about what he did to me and what I suffered is really embarrassing', adding, perhaps a little late in the day, 'I am ashamed that I let it go on so long.'

Collings's silence speaks volumes about the reign of terror that Bellfield waged over his female partners over the years – clearly backed up by his family and friends. What began as infatuation with the man who could be a 'Prince Charming' turned within weeks to fear and trembling at what he was capable of and what he might do. Just as it was true for Becky Wilkinson, so it was true for Collings. Both women would put up with the worst forms of humiliation in order to keep him and to survive.

One means Bellfield used to control them both was by keeping them constantly on edge. As Collings once vividly put it, 'You never know when he's going to come home what mood he'll be in. You live your whole life all the time on your nerves and in fear of him coming in and being off his head or even normal.'

That wasn't all. Bellfield would also routinely humiliate his female partners, forcing them into a level of subservience that belittled them to such a degree that they lost the ability to judge what was normal and what was not. One horrifying example concerns Bellfield's toilet habits, probably bred by his mother's habit of spoiling of her youngest son. After his arrest Collings told the police, 'He even made me wipe his arse when he had been to the toilet, I would have to sit on the bath next to him while he was on the toilet.' The degradation did not stop there. 'If I went to the toilet I didn't lock the door, as I wasn't allowed to' she confessed.

It wasn't even just his bathroom habits that his partners had to accept. It was also his serial infidelity, and his desperate desire to keep in contact with the mothers of his other children.

To an outsider it would have seemed that Bellfield was a man completely out of control, and growing more so by the day. He had started drinking strong lager in the mornings and then continuing to drink for the rest of the afternoon and evening, while adding cocaine to the mix as his day progressed and even – according to Collings – 'smoking heroin' on a regular basis. Bellfield was also still having regular brushes with the police – not only for his persistent harassment of Becky Wilkinson but also for a variety of minor offences, including common assault outside the nightclubs he worked at, where he would get carried away in fights with the customers. All the while, Bellfield was still 'ducking and diving', driving a string of cars and vans, all different, all for short periods, to throw any police officer who might begin to take an interest in him off the scent. He would scuttle through the back alleys and byways of west London in vehicles of all shapes and sizes, always on the lookout for young women, but never staying still long enough to attract too much attention.

Throughout the mid 1990s, when Bellfied was nominally with Jo Collings and their two children, he would flit from place to place, never content to stay anywhere for very long, always moving, always prepared to keep everyone around him on their toes and off guard, always unpredictable.

Bellfield was not a man to stray far from his familiar stamping grounds in west London. He took pride in 'knowing all the back doubles', as Collings explained later, and a similar pride in the fact that all his partners knew each other – Collings knew Wilkinson, and in 1996 both women knew that he had embarked on a relationship with the timid and impressionable Emma Jane Mills.

Like a Moorish sultan, Bellfield liked to surround himself with a contemporary version of a harem, where his women were always available to him, even if he chose to keep them in fear rather than in comfort. He was a creature of habit, and of limited horizons: his world was remarkably small. He liked it that way. Everyone knew everyone else – especially the girls in the nightclub queues.

Jo Collings, for example, first met Emma Mills at Rocky's in Cobham. 'She was very young, and I remember her as a very quiet, sensible, little well-spoken girl,' Collings said later. 'I remember she always used to drink water.' But it wasn't long after the birth of Collings's first child with

Bellfield in February 1996 that she learned Mills had become another of Bellfield's conquests.

'I knew he was seeing someone,' Collings would admit, 'but I didn't know who. He used to say he was going fishing. I caught him out and he finally admitted it. I was fuming and I was angry with both of them. I think she was scared of me because of what she had done. I did shout and swear at her but I never hit her.'

The relationships between the women in his life added fuel to Bellfield's growing sense of control and power. That power was one of the reasons for the 'rape kit' that he kept in the Collingses' garage in Strawberry Hill. In his own mind he was creating a fantasy about what he could do to every impressionable young woman that crossed his path, a fantasy that he became ever more anxious to carry out.

For the moment the possibility of abducting a complete stranger remained just that – a fantasy – something to sustain him in the darker hours of the night when he drove around west London, stalking potential targets. His business was drugs and violence, and providing them to the highest bidder. As his relationship with Collings waned in 1996, and his closeness to Emma Mills deepened, so his drug-dealing grew apace, extending from ecstasy tablets and cannabis to cocaine and heroin for a more select group than simply the girls in the nightclub queue, a client base that could afford higher prices.

In turn the drugs lead to other things – notably violence, and the use of weapons. If there was a fight at one of his nightclubs Bellfield would be the first to get involved. If there was someone who needed to be intimidated – for whatever reason – he was happy to help his friends do exactly that. His steroid-created frame, honed with a little bare-knuckle boxing, was enough to intimidate, but with the help of a baseball bat, a brass knuckle-duster and a knife he became a potentially terrifying figure, especially when he had been taking drugs himself.

Bellfield liked nothing more than to cast himself as a 'bit of a gangster', someone the local girls would describe as a 'bad boy' with a bit of a nervous giggle when they talked about him. They knew and he knew he was dangerous, and that added to his attraction. He relished the frisson his reputation created.

No one was more impressionable than seventeen-year-old Surrey schoolgirl Emma Jane Mills – who knew he was living with Jo Collings, just as she knew he was still in contact with his previous partner Becky Wilkinson. Indeed, she was to admit a decade later: 'In the beginning of our relationship together, when Levi was living with Jo, I sometimes dropped him off at Becky's house. Levi told me that there was nothing in it and that they were now friends.'

By July 1997, however, when Jo Collings gave birth to her child with Bellfield – a boy they named Henry – their relationship was all but over. The rows had become relentless, and he rarely stayed at the Strawberry Hill house, preferring to disappear to Emma Mills or a flat in Hounslow that he also had the use of.

Sheila Collings had watched her daughter's decline as the years with Bellfield had worn on, and though she had never actually witnessed his violence towards her daughter she was certain it was happening. 'There were occasions,' she would explain, 'when it was obvious that Johanna had marks and bruises, which she tried to hide. The problem was she wouldn't talk about things.'

As a consequence, Mrs Collings had to watch her daughter change from a 'lively happy girl to a scared nervous one', trapped with a man who liked nothing more than to boast about the fights he had had and how he had just beaten someone up.

It was into this maelstrom that the naive and impressionable Emma Mills walked as a teenager – only too keen to demonstrate to herself, and to her mother, that she was now a fully grown woman, and use her new relationship with Bellfield to prove it.

By the autumn of 1997, Mills was living with Bellfield in a small flat in a Victorian villa in Manor Road, Twickenham, not far from the Green. It was there that Mills got used to her new partner's attitude to his children, and his ex-partners. At that point Mills was six months pregnant with their first child, Lucy, who would be born just before Christmas that year – barely six months after Jo Collings had given birth to her own new son with the nightclub bouncer.

Bellfield's appetite for polygamy and fathering children with whichever partner happened to be dominant at that particular moment was by now well established. The overlapping children tied the women to him securely. They proved he was a man, and that he could conduct himself in any way he chose, when he chose. His children with Becky Wilkinson, Jo Collings and now Emma Mills not only meant that the women knew all about each other, it also, in turn, lead to tensions which none of them could, or chose to, escape, as well as to a series of extraordinary arrangements for allowing the children to see their father.

'If I picked up the children from Becky's house,' Mills explained later, 'I'd have to wait around the corner in the car. Becky used to call me "the stuck-up whore". I haven't done anything bad to her, and they were finished by the time I started seeing Levi. Levi would see the children in fits and starts, and there would be long periods where we wouldn't see the children or Becky at all.'

It wasn't just Becky Wilkinson that caused the now eighteen-year-old Mills trouble, it was also Jo Collings. Bellfield was still trying to keep all his options open – telling Mills that even though he still saw Collings they were 'no longer a couple'. That wasn't how Collings saw it. After all, she had a daughter of eighteen months and a baby of six months when Mills came on the scene.

For her part Mills was furious with her, and showed it. One day in the autumn of 1997 Collings remembered that Bellfield and she encountered Mills one day when Bellfield was driving her beige Austin Metro car and Mills was driving her car in the opposite direction.

'Emma saw me and Levi and she was not pleased,' Collings said. 'She jumped out of her car leaving it in the middle of the road and ran over to my side of the car. I was in the passenger seat, so I quickly locked the door. Levi also locked his door. He was laughing nervously at her.'

According to Collings, Mills leaned across the bonnet, screaming and swearing at them both. Bellfield laughed off the incident. As far as he was concerned it was another example of the control he had over the women in his life, further proof of his harem.

On another occasion, Bellfield was having a drink with Collings in a local pub when he phoned Mills to ask her to collect him in her car. Without a murmur Mills agreed – though what she did not know was that she was to get more than she bargained for.

'Levi came out of the pub with his ex girlfriend, Jo,' Mills recalled later, 'and they both came up to my car. Levi told me to wind down the window and I said, "No." The window was already wound down a little way. Jo said, "Oh wind down the window, Emma, I'm not gonna do anything to you."'

At that moment Bellfield went round to the passenger side of the car, opened the door and started punching Mills on the side of the head near her left eye and shouting, 'Do as you're told, do what you're fucking told.' It was the first time that the bouncer had hit his teenage girlfriend, though it certainly would not be the last.

Bellfield then climbed into the car and instructed Mills to take him to his mother's house, which the terrified teenager duly did, only for him to punch her repeatedly all the way there. The bruises that Bellfield caused were so bad that later that evening even he began to worry that she might need medical treatment. Without a moment's hesitation, he telephoned Collings to ask her to take Mills to the nearby Ashford hospital.

'Jo came in and sat with me,' Mills would explain. 'I gave her name and her address in Twickenham. I was seen by the doctor and told him that some girls had done it. I told that lie because I was frightened of them finding out Levi had done it in case he got into trouble.'

Bellfield's domination of his women was complete.

They would never betray his abuse and violence to the police or local social workers. They would put up with any humiliation he chose to heap upon them, no matter how terrifying. It contrived only to further increase the swagger in his stride. The fact that they were at each other's throats only increased his sense of power. Not one of them stood up to him, none questioned his actions, and – even more significantly – it was abundantly clear that the one woman whom Bellfield had always sought to please, his mother Jean, would never object. 'Levi could do no wrong as far as his mother was concerned,' one girlfriend declared in 1998, and it was entirely true.

What pleased Bellfield almost as much as his power over the women in his life, however, was his delight in physical violence, which in turn showed up in his brushes with the law. In March 1998 he was arrested for the possession of an offensive weapon, a baseball bat which he had used in his role as a nightclub bouncer, just as he had been charged with the use of a Stanley knife during another brawl four years earlier. Violence was as much part of Bellfield's life as the drugs that provided him with a regular income. But it wasn't just knuckle-dusters or knives. Bellfield also dealt in guns – though he was at pains to keep this quiet from most people. But not from Emma Mills, who was horrified one day when he returned home to her with 'a long gun like the ones used for clay pigeon shooting'. Bellfield started to saw off part of the barrel of the shotgun – with its 'great wooden handle' – on the kitchen table, and showing off as he did it. The sight terrified Mills, who was only too well aware that her children could be hurt. 'We had an argument about it because the children were in the house,' she was to say later. 'And Levi took it away the same day.'

'Levi was a big deal to his mates by the end of the 1990s,' one police officer who worked on the case was to say, 'a very big deal, not least because he wasn't afraid of dealing in guns.'

Nothing gave Bellfield greater pleasure. By the end of 1998 he was a 'face' to be taken seriously in his part of west London, and that bred a confidence that was to encourage him to fulfil his fantasy about hurting young women he didn't know and had never met – particularly blondes.

Levi Bellfield's fantasy was about to come to life.

7. Sex and Drugs

'They are as sick that surfeit with too much
as they that starve with nothing.'
William Shakespeare, *The Merchant of Venice*

Shortly after Levi Bellfield's thirty-first birthday in May 1999, he learned that his latest partner, Emma Mills, was pregnant again, with their second child, due in October. It would bring the total number of children he acknowledged that he had fathered to no fewer than seven – four with Rebecca Wilkinson, one with Jo Collings and now the second with Emma Mills.

There were rumours that he was also the father to a number of other children but Bellfield always denied it, just as he tried to claim that at least two of the children he had accepted as his own were 'actually other blokes''. Their mothers, Wilkinson and Collings, fervently disagreed.

It was typical of the man. Given to ever-increasing mood swings, he could be dismissive of his five infant girls and two baby boys at one moment and then, equally suddenly, become over-indulgent with them the next. Bellfield would shower them with presents bought with his profits from dealing – in everything from drugs to cars, weapons to violence; he was 'ducking and diving' in the twilight zone on the very edge of the law like a man possessed.

Now a 20-stone man whose head seemed to sit on top of his shoulders without a discernible neck, he was still a nightclub bouncer – most recently at a new club in Shepperton called The Barn – but that was only a means to an end. It provided him with the ideal cover to deal in drugs, but, more importantly, also gave him ample opportunity to try and seduce young girls into his personalized 'shagging wagon', his Toyota people-carrier complete with its orange quilt, mattress and purple neon lights. If the girls could be persuaded to accept his offer of a spiked Malibu or Red Bull then so much the better. He would have sex with them in the Toyota and then throw them back out into the nightclub car park, where they would rarely remember exactly what had happened to them. It was the perfect modus operandi: unlimited sex with very young women whom he could use as he chose – and who would never accuse him of anything. If he sometimes invited one or two of his 'mates' to enjoy the girls too, well that only made him more popular among the men who had increasingly come to follow his lead. 'Nothing to be lost,' he would boast to his friends with a knowing smirk. 'No one's ever any the wiser, specially not the girls.' The fact that it was the ruthless, unprincipled exploitation of vulnerable, innocent young women didn't cross his mind. Bellfield still felt the law 'doesn't apply to me'.

The truth, of course, was that Bellfield's brushes with the law had increased rather than slowed down over the years. Since the age of sixteen he had been charged with no fewer than sixteen offences, from theft to burglary, from actual bodily harm to possession of an offensive weapon. But not one of those charges related to his sexual obsession. He had also come into contact with the police on countless other occasions – particularly over the abuse of his partners. Nevertheless he had only spent one brief period of four months in jail as an adult and had even managed to keep control of Becky Wilkinson and his family while he was away, using his mother and sister to 'keep a close eye on her'.

In the summer of 1999 Bellfield was living with Emma Mills in a small flat in Clements Court in Hounslow, near the open space of Hounslow Heath, but he was looking for something bigger, only too aware that he would soon be the father of a toddler and a baby – even though that didn't stop him 'always going out in the evenings', as Mills described it, leaving her to take the responsibility of childcare.

But that wasn't the only responsibility Bellfield gave his then twenty-one-year-old lover. Inexorably, Mills was forced to hand over packages to strangers, not knowing what they contained, and only agreeing to do it because she was terrified of him. It was only later that Mills realized the full extent of what had been happening, and what he had been asking her to do. It came as a tremendous shock to the young woman from Esher, who had never taken an illegal drug in her life. Bellfield saw nothing wrong whatever in involving his young partner. Like everything else to him, it was not a big deal, just part of his wheeling and dealing.

As time wore on, and Mills gave birth to their son William in October, Bellfield made no effort to conceal his own drug use, openly admitting to his partner after nights out that he had had a 'bit of Charlie', as he called cocaine.

Not that Bellfield was incapable of feelings towards his

new young partner. During the previous summer of 1998, for example, he had taken Mills and their six-month-old daughter Lucy on a holiday to Ibiza, a holiday habit he was to repeat regularly in the years to come, although he came to prefer the island of Tenerife, as he maintained it was 'sunnier'.

For a far greater part of the time, however, Bellfield treated Mills like a slave, disappearing for long periods of time – especially at night – without giving her any kind of explanation. Mills was left to fend for herself, as Bellfield would often not reappear until the following morning. Sometimes he would even disappear for days at a time, going to stay with one of the men who had become his friends on the doors of nightclubs.

One of the men he met while working on the door at Royales, the Uxbridge club beloved of airmen from the local RAF base, was a man in his early thirties known for his girth and aggressive attitude named J— Spiers. Along with Bellfield, he worked a series of doors together at nightclubs on the outskirts of London including The Works in Kingston-upon-Thames.

One young woman who saw exactly what Bellfield was capable of on his nocturnal sprees with Spiers was named S— Atkins, who launched into an affair with him after she met him at Royales. She alleged later that Bellfield and Spiers enjoyed such a close relationship that he even would video Bellfield having sex with girls.

'Levi wanted to show me the video,' Atkins would recall later, 'but I told him I didn't want to see it.' Undeterred, Bellfield put it into the video-recorder and switched it on. Rapidly realizing what it was, she insisted he turn it off at once. Her refusal to watch it did nothing to dampen Bellfield's enthusiasm, however, as he also asked her if she would like to have a threesome with another man, although he did not mention which other man he had in mind, but again she refused.

They were the actions of a man without conscience, whose disregard for the law, indulgence of every conceivable vice, and stalking of young women demonstrated for all to see that he had lost contact with any moral code. They were the actions of a sociopath.

Bellfield boasted to Atkins that he could get hold of a date rape drug and asked if she had like to try it. Again she refused, even though he insisted that the 'sex was supposed to really great'. It made her 'feel uneasy about him'.

As well it might, for it was the formula Bellfield was increasingly using to seduce women in one of his many cars. Atkins herself admitted that the first time she had had sex with him was in a car on their way back from a nightclub.

Bellfield revealed another ever-growing aspect of his character to the young clubber that he had met in the queue – his increasing appetite for violence.

'He used to boast about throwing people out of Royales and beating them up,' Atkins said later, explaining that if the bouncers felt 'bored' and someone started a fight they would throw them out and beat them up. To prove how much he enjoyed violence, and was prepared for it, he produced a knuckle-duster from his pocket to show her.

Another man who saw the drug-dealing and violent side of Bellfield was Richard 'Yosser' Hughes. Hughes would become a father figure to Emma Mills and almost single-handedly helped her survive the torment of spending her life in the shadow of Bellfield's moods, his temper, and his relentless violence and sexual abuse. At the same time, however, Hughes remained Bellfield's confidant, going to unlicensed bare-knuckle boxing matches with his childhood friend.

Like Mills, Hughes was well aware of Bellfield's drug-dealing. 'I have seen him take cocaine on a number of occasions,' Hughes would recall later, adding: 'He also dealt in cocaine. He had a press at Little Benty, which he used to make blocks of cocaine. He mixed the cocaine with another white substance so that it would go further.'

No one was more aware than Hughes of his friend's temper and capacity for violence. After Bellfield's arrest that he would describe him as 'mainly being nice towards people' but adding that he 'soon turned if they upset him or his friends. It did not take a lot for him to loose his temper.' He went on to explain that he had witnessed Bellfield 'assault people on a number of occasions'.

One place Hughes saw this propensity for violence at first hand was at a mini-cab firm in Shepperton, Middlesex, called New Lion Cars, where he had started working early in 2000. Bellfield had joined him there shortly afterwards. It was another job that allowed him to come and go as he pleased as well as setting his own timetable. Who was to know exactly what a mini-cab driver got up to when he was out on the road on his own? There was, of course, the additional attraction that driving a mini-cab allowed Bellfield ample time to search for vulnerable young women.

In the mini-cab office Bellfield showed his true colours – defence of his friends and a capacity for violence. The company's twenty-three-year-old radio dispatcher reported a colleague to the police for using drugs after an argument in the office. After his arrest, Bellfield picked him up from the police station and went straight to Lion Cars office. There, he took a hot kettle full of water and hit the controller over the head with it, knocking him to the floor, and then laid into him behind the counter. The controller ran off, never to be seen again.

Not that violence was the only interest Bellfield had at the mini-cab firm. He also started an affair with one of the female drivers. Never one to miss an opportunity, he started having cards printed with his personal mobile number on them – rather than the company's – so that he could also 'freelance' as a mini-cab driver. He would distribute the cards to the girls in the nightclub queues, pointing out that he was always available to take them home. Those personalized cards were just another one of Bellfield's ruses to get young women into his car alone in the hope that they might be tempted to try the 'alcopop' drinks that he offered them 'to make a great end to the night'.

One of Bellfield's friends at the time remembered later that the bouncer had a number of cars and vans at his disposal – though he never knew exactly how he came to have so many. Bellfield would brag about them, calling them his 'GHB wagons'. This friend saw the inside of 'at least one' van, which was fitted out with a mattress, handcuffs and blacked-out windows.

Another of Bellfield's friends, who worked with him as a bouncer at both The Barn in Shepperton and at Royales in Uxbridge, would later confirm to the police that when they were 'working the doors' Bellfield never went home straight away as he would either have 'pulled' a girl while he was working that night or had one lined up already. It was he who first told the police of the Bellfield's habit of taking girls to hotels on the northern perimeter of London's Heathrow airport.

No one can say for certain how many girls Bellfield abused in this way – as few ever came forward to make a complaint against him to the police, not least because most could not even remember what happened to them. Even if these young women could remember dimly that something had happened to them many also felt a sense of guilt, knowing that they had bought ecstasy, cannabis or even cocaine from the giant bouncer.

But date rape drugs were not the only means that Bellfield used to conceal his intent. There was also the matter of his cars. He took enormous pains to ensure that he seldom used the same car twice when he went out at night. If the victims could identify his car – which was unlikely but just possible – he wanted to be sure that the car couldn't be traced back to him, and he did so by making sure that he had access to a large variety of vehicles, some bought, some borrowed, some even stolen for the night, that would make it difficult for any police officer investigating a complaint against him to trace him.

The officers who investigated Bellfield after his arrest in November 2004 came to believe that a 'significant' number of young women had fallen victim to his use of date rape drugs.

'We know he raped young girls in his cars after drugging them,' one officer would admit later, 'but we couldn't prove it. We also believe that he would even dress them up the victims as schoolgirls while they were unconscious to increase his pleasure, and then invite his mates round to abuse them too, but again it was enormously difficult to prove so long after the events.'

If that did happen, there can be little doubt that it increased Bellfield's hold over the group of men who were gradually forming around him as his 'known associates' – to use the official police term. Attracted by the bouncer's bravado and audacity, not to mention his complete lack of conscience and eye for a drugs deal, they saw Bellfield as man who was afraid of nobody and prepared to do anything. For his part Bellfield liked to sustain his image as a 'leader' by drawing them into his drug deals and sexual attacks – and thereby ensuring that they could never give evidence against him. If they were to inform on him they would only be guaranteeing their own arrest and imprisonment. But if they remained silent they could participate in the profits of the drug deals and the availability of young women who were not only beneath the age of sexual consent, but also drugged and incapable of giving it.

But Bellfield's sexual conquests under sixteen were children in the eyes of the law, which inevitably drew him into the dreadful, ugly world of paedophilia. At one stage he bragged to a friend that he had been to a paedophile 'meeting place' in a park where he could engage in sex with under-age girls. He confided that it was a place where paedophiles of all kinds could meet to indulge themselves but he didn't reveal the exact location, except to say that it was outside London and to the south with the word 'Hill' in its name. There is no doubt whatever that Bellfield knew of the existence of a paedophile ring in west London and at least one of its members, Victor Kelly, a man whom the police would later describe as 'one of Britain's most dangerous paedophiles'.

Operating out of a flat in Hayes, west London, Kelly, then in his early sixties, would groom young girls for sex after buying them presents of clothing or mobile phones and then giving them cannabis and cocaine. A career criminal, he supported his lifestyle by dealing in drugs and had been jailed for six years in 1982 and eight years in 1990 for drug offences. He was finally sentenced to eight years' imprisonment in November 2005 after a being convicted of giving a twelve-year-old girl cocaine so that he could have sex with her. The police knew of at least thirty other victims and believed that Kelly, known in west London by the nickname of 'Uncle Joe', may well have abused up to 200 young girls – all of them between the ages of twelve to fourteen – over a seven-year period stretching from 1997 until 2004. It was at precisely this same time that Bellfield was bragging to his friends about his own conquests of fourteen-year-old girls, and when he too, like Kelly, was sustaining his lifestyle by selling drugs. After Kelly's conviction at the Old Bailey in November 2005 Detective Chief Inspector Matt Sarti described Kelly as 'a ruthless man who presents a real threat to children' and called him a 'serial groomer and abuser of children', who used violence or the threat of violence to stop his victims revealing what had happened to them.

It is highly unlikely that Bellfield, who lived in exactly the same part of west London and was also involved in dealing in illegal drugs, didn't know of Kelly and his appetites. Indeed several of the bouncer's friends and 'associates' also knew Kelly and his reputation in the western fringes of the city.

But Levi Bellfield was adept at presenting himself to the world – and particularly to young women – as 'a big softy' who 'never hurt anyone'. It was this ability to groom those around him, both male friends and female victims, and to pass himself off as 'no more than a grown-up kid', that was to save him from being identified by the police and other authorities as a sexual predator for more than a decade.

Like the Gloucester serial killer Frederick West, Bellfield knew how to make himself inconspicuous, even helpful, to the police. Indeed by the time that he was finally arrested for the murder of Amélie Delagrange in November 2004 the police criminal records files showed that he had attracted the attention of the Metropolitan Police's officers on no fewer than ninety-two separate occasions before he finally found himself in Heathrow police station being interrogated by detectives from DCI Colin Sutton's double murder squad. There were criminal records of his possession of offensive weapons, of possession of stolen vehicles, of burglary and theft, of assault involving actual bodily harm, even accusations of rape and buggery, but Bellfield somehow remained 'comparatively harmless' in the eyes of the authorities in west London. And the reason was his natural ability to 'charm the birds off the trees'. Time after time Bellfield would play the part of the naughty boy, large of stature, certainly, but never threatening, when he came into contact with the police and social services. Indeed at one stage he even started to offer titbits of information to the officers at Hounslow police station – just as Frederick West had done to the officers in Gloucester. It was a ruse to make them underestimate him, to see him as no more than 'small-time', while the reality was completely the opposite. Bellfield was a very dangerous man indeed.

Every bit as importantly Bellfield had learned to mask his desires behind his image as a 'Jack the Lad' who really wouldn't hurt a fly. He might display his true self – the sexual marauder relentlessly searching for fresh prey – to his male 'associates', but he was careful to keep it hidden from everyone else. Photographs of Bellfield with partners and their children at this time show a man who seems to revel in his role as a father, rather than rapist on the edge of a psychotic break who was about to turn to murder. He presented himself to the wider world a man anxious to seem as 'normal' as possible, even though he knew only too well, in his heart, that nothing could be further from the truth. Underneath that apparent normality there lurked a far darker and more frightening character, and one whose appetite for sex and violence had been whetted and was about to be satiated.

So, as the millennium came to its end, Bellfield's appetite for sex with naive and impressionable young women had grown to consume his life completely. The more it did so, the less able he was to control himself, and the more his addiction to it increased. But why did it escalate? And why now? The obvious answer is that Bellfield had managed to go unpunished and undetected for more than a decade. He was now thirty-two years old and well aware of the satisfaction he got from indulging his violent sexual fantasies on three permanent partners, Becky Wilkinson, Jo Collings and Emma Mills.

Professor David Canter, one of Britain's leading psychological criminal profilers, explains in his 1994 book *Criminal Shadows*: 'The destructive mixture of a callous search for intimacy and an unsympathetic desire for control is at the heart of the hidden narratives that shape violent assaults.' The twin traits of the 'loving father' and 'controlling partner' lie at the centre of Bellfield's personality and provide part of the explanation of why it was about to fracture for ever.

His own lack of a father figure almost certainly contributed to his distorted view of what being a husband and father meant. The skinny child whose father died when he was eight, who was then vastly over-indulged by his mother, and then rejected by his first proper girlfriend – who may even have paid for it with her life – was about to 'compensate' by attacking women at random. It was, at least in part, his private retaliation against what Sigmund Freud called 'the mother he is afraid to challenge'.

This explosion of inner rage into violence against female strangers whom he neither knew nor cared about was to see him launch an unprovoked attack that would bring him to trial beneath the statue of a woman bearing the scales of justice in her hands above the Central Criminal Court in London's Old Bailey.

There could be no more appropriate image for the crimes of Levi Bellfield.

8. Sultan of Sex

'Men must have corrupted nature a little, for
they were not born wolves, and they have
become wolves.'

Voltaire, *Candide*

In September 2000 Levi Bellfield and Emma Mills, together
with their children, two-year-old Lucy and eleven-month-
old William, moved into the cramped cul-de-sac house
at 11, Little Benty, in the shadow of the M4 motorway. It
was to be their family home together – with one or two
exceptions – for the next four years.

On the surface Bellfield was still presenting himself to
the neighbours as a family man who liked nothing more
than to play with his toddler daughter while helping to
look after his baby son, the sort of father who liked taking
them out for 'treats' like a trip to the country in one of his
many cars, and taking family photographs to prove it.

As Emma Mills knew only too well, however, beneath
that facade, Bellfield was a darker and more threatening
character altogether, with a prodigious appetite for Ten-
nant's strong lager and recreational drugs. He was still
attacking her repeatedly, denying her money and disappearing for long periods of the day and night without
explanation. He had also developed the habit of never

parking whatever car he was using outside their house, but always 'round the corner', as if preparing for a quick getaway.

One person who saw at first hand the private torment of Mills's life at Little Benty was her mother, Gilly, who had been concerned about her daughter for the past four years, but hadn't been able to do anything about it. Concealing her private fears, Gilly Mills had kept her dignity and had even been present at the birth of both her daughter's children, alongside Bellfield, regardless of his temper and abuse – though she also knew that on both occasions he had made a rapid excuse to leave the maternity ward for the local pub.

Mother and daughter remained close, and Emma continued to visit her mother's house in Esher with her children after she had moved into Little Benty. But the visits to her mother only sharpened Bellfield's desire to control his partner and family. Whenever Emma went to see her mother, Bellfield would ring her repeatedly – on her mobile and her mother's landline – between six and eight times in just two hours, determined to break the intimacy between them and disrupt their conversations. In Bellfield's mind, Mills was his property and he was intent on making sure he alone controlled her.

Meanwhile, although he was living with Mills, he was keeping in contact with both Becky Wilkinson and Jo Collings. His appetite for multiple affairs was as much part of his character as his swaggering behaviour on the doors of the nightclubs he worked at. He was, it seemed to some, intent of being nothing less that a sultan of sex, as another young woman who came into contact with him in the first months of 2001 discovered very quickly.

In her early thirties with three children, the woman in question, A— Platt first encountered Bellfield at a funeral in May that year. The deceased was related to the Bellfield clan so they were strongly represented at the ceremony. Sensing an opportunity for another sexual conquest, the rapacious Bellfield asked Platt out for a drink 'to catch up on old times', and suggested she come out to Royales nightclub in Uxbridge with her 'mates' and he would make sure she got in free.

Though Platt was still married at the time, she was well aware that her marriage was failing and a couple of weeks later took Bellfield up on his offer. 'Levi made me feel secure,' she remembered. 'He would look after me. I saw him as someone who would protect me.'

She was then subjected to the familiar pattern of grooming that Bellfield had perfected over the past decade – and she exactly matched his preferred type, even if she was a little older. She was naive and intensely vulnerable – with three children from a previous marriage and a husband whom she alleged was violent towards her.

'Levi took an interest in me,' Platt was to confess. 'He kept on saying, "Come out for a drink." He used to buy me drinks all the time, and he was very pleasant. He would take me out for curries.'

Platt never met Emma Mills, although Bellfield did admit to her that she existed, and that they had two children together. 'He always kept her separate from me for some reason, I don't know why,' she was to admit later.

It didn't take very long for Platt's relationship with Bellfield to turn into a sexual one. He would visit her at her home while her husband was out at work, and there would be encounters in his car. But things did not go exactly to plan.

'The first few times we had sex I don't think he did ejaculate,' she said. 'He used to go limp and that was it. He said it never happened with other girls. But then as he got more comfortable with me he did, but it was almost like he didn't enjoy having sex with me. That was the impression I got. Although he made out that he was the big man around women and boast about it, with me he was completely opposite: he was shy, timid and gentle.' Platt explained, 'Levi would never take his top off and he would never let me take his top off because he was embarrassed about his stomach.' He even told her that his 'ejaculation problem' was because he was 'so close to me'.

But when she asked him about all the other women, Bellfield merely replied that it was 'different with them, just sex, it doesn't matter'. Three years later Platt would admit that it was 'more of an excitement thing, being with him. He was protective, and I was going through a bad time. It wasn't a very sexual relationship.'

That didn't prevent Bellfield from demonstrating his penchant for sex with other, much younger, women. Indeed one reason for his sexual difficulties with Platt could well have been that she was more than a dozen years older than his preferred 'schoolgirl' type. As an older woman she could well have led him to feel inadequate even though she made no secret of her vulnerabilities. In Bellfield's sexual pantheon a young impressionable girl was one thing, a mature woman quite another.

Bellfield's problems certainly weren't replicated when it came to the teenage girls in the queue at Royales. She used to watch him taking them up to the room above the night-club with its grotty sofa. 'He used to joke about it,' she would remember. 'But all the girls knew about Emma. He would always tell them he was with Emma, and they all willingly had sex with him.'

At one point Platt even warned him that he might catch AIDS, but Bellfield had his answer well prepared. 'No, no, no I'll never catch AIDS,' he told her. 'Why do you think I always go for the young ones? They're clean, that means that I'm clean.'

No matter how it may have appeared to his neighbours in Little Benty, behind closed doors Bellfield acted in exactly the same way that he had done for the previous decade. He manipulated the women in his life, intimidated them with violence, while dealing in drugs to sustain his lifestyle. He even extended his drug-dealing to Platt and her three daughters.

On one occasion when Bellfield was at her house, the oldest daughter woke up at nine o'clock one evening wanting some chocolate. Her mother told her to go back to bed, but Bellfield persuaded her to allow him to take her out and buy her some chocolate – on the surface the act of a caring man. The reality, of course, was altogether different. There was a drug deal to be done, and Bellfield took the girl, and Platt's car, and drove to Royales nightclub, staying out for about two hours. 'I was livid,' she would remember. 'The next morning I spoke to my daughter about it, and she told me that they were outside Royales, and Levi had tablets in a bag. I couldn't believe it. I thought: what am I getting into?'

Bellfield's oscillation between charm and menace was

still part of the intimidation technique that he depended on. It left Platt reeling, unable to predict how he would respond to her behaviour, and as the summer of 2001 continued that meant she would agree to accede to whatever demands he made on her – no matter how outrageous.

One way in particular that Platt would give in to him was by allowing him to borrow her car. Bellfield would tell her he had 'some business to do' and ask if he could borrow it, although he would never tell her what exactly the business was. It wasn't long before she found out. One day in July 2001 he came back with the car and said to Platt, 'Look what I've got,' and produced a long-barrelled shotgun with a brown handle, which he proceeded to hide under the units in her kitchen, by taking out one of the bottom boards, pushing it into the space beneath the units, and then replacing the board.

'What the hell is that doing in my house?' Platt asked him.

'I just need somewhere to put it for now,' Bellfield replied.

'Well you're not leaving that here,' she said. 'I've got the kids here. If someone found a gun in my house I would get into trouble.'

Bellfield wasn't to be dissuaded. 'It's only for a short time' he told her. 'It's just I don't want to move it right now, its daylight.'

That night the gun disappeared.

But the gun wasn't the only weapon that Platt saw in Bellfield's possession. One day she opened the glove compartment in one of the cars he was driving and found a brass knuckle-duster, which he told her was 'for my bouncing work', while on another occasion she found a flick knife.

'He said it was to protect himself,' Platt said later, 'but I told him if he got caught he would get into trouble.'

Unabashed, Bellfield told her: 'No one will ever catch me.'

To prove how unconcerned he was, Bellfield also started carrying a baseball bat in his car. 'He always said it was for his protection,' Platt would insist. 'Not that by the size of him he would need protecting.'

Bellfield's mood swings became steadily more severe as the end of the summer of 2001 approached, and it wasn't just Platt who felt it. Emma Mills did too, and all the time he was still indulging his passion for promiscuity. Throughout the summer he would see Platt most weekends, regardless of his relationship with Emma Mills. It was finally to tip Mills over the edge. Together with the verbal abuse, the disappearances, the mood swings and the endless violence, it finally convinced her to leave, and take her children with her.

In July 2001 Mills took her children to a women's refuge near her mother's home in Woking. She was to remain there for the next two and a half months, and while she was there she began to describe some of her experiences at Bellfield's hands to the female volunteers. But she couldn't keep it up. The memories were too painful.

The first person to hear about Mills's departure from Little Benty was Platt. Bellfield told her that Mills had suddenly walked out. 'She's sick and tired of the women: she knows I have other women.' But then he added that he really wanted Mills to stay with him because of the children. 'They're my kids,' he said. 'I love my kids and I want to bath them at night.'

As ever, Bellfield was not telling the entire truth. Another reason for Emma Mills's departure was his relentless violence.

'She's made out that I'm violent,' Bellfield told Platt.

'Well are you violent?' Platt asked.

'You know me, I'm a big softy,' he said, 'but I would never hurt anyone, I only hurt people who deserve to be hurt.'

It was a barefaced lie, but, at the time, Platt believed him.

'He had never been violent towards me,' she would recall. 'He just got very very nasty verbally towards me, like saying he was gonna burn the car and smash the windows. Silly things like that.'

Mills's departure sent Bellfield into a paroxysm of rage, raising still further his innate hatred for any woman that 'disrespected' him. Platt was not to know it, but it was a rage that was to come brutally to the surface in the weeks and months ahead. The FBI's behavioural psychologists call such an incident that incites violence a 'stresser', and there can be little doubt that Mills's departure with his children from the house at Little Benty turned Bellfield into an even angrier man than he had been in the past.

But Mills was not out of Bellfield's clutches entirely. She was obliged to allow him to see their children, which he did from the middle of August. There was also the problem that she could not stay at the refuge indefinitely, and so, towards the middle of September 2001, she left and settled in the flat at Collingwood Place in Walton-on-Thames.

The moment that Mills left the Woking refuge Bellfield started to stalk her – shadowing her in his car and then telephoning her mobile phone out of the blue to tell her exactly where she was and what she was doing. It was intrusive and manipulative, and typical of Bellfield's behaviour, but, tragically, the young woman who had been so brutalized over the past four years was still under his spell. Gradually – inevitably – Bellfield ensnared the young woman and her children back into his clutches. He insisted he would be 'a different person', and she watched as his violence towards her did come to an end. Mills was back within his spell.

Bellfield's violence towards her may have ceased, but the cycle of rage that her departure had initiated for the skin-headed nightclub bouncer was now to take another direction. He had got what he wanted – his partner and their children back – and so the rage he had felt at her loss was now mixed with a brutal arrogance at his success in persuading her to return. It was a lethal mixture, and one which would eventually come to tip him into mindless violence.

Shortly after 11.30 on the evening of Monday, 15 October 2001, just weeks after Bellfield had moved back in with Mills, the police later alleged that he committed his first blitz attack on a young woman that he had never met.

Her name was Anna-Maria Rennie. Slim, blonde-haired and only seventeen years of age at the time, she represented everything that Bellfield fantasized about in a teenage girl, and the police alleged that he came across her near a bus stop on Hospital Bridge Road in Twickenham, barely half a mile from the studio flat that he and Emma

Mills had shared in Manor Road and barely a mile from a flat he regularly used on the Oriel Estate in Hanworth. It was the heart of Bellfield's patch in west London, all of it on just one two-page spread in the *London A-Z*.

On that particular Monday evening Rennie had been having a row with her boyfriend, Richard Lewison, with whom she was living in a flat in Whitton, just off the A316 Chertsey Road that leads to the M3 motorway. Fiery by nature, she had decided to take herself off for a walk to calm down and left the flat shortly after 11 on that autumn night. It was cool outside, so she had grabbed her coat and flat keys, but not her handbag or any other belongings. She wasn't planning to be away for ever, she just wanted a bit of space to think.

It was dark but there was plenty of illumination from the street lamps as Rennie came out of her flat in Ross Road, turned left, walked west into Percy Road and then turned left again into Hospital Bridge Road, before crossing the main Chertsey Road and continuing south along the west side of the road where it crosses a bridge over the local River Crane. Just over the bridge was a bus stop, with red plastic seats and a shelter to protect waiting passengers from the rain, and Anna-Maria Rennie sat down. She had been out for about twenty-five minutes and had recovered some of her composure. Besides, it was late and she wanted to get to bed. So she started back towards home.

As she did so, Anna-Maria Rennie looked back and saw a car pull up about 10 feet behind her on her side of the road. A man climbed out of the passenger seat and walked to catch up with her, and she remembered later stopping to have a conversation with him. When she talked to the police about the conversation three years later she thought it might have gone on for as long as twenty minutes, because she was 'still upset' and crying about the row with her boyfriend.

At some point towards the end of their chat the man offered her a lift in his car, but she turned it down, telling him that 'a man of his age' shouldn't be offering young girls lifts at that time of night. The man told Rennie that he was only twenty-five, though if this was indeed Levi Bellfield, as the police allege it was, he was actually thirty-three.

At this point the man asked her to look at something he had in his car, and she walked back with him, where he introduced her to the man who was actually driving the car, which she thought, but couldn't be sure, was a dark-coloured Ford Mondeo. Anna-Maria Rennie couldn't be sure of the colour because it was dark, but she thought it might have been dark blue or black. After saying hello to the driver, she told the two men that she had to leave and set off back up the east side of Hospital Bridge Road towards Chertsey Road and her flat on the far side.

But she had only walked about 15 or 20 feet when the man who had engaged her in conversation grabbed her from behind in a bear hug with his left hand, while he put his right hand over her mouth and lifted her off the ground completely to carry her back to the car. It was an unprovoked attack on an innocent young woman on a well-lit main road with passing cars and buses, but he didn't hesitate for a moment. Anna-Maria weighed only 7½ stone, and was thin as a rake, and so it wasn't difficult for the man, whom she thought was over 6 feet tall and weighed at least 18 stone, to lift her. He certainly didn't have any difficulty whatever in carrying her to the car.

The seventeen-year-old was petrified, but she wasn't going to give up without a fight and started kicking and struggling violently. It worked, because about 3 feet from the car she managed to break free from his grip. Scared half to death, she ran into the park beside the River Crane and away from the two men and their dark car.

As she did so the man who had grabbed her shouted 'whore' after her, and followed her a little way into the park, but she was running too quickly to be caught by a man of 18 stone and escaped.

It was to be three days before Anna-Maria Rennie reported her attack and the attempted abduction to the police, and she only did so then when a local constable in uniform came to her flat to investigate something else entirely. She told the officer that she had been attacked by a man who said he was twenty-five, had short blond hair and a 'round face' that was fat. She also described him as about 6 feet 3 inches in height and with a tattoo on his lower right forearm. Rennie explained that he had been wearing a cap and a white or cream tracksuit and trainers and had a London accent.

Meanwhile Rennie's boyfriend told the officer that he had briefly gone out to look for her after she had left the flat that night but had given up and gone home. When she got back, he went on, she was 'distraught and crying'. He tried to cuddle her and help her to get to sleep, but 'she didn't manage to'. Apart from that her boyfriend didn't remember very much else, perhaps because – as Rennie was to tell the police later – he was smoking cannabis at the time and was a 'heavy user'.

The police tried to locate the dark Ford Mondeo Rennie she thought she remembered – which Anna-Maria thought might have a licence plate that began L561 – but without success. None of the fifty-four owners of blue Mondeos with that plate were anywhere near Twickenham or Hounslow in October 2001.

It was only after Levi Bellfield's arrest for the murder of Amélie Delagrange in November 2004 that they discovered that he had access to a number of dark-blue Mondeos at that time. Platt remembered him having not one but two, while a fellow mini-cab driver also recalled him having a Mondeo.

Indeed it wasn't until the end of March in 2005 that Bellfield, a man with a habit of never driving the same car twice if he could help it, was arrested for the attempted abduction of Anna-Maria Rennie, and it wasn't until she had identified him in a video identity parade that he was formally interviewed under a police caution at Milton Keynes police station before being formally charged with abduction.

In the words of prosecuting barrister Brian Altman QC to the jury at Bellfield's trial for Rennie's abduction in October 2007, 'Bellfield demonstrated himself quite prepared to approach and attempt to abduct a lone young female at night, albeit on a main road, even when he was in the company of another male.' In the end, however, the jury at the Old Bailey failed to agree a verdict on Bellfield's alleged abduction of Anna-Maria Rennie. He was cleared of attacking her.

What the jury did not hear, however, was information that had reached the police from the other man in the car that night – a man so afraid of Bellfield that he was not willing to testify. The man was B— Kingston, one of Bellfield's drug customers, who had been getting supplies of cannabis from him for a year or more. That night, he told the police in confidence, he was being given a lift home by the bouncer to his house, in what he thought it was a white BMW, not a dark Mondeo. That fact alone cast doubt on his validity as a witness, but he described exactly what happened to Anna-Marie Rennie and could hardly have done so in such detail had he not actually been there.

According to Kingston, Bellfield was driving along Staines Road and had just turned into Hospital Bridge Road when he suddenly told him, 'I want to talk to that slut,' and promptly stopped the car. Bellfield jumped out and approached a girl the informant thought was in her 'early twenties' near a bus stop, and they had what he called a 'heated' discussion. Kingston then saw his drug-dealer 'grab the girl and manhandle her' which so upset him that he got out of the car himself to speak to him. Bellfield told him – in no uncertain terms – to mind his own business. Disgusted, Kingston turned on his heel and walked away. By this time the girl had also run away.

A few minutes later Bellfield pulled up beside him in the car and began swearing and shouting at him. The bouncer told him bluntly, at the top of his voice, never to interfere and then drove off, leaving Kingston to walk home. Kingston also told the police that Bellfield had been perfectly calm and cheerful before the attack, but 'flipped' as soon as he saw the girl. Most significantly of all, he also told the police that on a number of occasions when he had been in a car with him, Bellfield had demonstrated what the man described as 'an unhealthy interest' in schoolgirls.

'He would wind down the window and shout abuse or obscenities at them' or 'he would jump out and speak to them direct', although the informant insisted he could never hear what was being said.

Just a few months later a thirteen-year-old schoolgirl was to disappear just across the road from a bus stop on the road that leads away from Walton-on-Thames railway station. Her name was Milly Dowler.

9. Vanished into Darkness

'The Sun's rim dips; the stars rush out;
At one stride comes the dark.'
                    Samuel Taylor Coleridge,
                'The Rime of the Ancient Mariner'

The morning of Thursday, 21 March 2002 dawned grey and damp in Hersham, one of the leafier south-western suburbs of London, but in a warm house there a family were getting ready for school. The two daughters, the often smiling thirteen-year-old Amanda Dowler – known as Milly – and her elder sister Gemma, who was sixteen, were packing their school bags and getting ready to climb into their mother Sally's car to drive to Heathside School in Weybridge, where Sally was a teacher and the girls were pupils.

It was a perfectly ordinary morning, on a perfectly normal school day, and both girls kissed their father, Bob, goodbye and disappeared happily with their mother. But what no one knew on that dull Thursday morning was that it would be the last time the Dowler family would ever be together. It was to be the last morning that the Dowler family would see their beloved Milly alive.

At 3.26 that afternoon Milly caught the train home from Weybridge, but instead of travelling through to Hersham, she got off at Walton-on-Thames, just one stop before her own, to share some chips with a group of her friends at the station café. It wasn't something Milly did every day, but it wasn't all that unusual either. She was simply one of a group of teenagers enjoying themselves. At 3.47 she borrowed a friend's mobile phone to call her father and tell him that she would be home in about 'half an hour' or so. Then she went back to gossiping with her friends. The chat went on a bit longer than she expected, but, just after 4 that afternoon Milly set off along Station Avenue to walk the half mile or so back to her home.

She never got there.

At about 4.08 on that grey March day Milly disappeared as she walked down the opposite side of the road from the first bus stop in Station Avenue – diagonally across the road from the station. One of her friends was standing at the stop and watched her pass on the other side of the road, but after that no one saw her again.

It was broad daylight. Cars were passing, people were making their way to the station, buses were collecting passengers, but no one saw what happened to the 5-feet-tall girl with brown eyes and shoulder-length brown hair. No one saw her stop to speak to anyone. No one saw her get into a car, or walk into one of the nearby blocks of flats. No one saw anything.

Milly Dowler simply vanished into thin air.

It was a disappearance that shocked the nation, provoking national appeals for information on television, thousands of pages of newsprint, a BBC *Crimewatch* reconstruction and countless theories. A video of Milly ironing her jeans at home while dancing at the same time became a hit on the internet, as did another of her playing the saxophone. But the publicity and the outcry across the country were to no avail. Milly Dowler had disappeared.

She wasn't to be seen again for six months, and when she was all that remained of this charming, effervescent teenager with a knack for making friends was her bones.

One man who knew all about Station Avenue in Walton-on-Thames in March 2002 was Levi Bellfield. The reason was simple enough. He was living there at the time with Emma Mills and their two children, Lucy and William. When Mills had left the refuge in Woking, she had moved into a flat that her mother had found for her. It was at 24, Collingwood Place, an unassuming brick-built flat on the ground floor of a low-rise block just off Station Avenue. The flats were constructed around courtyards, with small paths winding between them.

The easiest way to reach the flat on foot is to take the clearly signposted footpath just beside the first bus stop on Station Avenue – where Milly's friend saw her on that March afternoon – and follow it for about 30 yards, through a group of other flats, until you reach number 24. To drive there you need to go a little further along Station Avenue and turn left into Copenhagen Way, then left again.

Bellfield and Mills had by now reconciled to the point where he had moved some of his clothes and belongings from what Emma called 'the squat' of 11, Little Benty into Collingwood Place. They even shared Emma's Staffordshire bull terrier, called Cheyenne, always known as 'Chey'. It was, as far as one ever could be with Bellfield's appetite for different homes and different partners, a family home. Yet Bellfield did not conduct himself at Collingwood Place like a conventional husband, partner or father, any more than he had done so in their studio flat in Twickenham. He would disappear for hours, even days, at a time going about his 'business' in all sorts of borrowed cars and vans, and still keeping Mills as much in the dark about where he was and what he was doing as she had ever been, though he had be sure to keep in touch with her on his mobile phone – his appetite for controlling his female partners hadn't dimmed.

When she had moved there from the women's refuge, Mills had taken a six-month lease on Collingwood Place, but in early March had decided that she would go back to Little Benty with him and the children at the end of the lease in early May. She didn't want to go back to Little Benty straight away, however. She wanted it smartened up a bit. So in the last weeks of March she had planned to do some painting and decorating there to make the house more 'habitable' and less of a 'squat'. For his part Bellfield was perfectly happy with the arrangement, providing it left him free to come and go as he pleased.

On Thursday, 21 March 2002 Bellfield, Mills and their children weren't actually staying at 24, Collingwood Place, however. They were 'house-sitting' for her friend Christine Hawgood, in West Drayton in Middlesex, not far from Heathrow airport and their house at Little Benty, while Hawgood took a short cruise from Portsmouth to Bilbao in Spain and back. She had needed someone to look after her house and dog. Mills seized the opportunity because it meant she could spend time decorating Little Benty before moving back there without the bother of having to drive all the way over there from Walton-on-Thames. Bellfield went with her to Hawgood's house on Tuesday, 19 March, when Christine left, and was still there on the morning of Thursday, 21 March.

But on that particular March day, Bellfield too disappeared.

As Mills would tell the police three years later, 'Levi normally rings me every hour or every couple of hours just to say "hello" or to say he would be back at a certain time.' But on that particular March day he didn't. Bellfield simply left Christine's house in the middle of the morning and didn't appear again until late in the evening. And he didn't phone her once.

When Bellfield left he was driving Mills's red Daewoo car, with the registration number of N503 GLT. At the time it was the only one he had the use of, or so Mills believed, but that didn't mean he behaved in an exactly normal way. Just as he did throughout their years together Bellfield would seldom park the car outside where they lived, preferring to leave it 'round the corner'. In this instance that meant that Bellfield left the Daewoo on the main road or on Copenhagen Way and walked through to the flat, which took 'about a minute', according to Mills. 'You could see the main road from the kitchen, the living room and the bedroom,' she said later, even though the flat was protected from the road by a hedge.

'I remember that day,' said Mills, 'because I was trying to ring him all day from Christine's house, as I needed some money to go to the shop to get some milk and stuff. He had my car, and his phone was off all the time. I just thought it was weird . . . I thought he was up to something because he had turned his phone off. I thought he was in the pub or with another woman.'

That afternoon Mills took the dogs for a walk and kept on trying to get hold of Bellfield, but she didn't manage to. In fact it wasn't until 10.30 that evening that Bellfield reappeared at Christine's house, and when he got there he was wearing an entirely different set of clothes from the ones that he had left in that morning. Mills couldn't remember exactly what her partner had been wearing that morning, 'but I just knew he had changed,' she explained. 'He was wearing a white shellsuit-type top, I don't think it had a hood, and I think it may have had a stripe down the arm, maybe red or blue . . . I recognized the top as I had seen him wear it before.'

The fact that Bellfield had changed his clothes convinced the young mother that he must have been back to their flat in Collingwood Place during the day to change, because the clothes he was wearing that evening weren't among the ones he had taken with him for their few days of house-sitting for her friend Christine.

'He only had a couple of bits of clothing at Christine's,' she said, 'but not that top. That's why I remember and that's why I was suspicious.'

Mills had every reason to be – her partner's appetite for sex with young impressionable women, not to mention his ongoing relationships with Becky Wilkinson and Jo Collings, confirmed his lack of respect for monogamy. It was a convention that didn't apply to him. Mills also knew that Bellfield had the keys to Collingwood Place, as there was only one set, which were on her key ring, which also contained the keys to her Daewoo. 'Nobody else had access to the flat,' she was to explain, and Mills had certainly not been there herself, as she didn't have any transport.

'When he came home I could tell that he had had a drink,' she was to say. 'He wasn't drunk, but I could see that his eyes were bloodshot.'

But she didn't ask him where he had been. 'If you knew Levi, you don't really ask questions,' she said. 'If you do, it's none of my business . . . He didn't like me asking him questions about where he had been, but then he never liked me asking questions.'

Bellfield had brought home a Kentucky Fried Chicken meal for them and a few cans of lager, which they shared before going to bed.

Meanwhile back in their neat, tidy house in Hersham Milly Dowler's parents were beside themselves with worry. Milly had phoned her father just after 3.45, but there had been no sign of her since. So at 7 that evening Bob Dowler had phoned the police. Rather than fobbing him off with the idea that Milly might have gone to stay with a friend, or even that she had run away because of an argument at home, Surrey Police acted with commendable speed and rapidly launched a full-scale missing persons inquiry, later to be codenamed Operation Ruby. It was to become the most expensive single operation in their history, costing some £6 million. Police family liaison officers were despatched to speak to Bob and Sally Dowler, as well as Milly's sister Gemma, and plans were laid to launch a full-scale hunt as soon as it was light the following morning. No time was to be lost in tracking down the missing teenager.

In the early hours of the following morning, back in

Christine Hawgood's house in West Drayton, however, things were about to take an unexpected turn. Between three and four o'clock in the morning, Mills woke up to find Bellfield getting dressed.

'I thought, that's peculiar,' she remembered later; she asked him what he was doing.

'I'm going to go back to the flat,' he told her, 'because I'm going to have a lay-in.'

Mills couldn't understand why on earth Bellfield had to get out of bed in the middle of the might, because he could just as well have had 'a lay-in' at the house. But he wasn't to be dissuaded. So, at around 4 in the morning of Friday, 22 March Bellfield gave Mills a kiss, told her that he would call her when he woke up and left. She didn't notice what clothes he put on, because she was half asleep, but she did notice that he took their Staffordshire bull terrier with him.

Remembering the events almost three years later, Emma Mills couldn't recall exactly when Bellfield had returned to Christine's house the following day, although she was sure that they had slept there together on the Friday night because Christine was coming back from her trip to Bilbao on the Saturday evening, and Mills wanted to tidy the house for her.

Then things took another strange turn. Bellfield suddenly announced to his young partner that he wanted to go straight back to Little Benty rather than return to stay Collingwood Place – even though they had planned to stay on at Walton-on-Thames for another month.

Confused, and surprised, by his sudden decision on the Saturday morning of 23 March, Mills rushed around clearing up Christine's house before Bellfield gave her a lift back to Walton-on-Thames so that she could collect her own and their children's clothes. He dropped her off outside the flat but didn't go in with her. Once again he just disappeared, as he had done so often in the past.

Inside the flat Mills was in for another surprise.

'When I went into my bedroom I saw that all the sheets were gone off my bed,' she would remember. 'This included the duvet cover, the sheet and the pillow cases. They were all gone, and there was just the duvet in the middle of the bed . . . I thought at the time that he had had a woman in the flat so I rang him on his mobile.'

'Oh sorry, Em,' he replied, 'the dog had an accident. I've chucked it all.'

Mills didn't believe the story for a second. It was her dog as much as Bellfield's and it was house trained. Besides, there weren't any marks or stains on the mattress that would have shown that the dog had made any kind of mess the bed. Bellfield also told her that he had thrown the sheets, pillow cases and duvet cover out with the rubbish, but when she went out to look for them they weren't there, though she did think the rubbish bins were normally emptied on a Friday morning, the day before she had gone back to the flat.

By that Saturday morning the police search for Milly Dowler was well advanced. Surrey Police had set up a major incident room and appointed a detective chief inspector as senior investigating officer. They had searched through the family's computers, spoken to her friends and seized every piece of CCTV coverage of the area that they could as well as using police dogs to examine the local allotments and starting going from house to house in search of any information that could help to explain Milly's disappearance.

That morning four specialist officers had begun a fingertip search of the Dowler's house and garden, focusing particularly on Milly's bedroom. They meticulously checked her mobile phone to see if she had made or received any calls on 21 March – but she hadn't. They even removed no fewer than 140 separate items from the Dowlers' home, for closer forensic examination, but even that brought them no closer to finding Milly.

When Emma Mills arrived back at 24, Collingwood Place on that Saturday morning she could see the police cars and the television camera crews with their satellite trucks camped around Walton-on-Thames railway station. She half expected the police to knock on her door 'to see if anybody had seen anything', but they didn't and she didn't give it a great deal more thought. Mills simply gathered up her own bed, the children's bunk beds, the television cabinet and a little tumble dryer and loaded them into the red Daewoo when Bellfield returned and set off for Little Benty. She didn't approach the police to explain who she was or where she lived, although she was to discuss Milly's disappearance with Bellfield in the days that followed.

'I remember saying to him how terrible it was,' she would recall later, 'especially when you live opposite to where she went missing from.'

Bellfield certainly took an interest in the investigation. 'For example, when Levi was out,' Mills remembered, 'if he heard something on the news like a car had been seen, he would ring me and tell me.' Surprisingly, he even seemed to know where the Dowler family lived, but then his mother's partner, Johnny Lee, had lived in Hersham and knew the area well.

In the weeks that followed, however, Emma Mills started to notice a change in her partner. From a man who seemed not to have a care in the world and did exactly what he chose Bellfield started to display signs of nervousness, even fear. After they left Collingwood Place he started to develop what Mills later called 'panic attacks', attacks so severe that he 'couldn't even go into a shop'. When he was in the grip of an attack Bellfield looked as though he was going to faint, started sweating so that his skin went clammy and began shaking. The attacks would come on without warning: in bed at night, in the car during the day – anywhere. As far as Mills could see there was nothing that set them off, though he would claim to her that it was only because he was drinking too much at night.

'It's only since we came back from Walton that he's gone funny,' she would tell her friends later.

Panic attacks weren't the only problem. Less than a week after Bellfield had suddenly whisked them back to Little Benty, he came back into that cramped house beside the M4 to tell her that he didn't have her red Daewood car with him. He told her that he had spent the day drinking in a pub in Hounslow with a group of friends and hadn't wanted to drive home because he had had too much to drink. But when Bellfield went back to retrieve the car on the morning of Tuesday, 26 March it had disappeared. He rang Mills and told her: 'You're not going to be very happy, but the car's gone.' She remembered later that he 'didn't seem particularly bothered about it being stolen' and had even suggested that one of his 'cousins', Charlie Brazil, had stolen it because 'they'd had a row'.

Emma Mills could not have known it at the time, but the fate of a red car that looked rather like her missing Daewoo was to become the subject of national interest and speculation in the months that followed. The reason was that a red car had been caught on some CCTV footage turning out of Copenhagen Way and out into Station Avenue shortly after Milly Dowler had been making her way home on the other side of the road. Perhaps the driver had seen her, or spoken to her, or even perhaps offered her a lift. No one knew. Certainly the police tried everything in their power to track the car down and launched repeated appeals for anyone who might have been driving it to come forward, or for anyone who might have seen it to contact them, but without success.

The Operation Ruby squad looked at more than 250 CCTV tapes and sent some of them to the FBI's headquarters in Quantico, Virginia, to see if they could enhance the images of the cars, but without success. But Surrey Police weren't just looking at CCTV footage of cars as part of their search for Milly. They also visited 3,500 houses in the course of their inquiries, took an astonishing 4,941 statements, collected 4,800 exhibits and conducted thousands of interviews to see if anyone had any memory of seeing the schoolgirl on that fateful Thursday afternoon in March. But not a single person had seen her get into a car. They interviewed everyone that Milly had come across that day, whether at school, on the way back to Walton-on-Thames on the train or at the station café, but without success. They investigated sex offenders who lived locally, considered the male teachers Milly might have come into contact with, or workmen that she might have met at home or at school. They even interviewed the fathers of Milly's friends in search of a possible suspect, but to no avail. More than 100 police officers were drafted in to help in the investigation, and they searched no fewer than 300 sites in an attempt to locate her – thirty of them underwater, using specialist teams from the Metropolitan Police. They asked for, and got help from, other forces in Sussex, Essex and Bedfordshire, to check every car that was in the station car park that day: again without success.

Desperate to solve the mystery of Milly's disappearance, the police encouraged Bob and Sally Dowler to launch appeal after appeal on every conceivable television programme and channel for any information that would help to find her. The *Sun* newspaper backed that up by offering a £100,000 reward for anything that might help find Milly. Nothing positive emerged – nothing that is except for the occasional lunatic and timewaster who came out of the woodwork to infuriate the police and harass and upset Milly's parents and sister. A man called Paul Hughes, for example, was jailed for five years after sending letters to her mother claiming to have killed her daughter. The letters were sent whilst Hughes was in prison for indecently assaulting a twelve-year-old girl. Lianne Newman from Tewkesbury phoned Milly's parents, school and the police pretending to be the missing schoolgirl, and was sent to prison in April 2003 for five months after pleading guilty to five counts of making phone calls to cause annoyance, inconvenience or needless anxiety. Meanwhile Gary Farr from Nottinghamshire repeatedly emailed Milly's parents claiming that their daughter had been smuggled out of the country to work as a prostitute and stripper in Poland. In October 2006 he was sectioned indefinitely under the Mental Health Act for being a danger to the public due to a history of schizo-phrenia. Surrey Police even received 450 calls from people who called themselves 'psychics' and who claimed to know Milly's whereabouts.

Every one of these potential 'leads' came to nothing, and so, in an effort to reinvigorate the search, the police appointed a new senior investigating officer, to bring a new pair of eyes to the investigation, but even that did not do the trick.

By August, Surrey Police were forced to admit – in private at least – that they were at their wits' end. They had no body, no crime scene, no witness, and – even more astonishing – no significant suspect. The search for Milly Dowler had stalled.

Then, out of the blue, on Wednesday, 18 September 2002 – almost six months to the day since Milly's disap-pearance – a Polish couple named Mr and Mrs Wislocki found human remains while they were out picking mush-rooms in a secluded part of Yateley Heath Wood, near Fleet in Hampshire, 25 miles from Walton-on-Thames. The Wislockis found part of a skull and some rib bones well hidden within a thicket in the wood. Surrey Police immediately thought they might belong to their missing schoolgirl. The following day they launched a detailed search and quickly found other bones scattered around the immediate area. Not long afterwards they found more bones and other remains in a nearby stream.

The remains were taken to North Hampshire hospital in Basingstoke – not far away down the M3 motorway – and on the afternoon of Friday 20, September a forensic odontologist compared the skull and the dental records of Milly Dowler and came to the dreadful conclusion that the remains were indeed hers.

A forensic palaeontologist then told them that he believed the body had lain at that secluded site in a Hampshire wood since shortly after Milly's abduction six months earlier, because of the pollen that was found beneath her skull and the pattern of rainfall that summer.

Surrey Police's missing person's inquiry had become a murder hunt, and they renewed their efforts to track down her killer, searching the sex offenders register for locals to Yateley Heath, interviewing people who knew the area well, as well as retracing their steps and going back to interview those men who might have known her at school or through her friends.

No DNA from anybody else was found at the site where Milly's body was discovered. None of her clothes were found, nor any of her belongings: not her mobile phone, not her purse, not her backpack. She had been dumped there naked and alone, her mortal remains left to perish unprotected against the elements for six long months. To remind themselves of the tragedy of her death the police even kept a photograph of her skull darkened brown by its period in the open air, a stark contrast to her white teeth – the teeth that had been the only means of identifying her. No one who saw it could fail to be moved.

Surrey Police felt passionately that they had to do whatever they could to bring Milly's killer to justice and strained every sinew to do so. They even targeted her IT-recruitment-consultant dad Bob, subjecting him – though he did not know it at the time – to covert surveillance, bugging his phones and car, as they explored every inch of his relationship with his younger daughter. They trawled his computer for dark secrets, but found nothing incriminating whatsoever.

Milly's memory, meanwhile, was marked by a memorial garden at Heathside School, and her parents set up a charity in her name – Milly's Fund – to help educate young people about their personal safety, and how to protect it. Milly even had a deep-crimson sweet-pea flower named in her honour and to keep her memory alive. But in spite of the relentless publicity, the heartbreaking appeals from her parents, the television documentaries, the endless police interviews and the thousands of separate suggestions from the public, not a single suspect was found for her murder.

The Surrey Police investigation was to stretch on for years, but Operation Ruby drew a blank. Milly Dowler may have been found, but her killer had not.

10. Keeping Up Appearances

'Fine words and an insinuating appearance are
seldom associated with true virtue.'
Confucius, *Analects*

In the weeks after Levi Bellfield dramatically whisked
Emma Mills and their children back to Little Benty from
Walton-on-Thames on that Saturday in March 2002, his
panic attacks grew steadily more severe. Without warning,
and for no apparent reason, he would start shaking and
then break out in unexpected, drenching sweats that rendered him all but unable to move. He would do his best to
laugh it off, blustering that he 'didn't know what had come
over him', but Mills knew in her heart that something had
changed.

'Levi wasn't quite the same after we left Collingwood
Place,' she was to confess to her friends nearly three years
later. No matter how much he tried to keep up appear-
ances, in the darkness of the night there was no concealing
the fact that he had crossed some kind of Rubicon. Bellfield was still working as a nightclub doorman, now also
at a club called Park Avenue in Richmond as well as the
two original clubs, but he seemed distracted, not quite
the same big-mouthed, bullying 'Jack the Lad' that he had
been in the previous year. It was almost as though he

had frightened himself. He wasn't even quite as interested in Atkins, whom he had been seeing since the previous summer. In May 2002 their relationship just 'sort of fizzled out', and it looked for a moment as though this latest member of the harem of women he had taken such trouble to build up around him might be the last.

There were shakes and night terrors in private, but in public Bellfield did everything to prove that he was still firmly in control, and his temper certainly hadn't improved. His response to the panic attacks was to become even more violent whenever anyone annoyed him, and to do so with such force that he seemed to have lost all sense of self-control.

One friend who experienced his rapidly escalating violent nature was Kingston, the man who was later to insist that he had been in the car with him when Anna-Maria Rennie had almost been abducted on the edge of Twickenham. By the summer of 2002 Kingston was literally terrified of Bellfield, the man who had started off supplying him with cannabis and then had gradually drawn him into his drug-dealing business, and he had every reason to be. Kingston was assaulted repeatedly by Bellfield in arguments over the drug profits that one may have owed to the other.

The most dramatic example came in the summer of 2002, when Bellfield claimed that Kingston owed him £3,800 over a series of drug deals. The two men were at the house in Little Benty when the row started, but it quickly got out of hand – so much so that Bellfield produced a shotgun and proceeded to threaten Kingston with it. In fear of his life, Kingston ran out of the house and away down the cul-de-sac, with Bellfield chasing after him, still brandishing the shotgun – but no shots were actually fired.

It wasn't the only occasion when Kingston was threatened with a gun by Bellfield, but he never reported the bouncer to the police, nor did he break off their professional relationship over drugs. Kingston simply elected to suffer in silence, aware that after every tantrum Bellfield would suddenly become overcome with guilt, and apologize profusely for the violence he had threatened only moments before.

Like someone suffering from a form of bi-polar disorder the fat bouncer seemed to oscillate dramatically between extremes of emotion, ferociously angry at one moment, utterly repentant the next, apparently unaware of exactly how unstable he had become. Any control that he might once have had over his actions and emotions was slipping away.

Perhaps to convince himself that everything was exactly as it had always been Bellfield launched into another relationship with a teenager. In the summer of 2002, he started seeing a sixteen-year-old named J— Tilley. Like so many of the very young women in his life, Tilley first encountered Bellfield outside a nightclub and she was also aware that he lived – some of the time at least – in Little Benty with Emma Mills and their two children. Bellfield did not let that inhibit him, however. He had also recently rented another flat on the Oriel Estate in Hanworth, barely half a mile from where Anna-Maria Rennie had been attacked, to which he took his other young women.

Significantly, 39, Crosby Close, the new flat, was just as

difficult to find as his house at Little Benty, unless you knew exactly where to look. A visitor had to make his or her way through a maze of alleyways and car parks before eventually reaching it, tucked far away from the road. Bellfield's appetite to find a lair that made him hard to find had not deserted him.

He had reason to find one, because in the autumn of 2002 Bellfield decided to branch out from working as a nightclub bouncer and drug-dealer and take on another occupation which offered large amounts of ready money, providing he wasn't afraid to use intimidation. Bellfield turned his hand to wheel-clamping. As far as Bellfield was concerned the wheel-clamper's life was too good to be true. He could arrange clamping contracts with offices, clubs and shops across London which guaranteed the owners that no one would be able to park illegally on their property. If anyone were foolhardy enough to do so – against the instructions he would place on the parking area – he would clamp their cars and then charge extortionate prices to have the clamps removed. If the vehicles' owners objected it was not a problem. Bellfield would deal with them in precisely the same way that he did with angry clubbers in the queue at one of his nightclubs – with the threat of violence. After all, he was still carrying the knuckle-duster and the baseball bat with him in the car whenever he went to work.

According to his friend Spiers, who had worked with him on the doors at Royales in Uxbridge, Bellfield started in the clamping business with a man called Joe Smith, known as 'Jimmy Stockings', and his two brothers, Aaron and John, who taught him the business. Like Bellfield, the Smiths were travellers.

In no time at all Bellfield had left Jimmy Stockings behind him and branched out on his own with a company called Access Controlled Parking, and to help in his new business he recruited as many of his friends as he could.

One person Bellfield turned to for help was twenty-three-year-old L— Smith, who had been a friend of Spiers for the past four years, since they had met when he was a doorman at the Works nightclub in Kingston. Bellfield met Smith regularly at Spiers's house, and in late October 2002 told her that he was going into the clamping business and asked if she would like a job helping him.

'I would be there when Levi and Spiers were clamping,' she explained later, 'and I would answer their phones for them, calls from people wanting their cars unclamped. Basically I just sat in the car all day, but because I spent more and more time with Levi, I got to know him a bit better.'

As time passed Bellfield gradually signed up clamping contracts around some of the areas he normally worked as a doorman, including a nightclub in Park Royal, West London, a pub in Hounslow, an estate agent's office in Addlestone, a telecom shop in Woking and a carpet shop in Staines.

As his clamping business expanded, so the young Smith quickly came to see her new boss in a different light. 'To be honest I thought Levi was a bit of a prat and arrogant,' she was to say. 'He would wind people up a lot. I remember once that he clamped somebody even before they had got out of the car. We didn't get on too well.'

'Levi fancied me, he didn't hide that,' Smith admitted. 'He would say that he wanted to sleep with me and things like that. I would say I had better taste. I think that is why he didn't like me, because I turned him down.'

One other thing was clear. Smith didn't like being left alone with Bellfield and told Spiers so firmly. In particular Smith disapproved of Bellfield's habit of whistling at thirteen- or fourteen-year-old schoolgirls in short skirts when he saw them in the street. The fact that he would then shout 'Do you want some sweets?' distressed her. She remembered one occasion when she was with him outside a parade of shops not far from Little Benty when he had kept going into a shop where there were two or three girls in their school uniform. Smith told Bellfield to 'stop perving', but it didn't put him off in the slightest. 'He did the same sort of thing on a number of other occasions,' she would remember. 'It must have been really intimidating for the kids because Levi isn't a small man.'

It wasn't just Bellfield's attitude to schoolgirls that dismayed Smith, however. She also became increasingly angry about the fact that he wanted to have sex with her, even though she knew he was living with Emma Mills. 'He kept wanting to come over to mine to see me,' she would explain, 'which I didn't want. So I told him he was a fat idiot.'

The ever-touchy Bellfield – especially when it came to his weight – told Smith she should 'watch her back' because she would 'be sorry she said that', although, in fact, Bellfield never took revenge on the young woman. The two simply lost contact, while he reserved his anger for other women – young women who were complete strangers he had stalked at night. Bellfield's appetite for driving around west London at night looking for female prey hadn't dimmed. Far from it, as his clamping business expanded it seemed to grow in intensity. He took an ever-increasing pleasure in boasting to the friends who went out clamping with him about what he would do to 'the slags' when he caught up with them.

The clamping business also gave Bellfield the financial muscle to increase his collection of cars. The extra vehicles were necessary because he would often travel to a clamping site with both a car and a van to carry the clamping equipment. But there was the added attraction that it gave him access to a wide variety of vehicles, making his movements even more difficult to trace.

Wheel-clamping was a lucrative business. Bellfield charged up to £215 to remove a clamp, as well as up to £500 for a tow, and he always demanded the money in cash. Given the fact that he was clamping a minimum of thirty cars a day, he could certainly afford a new car. It was bringing him in more than £30,000 a week in cash. With the proceeds, Bellfield bought himself a second-hand silver five-door Vauxhall Corsa hatchback in early November 2002 to use for clamping. He signed the registration document in his own name and organized finance for the purchase in the name of his company, Access Controlled Parking. The car's registration number was Y57 RJU, and it would come to play a significant part in his life over the next few months, not least because he used it to drive around west London at night stalking potential victims.

One of Bellfield's favourite methods of stalking was to drive slowly past buses at night and look inside to see if he could spot a single young woman alone who was just about to get off. He would then follow her once she was on foot.

One young woman who may well have had the misfortune to come into contact with Bellfield in the last months of 2002 was Sonia Salvitierra, who happened to be walking up Hampton Road in Twickenham on 5 November at about 10.30 in the evening. Just as she arrived at the junction with Trafalgar Road – only a few hundred yards from Twickenham Green and close to a bus stop – a man appeared out of nowhere and hit her over the head with a blunt object before running off and then driving away in a car. The police later believed that it might have been a white Ford Sierra Estate car, although it might also have been a silver Vauxhall Corsa. They were not certain, and neither was the unfortunate victim.

Could the attack have been carried out by Bellfield on his nocturnal wanderings around west London? After his arrest in November 2004 on suspicion of the murder of Amélie Delegrange on Twickenham Green, DCI Colin Sutton's murder squad certainly became convinced that it was, but he was never to be charged with the offence.

The murder squad were equally convinced that another teenager had been another of his victims after she was hit on the head with a blunt object by a man that ran away and then drove off in a car just a few weeks after the Bonfire Night attack on Sonia Salvitierra. This time the vehicle that was used was probably a white Bedford pick-up truck – though, again, neither the police nor the victim could be certain. Jesse Wilson, who was only sixteen, was attacked at 8.45 p.m. on the evening of 8 January 2003 outside number 2, Walpole Gardens in Twickenham, once again near a bus stop, and just across Strawberry Hill golf course from the Salvitierra incident. She received massive head and facial injuries after being struck on the back of the head with a heavy instrument, quite possibly some form of hammer.

Significantly, Walpole Gardens was barely 50 yards from the shadowy alleyway leading down from Strawberry Hill railway station that Bellfield liked to hide in when he was 'stalking' victims while living with Jo Collings. Was she another victim? No one can be sure.

What is not in doubt is that Hampton Road in Twickenham and Walpole Road in Strawberry Hill were very much part of Bellfield's patch, the square mile or two of west London that he had lived in, drunk in and driven round endlessly over the years, a part of the capital where he knew 'all the back doubles'. It was an area in which he felt entirely at home. The forensic psychologist Professor David Canter of Liverpool University has pointed out: 'Where a criminal operates is one of the most distinctive features of the shadow that he casts.' Canter calls it their 'geographical centre of gravity', and this small section of West London was the epicentre of Bellfield's universe.

If these two random attacks were indeed carried out by Bellfield, they proved not only his appetite for random violence, but also his increasing belief that he could get away with anything he set his mind too. He was refining his skill as a stalker and a 'blitz attacker', and his confidence was growing by leaps and bounds. Like the increasingly obsessive Cuban criminal Tony Montana in *Scarface*, the 1983 film starring Al Pacino, the more he risked and the more he got away with it, the more convinced he became that nothing and no one could stand in his way.

Kingston saw that all too clearly in December 2002, when – after another argument about money – Bellfield held a revolver to his head at the house in Little Benty and threatened to pull the trigger. Again Kingston was literally terrified, but again didn't report the assault. And, as usual, Bellfield laughed it off afterwards, suggesting it was nothing but a 'bit of fun'.

Another 'bit of fun' took place on New Year's Eve that year in Laurel Lane, West Drayton, just round the corner from Little Benty. Kingston, and another of Bellfield's friends, Joe Ryan, were at a party in a block of flats in Laurel Lane just off the Harmondsworth Road, which crosses the M4 motorway on a bridge. The New Year's Eve party was described by Kingston as a 'free for all' for anyone who fancied it, which meant that he had no idea of the identities of many of the people who were there – except, of course, Bellfield and Ryan. The host was a keen fisherman, with a rather plump, ginger-haired, fourteen-year-old daughter. As midnight approached, the party came to what Kingston called 'an abrupt halt' when the father accused Bellfield of having 'touched up' his daughter in the flat's toilet. Kingston and Ryan – along with most of the other guests – quickly left the party and fled back to the safety of their own homes, but Bellfield remained at the flat. As far as Kingston knew, the police were never called, and the matter was 'resolved'. Afterwards Bellfield refused to discuss the incident with his friends, although the rumour among some of the guests was that he had actually sexually assaulted the girl. If he had, the incident served only to confirm his by now certain conviction that he could get away with anything.

It was a conviction that would lead to murder.

Part of the area that Bellfield knew very well was around Hampton in Middlesex, south-west of Twickenham and not far from the A316 artery out of London. His aunt had lived there in Fearnley Crescent, and his former partner Jo Collings had kept horses at the stables in Oak Avenue. His own sister had also kept a pony at the stables, and he had visited the stables regularly with her over the past two years. And it was here, barely half a mile from the stables, that shortly after midnight on Tuesday, 4 February 2003 a nineteen-year-old blonde named Marsha McDonnell was hit on the head by a random attacker outside number 60, Priory Road, just yards from her parents' front door. But, unlike Sonia Salvitierra and Jesse Wilson just weeks earlier, Marsha did not survive.

It was just 17 minutes after midnight on that February evening when Marsha got off the number 111 bus after her evening at the cinema with her friends. And at the very moment she did so the closed circuit television cameras mounted on the double-decker revealed a car driving towards it, which slowed as it passed and then stopped just a few yards further on at the entrance to Priory Road. The video footage showed the car stopping suddenly in the moments after Marsha got off, its red brake lights standing out in the inky night. As prosecuting counsel Brian Altman QC was later to tell the jury at Bellfield's trial for the murder of Marsha McDonnell, there was 'no obvious reason why at 12.17 a.m. the car should have slowed and suddenly come to a stop where it does other than . . . because of an interest in the bus and its disembarking lone female passenger'.

It was after midnight, the streets were quiet, there was no other traffic, and the CCTV cameras on the bus revealed that the car was a silver-coloured five-door Vauxhall Corsa hatchback. No one knows exactly what happened next. No eyewitness saw what happened in the next six or seven minutes – between the time that Marsha got off the bus and the time that she was suddenly and brutally attacked.

What is known, however, is that she was being stalked by the car that was caught on the bus's video cameras. There can be no doubt about that because, as she walked the few hundred yards home, she was also being watched by another CCTV camera, this time one mounted on a greengrocer's shop at number 72A Priory Road. The camera revealed that within a minute and a half of Marsha getting off her bus a car was parking in Priory Road at its junction with Bloxham Crescent.

It was just before 12.20 when Marsha was attacked without warning outside number 60 Priory Road. Someone had run up behind her and hit her brutally, and fatally, on the left side of her head – but that someone was not picked up on any of the CCTV cameras.

Immediately after Marsha's death the Metropolitan Police launched a full-scale murder inquiry to find her killer. One problem the police had was tracing the silver Vauxhall Corsa that had been captured on the video cameras. In spite of widespread publicity and persistent appeals for help from the public, no one came forward to say that they had been driving their Corsa down Percy

Road in Hampton in the early hours of that February morning.

It was to take the police more than three years to track down the car, and to do so they had to consider no fewer than 600,000 combinations of registration numbers until they finally identified the owners of 178 Vauxhalls that matched the video footage. One of them was the silver hatchback Y57 RJU that Bellfield had purchased the previous November to use in his new clamping business. But that hadn't proved easy to track back to him as, significantly, and for no apparent reason, Bellfield had sold the Corsa on 11 February 2002, just a week after Marsha's murder.

Emma Mills, who remembered going to buy the Corsa with Bellfield, later told the police that he had said he had sold it because he 'couldn't afford the repayments'. But he didn't charge top price for it – so keen was he to get rid of it. He sold it to a man called Sean James for £1,500 and an elderly blue Ford Escort van, which was probably worth £650, even though Bellfield had paid £6,300 for the Corsa just three months before.

But selling the Corsa wasn't the only sudden decision Bellfield was to take in the days after Marsha McDonnell's murder. He also announced to Emma Mills that they and the children were all going to take a holiday to Tenerife, the largest of the Spanish Canary islands in the Atlantic Ocean, even though their elder daughter Lucy was still at primary school. A trip abroad in term time was unheard of. Bellfield's explanation to Mills for the sudden trip was that he had been 'doing well at wheel-clamping', and the weather had turned for the worse, so he 'wanted a bit of sun'. He booked the holiday through Thomas Cook on Saturday, 8 February 2003, just four days after Marsha McDonnell's killing. The family were to leave Gatwick Airport on Friday, 14 February and return on 21 February and were to stay at a self-catering apartment in the Playa de las Americas. They even decided to take the family friend Richard 'Yosser' Hughes with them.

So Emma Mills and her children, Lucy and William, drove to Gatwick with Richard Hughes on the night of Thursday, 13 February and stayed at the airport Holiday Inn to be sure to be there in time to catch the morning flight. But Bellfield didn't go with them, he turned up later – carrying £2,000 in Euro notes for the holiday, which had already cost him £1,300.

In retrospect the reasons for selling the Corsa and taking a holiday out of the blue were clear enough. Bellfield was intent on disposing of a car that could have been incriminating as quickly as possible and then leaving the country in case the police came looking for him. It was a trick he had used before – 'making myself scarce' as he liked to put it – by disappearing from his usual haunts, just in case the police came looking for him.

As Brian Altman QC explained at the Old Bailey, the police and prosecution were convinced that the car driving past the bus after midnight on Tuesday, 4 February 2003 was not only a silver five-door hatchback Vauxhall Corsa but also Bellfield's Vauxhall Corsa, which, together with the evidence that the attack wasn't carried out by a pedestrian but the occupant of a car, 'should, we say, compel you to conclude that Levi Bellfield murdered Marsha McDonnell'.

As Levi Bellfield would discover in February 2008, the jury agreed with the police and prosecution and found him guilty of Marsha McDonnell's murder. But that day of reckoning was a long way off. For the moment, Bellfield was free to enjoy his holiday and, even more terrifyingly, to kill again.

11. Mr Treacle

'Sin has many tools, but a lie is the handle
which fits them all.
Oliver Wendell Holmes

No sooner had Levi Bellfield returned from his week's holiday on the Canary Islands with Emma Mills, their children and Richard 'Yosser' Hughes than he started to plan another holiday. It was as if he suddenly had no wish to stay at home and wanted to put as much distance as he possible could between himself and Little Benty.

Why? The answer is clear enough. The shadow of Marsha McDonnell's killing was hanging over him, and he wanted to escape it by any means possible. But that didn't just mean leaving the country, it also meant leaving Little Benty.

After the beginning of March in 2003 Bellfield started to spend more and more time at the flat at 39, Crosby Close, which he had rented from the man who had arranged for the finance to help him by the Vauxhall Corsa. He even took advantage of yet another flat in Hayes of which he had the use. And at the end of April Bellfield took Emma and the children back to Tenerife for another week, although this time he invited Christine Hawgood's fourteen-year-old daughter Gemma to go with them to the self-catering apartment in the Playa de las Americas. His aim was to present a calm, unflustered appearance to the world, for Bellfield was shrewd enough to realize that the appearance of nervousness – even to his clamping crew – could weaken him.

This meant that Bellfield went to enormous lengths to conceal his true intentions about anything – be it his clamping business, exactly where he was living, or indeed whom he was living with. He would dissemble about anything and everything, presenting the world with a tissue of lies so great that 'Yosser' Hughes nicknamed him 'Mr Treacle' for the sheer scale of his ability to conceal the truth.

Bellfield continued to expand his wheel-clamping business. He would clamp cars at random, and then tell the frightened motorist that they had parked illegally, when clearly they had not. It was a perfect scam for a man who was prepared to back up his lies with the threat of violence. The style was such a success that, at the end of March 2003, after coming back from Tenerife, Bellfield began taking on more extra staff to help him. One man he invited to join him was Noel Moran, then almost nineteen, who had been at school with another of his regular clampers, T— Morgan.

Moran remembered later that he started to work for 'Lee' – as he knew Bellfield – in March 2003 and went to a large number of clamping sites with him, including ones in Acton, Woking, Addlestone, Staines, Sunbury, Hounslow, West Drayton, Hounslow and Hersham, near Walton-on-Thames, as well as newer sites further away in Bicester in Oxfordshire and Chichester in West Sussex.

'I would get a day or two notice of which site to go to,' Moran would recall, 'and I would usually pick up one of his cars.' Moran would drive to whichever flat Bellfield was at on that particular morning and park his car. He would then use one of Bellfield's cars for the day before dropping it off later and collecting his own.

The fleet of cars and vans that Bellfield had at his disposal expanded as his wheel-clamping business became steadily more successful. They included a white Ford Courier van, a white Transit tow-truck with a red stripe on the side, a Citroën Berlingo, a Peugeot van, a green Metro, a red Peugeot 306 saloon, a black BMW, a red Toyota Land Cruiser and a white Toyota Previa 'space cruiser'. Both the distinctive Ford Courier van, with its blacked-out back windows and the registration number of P610 XCN, and the Toyota Previa 'space cruiser', also with blacked-out windows and with its registration number of K885 EFL, would come to play a crucial part in Bellfield's life over the coming months. But, for the moment at least, they were simply the tools of his rapidly expanding trade.

Clamping at so many diverse locations and using so many different cars and vans guaranteed that Bellfield remained elusive during the spring and summer of 2003. Never in one place for very long, and never permanently in residence at Little Benty, he would go to ever-increasing lengths to ensure that his whereabouts were a mystery to everyone – even his clamping crew. Bellfield also made sure that Emma Mills was never sure where he was, except when they went on holiday together, which they now did with astonishing regularity.

At the end of April, for example, and again between

late June and early August, they spent time in a caravan belonging to a woman they had met in Tenerife earlier in the year, Michelle Wickham. Her caravan was on a site in Kent, but it wasn't the only caravan that Bellfield had access to. He also used one belonging to his brother Richard, which was based at a site on the Isle of Sheppey. Caravans were difficult to track down and were part of the backbone of the 'travellers' life-style. They provided him with the perfect place to hide.

By the beginning of September 2003 Bellfield was back in Tenerife for another week, his third trip to the Canary Island in less than eight months. Once again he took Richard Hughes with Emma and the children, but this time he also invited their new friend, Michelle Wickham. His fellow clamper, Joe Ryan and his wife Rachel Brazil, who owned their own apartment in the same complex, joined them. All three of the trips to Tenerife were organized at the last minute by Bellfield and he never consulted Emma Mills about them. 'Levi wasn't like that,' she would admit later. 'You didn't question his decisions. You just accepted them.'

Certainly his neighbours in Little Benty were well aware that Bellfield was not a man to be questioned, or trifled with. Like Kingston, they had seen at first hand how violently he would react if ever his decisions were questioned. A Scot called Gary, who was in his thirties and lived next door at 13, Little Benty with his wife Trisha, found that out to his cost in the autumn of 2003.

Outside in the cul-de-sac – and on the green verge opposite the houses – Bellfield regularly worked on his clamping cars and vans together with two members of his clamping crew. One afternoon, as Spiers was to recall later, Bellfield's neighbour Gary made the mistake of coming out of his house to complain about the litter of cars and vans on their shared driveway and the green opposite. Bellfield's reaction was dramatic.

'I saw Levi run across the road and wrestle Gary to the ground in Gary's front garden,' Spiers remembered. 'Levi picked up one of Gary's flowerpots and smashed it over Gary's head.' He then calmly went back to working on the cars with the other clampers. Bellfield's attack left his neighbour with a cut to his head and a black eye. Not long afterwards he and his wife left Little Benty altogether to return to Scotland.

Bellfield's habit of suddenly escalating into violence, which had been growing rapidly since the move back from Walton-on-Thames, was by now well established, as was his equally rapid oscillation back to seeing it as 'a joke'. What was not a joke, however, was the fact that early in November 2003 a young woman named Dawn Brunton was hit over the head by a man at Hatton Cross, hardly any distance at all from Little Benty. The attack took place on Bonfire Night, exactly a year after the attack on Sonia Salvitierra, but Bellfield was never charged with either offence.

Just a few weeks later, however, came an attack which did see Bellfield face a charge. At about 7.40 on the misty evening of 16 December 2003, a thirty-four-year-old Albanian woman named Irma Dragoshi, who had lived in London for many years, was attacked in a remarkably similar way. That night Irma had left the hairdressing salon in Slough where she worked to travel home to the flat in west London that she shared with her husband,

Astrit. As usually happened when she worked late she was given a lift part of the way home by her employer, Ruth Baker, and so – at about 7.20 that evening – she was dropped off at a bus stop in Longford Village, on the old Bath Road, which runs from east to west parallel to one of Heathrow airport's runways and its perimeter road.

It was, of course, dark by the time Irma found herself waiting for a number 81 bus, not far from the White Horse pub on the north side of the road and near an old-fashioned telephone box. But Irma had her mobile phone with her, so there was no need for her to use the telephone box. There was a distinct chill in the air, and there was no one else around.

The bus Irma was waiting for should have arrived at 7.30, but on that particular night it was running late, and so she phoned her husband to tell him she had been delayed. As she did so Irma had the phone in her right hand and was listening with her right ear, with the hood of her coat up and facing in the direction of the White Horse pub and away from the road. By now it was about 7.40.

That was the last memory Irma had of the evening. The next thing she recalled was waking up in Hillingdon hospital in the early hours of the following morning suffering from a crippling pain in the back of her head, and with a large lump on her scalp to prove it. Her eyes were black and blue and swollen, and she had a terrible headache and was feeling perpetually dizzy. Nothing had been stolen, but her mobile had been damaged.

It was her husband who helped the police to piece together exactly what had happened to his wife. He told them that she had phoned him the previous evening to tell him that she had been dropped off by her boss and that there was now another woman standing beside her at the bus stop waiting for the number 81.

Quite suddenly, and out of the blue, Mr Dragoshi explained, he heard his wife scream, and the phone went dead. He immediately rang back, and it was answered by an Englishwoman who passed the phone to Irma, who by now was lying on the ground in Old Bath Road. He spoke to his wife for a minute or two, and she told him that she had been hit over the head from behind and that she was in great pain.

The moment Astrit Dragoshi rang off he called the emergency services and gave them the location of the attack on his wife. He then called a mini-cab and went to the scene himself, where he found her sitting in an ambulance with her head in her hands.

The couple were taken to Hillingdon hospital together, where Irma was able to tell a doctor what had happened before being sedated and left to sleep. But the following morning she had no recollection whatever of what had happened the night before, or indeed what she had said to the doctor.

The landlord of the White Horse pub was also able to tell the police something of what had gone on at the bus stop. He told them that he had found Irma on the ground, in floods of tears, and speaking in a foreign language. He was then joined by the English lady who had been in the telephone box when the attack took place, and they both tried to comfort Irma. Within a couple of minutes a number 81 bus had arrived, and a hysterical and disoriented Irma Dragoshi had insisted that she be allowed to get on to it. So the publican helped her on board and she sat down on one of the seats with her head in her hands, unable to move. At that very moment a second number 81 arrived, and, realizing that Irma was in no state to be moved, the other passengers on the first bus abandoned it and got on to the second. The English lady who had been in the telephone box joined them, and the second bus left.

Irma Dragoshi was left waiting for the ambulance and the police with the first bus driver and the publican, and it was while she was sitting on the bus that the police arrived, at 8.28 that evening, about forty-five minutes after the original incident. Irma managed to tell the two constables who found her that a man had tried to snatch the mobile phone out of her hand, but when she had struggled to hang on to it she had been struck on the back of the head by something – she didn't know what. The two officers rapidly carried out a search of the area but didn't find anything that might have been used as a blunt instrument in the attack. The officers then helped Irma into the ambulance, and she left for Hillingdon hospital with her husband.

To the police at the time it was an extraordinary, mindless piece of violence, an attack on an innocent woman without warning and for no discernible reason – but one which saw her brutally injured. Irma's injuries were so severe that she wasn't able to return to work for more than a month, and, even more significantly, she was never again able to remember anything about what had happened to her that night at the number 81 bus stop. What was not in doubt, however, was that the seriousness of her injuries meant that whoever had hit her over the head had intended to cause her the gravest harm.

As Brian Altman QC later explained for the prosecution at the Old Bailey at Levi Bellfield's trial for Irma's attempted murder: 'If you accept that Irma Dragoshi was struck over the back of the head with a blunt instrument with such force as to produce such a debilitating injury, that can only have been done with an intention either to kill her or at the very least to cause her really serious bodily harm ... Her attacker could hardly have intended anything less when he hit her over the head in that entirely deliberate and unprovoked way.'

But who had hit Irma Dragoshi over the head?

One man who claimed he knew was twenty-four-year-old Morgan, one of Bellfield's clamping crew, who later told the police that he had been with Bellfield on that December night in 2003. Indeed they had been driving around west London in Emma Mills's black Volkswagen Golf, registration number M404 WEH.

'We were driving in Bath Road,' he was to say, 'past the McDonald's. Levi ignored the No Entry sign, which only allows buses through ... I can't remember what time this was, but it was dark. Suddenly Levi just pulled over. He turned the headlights off and then the engine. Levi said, "'Ere, watch this." I didn't know why he had stopped or what he meant. Levi got out the car and as he did so he said, "Jump in the driver's seat." I got in the seat still not knowing what was going on.'

Bellfield had parked on the opposite side of the Old Bath Road, about four bus lengths down from the White Horse pub. But from where they had parked Morgan could clearly see a woman on a mobile phone. According to Morgan, Bellfield, who had pulled the hood of his tracksuit top up as he had got out of the car, 'jogged up to her and put his arm out and grabbed her shoulder'.

'I thought that he was going for her handbag, which, I remember, was over her shoulder,' he said. 'I still didn't know what was going on. Levi grabbed her with one hand and spun her around. It was one action.'

Morgan then saw Bellfield crouched over Irma pulling at her handbag, only to stand up and carry on jogging away from their car and past the pub. 'He went past the pub and then crossed the road,' Morgan explained. Then, still jogging, he came back towards the car.

'I was shocked. I couldn't believe what he had done,' Morgan went on. 'As he jogged back towards the car, he crossed over . . . to the driver's side. I jumped over the gear stick and back into the passenger seat. Levi got in. He turned the engine on but not the lights. He drove off past the pub then turned the lights on. Levi was laughing. I couldn't believe it.'

Bellfield then drove back to the garage area behind his house at Little Benty and parked the VW Golf, which took about five minutes. 'We never spoke about what had happened during the journey,' Morgan said later. 'He had stopped laughing and we sat in silence. We both got out and we both said goodbye.'

Morgan never told anyone what he had seen that night until after Bellfield's arrest on suspicion of murder, a year later.

'There was no way I was going to tell anyone about it,' he said, 'because Levi Bellfield has made me feel scared and bullied for as long as I've known him. He generally makes you feel like you have to do what he tells you . . . If you don't, he verbally threatens you. He lives off his reputation, and it is safe to say I am frightened of him. I felt that, if I'd have told someone about it and it had got back to him, he would have beaten me up.'

In fact there was another reason why Morgan was frightened of Bellfield. There was more than a hint of sexual jealousy between the two men, because Morgan's new fiancée, Tilley, had had a sexual relationship with Bellfield before she had left him to become Morgan's permanent partner.

'I was more scared for my girlfriend and still am,' Morgan was to tell the police, and he had every reason to be. He had seen at first hand Bellfield's attitude to young women and his capacity for violence against anyone who disobeyed him.

But when Morgan's recollection of the events of that cold, misty December night in 2003 were told to Levi Bellfield after his arrest on suspicion of attempted murder, his version of what happened was significantly different. The man 'Yosser' Hughes had nicknamed Mr Treacle insisted that it had been Morgan who had carried out the attack on Irma Dragoshi, and not him. Although the police were never to seriously suspect Morgan, it wasn't for want of Bellfield's trying. Bellfield admitted that he had been in the car with Morgan that night, but had been so shocked at what Morgan had done that he had driven the car away from the attack and then waited at the end of the road. He also insisted that his fellow wheel-clamper hadn't hit Irma over the head but had merely 'pulled' at her handbag, and she had hit her head on the ground when she fell.

So what was the truth? Mr Treacle was certainly capable of lying, and Morgan had no history of attacking young women out of the blue and without reason. But he had every reason not to tell the police, or anyone else, what had happened.

Bellfield had used the attack to prove to Morgan exactly what he was capable of and, just as significantly, to bind Morgan to the crime. If he continued to say nothing to the police, Morgan was therefore complicit in it and compromised. It gave Bellfield a considerable hold over an impressionable twenty-one-year-old.

In the end no one could be quite sure what had happened to Irma Dragoshi on that misty December evening. She said she had been hit on the head, but Bellfield insisted that she had hit her head on the ground, and the two police officers couldn't find a weapon. Meanwhile Morgan wasn't able to say with any conviction that Bellfield had hit her over the head during the struggle. In the end Levi Bellfield was not found guilty of the attempted murder of Irma Dragoshi.

As far as he was concerned in December 2003 the attack underlined once again that he could do whatever he wanted, whenever he wanted to. The police hadn't questioned him about Marsha McDonnell. His new wheel-clamping business was expanding, as was his drug-dealing operation, and he was now working as a doorman at The Sorting Room in Twickenham, as well as his other clubs. On top of that Emma Mills had discovered that she was pregnant again with their third child.

Perhaps it was the pregnancy, or perhaps it was simply a matter of habit, but no sooner had Bellfield learned that he was to become a father again – for at least the eighth time – he launched into a new relationship with another young blonde teenager. Her name was Terri Carroll, and she was only fifteen. Provocative, confident and certainly sexually aware, Carroll had first met Bellfield through their mutual friend Morgan, outside the school in Hayes, West London, where she was studying for her GCSEs. As she later told the press, 'I was instantly attracted to him. I thought it was cool that an older guy paid me attention. He was funny, charming and kind in the beginning.' Bellfield's apparent maturity clearly attracted Carroll, although once again his natural gift for bending the truth was at the fore: the thirty-five-year-old Bellfield told Carroll he was in fact twenty-eight. It was also his ability to spend money on his new girlfriend that won her over: 'He would take me out for dinner, pay for taxis home, and he bought me a mobile phone and presents.' Unsurprisingly, the young woman, who had spent some of her childhood in care, was bowled over by the overwhelming attention. As she became increasingly infatuated with him she chose not to tell her family or friends about the relationship, not least as Bellfield had insisted she keep it a secret.

Bellfield for his part maintained the appearance of a 'tough, yet nice' older man, explaining to Carroll that he was separated from his partner and had a 'couple of kids'. Whatever appearance Bellfield was keen to maintain was only a temporary mask, however, which was soon to slip. During one of their first dates together Bellfield took Carroll to a Kingston nightclub, impressing her by showing her into the VIP area of the club, where he proceeded to buy the teenager alcopop drinks throughout the night.

Later that night Carroll let Bellfield drive her to his flat in Hanworth, where he led her to the bedroom. Despite her protestations, the two had sexual intercourse. Afterwards, she explained, 'I felt sick and cheap. I had slept with one boy before Levi, but I was very inexperienced.'

It was a few weeks later that the mask fully slipped: 'After a few weeks, he took me to a hotel room, where again he got me drunk before we had sex. He kept hitting me and slapping me on my face and body while we were on the bed. I told him he was hurting me, but he just carried on and laughed. When he had finished, he called a male friend and told him to come round and that I would have sex with him. When I refused, Levi got so angry, he punched me in the face. He said if I didn't do what he said he would dump me and find another girl. Luckily his mate didn't turn up.'

Of course Terri Carroll was simply the latest blonde teenager to fall under Bellfield's spell, and as he was the inexperienced teenager's first boyfriend she was desperate not to lose him. It wasn't long, however, before love turned into fear, as Bellfield soon began to threaten to kill her or hurt her family if she left him.

Just three weeks after she had met him, Carroll was pressured by Bellfield to move into his flat. He ordered her to stop going to school, and Carroll was soon spending twelve hours a day alone in Bellfield's flat, strictly forbidden to leave without his permission.

Bellfield's possessiveness became obsessive. As Carroll explained, 'He didn't want boys coming near me. If he rang me from work and I didn't answer he would accuse me of having someone in the flat. Before we got a landline installed, he would call me on my mobile and make me flush the toilet to prove I was inside.'

Bellfield's constant changing of temper and behaviour towards Carroll kept her in thrall to him and terrified of leaving: 'One minute he would be cuddling me and telling me he loved me, the next he would throw me to the floor like a rag doll and kick me as I begged him to stop. He got off on rage and loved to control me. When I cried at his insults, he laughed and told me I should be grateful to have him. I was constantly on edge, never sure what mood he would be in when he came home from work.'

Meanwhile, Bellfield's clamping business was beginning to infuriate the local residents of Chichester. In the words of the local paper, the *Chichester Observer*, he was a 'notorious and uncompromising clamper, who targeted the vulnerable and the elderly'. He was charging £155 to remove a clamp and £265 to tow a car he had clamped. One of his victims, David Worcester, called him 'very unpleasant' and explained that he was 'extremely aggressive and uncooperative', while concluding: 'He was the sort of person who really should not have been let loose in society.' Mr Worcester's wife Phyllida had to rescue him from Bellfield's rage when he didn't have enough cash to pay the £155 fine. 'He was not going to budge an inch on getting the money,' she said. 'He was just a thug. It is not something you expect to find on the streets of Chichester.'

A matter of hours after the first of these stories about Bellfield's exploits in the comfortable West Sussex town appeared, the shopping centre which had hired him suspended his clamping agreement. But that didn't worry Bellfield in the slightest. He returned to London bragging that the expedition had brought him at least £30,000 in profit in less than two weeks. The truth was it had probably brought him much more.

Bellfield's relationship with Carroll continued, with his latest teenage girlfriend now a virtual prisoner to his bidding and another in a line of partners desperate for his affections. He was thrilled that he was the focus of so much attention from the women in his life, but he had the same perpetual feeling that all woman were nothing but trouble – only underlining the feeling of rage he felt towards them.

Shortly afterwards that rage may well have expressed itself in another attack.

Just after 10 o'clock in the evening of Sunday, 18 April 2004 a young woman in her early thirties named Adele Harbison, who worked as an accountant, was hit over the head with a blunt object by a man in Trafalgar Road in Twickenham, barely 300 yards down Hampton Road from Twickenham Green, at the epicentre of Bellfield's hunting ground. She was found by a passing motorist with a massive wound to the back of her head and facial injuries that were severe enough to required reconstructive surgery. The doctors' detailed examination showed that her injuries were the result of three or four heavy blows, but there were no defensive wounds to suggest that she had put up any kind of fight. Once again the attack clearly wasn't a robbery, as her mobile phone and handbag were still with her, and nothing had been stolen. In the wake of his arrest on suspicion of murder, the police became convinced that Bellfield was the young woman's attacker, but they could not prove it and he was never charged with the offence.

Barely a month later, however, another young woman was attacked at another of Bellfield's familiar stamping grounds – and this time he was charged. The young woman's name was Kate Sheedy.

12. Into the Abyss

'No man is angry that feels himself not hurt.'

Francis Bacon

Kate Sheedy was exactly Levi Bellfield's type. A slim eighteen-year-old schoolgirl with long blonde hair and a fair complexion, she was just over 5 feet 4 inches tall and weighed a little over 7½ stone, the sort of girl that reminded him of his own schooldays. With her oval face and friendly, open smile, Kate was even a pupil at the all-girl Gumley House Convent School in Twickenham Road, Isleworth, barely half a mile from the house he had grown up in. It was the very school that he had made a habit of driving past, leering at the teenage pupils and shouting 'slags' to whoever was in the car with him.

Though he would never admit it, there was little doubt that the Gumley House girls stirred a sense of resentment in Bellfield, a reminder of the anger he had felt when Patsy Morris had turned him down when he was a skinny, but sexually precocious, twelve-year-old. There was something about them that made Bellfield want to 'take them down a peg or two'. A part of him wanted revenge for past slights.

Bellfield was to turn Kate Sheedy into his latest victim – even though he had never met her, didn't know anyone who knew her and had no interest in her apart from the fact that she represented everything he both lusted after and yet at the same time loathed. For him she was an object of hate and desire; hurting her helped him to satiate his desire for revenge on every young woman who appeared to look down on him.

But Kate Sheedy was unaware of all this on the morning of Thursday, 27 May 2004 as she and her girlfriends began to celebrate the Gumley House leaver's day, their last official day of school before heading off for a period of 'study leave' before their A levels. As the school's head girl, Kate had the responsibility of organizing the day. There had been presentations, gifts from one girl to another and the inevitable tearful goodbyes. This was the end of their school lives, a moment never to be forgotten.

Kate was intending to go up to university that autumn. There was to be no gap year, as she wanted to get on with her life, and she had a part-time job in the Next store in nearby Kew and a boyfriend who lived in Lincolnshire to prove it. She was every inch the finest kind of schoolleaver, a balanced, happy, enthusiastic young woman, full of every kind of promise.

She and her friends had decided to go out after the school's official leaver's day ceremonies and have a private celebration of their own. So after leaver's day was over at about 4 o'clock, she went home to her mother's house to change. Kate's parents were divorced, and she and her sister lived with their mother in Worton Road, just south-east of Isleworth and the school.

Shortly after 7 o'clock on that Thursday evening, Kate left her mother's house with some of her friends, dressed in a pink jumper, a black skirt that went just below her knees and pink sling-back shoes. The girls caught the number H22 bus into Twickenham, where they first went to The Sorting Room pub in London Road, just down from the railway station, and then, at about 10.30, to the Hobgoblin pub over the road.

By the end of the evening the Gumley House girls were merry, but no one was drunk. Kate just remembered later being tired and 'a little sad' because they were all going their separate ways. Their lives at school were over, and the future lay ahead of them; it was both frightening and enticing at the same time. There were a few tears, and a lot of hugs and promises of 'never to forget you' before they agreed to leave together.

Kate left the Hobgoblin pub at about midnight with three of her friends to catch their respective buses home, but her friends caught theirs before Kate's H22 arrived to take her back to Worton Road. In fact it wasn't until about 12.20 in the early hours of the morning of Friday, 28 May that the bus finally arrived.

She climbed on to the single-decker and sat two or three rows back on the left-hand side, thinking about the day and remembering the evening. She had hardly been on the bus a minute when one of the three friends she had just been with her called on her mobile phone to say she was home already. Kate told her friend that she would be home 'any minute' as she was just a few yards from her bus stop in Worden Road, just past The County Arms pub.

Tragically, it wasn't to be the case.

As the bus came to a stop in the well-lit suburban street, Kate was the only person to get off, and, as far as she could see, there was no one else around, although she thought she remembered a car driving past her. So, lost in her own thoughts, she got her house keys out of her handbag as she walked along Worton Road towards her mother's house. It was then that she heard the sound of a car engine and noticed that on her side of the road about 50 yards ahead there was a large white vehicle parked facing away from her with it engine running, but without any lights on. It was a white people-carrier with blacked-out windows.

Kate Sheedy was a bright, sensible young woman, and it was well after midnight, so she crossed Worton Road to the other side so as not to walk past what she later called this 'dodgy' car. What she did not know was that the people-carrier had been stalking her on the number H22 bus on her way home, all too visible on its brightly lit lower deck to anyone looking in from outside.

As it turned out, Kate's worries about the blacked-out people-carrier with its engine running were justified. As she crossed the minor road that led off Worton Road into the Worton Hall industrial estate – and reached the traffic island in the middle – the white people-carrier switched its lights on and revved its engine loudly. For a moment Kate though it was about to drive off, and she started across the second lane of the road. It was a terrible mistake. Without any warning the people-carrier did a U-turn in Worton Road and drove directly towards the entrance of the industrial estate – straight at Kate Sheedy.

Kate screamed and made an attempt to run to the pavement opposite her, but the people-carrier got to her before she could do so. It struck her, knocked her down and drove over her. But that wasn't all. It then paused and quite deliberately reversed back over her prostrate body before racing away south down Worton Road.

Some local residents heard Kate's scream, but thought little of it as they lived near a pub where the departing patrons could be a little rowdy. What they did not know was that Kate was now lying on the ground at the entrance to the industrial estate gravely injured and in dreadful pain.

There was no reason that this bright, open-faced schoolgirl should be attacked in a quite residential road in a respectable suburb of west London without warning, but then there had been no reason for the attack on Marsha McDonnell fifteen months earlier. The attacks were the work of someone with scant regard for human life, and a rage against their fellow human beings that was almost tangible.

But Kate was nothing if not a resourceful eighteen-year-old. Though badly hurt, she tried to crawl home. It was a brave decision, but it didn't work. Within a few seconds, she found she could barely move. She did, however, manage to drag herself across to her handbag, which had been thrown across the road when she had been hit by the people-carrier, to retrieve her mobile phone. She then had the presence of mind to call an ambulance, before calling her mother.

The first words Kate uttered after having been run over were to the 999 control centre were: 'He ran over me twice.' She then went on: 'The car stopped and checked me out . . . I thought he was dodgy, so after he turned round and ran over me and hit me again . . . I thought he was going to take me in his car but . . . when he saw that I knew he was dodgy he just ran over me.'

The recorded time of Kate's call was 12.39 on the morning of Friday, 28 May 2004, and within a matter of minutes the paramedics had found her, and so had her mother and father, who had run from their respective houses.

Badly shocked and brutally injured Kate was taken to the nearby West Middlesex hospital, where she was diagnosed as having a collapsed lung and a broken collar bone and – much more worryingly – serious internal damage to her abdomen and liver. She nevertheless managed to tell a detective constable who had been sent to interview her that she had seen the vehicle ahead of her on Worton Road turn its lights off, but that no one had got out, which she 'thought was suspicious'.

That was the only description Kate was capable of giving on the night of her attack, and her injuries were so serious that she was rapidly transferred to King's College hospital in central London and placed in the liver intensive-care unit, where she had surgery to her liver, and then further surgery for an injury to her back.

Just as dawn was breaking on that Friday morning, an official police photographer took a series of photographs of where Kate had been knocked down. One showed just one of the pink sling back shoes that she had been wearing lying in the middle of the road, a poignant reminder of the tragedy that had struck this innocent young woman.

Kate Sheedy was to remain in intensive care for no fewer than sixteen days after the attack. She wasn't discharged from hospital until 21 June – a full three weeks after she had been deliberately run over in Worton Road. But that was just the beginning of her recovery. In the months to come she had to have continuous physiotherapy to help her walk again, as well as hydrotherapy to improve her fitness.

The attack left her with a large scar on her lower back, which was to leave her in constant pain, a right collar bone so badly broken that it was out of alignment and formed an unsightly lump in her chest as well as what one of her hospital consultants later described as 'severe and lasting psychological effects'.

Hardly surprisingly, Kate missed her A levels that summer, although the examination boards awarded her A-level grades on the basis of her predictions from AS level the previous summer and told her that she could not go up to university that autumn. In fact it was to be another year before she was able to follow her friends, and take up her place. Her life had been turned upside down in a matter of moments by the hit-and-run driver in Worton Road.

When detectives from the Metropolitan Police finally came to interview Kate Sheedy after her release from hospital, she was typically sensible, doing her very best to remember what had happened in as much detail as she could. She said the people-carrier was definitely white, with blacked-out windows and a number plate that included an M or an N. She also said that the wing mirrors were black, and the one on the driver's side may have had a broken casing or have been defective in some way. Significantly Kate also said that the driver 'was leaning quite far forward on the wheel, quite hunched over the wheel', and that she thought there were two men in the front seats — although she only saw their outline. They both had short hair and broad shoulders.

There were no other witnesses to the attack. No one came forward to tell the police that they had seen what happened and to confirm that the people-carrier had driven at Kate quite deliberately. All the police had were Kate's recollections.

They had a little other evidence, however. Two CCTV cameras were mounted on the front of The County Arms pub – one facing north, the other south – and video footage retrieved from them after the attack on Kate clearly showed a white Toyota Previa people-carrier with blacked-out windows stalking the H22 bus before it stopped at 12.33 a.m. and then, a minute or so later, disappearing at speed south down Hall Road. But the cameras had not captured the attack itself. That was out of range.

The footage did reveal, however, that the Toyota stopped behind the bus – rather than overtaking it – which meant that the driver had a clear view of Kate getting off at her stop. It also showed that the people-carrier then overtook her and stopped with its lights off and its engine running.

The images were strikingly similar to those of the Vauxhall Corsa that stopped behind the bus in which Marsha McDonnell had travelled home from Kingston just fifteen months earlier – the same view of the occupants from outside, the same pausing in a road junction as if waiting to see who got off the bus. But this time the car was a people-carrier, not a five-door hatchback saloon.

Levi Bellfield's wheel-clamping crew were certainly familiar with a white Toyota Previa people-carrier with blacked-out windows and the registration number of K855 EFL, because they had all used it over the preceding months. They also knew that he had used it as one of his 'shagging wagons'. This particular vehicle had been bought in April 2003 by Aaron Smith, a member of the 'travelling' family that Bellfield had gone into business with when he launched his clamping crew, and in May that year Smith had sold it on to Bellfield.

Emma Mills also remembered it, and the fact that Bellfield specifically had blackened its windows after he had bought it from Smith, only to sell it at Christmas to the father of one of his clamping team, Christopher Moran, who in turn then gave it back to his son Noel as an engagement present in early February 2004. Moran regularly used the Toyota Previa for clamping with Bellfield.

Terri Carroll also remembered the people-carrier very clearly. She was to tell the police that she had often been clamping in it in 2004, even though it was officially Noel Moran's car. 'When we were out clamping, Levi would teach me how to drive in the Toyota,' she was to say. 'Levi took me for driving lessons around March or April time.'

On the Thursday that Kate Sheedy was run down, Noel Moran later told the police that Bellfield was using the Toyota while they were clamping at The White Hart pub in Bicester in Oxfordshire. That was corroborated by a man whose car had been clamped in the pub's car park the day before. He remembered that a white Toyota Previa had pulled up in front of his van when he was examining the clamp, blocking him in. He later identified the driver – it was Bellfield.

Richard 'Yosser' Hughes also remembered that in early June 2004 Bellfield had suddenly decided to take the Toyota Previa to a 'car valeting service' to have it thoroughly cleaned inside and out, at a cost of some £60. The cleaning took two full days. Hughes had no idea why his friend had decided it needed cleaning – but then he hadn't been in Worton Road on the night of 27 May 2004.

There could be no denying that Bellfield knew Worton Road exceptionally well. When he was still with Jo Collings she would regularly drop him off at The County Arms, though she did not know why. He would disappear into a local alleyway without giving her any explanation. She also remembered collecting him there 'seven or eight times' during their time together.

Just as significantly, Kate Sheedy's school was less than a quarter of a mile from the entrance to the industrial estate where she was knocked down on that May night, and Bellfield certainly knew its girls.

Jo Collings would explain later: 'Throughout the time I was seeing Levi he would leer at the schoolgirls from Gumley Convent School. When he would see the girls walking along in their uniform he made comments like "Dirty little whores, they're begging for it." He would always call them sluts. Sometimes he would turn the car around and drive past them again, then roll down the window and shout things like "You know you want it."'

There was also no doubt whatever that Bellfield knew the two pubs where Kate Sheedy had spent the evening on the night she was attacked. He had been working as a doorman at The Sorting Room since the previous November and had also spent time working on the door of the Hobgoblin just across the London Road in January. Was that a coincidence? Or had he been stalking her from the moment she and her friends left the Hobgoblin pub that night? No one will ever know. But what is certain is that both Worton Road and London Road in Twickenham were part of what the forensic psychologist and criminal profiler Professor David Canter has called 'the geographical centre of gravity' of a serial attacker. They were familiar parts of Bellfield's patch of west London, places which gave him a sense of comfort because he knew them so well. It was a sense of comfort that gave him the confidence to kill.

As Brian Altman QC later explained to the jury at the Old Bailey at Bellfield's trial for the attempted murder of Kate, 'The prosecution submit you can be satisfied that the vehicle which ran over Kate Sheedy and left her for dead was a white Toyota Previa with distinctive non-standard blacked-out windows. That the driver of that Previa meant to kill her can hardly be an astonishing proposition. It is true that no blunt instrument was used to strike Kate over the head, but if the prosecution is right he used a different blunt instrument to attack her – the blunt instrument of a car . . . the prosecution submit that the evidence regarding this offence . . . should lead you to the view that this terrible crime was the work of no one other than Levi Bellfield.'

But when it came to his trial Bellfield resorted to precisely the same excuse that he had used to explain the attack on Irma Dragoshi – he hadn't been driving at the time. Bellfield claimed that he had lent the Toyota Previa to his wheel-clamping colleagues Morgan and Suraj Gharu for a 'birthday celebration' – although he did admit to driving it on Wednesday, 26 May in the car park of The White Hart pub in Bicester. On the night of Thursday,

27 May, however, when Kate was run over Bellfield insisted that he had lent it to Suraj Gharu, and so could not have been driving it.

In the end the jury did not believe his version of events and convicted him of the attempted murder of eighteen-year-old Kate, a young woman who had done nothing whatever to incite his interest beyond being a young blonde on a bus late at night when he was trawling the streets of west London looking for an appropriate target to focus his rage against schoolgirl 'slags'.

But that conviction for attempted murder was still four years away. As May turned into June in 2004, Bellfield was still a free man, free to give full vent to his anger against women, and in the weeks that followed the attack on Kate Sheedy he became more steadily more and more volatile, arguing violently with both Terri Carroll and Emma Mills, and even finding time to argue again with Jo Collings.

Just a few days after the attack on Kate Sheedy Bellfield's inability to control his violent temper became all too apparent when he launched an attack on his friend, and fellow drug-dealer, 'Spanish' Pete Rodriguez, a rakish thin man of 5 feet 7 inches in his late twenties with short dark hair. The two men had been sharing the flat at 39, Crosby Close, just off the A316 road out of London, though Rodriguez had been forced to sleep on a futon on the floor in the front room while Bellfield and Terri Carroll had shared the bedroom. Carroll later described Rodriguez as Bellfield's 'lapdog'.

Unbeknown to Bellfield, however, Rodriguez had struck up a friendship with Jo Collings and had arranged to go and live with her until he had 'sorted himself out', as she was to put it. The move was to take place over the week-end of 5–6 June – barely a week after the Sheedy attack.

Rodriguez had stayed with Collings on the preceding Friday night, leaving on the Saturday morning to collect his stuff. But Rodriguez didn't return to her flat when she expected him to that night. So, not certain what was going on, she phoned him from her mobile phone on the Sunday afternoon while she was at a horse show at Hickstead in Sussex. He told her not to worry – he would be coming round that evening.

Back home, Collings rang him again between 7 and 8 that evening, only for Rodriguez to tell her, 'It's all kicking off,' and that she should ring him again in an hour. At this point he was still in the flat in Crosby Close he had been sharing with Bellfield and Carroll.

As the evening wore on, Collings became ever more concerned and rang Rodriguez again between 9.30 and 10 o'clock. This time, however, he told her, 'I haven't got anything at the moment,' a code phrase they used to let her know that Bellfield was with him, and that she should ring off. She could hear Bellfield in the background as well as the voices of three other men. They were arguing, but she rang off fully, still expecting to see Rodriguez later on that evening. But he never appeared.

Exactly what happened to 'Spanish Pete' on the evening of Sunday, 6 June 2004 at the flat at Crosby Close has never been fully explained, but the aftermath was clear, and disturbing. The night ended with Rodriguez being rushed into hospital having been viciously attacked with an axe and a screwdriver, an attack that was to see him on a life support machine for the next six weeks.

What is also not in doubt is that Bellfield had been out wheel-clamping on that Sunday afternoon, and that Terri Carroll had been with him, as had Spiers and Noel Moran. They had spent the day in Hemel Hempstead and got back to Crosby Close at about 7.

Given Bellfield's appetite for lying, it's almost certain that the truth about what happened that evening will never be known, but the Metropolitan Police became convinced privately that Bellfield had fallen out comprehensively with his friend and fellow drug-dealer and had attacked him.

Part of the reason for the attack could have been that he had asked Rodriguez to store about 250 ecstasy tablets for him in the fridge at his mother's flat in Battersea, south London, and he had failed to collect them. At the time Rodriguez's mother is in hospital. But another reason could have been his discovery that 'Spanish Pete' was now close to his former partner Jo Collings, and yet another reason involved another very young woman.

That weekend, a fourteen-year-old friend of Terri Carroll had rung her to say that she had been thrown out of her home by her mother and asked if she could stay with her. Bellfield had immediately suggested that she could join them in Crosby Close. And on the night of Sunday, 6 June the visiting fourteen-year-old was allegedly sexually molested. To this day no one has been identified as responsible.

One thing is certain, however: the events on that Sunday evening so upset Bellfield that at about 1.30 a.m. in the morning of Monday, 7 June he phoned Emma Mills at Little Benty to tell her to 'get out of the house – they're coming'. He meant the police, for he clearly believed they would blame him at least for the attack, if for nothing else, and he wanted to make himself as scarce as possible. When Mills told him she didn't have a car, Bellfield told her to call his sister Lindy-Lou and get her to collect her even though it was the early hours of the morning and Mills was nearly eight months pregnant. Then, at 3 a.m. that morning, Bellfield took Terri Carroll and their fourteen-year-old visitor to stay at a hotel on the Heathrow airport perimeter road, before announcing that he was off to visit Rodriguez in hospital – though whether he actually went there is less certain.

Did Bellfield attack Rodriguez? The police who investigated the attack certainly become convinced that he did, although the myriad of conflicting statements they received from people who knew what had happened did not make the events clear.

Was the known paedophile Victor Kelly involved? There was a suggestion that Carroll's fourteen-year-old friend had been seeing the sixty-two-year-old and could have been attacked by him. Again, a set of conflicting statements from those who knew about the events brought the police no closer to the answer – even though everyone at Crosby Close that evening knew, or at least knew of, Kelly and his predilection for girls aged between twelve and fourteen.

In the end all the police could do was to suspect that there had been a deliberate attempt to cover up the events in Crosby Close that night, and that Bellfield had been in some way involved. Proving it was a different matter, however, although to help them do so they took away two of the cars parked outside the flat that evening, a Vauxhall

Vectra and the white Ford Courier van which Bellfield used for wheel-clamping.

Whatever the truth, one thing was quite clear. Bellfield had no intention of accepting responsibility for the attack. He insisted that 'the Paki had done it', meaning his fellow wheel clamper Suraj Gharu. He also told Emma Mills that Victor Kelly had also been involved in some way, although he wasn't specific about how he may have been, beyond warning Mills that Kelly was 'dangerous'.

In private Bellfield believed that he would be arrested for the attack on Rodriguez. He confessed to Mills that he was convinced the police 'are gonna do me for Peter', and she certainly recalls that he was arrested, then charged with perverting the course of justice and given bail. But even that didn't prevent him telling her repeatedly: 'You know I didn't do it, Emma.'

Mills also knew that no member of his wheel-clamping crew would tell her the truth. They were as closely bound together as a family of Dickensian criminals, all knowing secrets about one another, secrets that they would not share with anyone else – and certainly not the police. Their 'omerta' of silence was as much part of their creed as was Bellfield's devotion to his travellers' roots – a sense that they would never let one another down, and could only trust one another in any kind of emergency.

It was that loyalty to one another that made it exceptionally difficult for the police investigating the brutal attack on Rodriguez to penetrate. They took statements from the people who seemed to be involved, but none of them had seen anything of any significance. A blanket of silence and secrecy was thrown around the events of that evening, and the reason was plain to see: too many people had too much to lose by telling the truth about what really happened.

Nevertheless, the attack on 'Spanish Pete' demonstrated vividly exactly how far Bellfield was involved in the twilight world of under-age sex and drugs. It had been part of his life for the past fifteen years, and he was certainly not capable of breaking free of it. The Rodriguez attack was the final evidence of his descent into addiction.

One man who witnessed that descent at first hand was a friend of Peter Rodriguez called C— Mayell, who had first met Bellfield in April 2004 and had immediately been asked to join the clamping crew. It didn't take long for him to realize the nature of Bellfield's attitudes to sex and women.

'I would describe Levi as an animal,' Mayell was to say, and with good reason. No sooner had Bellfield introduced him to Terri Carroll and another of her young friends, who was then fourteen, than Bellfield had bragged that he had had sex with the fourteen-year-old. 'I remember being disgusted because the girl was so young,' Mayell remembered.

That wasn't all. Bellfield also asked him if he wanted to sleep with Carroll. 'Do you want to buy her off me?' he asked, but again Mayell refused.

Another man who witnessed Bellfield's rapacious sexuality was L— Drakeford, another friend of Rodriguez, who had helped to organize the clamping expedition to Chichester earlier that year. Not long after the attack on Rodriguez Bellfield asked Drakeford to pick him and a young girl up at a pub in West Drayton and take them to the flat in Crosby Close. On the way there Drakeford stopped to buy a kebab. When he came out of the kebab shop he discovered that Bellfield and the girl were having sex in the back of his car. 'I pushed the mirror so I didn't have to watch them and continued driving,' he recalled later.

But when they got back to Crosby Close, and after the girl had got out of his car, Drakeford suddenly saw the other side to Bellfield's sexual bravado. The bouncer and wheel-clamper burst into tears, begging him: 'Don't let her see me like this.' Bellfield confessed to Drakeford that he was deeply worried about what the police might find in the back of the battered white Ford Courier van, which he had used for clamping, and which the police had taken away in the wake of the Rodriguez attack. Bellfield admitted there was a hammer in the van, which he was clearly concerned about, telling his friend, 'I'm totally fucked. My life is over.'

Drakeford thought it had something to do with the Rodriguez assault and told him that if he hadn't done it then he had nothing to worry about – but that did nothing to stop the wheel-clamper's tears. That van was to play a role again in Bellfield's life in the weeks to come.

13. The Killing Ground

'It is long and hard and painful to create life:
it is short and easy to steal the life that others
have made.'
George Bernard Shaw, *Back to Methusela*

The Rodriguez incident left Levi Bellfield nervous, very nervous indeed. Part of him felt guilt that he had been involved in the fight that had seen 'Spanish Pete' hit over the head with an axe and stabbed three times in the stomach and knees with a screwdriver, and part felt relief that the man he had used to fetch and carry drugs for him wasn't able to tell the police exactly what had happened – as he was in a coma.

The six weeks Rodriguez remained unconscious became some of the most anxious in Bellfield's life, not least because he suspected that the police were certain he had played a much more significant role in the attack than he had admitted to them. The anxiety only added to the sense of dread that had been gripping him for months, making his panic attacks even worse.

Nevertheless Bellfield did everything in his power to behave as normally as possible. The by now sixteen-year-old Terri Carroll and he couldn't go back to Crosby Close, because it was an official police crime scene, so they went to live together in a hotel on the perimeter road north of Heathrow airport. It was familiar, and relatively cheap, but it was close to Little Benty, and he had every reason to want to be nearby. Emma Mills was about to give birth.

On 17 July 2004 Mills duly bore Bellfield a third child, a daughter they named Georgina, and who went back to Little Benty with her mother after leaving the hospital maternity unit. Mills and her children were still very much a family even though they didn't see a great deal of the man they all called 'Dad'. Bellfield would go and visit them on a couple of days a week, usually in the early evening after clamping and before he went off to work as a doorman and bouncer.

On the surface, as the summer of 2004 deepened, Bellfield's life continued relatively normally. He and his team, often accompanied by Carroll, would go wheel-clamping during the day at a vast range of sites across west London and beyond, while in the evenings he would still work the doors at Royales in Uxbridge or at The Sorting Room in Twickenham. He saw no reason to change his habits. After all there were still drugs to supply and teenage girls to be seduced.

Beneath the surface, however, Bellfield's mental and emotional disintegration was gathering pace. The memories of the attack on Kate Sheedy at the end of May, the battle with Spanish Pete Rodriguez barely a week later, the subsequent police investigation and the fact that they were still examining his white Ford Courier van had all contrived to accelerate the mental 'break'.

He kept telling Noel Moran, 'I'm fucked, utterly fucked.'

By now Bellfield was a man on the very edge, a man

(*above*) Bus stop killer Levi Bellfield, who is likely to remain imprisoned for the rest of his life.

(*left*) Bellfield with two of his children by Emma Mills. He is father to at least nine children.

(*below*) The road where Bellfield lived in Little Benty, West Drayton.

Kate Sheedy, who suffered horrific injuries when she was run down by Bellfield in May 2004, just three months before he killed Amélie Delagrange.

The families of Marsha McDonnell and Amélie Delagrange at a press conference in 2008, shortly after Bellfield was found guilty of both murders.

(*left*) The police handout of nineteen-year-old murder victim Marsha McDonnell.

(*above right*) Marsha getting off the bus, shortly before Bellfield murdered her in London in February 2003. She was found just yards from her home after being clubbed to death.

(*left*) The Vauxhall Corsa used in Bellfield's attack on Marsha McDonnell.

(*below*) A floral tribute at Marsha's funeral. Her brutal murder caused shockwaves throughout Hampton.

The photo of French student Amélie Delagrange used by the Metropolitan Police during the early stages of their investigation.

A CCTV grab of Amélie boarding a bus after a night out with friends in Twickenham, shortly before she was found with fatal head wounds.

Police search for clues in leafy Twickenham, where Amélie was bludgeoned to death.

The intense search operation led police to the banks of the River Thames near Walton Bridge, where some of Amélie's belongings were found.

Amélie's parents, Jean-François and Dominique Delagrange, outside Bow Street Magistrates' Court in 2006 after Levi Bellfield was charged with their daughter's murder.

Amélie's parents lay floral tributes at the base of a tree planted in her memory on Twickenham Green.

Just your average teenager, Milly Dowler had her whole life ahead of her.

Milly got off the train one stop early at Walton-on-Thames to meet friends at a café. She was last seen by a friend waiting at a bus stop.

Leaving school on the day she was kidnapped in Walton-on-Thames in broad daylight, just after phoning her dad to let him know she was on her way home.

A nationwide search followed Milly's disappearance. The investigation was the largest ever mounted by the Surrey Police.

It was six months after Milly went missing that her body was found in Hampshire and identified by dental records. None of the clothes she was wearing, nor her schoolbag or mobile phone have ever been found.

Milly's father Bob, sister Gemma and mother Sally walk behind her coffin in the funeral procession.

A court drawing of Levi Bellfield in the dock at the Old Bailey as he pleads not guilty to the murder of Milly Dowler.

Milly's father Bob Dowler reads a statement outside the Old Bailey following the jury's guilty verdict.

without conscience, a victim of his own sexual desire and his addiction to violence – an addiction he was keeping at bay by smoking crack cocaine and cannabis, as well as consuming ever more copious amounts of extra-strength lager at all times of the day and night.

But his use of drugs and lager wasn't driven by guilt alone, it was also driven by the narcissism that had gripped since his childhood, when his mother had instilled in him the utter conviction that he was the only significant person in his life – which convinced him he was a man who could literally 'get away with anything'. Like Tony Montana in *Scarface*, Bellfield was now creating his own psychological reality.

'The law doesn't apply to people like me,' he would brag to his wheel-clamping colleagues while they were out working. 'They'll never lay a finger on me.' That was partly braggadocio, for in private Bellfield believed that he could see himself in prison over the Rodriguez attack – after all he was already on bail and due to appear in court in August on a charge of perverting the course of justice.

Mills recalled later that he was 'quite down' and 'crying all the time' during the summer of 2004 and that he 'worried he was going to get into trouble for the Peter thing' – especially when Bellfield started to ring her in the middle of the night to cry his heart out. He had developed the habit of ringing her in the early hours of the morning to confess how anxious and unhappy he was.

'Levi was just in a bad way,' Mills would explain. On his mobile phone Bellfield would tell her that he 'didn't want to live any more'.

In truth, Bellfield descended into a frenzy of both

self-pity and anger during July 2004, losing whatever frail sense of proportion and reality that he may once have had. He was not insane, however – quite the reverse. He was still Mr Treacle. He still had the ability to lie at will, to cover his tracks, to plead his innocence no matter how guilty and to 'charm the birds off the trees'. That was his well-practised 'reality', the face that he presented to the world.

Behind that reality, however, his addiction to sex and violence towards young women had escalated to murderous proportions. The practised charm meant nothing. It was a mere false benevolence that concealed his true feelings towards young women. He wanted to hurt them – badly.

On 21 July Bellfield's superficial confidence received an extraordinary boost when the police returned his white Ford Courier to Little Benty on a car-transporter. They hadn't discovered anything unusual, or worthy of further investigation, and they certainly hadn't found a hammer. Bellfield could hardly believe his good fortune when he asked Mills to take delivery. The gods were smiling, he thought: he genuinely could get away with anything.

It was a stroke of good fortune that also encouraged Bellfield to believe that the van was 'lucky'. Without delay he started using it not only for wheel-clamping, but also for his by now habitual nightly drives around west London and his old stamping grounds of Twickenham Green and Strawberry Hill. The van was his talisman, his good luck charm, ensuring that no one would notice him as he stalked the minor roads.

Yet there could be no doubt that the Ford van was, in fact, distinctive, as many of the clampers remembered.

Spiers, for example, used to drive it regularly. 'The third gear was knackered,' he would recall. 'The back doors had a checker plate on them. The windows were blacked out. The seats were torn. It was a pigsty.' For good measure the nearside front hub cap was missing and the left head-light didn't work. It had also been used as a vehicle at Heathrow airport and had a mark on its roof where a yel-low beacon light had once been fitted, as well as a small gap in the blacked-out rear windows to allow someone to sit inside and watch a clamping site.

The white Ford Courier van was to become the link that would eventually lead DCI Sutton's double murder squad to Little Benty – as they were particularly interested in the van's whereabouts on the evening of Thursday, 19 August 2004.

That afternoon Emma Mills and her three children went to a children's party at her friend Christine Haw-good's. There were about fifteen small children there, and during the party Bellfield rang on her mobile phone to ask what she was doing. When she told him about the party he said that it all sounded 'pretty noisy', but explained that he was busy wheel-clamping and that he would call her later.

Later that evening, back at home in Little Benty, Mills decided to go the large local Tesco in Hayes. She needed nappies for her new daughter, who was only four weeks old, as well as other things for the children. She had hoped that Bellfield would have come back from clamping to take them, but he hadn't been in touch, and so shortly after 7 that evening she phoned a local taxi firm. Minutes later Bellfield suddenly rang to say he would have taken her and to ask why she was wasting her money on taxis. It was too late, however; the cab had been ordered, and Mills set off in it with her three children. She had bought baby wipes and Jaffa Cakes, chocolate milk and fish pie, ham and yoghurts – a typical family shop – and the bill had come to just under £70.

Just as she finished shopping Bellfield arrived at the store to collect her and immediately took his two older children across the road to the nearby Toys 'R' Us to buy them each a present. He then gave them a lift back to Little Benty in the white Ford Courier van. But Bellfield didn't stay with them. Shortly after 9 o'clock that evening – as he had done so many times in their years together – Bellfield made an excuse to Mills about having 'business to do' and climbed back into the white Ford van and disappeared into the gathering dusk. It was a dusk that he was to wrap around himself like a dark cloak.

By 9.30 on the evening of 19 August Bellfield was driving his white Ford van up the Hampton Road towards Twickenham Green. But he wasn't going anywhere specific, he was simply driving around. Perhaps he was annoyed at having to collect Mills and their children from Tesco; perhaps he had argued with the teenage Terri Carroll, who always wanted to know where he was and what he was doing every moment of the day or night; but, far more likely, the rage against young women that he had felt for years was gnawing away at him ever more fiercely on that balmy summer evening. What is not in doubt is that Bellfield was out searching for a victim that night.

The area he had chosen was all too familiar – not far from where Mills and he had had their first small flat together on Manor Road, near two of his favourite pubs on Hampton Road and not far from the A316 out of London, where Anna-Maria Rennie had been attacked. Jo Collings's house in Strawberry Hill was only half a mile away.

That evening Bellfield started driving in a sort of triangle up and down Staines Road and Hampton Road with Twickenham Green at its apex – on the lookout for a young woman alone. At 9.45 he found one – the French student Amélie Delagrange – getting off a London United R267 red double-decker outside the Fullwell bus garage on Hampton Road.

Amélie was an attractive young woman of twenty-two with short blonde hair – very much Bellfield's type, if a little older than his absolute ideal. Her parents lived in the French countryside outside Amiens on the River Somme about 70 miles north of Paris; she had an older sister, Virginie, who had married in September 1999. Amélie had a passion for English, studying it at school as part of her baccalaureate and then following up with a period of study in Manchester. She had then gone off to Spain to learn Spanish, before returning home to France. But in April 2004 she had decided to come back to England to improve her English still further. She planned to use her fluency in French, Spanish and English to become a tri-lingual personal assistant.

Amélie had decided to rent a room in a house in Gould Road, just north of Twickenham Green. She liked the area, which she felt was 'very safe', and her landlady described her as a 'sensible, intelligent girl', who was both 'independent and sociable'. Amélie then found a job at a café and patisserie called Maison Blanc in Richmond and proceeded to develop a close circle of both English and French friends.

On the evening of Thursday, 19 August 2004 she had agreed to meet a group of them at the Crystalz wine bar on London Road in Twickenham, just across the road from The Sorting House pub, where Kate Sheedy had had met her friends just three months earlier.

Amélie and her friends decided to sit outside because it was such a nice evening. It was nearly the weekend, and they were intent on having a good time without going too far. Indeed, one of Amélie's friends, Benjamin Blatrix, remembered that she only had three or four glasses of wine, as 'she was working the following day'. Nevertheless, another of Amélie's friends, Floriane Merzougi, recalled later that had admitted to her that she was 'a little bit drunk', even though she had had the good sense to eat a plate of chips.

At about 8.30 Amélie called her new boyfriend, Olivier Lenfant, who worked with her at Maison Blanc, and invited him over to her house for the night because her landlady was away. Olivier turned down the offer, saying he was tired, having just moved flat, but they arranged to meet the next day.

Then, about an hour later, at 9.30, just as it was just getting dark, Amélie asked another friend, Vanessa Roche, to walk her across the road to the bus stop outside The Sorting Room pub to catch the R267 bus back to Twickenham Green and her room in Gould Road. As she stood at the bus stop she waved to her friends still sitting outside the wine bar on the other side of the street.

The closed-circuit television on the R267 that arrived

to collect her shows Amélie climbing on board at 9.39. She got off just six minutes later, at 9.45, half a mile or so past her normal stop. Perhaps the bus was hot and the wine had made her a little sleepy; perhaps she was pre-occupied by thinking about Olivier, or work the next day. It was a minor lapse of concentration, but one that was to have tragic consequences.

It was a perfectly ordinary night, and Amélie was a sensible young woman. Hampton Road was busy as she made her way back up towards Twickenham Green, and there was no reason whatever for her to fear for her safety. Her inhibitions would certainly have been lowered by the wine, but this was not a dark alley in the East End of London after midnight. It was an eminently middle-class road, home to the respected Mall School.

Amélie did not realize it, but her entire progress up Hampton Road was caught on a variety of CCTV cameras along the way – as was the progress of a white Ford Courier van. At 9.49 she was seen in the video footage from a R281 bus travelling south. Two minutes later she walked past the Loch Fyne restaurant, where she was caught on camera again, and two minutes after that a passing police car travelling south video-recorded her walking north towards the Green. At 9.58 the cameras on another R281 captured her still walking towards the Green, and two minutes later she appeared again on the CCTV system outside a shop known as The Accountants. At 10.01 she appeared on a bus camera again – a Tellings R70 bus – and she was still on the east side of Hampton Road, now very close to Twickenham Green.

It was to be the last image of Amélie Delagrange alive.

By the time this vulnerable young Frenchwoman, who was a little unsteady on her feet, had reached the edge of the Green and started to cross it towards her home in Gould Road one of the vehicles driving up Hampton Road towards the Green had taken a particular interest in her – Levi Bellfield's distinctive white Ford Courier van.

It was first spotted by CCTV cameras in Hampton Road just before 9.30 that evening, before Amélie got off her R267 bus. Not long afterwards, it was seen not far away in Staines Road. Then, at shortly before 10, this same distinctive white van – with its left nearside headlight not working – was spotted by CCTV cameras on an R281 bus driving along Hampton Road towards Twickenham Green, and then again on the cameras outside The Accountants shop.

The Ford Courier passed the shop about a minute before Amélie was seen on exactly the same camera – which means that it had passed her as she walked towards the Green. But the white Ford Courier didn't drive round the Green and back along Staines Road this time – the triangular circuit it had been taking. At 10.05 the van was spotted parked in the bus lane on the Hampton Road side of the Green by the CCTV cameras on an R281 bus, and two minutes later by the cameras on an R70. It was clearly waiting for something, or someone, and that someone was Amélie Delagrange.

Though the shop fronts on the far side threw out a lot of light, the Green itself is ringed by trees, and it was dark as Amélie set off diagonally across it towards her home. Nevertheless she could hardly have expected anyone to interrupt her progress across that most respectable of all

English venues, a cricket pitch. Why would she? This was a part of the world that she and her friends had decided during their conversation at Crystalz wine bar that evening was 'very safe'.

Tragically that did not turn out to be the case for Amélie Delagrange.

By 10.08 that evening, the white Courier van had disappeared from its place in the bus lane on Hampton Road, and Amélie lay seriously injured on the north side of the cricket square. Despite all the best efforts of the staff at the West Middlesex Hospital to resuscitate her, this pretty blonde French woman with a talent for languages died just two hours later later, at two minutes past midnight on the morning of Friday 20 August 2004.

Within hours a full-scale police operation to track down her killer had been launched, and just before 7 o'clock on that Friday morning Detective Chief Inspector Colin Sutton, a senior investigating officer with more than eight years' experience in the role, was contacted at home and asked to take charge of the inquiry. By 9 o'clock he was at Twickenham police station, just yards from where she had spent her last hours at Crystalz, being briefed on the case, and that afternoon he went to the post-mortem examination at Kingston hospital.

By a strange coincidence, the pathologist who examined Amélie's body was exactly the same man who had conducted the post-mortem on Marsha McDonnell a year earlier, Dr Roger Chapman, and he discovered remarkably similar injuries. Both young women had died from a severe blow to the head made by a blunt object, and neither of them had defensive wounds on their hands.

Dr Chapman also told DCI Sutton that Amélie had been 'hit from behind' and that there was also evidence of another impact just behind her right ear, as well as further bruising on the top of her right shoulder, consistent with two other, but less traumatic, blows from behind by her attacker.

As Sutton was to say later, the atmosphere at the post-mortem was even more morose than usual, 'as we looked on at an examination of a beautiful young girl, perfect and healthy in every way until an animal left her with a skull like a dropped Easter egg'.

The question was: was Amélie's murder a one-off crime, or part of a pattern of crimes? DCI Sutton wasn't sure, but he was aware that during the year before the police had launched an inquiry called Operation Upwey into three similar assaults in the area between Twickenham Green and Hampton – on Marsha McDonnell, Jesse Wilson and Adele Harbison – because they felt the offences were linked in some way. As DCI Sutton was to write in notes to himself after that first briefing at Twickenham: 'Attacks like this, where a stranger commits a murderous assault in the street, are extremely rare . . . Here we had three very similar attacks in very similar circumstances on very similar victims, and all in a small, very suburban and safe corner of London. And now there was a fourth. To me there was every reason to think that they might be the work of one person.' But for the moment he confined his thoughts to trying to find the man or woman who had killed Amélie Delagrange.

'My first task was the new one,' he said later, 'an offence where I could start from the beginning and where there would be new opportunities. Once we had found Amélie's killer then and only then might it be worth revisiting the old attacks.'

Within two days DCI Sutton had assembled a murder squad of more than eighty officers – double the normal size in the Metropolitan Police – and they had begun searching for evidence at the scene.

The squad's first break came when they traced the signal from Amélie's mobile phone. The police discovered that it had last contacted the T-Mobile network, to which it was connected, at 10.22 p.m. on the evening that she had been killed – after the passing patrol car had found her body, without her mobile phone. There could hardly be any doubt that the phone had been taken by her killer. On the morning of Saturday, 21 August Sutton and his team met again at Twickenham police station to discuss the discovery. The Telephone Intelligence Unit at New Scotland Yard had pinpointed the area where the phone had last contacted its mobile network to an area of about 500 square yards just north of Walton Bridge over the River Thames.

Nothing had been heard from Amélie's mobile phone since. It had simply disappeared from the network, but there had also been no sign that it had 'powered down' by being deliberately switched off. The murder squad immediately realized that it could have had its battery removed, been damaged in some way, or – quite possibly – been immersed in water. On that Saturday morning DCI Sutton's murder squad took the decision to send a team of police divers to Walton Bridge to see if, by chance, Amélie's attacker had thrown the phone into the Thames. It proved a wise move.

On the following Tuesday, 24 August, a team of police drivers searching under Walton Bridge quickly found – quite close together – a CD player with headphones, a bunch of keys, an a purse. Inside the purse was a receipt for a mobile phone SIM card as well as an ATM receipt for the withdrawal of £50, and – most telling of all – a receipt from Next for a red camisole top. Amélie's handbag and her mobile phone, however, were never recovered.

It was a break in the case, but it wasn't decisive. The murder squad now needed to know how Amélie had arrived at Twickenham Green. So they started to assemble the closed-circuit television evidence from the buses that had passed along Hampton Road beside the Green on the evening of her murder, and it wasn't long before they found footage of her getting off the R267 at the Fulwell Bus Garage. Now the murder squad knew that Amélie had walked to Twickenham Green, and that her mobile phone had then been taken back to Walton-on-Thames, where it had been located barely twenty minutes after her attack. The obvious conclusion was that the phone had been taken by her murderer, who must have had some kind of vehicle, because the phone couldn't have reached Walton so quickly in any other way.

That realization was to prove a turning point in the search for Amélie's killer, for, as DCI Sutton was to put it later, 'Despite London's much-reported mass of CCTV cameras (one's image is captured around 300 times a day in the city on average) the identification of pedestrians is often difficult – particularly at night.' The identification of vehicles, on the other hand, is 'rather easier', as the make, model and colour are regularly discernible, and 'occasionally even the registration number can be seen'. 'I knew the killer's car would be on those recordings somewhere,' DCI Sutton was to put it, 'and if we didn't secure them immediately they would be lost for ever.'

It was the subsequent search by six officers specifically assigned to look at the CCTV footage that was to lead Sutton and his team to a white Ford Courier van with the registration number P610 XCN. The murder squad painstakingly pieced together the CCTV evidence to show that this white Ford Courier van had been parked on Hampton Road by Twickenham Green just after 10 p.m. on the night of Thursday, 19 August but had gone eight minutes later. They also quietly gathered evidence that it had been in the area for almost half an hour, 'cruising the area with no obvious destination', and yet had suddenly come to a stop at Twickenham Green – but only for a matter of minutes. It had last been captured at 10.08, parked at the beginning of the bus lane beside the Green. Yet less than thirty seconds later it was seen speeding away from the Green. Within five minutes it was spotted by CCTV cameras in Hampton and at 10.39 it was seen by another set of cameras passing the Toshiba factory in Sunbury, on the way towards Harmondsworth and Heathrow airport.

In the wake of their discovery the murder squad set out to trace the ownership of the white Ford van, but they also discovered that the van had received countless parking fines and committed other offences between June 2003 and August 2004. Indeed on Tuesday, 17 August 2004 a traffic camera had shown it driving in a bus lane in London Road in Twickenham, outside Crystalz wine bar, at 10.56 in the evening.

It was only a matter of time before the murder squad discovered that Levi Bellfield regularly drove the white Ford van, although he wasn't the registered owner. Once they had done so they set out to track the whereabouts of his mobile phone on the evening of Thursday, 19 August. If they could put his mobile at Twickenham Green that night they had the outline of a case against him for Amélie's murder.

It didn't take the murder squad long to discover, however, that Bellfield had as many mobile phones as he had vehicles, and that he changed them repeatedly. Nevertheless they managed to establish that he was using one which ended in the three numbers '452' that evening. Bellfield had taken the phone over from Terri Carroll. The mobile phone records for '452' showed that it had been at Tesco in Hayes that evening and that from there it had made the journey to Twickenham – with Bellfield and P610 XCN. Indeed at 9.37 that evening Emma Mills had called it from the landline at Little Benty, when it was on video driving close to Twickenham Green.

That was their best hope for evidence, because in the days after Amélie's killing not a single witness came forward to say that they had seen anyone attack her on Twickenham Green. There may have been people walking their dogs, courting couples arm in arm, men standing in the shadows of the cricket sight-screen smoking, but no one had seen anything.

That presented a special test for the detectives – one which no senior investigating officer could turn down. As DCI Sutton himself put it later: 'For senior investigating officers, the huge wave, the massive trout and the hole-in-one is the Category A+ murder, the high-profile stranger attack where there is no connection between killer and victim, save for the misfortune that their paths happened to cross . . . The greatest possible test, the most unpredictable challenge: to take out a madman who was killing young women at random and for who knew what twisted reason.'

It took Sutton's squad almost three months of hard work, but by early November 2004 they were in no doubt whatsoever that Bellfield had been driving the white Ford Courier van they had picked up on CCTV parked beside Twickenham Green that evening, and his mobile phone records proved it. It was the trigger to allow them to launch a full-scale surveillance of Bellfield.

After all, as Brian Altman QC was to ask the jury at his trial for the murder of Amélie three years later, 'What had been its driver's purpose in stopping by the Green for no more than eight minutes at the very time we suggest Amélie was struck down? We suggest the answer is perfectly clear. Bellfield was driving the van and spotted Amélie at some point along the route and determined to engage her. There was more than enough time for him to wait for her in his van by the Green, wait for her to catch up and, when she walked across the Green, intercept and attack her, steal her possessions and return to the van and drive off.'

The white Ford Courier van and the mobile phone that ended with the numbers '452' were to lead DCI Colin Sutton and his double murder squad to the front door of number 11, Little Benty at 5 a.m. on that November morning in 2004.

By that time Levi Bellfield had done his very best to conceal any connection there might have been between him and the white Ford Courier van, which – like Emma Mills's red Daewoo in Collingwood Place in Walton-on-Thames in March 2002 – had disappeared into thin air, never to be seen again.

14. The Noose Tightens

> 'Justice is truth in action.'
> Joseph Joubert, *Pensées*

Just after 11 o'clock on the evening of Amélie Delagrange's murder Levi Bellfield arrived back at Little Benty,
but he didn't stay at the house with Emma Mills, their new
daughter Georgina and his other two children. In fact, he
didn't even go inside to see them. Instead he parked the
white Ford Courier van round the corner by the garages,
called her on his '452' mobile phone and then called the
local LHR Express mini-cab firm to take him to Crosby
Close and Terri Carroll.

When the mini-cab driver, whose name was Patrick
Kelly, arrived to collect him at 11.21 p.m. he watched as
Bellfield emerged from the darkness at the side of Little
Benty carrying two large black bin-liners knotted at the
top which didn't appear to be very heavy and which he
proceeded to put on the back seat. He was also carrying
two bottles of beer, drinking from one of them.

Bellfield didn't go straight back to Crosby Close, however. There was something he needed to do first, although
he didn't explain what he was. He simply told the mini-
cab driver to take him to a dead-end road not far away in
Hanworth.

When they got there, he got out of the car, made another mobile-phone call, took something out of one of the bin-liners in the back of the mini-cab and disappeared into the darkness to 'meet someone'. The mini-cab driver didn't see who he was meeting, but within five minutes Bellfield was back and asking to go to Crosby Close.

Could it be that during those five minutes in Hanworth, Bellfield gave the keys to the white Ford Courier van to someone and asked them to dispose of it, or, at least, to make sure that it was out of sight should anyone come looking for it in the wake of Amélie's murder? No one will ever know – but what is known is that the where-abouts of P610 XCN were to remain a mystery from that night on and a matter of intense interest to DCI Sutton's double murder squad.

By the time that the squad began to assemble at Twick-enham police station the next morning, Friday, 20 August, Bellfield was on the move again, this time asking the same mini-cab service to pick him up from one of his usual haunts, a pub in West Drayton called the Fox and Pheasant. Acting as though he didn't have a care in the world, Bellfield went back to Little Benty, collected another of his cars and set off to sign up a new customer for his wheel-clamping business in Potters Bar in Hertfordshire. On the surface, at least, business was going on as usual.

In spite of his superficial confidence, however, the panic attacks that had troubled him since his sudden departure from the flat in Walton-on-Thames in March 2002 were now plaguing him night and day, and although he would bluster that he was 'perfectly all right' to his clamping crew, back home in the darkness of the night things were very far from it.

Emma Mills knew that. She remembered his attacks happening 'all the time' in 2004. 'All through the day he had little what he calls fits,' she would explain. To control them Bellfield had started smoking even more cannabis and drinking even more heavily than he had done before. But the Diazepam drugs that he had been prescribed to help with the attacks weren't working.

'Levi would take too many in one day,' Mills would remember. 'He was hooked on them really. He had had the odd one now sort of every now and again, but I mean now he gets them all the time, you can't go anywhere without him having one.'

No matter how calm Bellfield might have appeared to his wheel-clamping crew, in the days after Amélie's murder his attacks took an even more powerful hold, and his mood darkened steadily – so much so that he left Carroll at Crosby Close and went back to Little Benty to seek solace with Mills and his children.

By the middle of the following week, which led up to the August Bank Holiday, he was all but inconsolable, his mood not helped by the fact that he was also due to face a charge of perverting the course of justice over the Rodriguez affair at Isleworth Crown Court that week. Bellfield's life was out of control.

Matters came to a head on Wednesday, 25 August – less than a week after Amélie's murder – when his friend 'Yosser' Hughes went round to visit him at Little Benty around lunchtime.

'I went to his bedroom and saw him lying on the bed in his shorts,' Hughes said later. 'He was crying his eyes out, and I asked him what was wrong. He said, "I think I need some help."' Hughes was to spend the next half an hour or so trying to calm Bellfield down. 'I thought he was in this state because of drink or possibly drugs,' Hughes added, and he tried to persuade his friend to go to hospital. But the sobbing Bellfield refused, and Hughes left. He wasn't gone for long.

Three hours later Hughes returned to find Bellfield in exactly the same state, but this time he agreed to go get help, and Hughes took him to the nearby Hillingdon hospital. Choking back the tears during their trip to the hospital together, Bellfield told Hughes, 'You don't know what I've done.'

Bellfield arrived at Accident and Emergency in Hillingdon just before 7 o'clock that evening and told the staff he had a history of panic attacks over the past two years and had used Diazepam to control them. He also admitted that he had been feeling suicidal over the past few days and that he planned to hang himself. Significantly, Bellfield told the nursing staff that the stress he was under was partly the result of his 'domineering' mother and the fact that he was 'getting grief' from both his mother and his wife, which he couldn't control. He also admitted that he was in '£20,000 worth' of debt. As a result, that evening he was admitted to the Pinn Ward of the hospital's Riverside Centre, the mental health division of the Hillingdon hospital. Hughes stayed with him to keep him company until about 3 o'clock in the morning and then went home.

When Hughes went back to visit Bellfield the following morning, he learned that the hospital's doctors were going to discuss whether Bellfield should be 'sectioned' under the terms of the Mental Health Act to prevent him doing himself harm. But when he told the wheel-clamper, Bellfield became tremendously agitated and demanded that Hughes got him out of there. That was exactly what happened. Without official consent Bellfield checked himself out of the hospital, and Hughes took him back to Little Benty.

Then, in spite of his promising faithfully to return to Hillingdon the next day, Bellfield announced that he and Mills and their three children were going to Kent the very next day to stay with their friend Michelle Wickham. The decision came as a distinct shock to Mills, who had been planning to go to a birthday party for her grandmother that Friday afternoon, but she didn't object.

The question was: how were they going to get there? Bellfield was very vague about the whereabouts of the white Ford Courier van and insisted that Mills ask Hughes if she could borrow his Vauxhall Astra. But she wasn't allowed to tell him – or anyone else for that matter – exactly where they were going. Ever anxious about her children, Mills warned Bellfield that she wanted to be back early the next week to get them ready for school. Her daughter Lucy was going into a new class, and her son William was going for the first time – into the reception class. Bellfield agreed, or appeared to, and so, on the afternoon of Friday, 27 August, they set off for Kent, leaving 'Yosser' to look after their dog Cheyenne at Little Benty.

There was, of course, an all-too-familiar pattern to Bellfield's behaviour. Just as he had done after the murder of Marsha McDonnell – when he had suddenly whisked the family away to Tenerife – he was intent on making himself as scarce as possible should the police come looking for him. He specifically told Mills to lie about where they were going, telling her to say they were at the caravan site in Leysdown on the Isle of Sheppey if anyone asked.

'We were due to have a weekend away,' Mills was to explain 'but he just never wanted to come home. He said, "When I go home the police will be looking for me."'

In fact, Bellfield, Mills and their children stayed away from Little Benty for almost three weeks, and while they were away the couple rarely went out, although Mills did persuade him to allow her to take Hughes's car back, which was replaced by another white van – this time a Citroën Berlingo. There was still no sign of the white Ford Courier with the broken headlight. But Bellfield wouldn't even park the Berlingo outside Michelle Wickham's house. He preferred to leave it down the road out of sight, telling his partner 'not to worry about anything' and to leave everything to him. He also refused to use his mobile phone while they were in Kent, relying instead on the local telephone box and clearly worried that the police might track his mobile phone's signal if he switched it on.

In the end, however, the trip to Kent seemed to settle Bellfield's mind, and he finally agreed to return to London on 16 September, although Mills's two elder children didn't actually get to school until Monday, 20 September, a fortnight after the school term had started.

By that time Bellfield was back wheel-clamping. As far as the outside world was concerned everything was back to normal – so normal, in fact, that even though he attended one follow-up appointment at Hillingdon hospital in late September, he failed to appear for two subsequent appointments in October and November 2004. Bellfield's suicidal thoughts had apparently dissipated.

Bellfield was also back living with Terri Carroll. They had returned briefly the flat at Crosby Close, but it was suddenly repossessed at the end of September and they had to find themselves somewhere else. Once again Bellfield fell back on his usual haunts: he arranged for them to return to another hotel on the Heathrow perimeter, from where he could pay his periodic visits to Emma Mills.

One thing that struck Carroll as strange as they moved into the hotel at the beginning of October was that Bellfield had shaved all his hair off. When she asked him why he had done it, he didn't give a reason beyond saying that he had been in trouble with the police – 'something to do with fraud and clamping'. The true reason might have had far more to do with his reluctance to leave DNA evidence anywhere he went.

Nevertheless Carroll remained with him, sometimes staying in the airport perimeter hotels but just as often sleeping on the floor of the bedroom in Spiers's flat. On other nights she had go back to her mother's while Bellfield went to stay with Emma Mills at Little Benty.

Bellfield was still intent of preserving the appearance of a family life there with his three latest children, however, and was still taking an apparent pleasure in having family photographs with them whenever the chance presented itself. There was still a part of his personality that depended on his being seen as a 'family man', even though the horrifying reality of his true attitude to women – and particularly young girls – was far removed from this comfortable stereotype.

As autumn turned to winter in 2004, Bellfield's life settled into a by now familiar pattern, and for the time being he seemed to have given up his nocturnal drives around west London, perhaps only too aware that the police might be looking for a man driving the streets on the lookout for vulnerable young women getting off a bus.

On the night before his arrest in November 2004 Bellfield took Carroll to her mother's and went to stay with Emma Mills, where their friend Michelle Wickham from Kent had been staying for the weekend. He had spent the day wheel-clamping in the Woking area of Surrey with Noel Moran and acting as though he had barely a care in the world – in stark contrast to the man who had been taken to Hillingdon hospital just three months before. The police hadn't turned up at Bellfield's door in those three months, and the shadow of the prison cell seemed to have faded from his consciousness.

That did not mean that DCI Sutton's double murder squad had been idle, however. While Bellfield had been hiding in Kent, they had been trying first to identify and then to track down the white Ford Courier van by meticulously piecing together the CCTV footage from the buses on Hampton Road and Twickenham Green at the time of Amélie Delagrange's death. And it was precisely that old-fashioned police work that was eventually to lead them to Bellfield's door at Little Benty.

There was no direct evidence linking him to Amélie's murder – no murder weapon, no eyewitness, no DNA, nothing directly to suggest that he was a prime suspect.

But there was the van, P610 XCN, and the CCTV images, which showed a man who looked remarkably like Levi Bellfield driving it on the night of 19 August on the roads around Twickenham Green. It was those CCTV images and the knowledge that the white Ford Courier van had been in Bellfield's possession at the time of Amélie's murder that led the detectives of a Metropolitan Police murder squad to bang on the door of number 11, Little Benty at five o'clock in the morning of Monday 22 November 2004.

By the time that Bellfield had been discovered hiding under the yellow fibreglass insulation in the attic by Sergeant Norman Griffiths and been driven back to the custody suite at London's Heathrow police station, the murder squad were well prepared to ask him a string of questions about the Ford van, his mobile phone and his whereabouts on that warm August night when Amélie met her death. What they were not prepared for was Bellfield's aggressive response. The more questions they asked the angrier he became. He resented his arrest, he told them; he had nothing to say; he was innocent; they had made a terrible mistake; it was a 'stitch-up'. But as the hours passed Bellfield's tantrums turned into a sullen non-cooperation.

As the police questioning wore on, Bellfield started to refuse to answer any questions whatever, restricting himself to saying 'no comment' repeatedly, in his distinctive high-pitched voice. Time after time he would then turn directly away from his police interrogators in the interview room, finally turning his back on them completely in an act of blatant defiance. No matter how hard the police tried to cajole a cooperative answer from him, Bellfield remained adamant. He wasn't saying a word.

Question: Tell us where you went at 9 o'clock when you left Little
  Benty . . .

Answer: No comment.

Question: . . . in a hurry. Because there may be somewhere you went
  that we can check up on.

Answer: No comment.

Question: Is there anyone you could tell us that was with you at this
  time that can say 'No, Levi was with me'? It would be a good time to
  tell us if there was, wouldn't it?

Answer: No comment.

Question: What were you doing after that, Levi? After leaving Little Benty?

Answer: No comment.

Then, a little later:

Question: Did you have a phone with you that night?

Answer: Ahh, no comment.

Question: What do you mean by 'Ahh'?

Answer: No comment.

Question: At 2138 the landline at Little Benty calls the 452 phone . . .

Answer: No comment.

Question: What's that about then?

Answer: No comment.

Relentlessly, and for weeks on end, Bellfield refused to explain his actions on the night of Amélie's murder, beyond saying that he had gone to look at a car he was interested in buying and that he might not have been in possession of the white Ford Courier for part of that night, although he was less than forthcoming about who had had it that night, beyond saying that he thought it might have been Morgan and Suraj Gharu.

Question: So who had the van?

Answer: No comment.

Question: Who had the van?

Answer: No comment.

Question: Had you sold the van by then?

Answer: No comment.

Inevitably, the murder squad detectives put the obvious question to him.

Question: If you weren't driving the van on the 19 August, then anybody would surely be keen to say, 'I didn't have the van: I got rid of the van; such and such was driving it; I don't know who was driving it; it could have been any one of them . . .'

Bellfield's answer was: 'No comment.'
He saw no reason to elaborate on any of his answers to the police, relying instead on presenting himself to them as a man who had been 'wronged' by their 'vicious

accusations', a victim of their mistaken belief that he was, in fact, capable of murder.

DCI Sutton's murder squad weren't to be put off their task, however, but it wasn't the murder of Amélie Delagrange that was to keep Bellfield on remand in custody in the weeks and months that followed his arrest at Little Benty, it was his repeated sexual abuse of his three principal female partners over the preceding fifteen years. Gradually, as Becky Wilkinson, Jo Collings and Emma Mills – the mothers of eight of his children – told their stories to the murder squad, Bellfield's pattern of the rape and abuse of his partners emerged into the harsh light of day. As a result Bellfield was charged with rape, which allowed the police to ask for his remand in custody – which was granted repeatedly – while continuing their investigations into the murders of Amélie Delagrange and Marsha McDonnell, as well as the attacks on Kate Sheedy, Irma Dragoshi and Anna-Maria Rennie.

While those investigations continued it was also becoming all too clear to the murder squad officers that some of the other members of Bellfield's wheel-clamping crew were not entirely blameless when it came to matters of serious sexual misconduct and violence. In November 2005, for example, Suraj Gharu, who had worked with Bellfield since the wheel-clamping business began, was imprisoned for five years for having sex with a fourteen-year-old girl from a Hillingdon Council children's home. Friends of Bellfield, particularly Terri Carroll, told the police stories of Suraj Gharu ringing the wheel-clamper repeatedly to 'offer him' girls. 'Suraj would ring Levi and tell him that he had a girl with him,' Carroll was to say, 'and he would ask if Levi wanted to shag her.' Bellfield's habit of sharing sexual conquests with his friends had not died out – indeed it was clearly reciprocated.

Throughout the clamping years Bellfield had also kept up his connections with the sixty-two-year-old paedophile Victor Kelly, from whom he would sometimes buy drugs, and who had also been sent to prison for eight years in November 2005 for giving a twelve-year-old girl cocaine in order that he could have sex with her. At least one member of Bellfield's clamping crew believed that Suraj Gharu was one of the people who had helped Kelly procure young girls for under-age sex.

It was not just Bellfield's 'known associates' that interested DCI Sutton's murder squad, however. They were also intent on tracking down the three important vehicles that were linked to attacks they now saw as part of a pattern, and which were all linked to Bellfield. The more the squad had looked at the violent attacks committed in west London over the past few years the more convinced they had become that they were investigating one man – Levi Bellfield.

As DCI Sutton was to explain: 'The fact is, happily, that attacks like this where a stranger commits a murderous assault in the street are extremely rare,' a fact that had convinced him that Bellfield was responsible for all the attacks, even though the officers who had investigated before him believed it was 'unlikely' that the McDonnell and Sheedy attacks were linked to Amélie. Sutton disagreed. 'To me,' Sutton was to say, 'there was every reason to think that they might have been the work of one person.'

So Sutton and his team started to take an interest not

only in the missing white Ford Courier van, P610 XCN, seen near the attack on Amélie, but also the white Vauxhall Corsa, Y57 RJU, seen near the attack on Marsha, and the white Toyota Previa people-carrier, K855 EFL, that may have been used in the attack on Kate Sheedy. If they could link them to one man they would have a strong case to convince the Crown Prosecution Service to press for charges of murder.

The squad had to search through nearly 25,000 possible Ford Couriers before finding the one that had shown up on the CCTV cameras on the buses that passed it on Hampton Road in Twickenham on the night that Amélie was killed. They also had to search through 600,000 possible Corsas for the one that passed Marsha McDonnell's number 111 bus at its stop in Percy Road in Hampton. It was painstaking work.

The squad never located the missing white Ford Courier van, they simply found ample evidence after interviewing his partners, his friends and his clamping crew that it had been used by Bellfield in the first weeks of August 2004. Their statements helped to convince the squad that he had had use of the van on that August night.

The police had rather more luck with the Corsa, although they had to travel the length and breadth of the country to interview the legal owners of 178 possible Vauxhall Corsas that could have been the one seen stalking Marsha in the early hours of that morning in February 2003 before they could pin the single one down that was decisively linked with Levi Bellfield.

As for the Toyota Previa, the police finally tracked it down to a traveller named Jimmy McCarthy, who had bought it from Bellfield's clamping associate Noel Moran for £1,100 in July 2004 – two months after the attack on Kate Sheedy. They also established that the Previa had been used by Bellfield's clamping crew at the time of the attack and had a damaged wing mirror – which Kate had identified as significant on the people-carrier that drove over her.

The cars and vans were central to the police investigations into the attacks, but there was another element that helped to convince the murder squad that they had tracked down the right suspect – the use of mobile phones. In spite of Bellfield's appetite for having as many different phones as he had vehicles, seldom using the same one twice, a pattern of use did emerge that enabled the detectives to be sure that his '452' mobile phone had been in the Twickenham area on the night of Amélie's murder.

It was this attention to detail that eventually persuaded DCI Sutton's murder squad that they had enough evidence to convince the Crown Prosecution Service that they should charged Levi Bellfield with the attacks. But it was to take the CPS some time to agree with them, for there was little in the way of corroborating evidence to help – there was, of course, no DNA evidence; there were no witnesses to the attacks; no weapons had been discovered to link him to the crime. Indeed there was no confession from Bellfield himself.

It was not until 2 March 2006 that DCI Sutton formally charged Bellfield with the murder of Amélie Delagrange. And it was to be another two months before he formally charged him with the murder of Marsha McDonnell, on 25 May 2006. Both dates are for ever etched on Sutton's mind – the days when his long battle to uncover the man who had brutally murdered two total strangers in the respectable, leafy streets of west London for no apparent reason finally came to its end.

By that time Bellfield was on remand in custody at the high-security Belmarsh prison in south-east London, and while he was there the police had also begun to hear stories of his bragging to other prisoners about what he had done. One fellow inmate in particular told the police murder squad privately that Bellfield had 'confessed' to killing Amélie Delagrange. Significantly he had also told them that Bellfield described women as being like 'pet dogs': 'You feed them and you keep them, and you can do what you want with them,' he told him. It was a 'confession' that struck a chord with the officers who had been taking statements from Becky Wilkinson, Jo Collings and Emma Mills about Bellfield's behaviour towards them during the course of their relationships – further confirmation that they were dealing with a man who saw himself as above the law.

Bellfield was not alone in that conviction, however. On 2 January 2006, his fellow wheel-clamper and close friend Noel Moran, then still only twenty-two, attacked a man with a Samurai sword after a disagreement at a New Year's Eve party at the Fox and Pheasant pub in West Drayton, one of Bellfield's favourite haunts, the place he had been picked up from on the morning after the murder of Amélie Delagrange. Wielding swords, Moran and a friend called Gavin Ward had broken into the home of computer expert Christopher Mills – known to his friends as 'Millsy' – and attacked him viciously, severing an artery in his left leg. The pair insisted that he had 'disrespected' them at the pub on New Year's Eve. They carried out the attack in front of Mills's girlfriend, who was so frightened that she had to hide in the wardrobe with her five-year-old daughter.

After fatally wounding Mills, Moran and Ward went in search of another man whom they thought was equally guilty of disrespect, but failed to find him. They then disappeared to southern Ireland, but were tracked down by a Metropolitan Police murder squad and charged. In June 2007 both men were found guilty of murder at the Old Bailey. The following month both were sentenced to life imprisonment, and Moran was told he would have to serve a minimum of fifteen years.

Meanwhile Bellfield steadfastly maintained his innocence in Belmarsh prison – calling his mother Jean up to four times a day while he was on remand to insist it was 'all a stitch-up' by the police and that he had had nothing to do with the killings of any young women in west London.

Bellfield told the same story to Terri Carroll, whom he also spoke to on the telephone in the first few months of his remand, telling her tearfully that he 'still loved her' and that he was innocent. But their relationship gradually came to an end as the months on remand in Belmarsh turned into years.

It was to be almost three years before he would face a jury accused of murder, but throughout those years he maintained his innocence.

As Emma Mills was to say later, 'I don't think he'll admit to killing anyone. He's not the type to own up to anything. He's a control freak. He likes to have the power and control over everything – and that includes women.'

Ironically, it was to be in front of a female judge of the High Court that Bellfield would learn his fate at the Old Bailey, sitting in one of Central Criminal Courts' famous wood-panelled courtrooms beneath the statue of the figure of another woman holding the scales of justice.

15. Trial by Jury

'Human blood is heavy; the man that has shed it
cannot run away.'

African proverb

Levi Bellfield was destined to spend almost three years on remand in custody at Belmarsh prison before finally being brought to trial for the murders of Amélie Delagrange and Marsha McDonnell, as well as the attempted murders of Kate Sheedy and Irma Dragoshi and the kidnapping of Anna-Maria Rennie.

Throughout those years in jail, awaiting trial by a jury of his peers, he steadfastly maintained his innocence, telling his defence team time and again that the Crown's cases against him was 'all a mistake', and a 'stitch-up' by the police. 'It was not the behaviour of a man consumed by guilt, but the reaction of someone who knew that he had to work the judicial system to stand any chance of being found innocent of five terrible crimes.

As a result Bellfield took an exceptional interest in the presentation of his legal case. He would study the myriad of papers surrounding the evidence with exceptional care, answer any queries that his defence team put to him quickly and clearly and insist that they leave no stone unturned in their effort to defend him. This was a man consumed with

the idea that he might still be able to get away with anything, a man determined to defend himself and not give
away his true feelings for one moment. As one senior
police officer put it as the trial began, 'Bellfield is a smart
man and knew exactly what was necessary to present
himself in the best light.' Any appearance of the rage and
anger that he had demonstrated towards the women in
his life on so many occasions must never be allowed to
surface.

Bellfield also had no intention whatever of incriminating himself, and so throughout his years on remand in
prison he remained as silent as he had been during the
majority of his police interviews – ignoring requests for
information, refusing to answer questions put to him by
the Crown as it prepared its case, turning away from his
interrogators. He was allowed to do so by law and knew it.

But Levi Bellfield also never demonstrated for a moment
that he was a man overcome with grief or remorse at the
crimes he was charged with. To anyone from the prosecution team that came into contact with him he remained
tight-lipped, a man who knew that if he demonstrated
remorse it was tantamount to an admission of guilt. He
had no intention of making that mistake. He was – in the
words of one of the senior police officers who talked to
him – 'a cunning, devious man' who knew how to manipulate the law in his own best interests.

It was a trait that he intended to adopt at his trial –
when it eventually came.

In fact, it was not until 2 October 2007 that Bellfield
was finally loaded into a long wheelbase white prison
van along with three prison officers to be taken from

Belmarsh to Britain's most famous court, just 200 yards from St Paul's Cathedral in Central London, and always known as the Old Bailey. He was thirty-nine years old.

The first court on the site had opened its doors in 1539, beside Newgate prison, in a road named Old Bailey for its place as part of the walls of the City of London. The original building was paid for by the then Lord Mayor of London, Sir Richard Whittington, whose memory was famously immortalized in a theatrical pantomime. Until the middle of the nineteenth century those condemned to death in its courts were hanged in the street outside.

The present Portland stone building was built on the site between 1902 and 1907 with a great dome at its peak, and 212 feet above the ground atop the dome stands a bronze statue sculpted by F. W. Pomeroy. The statue shows a woman with the scales of justice in one hand and a sword held upright towards the sky in the other. Legend has it that the lady is blindfolded, though in reality she is not, but her statue has stood guard above some of the most dramatic murder trials in modern British history.

It was at the Old Bailey that Dr Crippen was sentenced to death in 1910; where William Joyce, the Nazi Party's propagandist 'Lord Haw-Haw' was sent to the gallows in 1945; where James Christie of the infamous 10 Rillington Place was condemned to death in 1953; and where Peter Sutcliffe, the so-called 'Yorkshire Ripper', was sentenced to life imprisonment without hope of parole in 1981.

The courts were damaged in an IRA bomb attack in 1973, just after a set of new courtrooms had been opened next door, which mean that the original grand main entrance is no longer used – but above it still stands the original inscription: 'Defend the Children of the Poor & Punish the Wrongdoer'.

And it was here, in the wood-panelled splendour of Court 6, that Bellfield was finally brought to justice.

As he walked into the glass-panelled dock that faced the judge across the room, he looked every inch an honest man. There was no sign of his familiar tracksuit bottoms or T-shirts as the prison officers sat either side of him. He had chosen instead to wear a neat grey suit with a white shirt and a selection of pastel ties and he took particular pains to speak in the politest of voices, and certainly never to shout or display anger. He made certain that the jury would not see some sort of scowling monster. Bellfield knew exactly the image he wanted to present – an upright member of the community who had been falsely accused. On one occasion in the dock he even chose to sport a pink-and-grey Pringle V-necked sweater and a pink tie that wouldn't have been out of place at one of the golf clubs in west London that he drove past so regularly.

There was certainly not a trace of a smirk on his round, white face as he sat waiting for the prosecution to open its case against him. Brian Altman QC, a Senior Treasury Counsel, who is charged with prosecuting the country's most significant criminal cases, was to prosecute him, while the much respected William Boyce QC, who had himself been Senior Treasury Counsel, appeared for his defence. The judge was the Honourable Mrs Justice Rafferty QC, who had been the first female chairman of the Criminal Bar Association when she was still practising as a barrister and before she had ascended to the bench as a judge in the High Court in 2000 had a reputation for formidable intelligence as well as scrupulous fairness. Certainly the fifty-seven-year-old Dame Anne Rafferty, product of the Wolverhampton Girls High School and the University of Sheffield, was determined to give Bellfield far more chance to defend himself than he had given the young women the prosecution alleged that he had attacked.

But the trial did not begin straight away. It took almost two weeks for the prosecution and defence to select the twelve members of the jury from a pool of 120 candidates. No one who had any connection with the Metropolitan Police or the Surrey Police was allowed to become a jury member, and neither was anyone who was not prepared to devote the next four months to daily attendance in court. So it wasn't until Tuesday 16 October 2007 that Brian Altman QC rose to open the case against Bellfield. His first words to the jury were all too clear.

'Between October 2001 and August 2004, five women, four of them young women aged between seventeen and twenty-two, were violently attacked. Two of these young women were brutally murdered by being battered about the head with a blunt instrument. One young woman survived the horrific attack on her when she was driven at and run over. One other woman suffered a nasty injury when she was struck on the head; another young woman escaped the attack upon her without injury. The prosecution say that this defendant, Levi Bellfield, was the attacker in each case.'

Over the next two days Altman meticulously laid out the Crown's case, pointing out the similarities between the attacks, the small area of west London in which they all occurred, the fact that Bellfield knew the area well, that all took place at or near bus stops, that all were committed in the hours of darkness between 7.30 p.m. and 12.30 a.m., and that all had been committed by an attacker who was 'a stranger to the victim'.

'Therefore we submit to you,' Altman concluded, 'when you examine all the elements of the evidence across all the attacks you will find evidence of similarity and system such that you can be sure that what you are seeing is the work of one man – Levi Bellfield.'

Among the spectators in the packed public gallery high above the courtroom were Amélie Delagrange's parents, as well as Levi Bellfield's mother, brother and sister. They watched in silence in the following days as Altman proceeded to call the prosecution witnesses, starting with Anna-Maria Rennie and progressing through Irma Dragoshi to Kate Sheedy. The court also heard from members of Bellfield's clamping crew, including T— Morgan, Suraj Gharu, as well as Noel Moran.

But two witnesses who did not appear before the court were the two teenagers that Bellfield had talked to at a bus stop during the period of police surveillance prior to his arrest in November 2004, the two girls he had made leering 'sexual suggestions' to and who had told him they didn't want to take a lift with him.

Her Honour Judge Rafferty ruled in private that their evidence might prove too prejudicial to Bellfield's case and, therefore, unduly affect the jury's deliberations. She had no wish to see an appeal against any verdict that they might reach on the basis of allowing their evidence to be heard. It was a clear sign that the judge was determined that Bellfield should be seen to have as fair a trial as she could arrange. But Mrs Justice Rafferty did allow the prosecution to present the five cases to the court as a whole – rather than independently – meaning that they could take into account the 'similarity' between the offences as part of their deliberations.

'If you are satisfied that the defendant was responsible for one or more of the offences,' Altman explained to the jury, 'you are entitled also to take those findings into account when deciding whether it is more likely than not that the defendant was responsible for the rest – whether he was disposed to behave in the way the prosecution say he did not once but on several occasions.'

This legal point, known as 'cross-admissability', was to play a very significant – possibly the most significant – part in Bellfield's trial as it progressed from October into November and then December 2007.

Yet it was to be the evidence of two of the Crown's principal witnesses, Emma Mills and Richard 'Yosser' Hughes, that was to provide the most dramatic moments. It was on Monday, 10 December 2007 that thirty-year-old Emma Mills finally took her place in the witness box to describe to a hushed courtroom in her rather weak little voice the extraordinary behaviour of the man who was father to her three young children.

In effect, Mills was fighting for her very life in witness box. If Bellfield was found innocent there was every possibility that he might come back to haunt her, and her children, in the years to come. As one of the police officers who had interviewed her before the trial was to put it later, 'Giving evidence against him was the only way that Emma was ever going to escape from Bellfield's clutches.

She had to tell the truth. If she didn't, and he wasn't convicted, she would never be free of him.'

In the public gallery the spectators seemed to hold their breath on that Monday morning as Brian Altman QC lead the pale-faced young woman through the details of her ten years with the man standing in the dock opposite her – details of the rapes and sexual assaults, details of the beatings, details of the disappearances and the strange telephone calls, the men calling for drugs at her door and the succession of young women who also had sexual relationships with the man her children called 'Daddy'. She spent more than four hours giving evidence and left clearly exhausted.

Just one week later 'Yosser' Hughes told an equally silent courtroom about the time in August 2004 that he had taken a distressed Bellfield to Hillingdon hospital and the defendant had confessed to him in tears that 'You don't know what I'm capable of.'

Mills and Hughes played a decisive part in the trial. 'They were plainly telling the truth,' one senior police officer said afterwards, 'and they obviously made a very strong impression on the jury.' It was an impression that Bellfield simply had to contradict if he was to convince the jury to find him 'not guilty'. But it was to be some time before he got the chance.

It wasn't until Friday, 11 January 2008 that Altman called one of his last witnesses, the man who had brought Bellfield to the dock at the Old Bailey – Detective Chief Inspector Colin Sutton, who would lead the double murder squad that had painstakingly tracked down his cars and his mobile phones and pieced together the details of his motiveless attacks on innocent young women.

On the morning of Tuesday, 15 January the rotund, benign-faced William Boyce QC rose to call his first witness for the defence – Levi Bellfield. The defendant was to remain in the witness box for the next week, first examined by Boyce and then cross-examined for the prosecution by Altman. Standing in the witness box, Bellfield systematically insisted that the prosecution case was a tissue of lies, that he hadn't attacked any of the five young women, that other people had been responsible, and that his trial was a travesty of justice.

'No airs and graces,' he told the jury. 'This is me. I'm not trying to fool anyone. I'm not an angel. I'm not claiming to be an angel. But I'm not a killer. No way.' It was Bellfield's attempt to present himself as a victim – a man who may have had a chequered past, but who was not guilty of these heinous crimes.

But the most compelling moment of all came when – under intense and persistent cross-examination from Altman – Bellfield seemed to snap.

'You don't understand,' he told the prosecuting barrister. 'I'm fighting for my life here.'

The hush in Court 6 was complete.

Yet it was not the only ill-judged remark Bellfield was to make during his evidence. At another point he condemned two prosecution witnesses as 'attention-seeking liars' who had 'enjoyed their day out at the Bailey'. On another he brutally condemned two of the police officers called to give evidence against him as 'downright liars'.

Over six days in the witness box, Bellfield repeatedly insisted that the witnesses called against him were mistaken, and that he was an innocent man, the victim of a series of terrible mistakes.

After he left the witness box on 22 January, there were just three more days of defence witnesses before Her Honour Judge Rafferty called the prosecution to sum up its case to the jury. It was not to prove comfortable listening for Levi Bellfield for it systematically tore apart his relentless equivocations in the witness box.

As Brian Altman QC put it, 'This is a man who could hardly give a straight answer to a straight question. He made speeches, he obfuscated and confused – black became white and white became black; he was dishonest yet truthful. Bets were hedged, sands shifted, goal posts moved, and behind it all there wasn't a shred of hard evidence to support a word he says. It was a cleverly rehearsed smokescreen, an attempt to blind you from the obvious. It was ultimately a performance with one end in sight – to fool you twelve, his jury, into thinking he was telling the truth in order to secure what the prosecution say would be a false acquittal. You may think, having watched him over those six days, that this is a man who displays cunning, cunning that meant the law did not catch up with him until November 2004.'

'He blamed everyone but himself,' Altman concluded. 'Every witness whose evidence was inconvenient to him was either mistaken or lying ... every one of them is wrong ... there's only one person who is right and truthful according to the defendant and that's Levi Bellfield.'

It was a forensic deconstruction of the defendant's

attitude, and one which concluded with the central, and most telling, plank of the prosecution's case against him.

'These are not offences which are unconnected in the sense that they have been committed by more than one man, each unrelated to the other,' Altman concluded. 'That we submit would be too fantastic a conclusion. Why do we say that? We submit to you the following. The locations for the offences are proximate to each other. These were areas with which the defendant was familiar . . . All these attacks on these victims took place whilst they were or had been at or near bus stops or once they had alighted from buses. Amélie had got off a bus; so had Marsha and Kate; Irma was standing at a bus stop; and Anna-Maria had been sitting at one moments before her attempted abduction. In all cases there is evidence that the offender emerged from and returned to the type and vintage of vehicle with which the defendant was linked at the material time, Anna-Maria – a Ford Mondeo; Irma – a VW Golf; Marsha – a Vauxhall Corsa; Kate – a Toyota Previa; Amélie – a pre-2000 Ford Courier . . . Is all that just chance? Or is it evidence that the same man was at the control of those vehicles committing similar if not identical crimes?'

Altman answered his own question by concluding: 'The behaviour of the vehicles in these cases is so strikingly similar that they prove one man had to be involved.'

The prosecuting barrister then reminded the jury of his opening remarks four months earlier about the extraordinary similarities between the women.

'Apart from Irma Dragoshi (who was hooded at the time of the incident) the victims were young,' Altman explained. 'Anna-Maria was seventeen, Marsha McDonnell was just nineteen, Kate Sheedy was eighteen, Amélie Delagrange was twenty-two. All were alone and vulnerable.'

Altman went on to point out the similarities in their build and physical appearance. Then he pointed out that all the attacks were carried out during the hours of darkness and between 7.30 p.m. and 12.30 a.m., and all in quiet residential areas. The attacker was 'a stranger to the victim in each case', he continued, and bore the hallmarks of someone who, 'having targeted the victim, would conduct himself with sudden and unexpected violence towards them'.

On 31 January 2008 Brian Altman QC concluded his remarks by saying bluntly: 'So it is that we submit to you when you examine all the elements of the evidence in all the attacks you will find evidence of similarity and system such that you can be sure that what you are seeing is not the work of several unconnected men carrying out unrelated attacks but the work of one man, that man being Levi Bellfield.'

It was a compelling argument – but that did not make it decisive. There were no witnesses to any of the attacks, no evidence directly linking Bellfield to the women, no forensic evidence to put him at the sites, no DNA evidence saying he had been present, no CCTV footage of the attacks themselves, no murder weapon in two of the cases, and – perhaps most significant of all – no clear motive. Why had Bellfield decided to attack these five innocent young women whom he did not know, without warning and for no apparent reason? After a four-month trial it was a question that the jury now had to decide. It was to prove no easy task.

Indeed after two days of deliberation the jury found it quite simply impossible to agree about whether Bellfield had or had not attempted to kidnap Anna-Maria Rennie from Hospital Bridge Road. They did not acquit Bellfield of the crime, but they could not be sure that he had committed it, leaving Mrs Justice Rafferty no alternative other than to allow the crime to be 'lie on the file'. He had not been found guilty, but he had not been found not guilty. The case against him for the attempted kidnap of Anna-Maria Rennie might one day again be presented to a jury, but for the moment it was dormant.

The same proved true for Irma Dragoshi. Once again, even though the judge allowed them to reach a majority verdict of ten votes to two if they wished to, the jury failed to agree. They did not find Bellfield not guilty, it was simply that they could not agree on whether or not he had committed the crime. Again, it left the judge no alternative other than to allow the crime to be 'lie on the file', waiting for the possibility that he might be tried for it again in the future.

Those two decisions left the prosecution, the Crown Prosecution Service and the Metropolitan Police distinctly nervous that their case might collapse completely if the jury could not agree that Bellfield had indeed committed the murders of Amélie and Marsha and had attempted to murder Kate. Indeed Bellfield might well have felt that there was now at least a chance that he would be acquitted on the remaining three charges. It did not turn out to be the case.

Another dramatic hush fell in Court 6 of the Old Bailey on the morning of 25 February 2008 when the foreman of the jury stood to read out the verdict in the cases of Marsha McDonnell and Kate Sheedy. Nodding to the foreman, the clerk to Mrs Justice Rafferty asked if they had indeed reached a verdict, and was told, 'We have, Your Honour.' The jury found Bellfield guilty of the murder of Marsha and the attempted murder of Kate by a majority of ten votes to two.

The courtroom erupted, with shouts from the public gallery from the defendant's relatives and friends, as well as from the relatives of the young women who had been attacked.

The jury then retired for a final time to consider their verdict on the murder of Amélie Delagrange, the murder that had brought DCI Colin Sutton and his double murder squad to the case in August 2004.

Her parents had sat in dignified silence in the public gallery throughout the trial – much to Bellfield's fury. At one point he had even shouted at them – accusing them of being 'fucking leeches'. The outburst was to do him no good.

This time the jury were in no doubt. When they returned to the court for a final time, it was with a unanimous verdict – that Levi Bellfield was guilty of the murder of Amélie, an innocent young woman who had done nothing more sinister than miss her bus stop and walk home across Twickenham Green on that balmy August evening.

Again the public gallery erupted, not least with relief from Amélie's parents, who had watched in horror as the man they believed had killed their daughter twisted and turned in an effort to convince the jury that he was innocent. As her father Jean-François was to tell his friends outside the Old Bailey on Monday, 25 February 2008, 'It is late, but there is justice.'

Mrs Justice Rafferty calmly brought the court to order before she addressed Bellfield.

'You have reduced three families to unimagined grief,' she told him firmly. 'What dreadful feelings went through your head as you attacked them and in two cases snuffed out a young life is beyond understanding.'

She then told the defendant that she would pass sentence the following morning.

When that morning came, however, Levi Bellfield refused to come out of the cells hidden in the bowels of the Old Bailey to stand in the dock to hear the punishment the judge would deliver. The reasons he gave were that he 'hadn't had a fair trial'.

So he was not there to hear Mrs Justice Rafferty sentence him to three 'full life' terms of imprisonment, which meant that he would spend the rest of his life in prison, never to be released.

With that sentence Bellfield joined an exceptional and very small group of British murderers. Fewer then forty people, and only one woman, have been sentenced to 'full life' terms of imprisonment, including the Black Panther, Donald Neilson; the murderer of five Ipswich prostitutes, Steve Wright; the Moors Murderer, Ian Brady; and Rosemary West.

Outside the Old Bailey life a jubilant DCI Sutton told the waiting media: 'Levi Bellfield is a predator who preyed on women over a period of time. He targeted his victims at random, attacking those much smaller and weaker than him.' Clearly relieved at the verdicts, Sutton went on: 'He refused to face what he had done, lied repeatedly to try to save his skin and treated his victims and their families and the authorities with contempt.'

It was a contempt that Bellfield had carefully hidden throughout his trial, but now it came out into the open as some of his former partners started to tell the media about their experiences with him. Jo Collings, for example, told one newspaper that Bellfield had kept her as his 'sex slave' for two and a half years, adding that he had attacked 'at least 100 women' and had even bragged to her about raping a disabled girl on a car bonnet in a nightclub car park after lifting her out of her wheelchair. Bellfield liked to boast to her, Collings went on, that he had 'had another little slut' when he got home from his job as a bouncer and insisted that all blonde girls were 'evil fucking bitches who must die'.

Even his last full-time partner Terri Carroll, who had been wheel-clamping with him and stayed with him throughout the last tumultuous eighteen months of his freedom, confessed to a newspaper: 'I can't believe how lucky I am to be alive. I know I came terrifyingly close to becoming one of his victims,' adding 'He made it clear he would kill me and hurt my family if I ever left him.'

Carroll's comments gave a lie to the behaviour of the modest, quietly spoken defendant from Court 6 who was now resting in the cells beneath the Old Bailey, condemned to spend the rest of his life behind bars.

To the media Levi Bellfield had become a modern-day Bluebeard, a man with no respect for women and who wanted nothing more than to end the lives of some of them. It was a reputation that was to follow him to prison.

After Bellfield's conviction he was moved from remand at Belmarsh in London to serve his sentence in the equally austere surroundings of the gaunt red-brick Victorian buildings of Wakefield prison in West Yorkshire, known among its inmates as the 'monster mansion' in tribute to the crimes of the men incarcerated there. Sitting on the bizarrely named Love Lane, Wakefield is the single biggest high-security jail in western Europe and houses some 740 inmates, including 100 Category A prisoners, who are regarded as very dangerous, and ten so-called 'high-risk' Category A prisoners, who are seen as extremely dangerous. Wakefield houses one of the highest concentrations of violent criminals anywhere in Europe and is home to the notoriously violent Charles Bronson – often described as Britain's single most dangerous prisoner – as well as Roy Whiting, whose sentence for murdering eight-year-old Sarah Payne has been commuted to forty years, Robert Black, the Scottish serial killer and child molester, and Carl Manning, the killer of eight-year-old Victoria Climbié. It is also home to kidnapper Michael Sams, still suspected of having abducted and killed London estate agent Suzy Lamplugh, as well as Britain's single most famous homosexual child killer, the now frail eighty-four-year-old Sidney Cooke, memorably known to his fellow prisoners as Hissing Sid, who is one of the most hated men in the prison. These were the men Bellfield was to join behind its 15-feet-high brick walls topped with razor wire.

Although Wakefield has been steadily upgraded by the Prison Service over the past ten years, it is still a gloomy, ominous place, a prison that seems to seethe with violence. Suicides among its prisoners are all too familiar.

It was here that the notorious serial-killer doctor Harold Shipman – convicted of the murder of fifteen of his elderly patients, but alleged to have killed as many as 235 – killed himself in January 2004.

Not surprisingly, therefore, Bellfield was put on 'suicide watch' when he first arrived as a new prisoner facing a life behind its bars. But he was not in the least overwhelmed by his new surroundings, rapidly establishing himself as a popular prisoner, with a ready line in conversation, and not one to be easily intimidated. The years of steroids and muscle building stood him in good stead among the prisoners in Wakefield, as did his appetite for relentless sexual innuendo, with one newspaper reporting that he had developed a taste for gay relationships behind its walls.

But one dark shadow still hung over the bouncer and wheel-clamper – the case of the thirteen-year-old Surrey schoolgirl Amanda 'Milly' Dowler.

On the day of Bellfield's convictions in February 2008 the Surrey police had announced that they were 'very interested' in questioning him about her abduction and murder and regarded him as a prime suspect. If he were to be found guilty of that crime, Bellfield knew only too well that his life in Wakefield would become far more difficult, as the prisoners' loathing of child killers had seen a string of attacks on them – recently on Ian Huntley, the Soham killer. Bellfield had never been convicted of killing a child and so he wasn't – in prison parlance – a 'nonce'. He had every intention of preserving that reputation, not least for his own safety.

But on 30 March 2010 Bellfield was indeed charged

with the abduction and murder of Milly Dowler, as well as the attempted abduction of another eleven-year-old school-girl named Rachel Cowles, on the day before in Shepperton, west London, not far from Milly's home in Hersham. On 6 October 2010 he appeared at the Old Bailey by a video link from Wakefield to have those charges confirmed.

Once again, Bellfield pleaded not guilty, and once again began to prepare himself for a trial. But his experience had taught him a great deal about the workings of the law, and he elected to replace his defence barristers for the new trial. He picked Jeffrey Samuels QC, a feisty Manchester-based barrister, who had acted as junior counsel to the formidable William Clegg QC in the defence of Barry George, whom Clegg had persuaded the court to release after he had originally been convicted of the murder of the television presenter Jill Dando. Prison legend had it that George and Bellfield had been prisoners together at Bel-marsh, and George had urged his fellow inmate to 'get one of my briefs, they're really good'.

So it was that on 19 April 2011 Bellfield once again stepped into the dock of the Old Bailey to hear Jeffrey Samuels QC attempt to get the case against him dismissed because of the paucity of evidence against him. Again he took care to dress in his neatest suit and replied to the questions asked of him in the most respectful voice.

The days in Wakefield had seen him lose a little weight, but he didn't particularly appear as a man who had suffered dreadfully at the hands of Her Majesty's Prison Service. If anything, he looked a little younger than his forty-two years and joked with the prison officers as they lead him into the glass-fronted dock of Court 9.

The prosecuting counsel was his nemesis from three years before, Brian Altman QC, but there was to be a different judge – the Glasgow-educated, sixty-three-year-old Sir Alan Wilkie QC, who had recently joined the Old Bailey's band of High Court judges from a senior position on the Newcastle bench. Thin-faced, and with an expression of measured interest, he had earned part of his expert reputation as a Law Commissioner.

If Mr Justice Wilkie dismissed the case against him, Bellfield could return to Wakefield, his reputation safe from accusations of being a 'nonce'. If he did not, then he would face a full-scale trial for the murder of Milly Dowler, a trial that – if he were convicted – would usher him into the pantheon of child killers and for ever brand him one of the most pernicious serial killers in British criminal history.

In fact the words 'serial killer' were uttered only once during the day-and-a-half hearing before Mr Justice Wilkie on those two hot April days just before Easter 2011, and they came from the mouth of prosecuting counsel Brian Altman QC. They were said so softly that it was almost possible to miss them, almost as though the description was too horrifying to contemplate.

The hearing was conducted with studious balance, although Jeffrey Samuels QC did allow himself to question repeatedly the prosecutions arguments that the case should be presented to a jury, describing them as 'thin', to the obvious delight of his client, who proceeded to thank him warmly at the end of the first day's hearing.

Bellfield's pleasure was to prove short-lived. Shortly after noon on the second day, 20 April 2011, Mr Justice

Wilkie announced, with the soft hint of the west of Scotland still in his voice, that the defendant would indeed stand trial for the murder of Milly Dowler. It was to start before him on Thursday, 5 May 2011.

Once again Levi Bellfield was to stand in the dock of the Old Bailey charged with a crime that would once have seen him hanged – the murder of an innocent schoolgirl.

16. The Reckoning Begins

'All virtue is summed up in dealing justly.'

Aristotle, *Ethics*

It was just before noon on the warm spring day of Friday, 6 May 2011 when Levi Bellfield finally got to his feet in the armoured-glass-fronted dock of Court 8 at the Old Bailey to face the charge that he had kidnapped and murdered the thirteen-year-old Surrey schoolgirl Amanda Dowler – known to her family as Milly – on 21 March 2002, nine years before. The Court Clerk, dressed in wig and black gown, asked him to confirm that he was indeed Levi Bellfield and proceeded to read out the indictment against him. Then she asked: 'How do you plead?'

Wearing a grey suit, a white shirt, a quiet striped tie and an expression that suggested the charges were ridiculous, Bellfield answered in his softest, least belligerent tone: 'Not guilty.'

The clerk put to him that he was also charged with the attempted kidnapping of another Surrey schoolgirl, eleven-year-old Rachel Cowles, on the previous day, 20 March 2002. Once again Bellfield answered softly: 'Not guilty.'

Bellfield then resumed his seat in the dock, flanked by two male prison officers and a female officer, picked up the small notepad that he used to write notes to his solicitor and defence counsel, who were sitting in the well of the court just feet in front of him, and waited for the case against him to begin.

He had spent the first part of the morning watching as the jury had been chosen and sworn in. They were made up of seven men and five women, chosen from a jury pool of fifty, and ranged in age from their early twenties to their late forties. Two of the women jurors were black and one was Asian, while the male jurors were all white. These were the twelve who were to decide his fate in the weeks that lay ahead of him, the men and women who had to determine whether he had indeed spirited away and killed Milly Dowler on her way home down Station Avenue on that March day all those years before.

It was just eleven days before Bellfield's forty-third birthday, and the court itself was hardly packed. Only the judge, Mr Justice Wilkie, the jury, counsel for the prosecution and defence, the court staff and one or two reporters were there to see him finally arraigned for the murder that would come to define him. The public gallery was deserted, but for one single person. Sitting quite alone was his elder brother Richard, pale and impassive, watching his brother stand accused of one of the highest-profile murders in Britain so far in the twenty-first century. From time to time, brother and brother would look across at each other, but for the most part they stared silently ahead of them – waiting for the trial to unfold.

Now staying, once again, at Belmarsh, where he'd spent his remand during his first trial at the Old Bailey, Bellfield was now well practised in the ways of the British justice

239

system and had taken particular care to study all the documents provided to him by both the prosecution and defence teams. His cell was positively crammed with legal papers – so much so that the joke in prison was that the authorities had privately declared it a fire hazard.

It wasn't until shortly after 10.30 on the following Tuesday morning, 10 May, that the Senior Treasury Counsel, Brian Altman QC, rose to his feet to open the prosecution's case against the former nightclub bouncer and wheel-clamper – whom the jury had now learned was also a double murderer as a result of the judge's decision to allow them to know about his convictions in February 2008.

In soft, measured tones, with their hint of the English Home Counties, Altman began by telling the jury about the day Milly disappeared, and how – just moments after leaving Walton-on-Thames railway station after sharing a plate of chips with one of her best girlfriends and fellow Year 9 pupil at Heathside School in Weybridge – she'd left to walk along the road when, 'just a few minutes after 4 p.m., she vanished: gone in the blink of an eye'. It was to be the phrase that would dominate the newspapers' headlines the following morning as the first reports of Bellfield's trial appeared. 'Milly had simply disappeared in a flash from a street in a suburban town in broad daylight,' they quoted Altman as saying, adding his phrase that it was 'every parent's worst nightmare'.

In his calm voice Altman went on to tell the jury: 'For six long months the Dowler family suffered the excruciating agony of not knowing what had become of their daughter until, on Wednesday, 18 September 2002, some mushroom-pickers found, quite by chance, the unclothed and badly decomposed body of a young female . . . lying in the undergrowth of Yateley Heath Wood in Hampshire. The body was soon identified as that of Milly Dowler.'

This innocent thirteen-year-old had been stripped naked and dumped, and the prosecution case was that the 'person who abducted and killed Milly Dowler was the defendant, Levi Bellfield', who was living at the time in a flat in Collingwood Place in Walton-on-Thames, just a few yards from where Milly had vanished, with his partner Emma Mills, their two children and a Staffordshire bull terrier dog.

Altman did not look behind him at the prisoner in the dock, but the jury could hardly take their eyes off him. For his part Bellfield sat dead-eyed, pasty-faced and sullen, his eyes often cast down, or looking at the notes he was writing to himself on his knee. From time to time he would push one of them through the gaps in the glass of the dock to his solicitor sitting in the well of the court in front of him.

Milly Dowler's disappearance had started what Altman told the jury was 'a massive missing person's inquiry and a police investigation on a national scale'. Her wide, open face, with its gentle smile and slightly raised eyebrows, had stared out of newspaper front pages and television news broadcasts for weeks.

But it was not only Milly who had been approached by Bellfield in those late March days in 2002. Altman also told the jury that another schoolgirl, Rachel Cowles, aged eleven, had been stopped by a man driving a red car in Upper Halliford Road in Shepperton just before 4 in the afternoon on the day before Milly had disappeared and tried to trick her into getting into his car by claiming to be her new neighbour and offering her a lift. Rachel had declined. It was quick thinking, the prosecution said, that had 'probably saved her life'.

'The prosecution say there can be no doubt that Levi Bellfield, and no one else, was responsible for both,' Altman said. 'He has proven to be a predatory and violent offender towards young women, with convictions in 2008 in this very court.'

Bellfield barely moved a muscle or blinked an eye, remaining studiously impassive, almost as if he were a little bored.

Altman then proceeded to sketch the background to the case, telling the jury that Milly had been born on 25 June 1988; she would have been almost twenty-three now, had her life been spared. She had lived with her parents, Bob and Sally Dowler, and her older sister, Gemma, in Walton Park in Hersham, Surrey, and was a pupil at Heathside School in Weybridge, as was her elder sister. Their mother taught maths there.

'Milly was slim, pretty and intelligent,' the prosecuting barrister went on, 'she was popular with her friends' and was 'attaining the usual milestones to be expected of a young teenager. To all intents and purposes she was an ordinary girl who was developing into a fine young woman.'

Moving on to Rachel Cowles, Altman told the jury that she was just two weeks shy of her twelfth birthday, having been born on 4 April 1990, and was a schoolgirl at Bishop Wand Church of England School in Laytons Lane, Sunbury, a few miles north of Walton, and she lived with her family in Shepperton. He also pointed out that she bore an 'uncanny resemblance' to Milly Dowler in her school photographs – her uniform was just like Milly's and she had had her hair done up in a ponytail, just as Milly had done on the day she vanished,

The jury then heard that Bellfield himself was born on 17 May 1968 and had worked as a doorman and wheel-clamper in west and south-west London for 'most, if not all, of his life and knows that area, as well as Walton and Shepperton, extremely well'. Altman also told them that he was 'left-handed, around 6 feet 1 inch in height', and 'big built'.

In fact, sitting in the dock, Bellfield looked a little slimmer and fitter than he'd done in the last days of his first trial for murder in February 2008; the fitness regime and rather more healthy diet on offer at Her Majesty's Prison in Wakefield had clearly had their effect.

As Tuesday turned into Wednesday, another warm spring day outside the windowless air-conditioned court room, Altman laid out the prosecution's case to the jury. He explained in detail how Emma Mills lived with Bell-field at 24, Collingwood Place, Walton-on-Thames at the time Milly went missing and Rachel had been approached – although they were in fact house-sitting at the time for a friend named Christine Hawgood in Harmondsworth, Middlesex, just north of Heathrow airport, on the very day of Milly's disappearance.

Altman then described in detail what the prosecution believed had happened on that fateful day. Milly's mum, Sally, had given her and her elder sister Gemma a lift to school, as usual, leaving home at around 7.40 in the morning – when

her dad Bob had given her a kiss goodbye. An IT recruit-
ment consultant, he had a meeting in Basingstoke that day
and was going there instead of making his usual trip into
his office in London.

At the end of the school day Milly had intended to stay
on and wait for a lift home with her mother and sister but
had completed some outstanding homework early and
decided to take the train home instead with some school
friends from Heathfield, including Danielle Sykes.

On that Thursday afternoon she'd walked across the
woods from school to the Weybridge railway station with
her friends, wearing her school uniform of a short grey
skirt, white blouse, blue V-necked jumper, navy-blue
blazer and black school shoes with white trainer socks.
She was carrying a beige and black Jansport rucksack containing her 'glittery' pencil case and her Nokia mobile
phone. Milly and her friends caught the 3.26 train from
Weybridge – which was running a little late – and arrived
at Walton shortly after 3.30.

'Ordinarily,' Altman explained, 'Milly would have continued her journey to the next train stop at Hersham,'
which was nearer her home, but on this day 'she was persuaded by Danielle' to leave the train at Walton and buy
some chips at the station café. While she was in the café
Milly had borrowed another pupil's mobile phone –
because hers had run out of credit – to phone her father
at 3.47 to tell him that she would be a bit late home.

Barely a quarter of an hour later, shortly after 4, Milly
left the café to walk home; Danielle asked her if she'd be
all right to walk home alone. 'Yeah, I'll be fine' she told
her friend. Tragically that wasn't to be the case.

Milly set off in the opposite direction from Danielle, down Station Avenue towards her home in Walton Park, and as she did so another schoolgirl from Heathside, Katherine Laynes, who was waiting at the bus stop in Station Avenue, saw her walking down the other side of the road away from the station. By now she'd taken her blazer off: after rain showers in the morning, the sun had suddenly come out. Katherine Laynes was the last person, other than her killer, to see Milly Dowler alive.

As Brian Altman pointed out to the jury: 'If that evidence is accurate and reliable, then it means Milly had to have been taken from that part of Station Avenue, right outside Collingwood Place, and right on the defendant's doorstep.'

When Sally and Gemma Dowler got home from school at 4.45 that afternoon Milly wasn't there, and just after 7 that evening Bob Dowler reported his daughter missing to the police. Meanwhile, according to the prosecution, Levi Bellfield had disappeared for more than nine hours to hide his 'wicked and terrible deed'.

In the afternoon session of Wednesday, 11 May, Altman then explained the events of the day of Milly's disappearance through the eyes of Bellfield's partner Emma Mills – who was to come to court herself to give evidence.

On that critical afternoon of 21 March 2002 Bellfield had 'just disappeared during the day', which was, according to Mills, 'unusual' as they would normally talk on the phone 'a number of times' every day. He was driving her red Daewoo Nexia car at the time, and she'd told the police that she hadn't, in fact, seen him again until between

10.30 and 11 that evening, when he had returned to Christine Hawgood's house with a Kentucky Fried Chicken takeaway and some lagers for them to share.

'Emma noticed immediately that he had changed his clothing,' Altman told the jury, 'which made her think that he must have returned to Collingwood Place because that is where he had his clothes.' She was suspicious that Bellfield had been with another woman, as she knew he had the only keys to the Walton flat on her key ring along with her car key. 'But she did not ask him where he'd been.'

During the early hours of the following morning, Friday, 22 March, Emma woke up to find Bellfield getting dressed and had asked him what he was doing, Altman went on. 'I'm going to go back to the flat, 'cause I'm going to have a lay-in,' Bellfield had told her and left at about 4 a.m., taking the Staffordshire bull terrier with him.

'You will want to ask yourselves what was it that was so important that in the middle of the night he decided to get up and drive over to Walton,' Altman said, 'a trip which a timed run demonstrated took just over twenty-seven minutes at that time in the morning and covered a distance of some 13.7 miles.'

'You can be sure it was no lie-in,' he concluded firmly. 'So why return to Collingwood Place in the dead of night? To walk the dog? To lie in?' Altman asked, and then he answered his own question. 'If the prosecution is right that he abducted and killed Milly Dowler, then he had to dispose of her body and clean up.'

Later on that Friday morning, Altman explained, Bellfield had asked a friend called Malcolm Ward to help him remove a mattress and some clothes from the Collingwood

Place flat, and when Emma Mills went there later in the day she found the bed with no sheet, pillowcases or duvet cover. When she challenged him about it, Bellfield told her that the dog had had an 'accident' and that he had 'chucked it all'. On that very Friday, Bellfield also told Emma Mills that he wanted to move back to their house at 11, Little Benty immediately, 'even though they had not planned to move back for a month'.

'You may wish to ask the question, why was the defendant in such a rush at this time of all times to make an unplanned and accelerated move away from Collingwood Place?' Altman provided his own answer. 'In fact, this was identical to how he was to behave following the murders of Marsha McDonnell and Amélie Delagrange in 2003 and 2004, when he left home with his family to take sudden holidays or move them from home, as we shall see.'

'What then became of the red Daewoo Nexia?' Altman went on. Bellfield and Mills used it to transport most of their belongings to 11, Little Benty, but a week later it was reported stolen, 'and it has never been traced'. The significance of the prosecutor's remark wasn't lost on the jury for a moment, as just minutes later there was a hushed silence in court as he went on: 'If the defendant abducted and killed her then he needed the red Daewoo Nexia to dispose of the body, and so the disappearance of that car so soon thereafter is no coincidence.'

On Wednesday, 18 September, almost six months to the day after Milly disappeared, a skull and some small bones were discovered off a little-used pathway in a wooded area in Yateley Heath Wood near Fleet in Hampshire, Altman continued. Police searched the area the next day and discovered other bones, which were identified as those of Milly Dowler. Altman told the jury that Bellfield knew the area well, as he would make regular trips to Blackbushe Market and Blackbushe Car Auctions, just north of Yateley, when he was still living with his former partner Johanna Collings. 'They would walk her dogs there,' Altman said firmly.

Drawing his remarks to a close, Altman then explained the five 'features of similarity' that marked Bellfield's 'offending' and made the prosecution's case against him so strong.

There were the geographical links that connected his other murders to south-west London. He had links with both Shepperton, where he'd worked as a mini-cab driver, and Walton Bridge over the River Thames, where he'd disposed of some of Amélie Delagrange's belongings. Then there was the fact that he targeted young female victims who were strangers to him; that he used vehicles to target them; his behaviour of the time of his offences; and that he acted with 'speed and motivation'.

'There being no actual or attempted sexual interference with any of the victims, the defendant's motivation for killing or attempting to kill was not obvious,' Altman added, 'but it is, you may conclude, at the very least consistent with someone who harbours a very great animosity towards women of the description of those victims and who goes on to act upon it.'

Drawing the jury's attention to Bellfield's previous murders as significant to the evidence in the Milly Dowler and Rachel Cowles cases, Altman pointed out that without those convictions the jury could not understand the full implications of the evidence overall: 'how it might be that in broad daylight, and within a flash, a thirteen-year-old girl can be plucked from the street unless you know that the defendant was capable of and had indeed gone on to kill, not once but twice, and nearly a third time, with decisive speed and without real concern for being seen to do so'.

'The evidence also allows you to conclude,' he went on, 'that it would be contrary to common sense to say that there must have been two men with such capabilities appearing by happenstance in the same place at the same time.'

'We say,' Altman concluded, just before he sat down in his seat in front of the judge, 'you can be satisfied that the abductor of Rachel Cowles and the abductor and killer of Milly Dowler was this defendant, Levi Bellfield, and no one else.'

For his part Bellfield looked straight across the court at the judge, his face still.

Outside the Old Bailey the television crews and their reporters told a watching world about the prosecution's allegations, and the following morning the newspapers speculated that Milly 'probably spent her final, terrified moments inside her killer's lair' after Bellfield had 'dragged her off the street or lured her into his ground-floor flat' as she walked innocently home in the sudden sunshine. There, some newspapers alleged, she was 'killed, stripped naked, and bundled into his car, before Bellfield drove her lifeless body to a remote patch of woodland 25 miles away and dumped it in the undergrowth'.

The trial of Levi Bellfield had begun in earnest, but in

spite of the prosecution's devastating opening the defendant himself was far more interested in ensuring that he manipulated the prison and the judicial systems to his advantage at all times. As part of his opening speech Brian Altman had explained to the jury that the day after he'd finished addressing them they would all be going on a 'site visit' to look at the scenes of both crimes – it was a familiar procedure in major murder trials. But what was not so familiar was the defendant's response. He insisted on going too. Bellfield firmly exercised his right to attend the visit along with the judge, jury and the barristers for both sides. That meant he had to be transported there, allowed to change out of his prison uniform (as he was allowed to do in court) and be escorted among the general public as the jury were shown the scenes of his alleged crimes.

So it was that, on the morning of Thursday, 12 May, accompanied by three prison officers and two Surrey police officers, Bellfield was escorted – his hands in cuffs – around Upper Halliford Road in Shepperton, where Rachel had been propositioned, and then Station Avenue in Walton-on-Thames, where Milly had disappeared. Bellfield cut an extraordinary figure walking just yards behind the judge and jury in full view of vast numbers of innocent, and utterly bewildered, bystanders.

In a quite extraordinary display of hubris, Bellfield joked with passers-by and even offered a word of encouragement to a television reporter covering the scene. A faint smirk never left his face, confirming his private conviction that he alone was in control of these events, in spite of the guards surrounding him. It was the perfect example of Bellfield's arrogant, brutal desire to take every opportunity to bend British justice to his will and demonstrate that he could always get what he wanted – no matter what the cost might be to the court, the jury or the witnesses.

Indeed, as the trial began, he started to complain loudly and repeatedly to his counsel each morning that he was not being treated 'properly' by the prison service, and in particular that he was not reaching the Old Bailey early enough to hold a meeting with his defence team before the beginning of the court's day at 10.30.

The perpetual complaints underlined Bellfield's sense of self-importance, the feeling that he was the equal of any of the legal brains involved in his case, and that they – and the court – should dance to his tune and to nobody else's.

At one point during a break in proceedings Bellfield even beckoned to me, exactly as I imagined he had done to Milly Dowler on that Thursday afternoon in Walton-on-Thames, careful to present a picture of innocence and humility – before the true horror of his intentions became nightmarishly clear.

'Mr Wansell,' he said in that distinctive squeaky voice.

'Yes, Mr Bellfield,' I said, walking towards the glass around the dock so that I could hear him.

'You will make sure it is a fair and accurate account,' he said, leaning towards me, for he knew full well that I was writing a book about him. I had asked to see him before the trial through his defence team. But he had refused to see me.

'That's what I'm intending to do, Mr Bellfield,' I said, and he nodded appreciatively.

'Good,' he muttered as he walked back to his seat in the dock, smiling across at me. It was part manipulation, part veiled threat, but utterly typical of his desire to turn everything to his own advantage. The implication was clear. Everyone should dance to his tune and his tune alone. He wanted to manipulate the court, and me, in exactly the same way as he had done the women in his life for so many years.

How must the 'polite' Milly Dowler have felt as she was beckoned across Station Avenue by this man who took such pains not to seem a threat to anyone? It was a thought almost too terrifying to contemplate. This was a man entirely capable of appearing nothing more than an affable giant at one moment, then turning into a monster the next, with barely the blink of an eye between. It was a brutal transformation that Milly Dowler must have seen at the closest quarters and my heart went out to her.

But Bellfield was very careful to make sure that his displays of hubris were never on display when the jury were in court – Bellfield knew only too well that he had to gull them into seeing him as a gentle, softly spoken man who had been wronged, not someone intent on manipulating the legal system.

Bellfield was certainly at pains to be the picture of innocence as the jury took their seats in court and the first of the prosecution's witnesses entered the court shortly after 10.30 on the morning of Friday, 13 May. Bellfield's brother's male friend had now joined his brother in the public gallery, sitting next to one another, and, of course, the jury did not know who they were.

One thing was clear to the jury, however. Rachel Cowles

now wasn't the eleven-year-old schoolgirl whom it was alleged he'd approached on Upper Halliford Road in Shepperton on Wednesday, 20 March 2002, the day before Milly Dowler disappeared. She was instead a cheery-looking, chubby, twenty-one-year-old with dark-red hair, glasses and a wide-eyed stare. In a firm, clear voice she told the court that on that afternoon a car had pulled up beside her as she was walking home from school, and the driver had leaned across the passenger seat to say to her – through the car's open window: 'Hello, I've just moved in next door, would you like a lift home?'

'I said, "No thank you, it's all right,"' Rachel explained. It was a decision the prosecution alleged saved her life.

She then told the court that a police car had driven past just as she was talking to the driver and that he'd driven off without saying anything more. She couldn't really describe the car, or its registration number. But she could remember that the driver was a man between thirty and forty years old, with a bald head and a rather 'round' chubby face and was wearing a gold loop earring in his left ear.

The encounter left the schoolgirl feeling 'shocked and confused', and she'd told her mother all about it fifteen or so minutes later when she'd got home. Rachel also told the court that she'd made a point of looking for the car near her house – 'to check if he'd been telling the truth'. But she couldn't see it anywhere.

Worried by what had happened, Rachel's mother Diane had phoned her father at work to tell him, and then called the police to report the incident. When she did so, she passed the phone to her eleven-year-old daughter, who started crying when she spoke to the officer. The tape of her call to the police was to be played to the jury during the trial.

'I felt scared,' Rachel said in the witness box, 'because I suddenly realized the enormity of what had happened.'

Jeffrey Samuels QC then rose to his feet to cross-examine the witness on behalf of the defence. It wasn't an experience she was destined to enjoy as, working directly upon Bellfield's instructions, he sought to cast doubt on her evidence – and on her description of the man she had said had offered her a lift home on that March afternoon nine years before. In particular, Samuels pointed out to Rachel that when she'd made a statement to the police about the events in March 2005 – three years later – she had indicated that he had had a beard, and that she may have been affected by a recent television report about Milly's disappearance.

Uncomfortable, and uncertain, Rachel told Samuels: 'I was stressed that day.'

The court also heard that she'd later been asked by the police to attend an identity parade but had been unable to pick out Bellfield.

As she left the witness box, the twenty-one-year-old whose life may just have been saved by her own clear thinking nine years earlier looked chastened and on the verge of tears.

In stark contrast, sitting across the court from her in the dock, Bellfield looked rather pleased, as though his plan to make everyone who was to give evidence against him suffer was succeeding. The following week, the world and the court would see his plan take its first casualties – Milly Dowler's family.

17. The Dowlers On Trial

'Wrong must not win by technicalities.'
Aeschylus, *The Eumenides*

Trapped in the windowless Court 8 at the Central Criminal Court, with no sign of the weather or indeed the world at all beyond its pale wood-panelled walls, it was easy to forget the terrible price that the Dowler family had paid to be there. It was, after all, their thirteen-year-old daughter Milly who had disappeared on that early spring day in March 2002, a girl they plainly loved, and whose videotaped antics of dancing while ironing a pair of jeans, or playing the saxophone, had touched the nation's hearts during the six months she'd been missing and before her skeletel remains were found in wooded heathland just off the M3 motorway.

For nine long years the Dowler family had waited to see the wheels of British justice bring a man to trial for the abduction and killing of their daughter, years which had seen them struggle to cope with the dreadful demons that any parent would feel at the loss of a child – snatched from them for no apparent reason, suddenly, brutally and without warning or explanation from a leafy suburban street in Surrey.

The Dowlers had lost their daughter Milly and were now coming to the Old Bailey to see the man they believed had taken her stand trial, and they walked confidently towards court hand in hand, the tall figure of Bob Dowler towering above his wife Sally and his only surviving child, Milly's elder sister, Gemma. They were in search of justice, an end to the torture of their daughter's disappearance and murder, but what they did not know as they made their way towards the Old Bailey in the early afternoon of Monday, 16 May 2011 was that it was they who would find themselves on trial almost as much the prisoner sitting pale-faced and apparently emotionless in the dock. They were to become the victims of the justice they craved.

The court's day had begun quietly enough – with a lengthy legal argument behind closed doors. Nothing threatening in that, the Dowlers would have imagined, but they were to be proved wrong, dreadfully, heartbreakingly wrong. For the argument held in private partly centred around material that Levi Bellfield's defence team were anxious should be allowed into evidence in open court.

There was no hint of that, however, shortly after two o'clock when fifty-nine-year-old Bob Dowler walked across the floor of the court to take his oath in the witness box. Bald now, and with what little was left of his hair turned grey, he might almost have been a police officer as he stood to give his evidence in a clear voice.

Bob Dowler told Brian Altman, who was questioning him for the prosecution, that he had met his wife in 1981 and they had married three years later. They had then gone on to have two daughters, Gemma, born in January 1986, and Amanda, whom they always called Milly, in June 1988. It meant that she'd been thirteen when she disappeared on Thursday, 21 March 2002.

That day, Bob Dowler explained, he'd been due to go to a meeting in Basingstoke rather than travel up to his office in London, which meant he'd been at the family home when his wife Sally had left to drive their daughters to Heathside School. Bob Dowler had kissed his daughter Milly goodbye that morning: 'It was very important I gave Amanda a kiss in the morning,' he told the jury. 'It was a bit of a family habit with her.' He'd forgotten the previous morning, he confessed, and she'd reminded him about it.

Dowler then explained that he had got back home to his house in Hersham at about 3.15 that afternoon and had taken a call from Milly at 'about 3.45', saying she was at the station café in Walton-on-Thames and would be home in 'about half an hour'. She hadn't asked him to come and collect her in his car, and he hadn't offered to do so.

'It was a totally normal conversation,' he said, his fingers extended downwards in front of him, as if he were trying to balance on them.

He also told Altman that he'd been making a series of business phone calls that afternoon 'which were very stressful' and hadn't noticed whether Milly had come in or not, though he had been aware that Sally and Gemma had arrived. His wife had been due to babysit for her brother and had gone off shortly after 5 that afternoon, leaving him a Post-It note asking, 'Where's Milly?'

At 5.21 Bob Dowler called Milly's mobile and left a message; 'Where are you?', and half an hour later he left another. By then he was becoming anxious, and by 6 had gone out to search for her in his car. She was nowhere to be found, and so, just after 7 o'clock that evening, he called the local police station to report her missing.

The tragedy that was to engulf the Dowler family had begun. But it was now about to get even worse. The loss of a daughter brought them almost unbearable grief, but their all too human frailties were now about to be exposed to the world – in front of the media – at the instruction and encouragement of the very man that they believed had kidnapped and killed her, Levi Bellfield.

Rising to his feet in front of the jury, Jeffrey Samuels QC, acting on Bellfield's specific instructions, and thereby doing the job that he was required by law to do on behalf of his client, began his cross-examination gently. He asked Bob Dowler for details of his day, but then suggested, resting his arms on the cardboard box of files in front of him with his hands clasped together: 'You became the focus of the police inquiries for a time.'

Bob Dowler blanched but accepted the suggestion was true – he had been the focus of inquiries – just as he agreed with Samuels that the police had even told him: 'You are a suspect, whether you like it or not.'

The tall, confident figure of Bob Dowler then started to crumple slightly as Samuels put it to him that his daughter Milly wasn't 'an entirely happy-go-lucky character'.

'She had her demons, did she not?' Samuels put to him. 'I think she had natural childhood fears,' he replied.

In a firm, yet unhectoring voice, Samuels then read to Bob Dowler, and the jury, a poem that Surrey police had discovered in Milly's room after her disappearance. 'I don't know what it is I do,' it began, 'they all just seem to hate me. All they do is slag me off and force everyone against me. I know I am pathetic and helpless and I know I'm not pretty or fit. But what do they have that I haven't? Let's face it, I am just totally shit. I know what people think, I know how they feel.' It was as if Milly's own voice were echoing around the courtroom from beyond the grave in the hush that descended. 'What the fuck, I don't know. What do I do to make them hate me? Maybe I should just go. Sometimes I think how life would be without me, for Mum and Dad to have a beautiful little girl who is something like Gemma. She would be everything I am not, everything I dream to be: pretty, smart, intelligent, wanted, loved.'

It was the anguished cry of a typical teenager, the outpouring of the agony that growing up can be for a girl on the verge of adulthood and uncertain how to cope with it, a cry for understanding and affection that virtually every one of her school contemporaries would have made at one time or another, but none the less painful or poignant for that.

It ended: 'Then I hit myself and wake up to reality and how bad school's going to be in the morning. I hate it, but not nearly as much as I hate myself.'

Controlling himself as best he could, Bob Dowler accepted that the notes were 'very sad'.

But that was not to be the end of his torment in the witness box, for Jeffrey Samuels then proceeded to read to him another document found by the police in Milly's bedroom in the family home – one which was even more distressing.

'Dear Daddy and my beautiful Mummy,' it began. 'By the time you find this letter I will be up there, or down below. I have always been that way, below other people. I am sorry, you deserve a better daughter. So I have left.

If anything, you should be happy now, you can concentrate on lovely Gemsy, without me getting in the way. You should have had an abortion, or at least had me adopted and at least I would not have made your life hell as well.' It was certainly the letter of a young woman with her 'demons', as the defence had called them, for it ended: 'I think it would be best if you tried to forget me. It is nothing you have done. I just feel I had to go. Please don't let any harm get to any of you. Lots of love, as always, your little disappointment. Amanda.'

The very life seemed to ebb out of Bob Dowler as the letter was read out to him. By the time it was finished he was sobbing uncontrollably, tears running down his broad, open face. The man who had lost a daughter was now seeing her memory stained for ever at the instigation of the man he believed had taken her, Levi Bellfield, who sat in the dock motionless as the letter was read out.

But Bob Dowler's agony did not even end there, for Samuels then went on to point out to him that the police had also found a note from his daughter describing what she called 'this whole Dad thing', which had been written after she'd found pornographic magazines in his and his wife's bedroom. In a steady, firm voice Jeffrey Samuels put it to Bob Dowler that the magazines weren't 'mainstream or top-shelf pornography' but rather 'extreme pornographic material of a fetish nature', which featured bondage and latex.

Now clearly distressed, Dowler coughed nervously and took a drink from the plastic water cup in front of him. He accepted that his daughter would have found the magazines 'horrible and disgusting'.

The dissection of Bob Dowler's private life wasn't over, however, for Samuels then went on disclose to the jury that the police had also found pornographic videos in the house as well as a bag in the loft that contained items of clothing and equipment 'associated with bondage-style sexual practices', including a 'rubber hood and a ball-gag'. Looking across the courtroom towards him, Samuels pointed out that he could not 'exclude the possibility' that Milly may have discovered the content of the bag, nor could he exclude the possibility that she might also have found a 'specialist contact magazine' which was also in the loft for 'those who provide such services' and which had been 'annotated by you indicating that you may have used such services'.

By now Bob Dowler was a shadow of the confident man who had walked across Court 8 barely an hour earlier. He shamefacedly accepted that the discoveries amounted to 'a complete betrayal as a father', although he firmly rejected the suggestion that they may have contributed to her disappearance.

The implications in the questions were clear: Milly may have run away after finding the 'extreme' bondage pornography.

'Are you in any way responsible for Milly's disappearance?' Jeffrey Samuels asked him directly.

'The only way I can be responsible is if she had seen some of this material,' Dowler repeated, recalling what he had told the police when first confronted with the Milly's notes and the discoveries. 'But I have no other involvement with Milly's disappearance whatsoever . . . God forbid she decided to take her own life or run away.'

Yet even those frank admissions didn't halt his ordeal, for the defence proceeded to remind him that he'd made a further statement to the police not long after Milly's disappearance. It stated that on his way back from his meeting in Basingstoke on the afternoon of her disappearance he'd stopped at the Fleet services on the M3 motorway, where CCTV cameras had captured him looking at 'magazines of a sexual nature'.

'You'd been aroused by them,' Samuels continued calmly, so much so that, when you returned home, 'you masturbated in the bedroom' before you embarked on the series of business phone calls and just 'shortly before you got the call from Milly saying she was going to be a little late'.

Now utterly humiliated, Bob Dowler could only hang his head and admit that it was true.

If anyone had been on trial in Courtroom 8 of the Old Bailey that afternoon it had not been the defendant, but rather the man whose daughter had been abducted and murdered.

Rising to re-examine him in the wake of his fierce mauling at the hands of the defence, Brian Altman quietly asked Bob Dowler if there had been any change in Milly's relationship with him in the wake of her discovery of the pornographic magazines.

Struggling to hold himself together, Bob Dowler told the court that he hadn't been aware of any change. Nor was he aware, Bob Dowler continued, that Milly had any reluctance to be in the house with him, and that there was nothing whatever in her voice when she called from Walton-on-Thames railway station on the way home that afternoon that she was in any way disappointed with him.

Then, to complete his humiliation, Bob Dowler was asked if his wife knew about the 'items' found by the police in the loft of the family home.

'No,' he said firmly. He told her after the police had found them and described her reaction by saying: 'Distressed is hardly the right word.'

After just eighty minutes in the witness box, Bob Dowler walked out of the court, not even glancing at the impassive face of Levi Bellfield in the dock. The pain on his face, and the slowness of his stride, spoke volumes about how he felt.

His humiliation was to be completed the following morning when the press went into considerable detail about his admissions. The *Daily Telegraph* chose the headline: 'Pornography made Milly's father first suspect'.

But the Dowler family's anguish was not over. Minutes after Bob Dowler left the court, his fifty-one-year-old wife Sally was led in by a Surrey Police team. Clearly aware of what had happened to her husband, she was already distressed as she walked towards the witness stand wearing a smart grey dress, a gold necklace and gold earrings, with her short hair tinted blonde.

A maths teacher at her daughters' school – though she did not teach either Gemma or Milly – Sally Dowler told the court that her daughter was a confident girl, who had been very happy in the days before she had gone missing in March 2002. The family had spent the Sunday before on a 'fun run', where Milly had been asked to play the saxophone at the party afterwards.

'At one stage tears were running down her face she was so happy,' she told the jury. Indeed Milly had told her afterwards that it had been 'one of the best days of her life'.

It was in stark contrast to the portrait of the suicidal girl built up less than an hour beforehand in court as Milly's poem and letter had been read out by the defence. 'Overall I would have said she was happy,' Sally Dowler explained.

For the prosecution Brian Altman then asked Milly's mother about the day her daughter disappeared. On the way to school, she told him, Milly had been in a 'lovely frame of mind', joking with her and her sister Gemma in the car about a radio programme they were listening to. Once they'd reached Heathside, the three split up, and Sally didn't see Milly again until after the end of the school day, when she left her gym bag with her and told her that she had decided to go home by train rather than wait an hour or so for her mother and sister. She had told her mother she would probably get home by about 3.40 – but, of course, she never arrived.

Sally and Gemma Dowler had arrived back at the family home at about 4.45 to find her husband in the dining room with the door closed, making 'phone calls'. Gemma called out to her sister when she got in, but there was no response, so she knew Milly wasn't at home, but that didn't worry Sally Dowler unduly, as she thought she'd probably gone to visit a school friend's house.

Treading as carefully as he could, Altman then raised the question of the pornographic magazines with Sally Dowler, whose eyes were now cast down as if she were being hunted by a hungry animal. She told the prosecution counsel that Milly had come to tell her that she'd found the magazines 'maybe about a year ago', and that her daughter had been 'taken aback', as she didn't know they were there.

Sally Dowler had told her younger daughter: 'It doesn't mean that Daddy doesn't love me.' She also insisted that Milly's attitude to her husband hadn't changed after the discovery, and that she hadn't had any other discussion with Milly about the magazines. 'Absolutely not,' she told the prosecution counsel firmly.

As the afternoon session in court was drawing to a close, Brian Altman then asked Sally Dowler whether Milly would have got into a vehicle with a stranger and was told she didn't think she would 'unless there was a very good reason'. Then, after a moment's thought, she added: 'But she was a polite girl.'

It was virtually the last exchange of the court's afternoon, for shortly after 4.15 Jeffrey Samuels asked if he could begin his cross-examination of Sally Dowler for the defence the following morning, when the witness and the jury would be fresher. Mr Justice Wilkie agreed, and the court rose for the day, leaving the Dowler family all but destroyed in a trial that had been supposed to bring them justice.

What their feelings were as they made their way home to Surrey only they could know, but the feelings in the press benches in court was that their treatment had been 'hideous' – all the more so because it had been deliberately orchestrated by a man who would do anything to convince the world that he was not responsible for their daughter's death – Levi Bellfield.

The court did not sit the following morning because two of the barristers had prior appointments at the Court of Appeal, and so it was not until shortly after two o'clock in the afternoon of Tuesday, 17 May that Sally Dowler returned to the witness box to face the defence – and its cross-examination.

The prospect alone must have given her a sleepless night, for she looked tired and strained as she walked across the courtroom towards the witness stand, steadfastly looking straight ahead, determined not to catch a glimpse of the man she believed had brought her there – the defendant sitting impassively in the dock.

Jeffrey Samuels did not waste any time. His first questions concerned the discovery of the pornographic magazines hidden under the chest of drawers in the bedroom that she shared with her husband at the family home.

'Do you recall the nature of the magazines?' he asked.

Sally Dowler's pale face wrinkled in despair as she explained that she did, and repeated that she'd told her daughter Milly, who'd found them, that: 'It doesn't mean Daddy doesn't love Mummy.'

Asked if she thought finding the magazines was distressing for a child of Milly's age, Sally Dowler conceded that it would have done, but went on to explain that she and her daughter hadn't discussed the subject again. But she had talked to her husband about the magazines.

'Bob said that he would remove them, and that was the last of it,' she told Samuels.

'You didn't demand that he threw them away?' the defence barrister asked.

'I can't recall exactly what I demanded of him,' she said, her eyes filling with tears.

There was a pause, and Samuels asked her if she remembered telling the police the month after her daughter had disappeared – and long before her skeleton was found – that she had noticed a 'sort of change' in Milly at the time of the discovery, 'but then it went back to normal'.

By now the tears were coursing down Sally Dowler's cheeks.

'Is it fair to say,' Samuels then added softly, 'that you may have shut your eyes to that material and what effect it had on Milly?'

'It was ten years ago, and it's really hard to recall it,' she almost screamed 'and as a result of this I've had a nervous breakdown.'

Sally Dowler did what she could to gather herself and insisted that she had always had a 'good, open relationship with her daughter'.

It was the admission that Samuels was clearly looking for, as he instantly turned to the poems and 'suicidal' letter that the police had found in Milly's bedroom during their search of the Dowler home.

'A lot of girls write that kind of stuff,' Sally Dowler said bravely. 'It's not that unusual.'

'But did it produce a picture of your daughter which you did not recognize as her mother?' Samuels asked.

'Yes,' Sally Dowler admitted, still struggling to control herself.

Citing the letter and poem, Samuels went on: 'Were you aware that Milly may have felt that you favoured her elder sister over her?'

The piercing, plaintive wail that suddenly emerged from Sally Dowler's mouth as she started to reply echoed around the courtroom.

'But it wasn't true,' she wailed, tears coursing down her face again. 'It was not true at all.'

No one could have failed to have been moved by the emotion in Sally Dowler's voice as she addressed the court, but Levi Bellfield sat, as he had throughout her testimony, utterly impassive. It was his revenge on the Dowlers, proof that he would extract a terrible price from anyone who dared to question his right to do as he pleased. They believed he had taken their daughter, so now he was destroying their life.

But Sally Dowler's ordeal wasn't at an end. On behalf of his client, Jeffrey Samuels then carefully painted a picture of Milly Dowler's 'double life' away from the eyes of her parents. Milly Dowler had created an e-mail address, he suggested to her, with the username of 'sexmeslow28'; she had visited internet chat rooms, and written e-mails about feeling 'ugly' and bullied – while all the time she appeared to be 'a happy girl' to her mother and father. Samuels also reminded Sally Dowler that she had admitted to her brother that Milly 'seemed to be living a double life'.

Then came the final twist of the knife, as Samuels reminded Sally Dowler about a call she had made to the police in early hours of the morning on 25 May 2002, two months after her daughter had disappeared, in which she had told them that she might have recalled that she might have caught a 'fleeting glimpse' of Milly with a 'group of boys' before she had vanished 'in the blink of an eye'.

Red-eyed and distraught, Sally Dowler confessed that she had asked the police to hypnotize her in an effort to get to the truth.

'I was so desperate to recall something,' she said. 'My mind was going over and over again trying to remember the minutiae.' Sally Dowler then paused for a moment. 'I was on the brink of insanity at this stage. I was driving myself mad.'

The court was to hear that barely two weeks later Sally Dowler had withdrawn her request to be hypnotized.

Rising to re-examine her for the prosecution, Brian Altman asked her if there had been any problems between Milly and her husband, Bob.

'No,' she replied firmly.

'Did she ever threaten suicide?' Altman went on.

'No.'

'Did she ever threaten you with running away?'

'No.'

'Was she a dark and depressed person?'

'No.'

Then, after a pause, Sally Dowler added: 'We were a happy family,' and with that she broke down again in tears, the emotion flooding across the courtroom in a tidal wave.

Thanking her for her evidence, Altman released her from the witness box, and Sally Dowler started to walk across the court, but as she did so she bent double as though the pain of the ordeal had cut through her like a sword. Bob Dowler and a police officer took her arms and helped her to the doorway, but as she left the sound of her anguished cries resonated around the panelled walls of Court 8. She had been there less than eighty minutes, and the blank expression on Bellfield's pale, round face hadn't flickered for a moment.

Outside the confines of the court, Sally's daughter Gemma was waiting to give evidence, but as she saw her mother helped out of court she too broke down in tears, becoming so hysterical that at one point she lay on the floor screaming in utter despair.

It was all too clear to the prosecution and the defence that Gemma Dowler was now in no emotional state to take the witness stand, and it was rapidly agreed between them that she would not be called to give evidence in person, but an agreed statement on her behalf would be read to the court the following morning.

The Dowler family had paid a heavy price for their desire for justice for their daughter Milly – a public humiliation orchestrated by the man they believed in their hearts had killed her, Levi Bellfield.

18. Witness for the Prosecution

'In law, what plea so tainted and corrupt
But, being seasoned with a gracious voice
Obscures the show of evil.'
William Shakespeare, *The Merchant of Venice*

Gemma Dowler never made her way to the witness box in person to give evidence in support of her murdered sister, but she did – finally – have her say in front of the jury when her agreed statement was read to the court on the morning of Wednesday, 18 May, the day after her mother's collapse.

In fact Gemma was in court at the time, sitting beside her father, and she listened intently as her words were read out to the jury by Brian Altman on behalf of the prosecution. She stared straight ahead and didn't turn to her left for one moment to look at the man she believed had killed her sister sitting in the dock no more than six feet away.

Gemma Dowler's statement brought her sister back to life in a way no one could have imagined in that quiet courtroom. For she went to some lengths to describe the famous video of Milly ironing a pair of jeans in the family home that had been played on television time after time during the long six-month search for her.

'She'd never ironed anything in her life before,' Gemma told the jury, and that was the reason her mother had made a videotape of her doing it for the first time. It was a unique event in the teenager's life, and it had taken place on the Monday evening of the week Milly had vanished while she'd been preparing to go to a Pop Idol concert starring Gareth Gates on the following evening.

Describing the day Milly actually disappeared, Gemma confirmed that, when she and her mother had got home from Heathside, she had expected to find her sister at home and had called out: 'Amanda, Amanda, where are you?' But there had been no reply. Within two hours – after trying to reach her on her mobile phone and then going out to look for Milly herself – Gemma had sensed something was dreadfully wrong.

'I knew immediately that something bad had happened to Milly,' she said, 'and that she'd been abducted. There is no way she would ever have run away from home or gone off with someone without telling us. Mum and Dad really drummed it into us that we must telephone one of them to let them know when we would be late.'

Confirming that Milly didn't have a current boyfriend, and that she also hadn't met anyone in an internet chat room, Gemma added: 'I do not think Milly would have ever got into a stranger's car or gone off with a stranger unless he told her something really convincing, although she may have got into the car of someone who she knew or trusted.'

Then, at the end of Gemma's statement, Milly Dowler herself made an appearance in court as the jury were shown the videotape her sister had described so movingly of the young teenager ironing a pair of jeans while she danced behind the ironing board. It was as if her ghost had walked across the green-carpeted floor of the court-room, past her father Bob and her sister Gemma, and taken her own seat beside the jury.

Milly Dowler's ghost was to remain there for days to come, as the evidence of her school friends, the last people to see her alive, was revealed to the jury. Indeed when the striking, blonde figure of twenty-three-year-old Danielle Sykes, one of Milly's friends, walked into court to give her evidence in person it was impossible not to imagine that Milly Dowler might have looked exactly like her, had her life not been brutally snuffed out at the age of just thirteen.

Danielle had been with Milly on the ill-fated train jour-ney from Weybridge station to Walton-on-Thames on that Thursday afternoon. They had even hugged each other goodbye on the train, as Milly had planned to go on to the next stop at Hersham, nearer her home. It had been Danielle who had persuaded her not to, and to get off at Walton, a decision that was to cost the thirteen-year-old her life. Just as the train was pulling in to Walton station Danielle had suddenly said to Milly: 'Would you like to come and have chips with me at the café?'

'I'd better not,' Milly had told her.

'OK, fine then,' Danielle replied, teasing her friend.

A split-second later, Milly changed her mind. 'Ah, no, actually I will come. I've got nothing better to do.'

It was a joke between two teenagers that was to change their lives for ever.

Once off the train, Milly and Danielle had made their

way to the Travellers' café on Walton station and ordered a 90 pence plate of chips each, although Milly had to borrow 10 pence from her friend to do so. Then they'd spoken to three male pupils from school who were there already, and Milly had borrowed one of their phones to ring her father. Not long after four that afternoon the two friends left the café, and Danielle had given Milly a final hug.

'I asked her if she would be all right to walk home on her own,' Danielle told the jury, 'and she'd replied, "Yeah, I'll be absolutely fine."'

They were almost the last words anyone said to Milly Dowler. For, as the jury also heard, her killer was the only person who could have spoken to her after that. The last that Danielle saw of her friend was as Milly left the station and walked towards Station Avenue.

In the wake of the Dowlers' ordeal in the witness box, it was inevitable that Brian Altman would have to ask Danielle about the pornographic magazines found under father's chest of drawers, and whether the discovery had upset her friend. Danielle told him frankly that they'd left Milly feeling 'disappointed' and 'weirded out'.

'But then no one wants to think of their parents in that light,' Danielle went on.

By now close to tears, with the memory of her dead friend all too fresh in her memory, Danielle explained that Milly always found a way to laugh things off.

Yet, on the following morning, the jury heard from the girl who had been Milly's closest friend that she didn't laugh at everything, and that she did indeed have 'a dark side'. Hannah McDonald, who was now twenty-two, had been another pupil in Year 9 at Heathside with Milly, and she told the court that they'd become 'really, really close' and confided 'secrets' to one another. When Hannah was asked by Jeffrey Samuels for the defence whether Milly was ever upset, she confessed that her friend sometimes 'used humour to mask her lack of self-confidence'. Hannah also said that her friend had been upset by bullying and name-calling at school. In particular, Milly was self-conscious about the size of her nose, and didn't like being called 'big nose' at school.

Did that upset her, Samuels asked, and Hannah admitted that it did.

'Just like any thirteen-year-old, she would take it to heart more than an adult would. Looking back, it was pretty trivial, and there was no need to get upset by it,' she said.

But Hannah then went on to explain that Milly had even tried to 'slit her wrists with a dinner knife' because of the name calling.

Despite this, Hannah also explained that: 'Milly did like to exaggerate things, and she only told me a year or so after the event. She didn't break the skin, or so she told me.'

In fact the jury learned that the attempt had taken place two years before Milly disappeared, and that she'd been much happier since then. Nevertheless the image of an almost teenage girl trapped in anguish on the edge of puberty seemed to float across the court, no matter how hard Hannah tried to brush it aside.

'She was a joker. She would always make you smile,' Hannah explained defensively. 'She had funny voices she used. She liked to be liked. I don't think anyone wants to be disliked.'

Hannah also told the court that on the day Milly disappeared they had been looking forward to a rock gig they were going to the following day, Friday, 22 March, and that Milly had been 'just normal'.

Two of Milly's other friends then confirmed to the court in written statements that she had been perfectly happy on the day she had gone missing. She may have had her secret moments of anguish, but her school friends confirmed that on the day that she disappeared she had been as happy as the girl dancing behind the ironing board.

Then came another moment of poignancy, as the jury heard from the very last person to see Milly alive – apart from her killer – another Heathside pupil, the now twenty-four-year-old Katherine Laynes, who was two years above Milly at school, in Year 11. Katherine told the jury that, on the afternoon of Thursday, 21 March 2002 she had been sitting at the bus stop diagonally opposite Walton-on-Thames railway station – and, incidentally, right outside the entrance to 24, Collingwood Place – when she had spotted Milly walking down Station Avenue away from the station on her way home. The two girls knew one another because Katherine was a friend of Gemma, and she had been to visit her at the Dowler family home.

Looking composed, Katherine explained that she had stayed behind at school that afternoon to work on a Design and Technology project and had then got the train to Walton from Weybridge to catch the 556 bus home to Shepperton. Katherine had walked across the road to the bus stop and sat down to wait. There was nobody else with her as she watched Milly walk past on the other side of the road.

'We made eye contact,' she told the court. 'I didn't wave or anything but I thought we both recognized each other.' At the time, Katherine remembered Milly's hair was tied up in a ponytail; her blazer was over her left arm, and her rucksack was on her back.

Katherine remembered that the blue single-decker bus she was waiting for came along quite quickly after Milly had passed out of her sight – obscured by the advertising hoarding on the bus stop – and she'd climbed on, paid her 50 pence child's fare and sat down on the left-hand side of the bus looking out across to the side of Station Avenue where she had last seen Milly. As the bus drew away along the road, however, Katherine couldn't see any sign of Milly. 'It was quite weird I hadn't seen her,' she explained. 'I could see quite clearly down the road but I still couldn't see her.'

What made Katherine Laynes so significant to the jury was that she was the only witness who claimed to have actually seen Milly Dowler walking down Station Avenue. That meant that she was certainly one of the last people to see her alive before Milly met whoever was to take her life.

Over the next two days the jury also heard statements – read out to them – from other people who had been in Station Avenue on that Thursday afternoon in March, as well as from some of other residents of the flats in Colling-wood Place, which lay just behind the bus stop where Katherine Laynes had last seen Milly Dowler.

But it was to be Levi Bellfield's partner in March 2002 Emma Mills – the true tenant of 24, Collingwood Place – who was to provide the jury with the greatest insight into what might really have happened on the afternoon of Milly's disappearance. Mills was to become the signal witness for the prosecution, but she asked for 'special measures' from the court to allow her to do so. She was now so terrified of Levi Bellfield that she wanted to be allowed to give evidence to the jury from behind black curtains, which would prevent her from seeing or making any kind of eye contact with the man she'd shared almost ten years of her life with and with whom she'd had three children.

This wasn't unusual in a major murder trial, and the defence raised no objections.

Levi Bellfield did, however. When discussing the arrangements with Mr Justice Wilkie at the end of Tuesday, 24 May – after the jury had been dismissed for the day – Brian Altman, for the prosecution, explained the procedure that would be put in place in court the following morning. Emma Mills would be brought into court first, and allowed to sit behind a curtain until she was called into the witness box, where she would be screened by a further curtain so that she could not see Bellfield when he was brought into the dock, and he could not see her.

'If there is any difficulty,' Altman said quietly, 'the usual practice is for the defendant to move along the dock slightly so there can be no chance of eye-contact.'

That was too much for Bellfield.

'I'm not moving along the box,' he announced in a loud, belligerent voice, following the declaration with an expletive or two for good measure, and then kicking one of the empty chairs beside him in the dock.

'That is Mr Bellfield's view,' Altman commented calmly.

It did not affect the court's view, but it did, once again, underline Bellfield's darker, angrier, side — a side that he had been at pains to conceal from the jury.

The following morning, Wednesday, 25 May, black curtains were indeed place around the witness box as Emma Mills was ushered to her seat behind them, but Bellfield had not moved his seat in the dock. He was still clearly determined that he should command as much of the legal proceedings as he possibly could and prove that he wasn't concerned what this particular witness had to say. Indeed, for the first time he chose not to wear his suit in the dock. In its place Bellfield had chosen a blue-and-white striped polo shirt with short sleeves. He was a man in control, a man who would not be intimidated — by anyone.

And so, shortly after 10.30, the slight, brunette figure of Emma Mills climbed into the witness box and took the oath in a soft, timid voice. The mousey looking thirty-three-year-old was clutching a tissue in her left hand and looked for all the world like a frightened fawn as she cowered behind the black curtains.

Brian Altman began by asking her gently about how she'd come to meet the defendant, and how their relationship had started.

Emma Mills told the court how she first met him at Rocky's in Cobham, when she was about eighteen, then moved into his uncle Charlie Brazil's house with him before they got a small flat together in Manor Road, Twickenham, and then into another in Clements Court in Hounslow, before finally moving to 11, Little Benty at the 'end of 1999 or early 2000'.

With each answer her voice seemed to falter, as if she

was trembling on the brink of some terrible abyss of despair. Then, from time to time, she would blow her nose with the tissue in her hand, to recover her poise. The attempt didn't often work.

Turning to events in 2001, Emma Mills told the jury that she had moved out of Little Benty that summer and gone to a woman's refuge – because 'her relationship with Bellfield had broken down'. Then in September her mother Gillian had found her the two-bedroom flat at 24, Collingwood Place through a friend at the local estate agents. Emma had become the tenant, and signed a one-year lease with a break clause which allowed her to move after six months, providing she gave the landlord's agents two months' notice in writing. Her mother had paid the deposit and the first month's rent, while the local Elm-bridge Council had paid the rent from them on, as she was a single mother with two small children.

But by Christmas 2001 Emma had resumed her relationship with Levi Bellfield as a result of their meeting regularly so that he could see their children. As the New Year turned he'd started to 'stay over' with her at Colling-wood Place 'most of the time', she told the jury quietly. He had brought with him his dog, a Staffordshire bull-terrier, which was black with a white bib and two white socks and was called 'Chey', short for Cheyenne, though she pronounced it 'Shy'. 'Levi took it about with him,' she told the jury.

After Emma had left the refuge her mother had also bought her daughter a car for £800, a Red Daewoo Nexia, N530 GLT, which Bellfield had taken to using. There was only one key for the car, just as there was only one set of the keys that opened the front door at 24, Collingwood Place, and they were all kept on one key ring.

Her voice still trembling, Emma then told Brian Altman that the car was always 'untidy' and littered with children's belongings, crisp packets, magazines and 'general day-to-day rubbish'. It also had a solid car seat for her young son William and a smaller 'booster' seat for her daughter Lucy.

By the beginning of March 2002, Emma Mills had also agreed with Bellfield that they would move back to what had been the family home in Little Benty, but that she hadn't wanted to go back there at once as 'it was a bit of a squat really'. So they had decided to redecorate it and then move back together 'as a family', and she'd given notice to the local estate agents on 20 March 2002 indicating that they intended to stay at Collingwood Place for 'a couple of months' and leave in late May.

Brian Altman then asked her about the events of the week that Milly Dowler had gone missing, and, in particular, where she, Bellfield and their children had been at the time. With her voice still on the verge of breaking, and with the white tissue now in her right hand, she replied that they'd been house-sitting for her friend Christine Hawgood in Harmondsworth Road, West Drayton, just round the corner from Little Benty. Being closer to Little Benty would make it easier for them to supervise the redecoration work there. So she, Bellfield and the children had gone to stay at Christine's on Tuesday, 19 March 2002.

Everything was normal on Wednesday, 20 March, Emma Mills explained. Bellfield went off to work, as he usually did, and she hadn't noticed anything out of the ordinary. But on the day Milly disappeared Emma told the court that she had found it difficult to get hold of Bellfield on his mobile phone. He had 'disappeared' and turned his mobile phone off. She remembered it clearly, she explained, because she hadn't got any money at the time and Bellfield had her red Daewoo Nexia, so she couldn't drive out to get some. She added that his behaviour that day had been 'unusual'.

'Normally he would ring me or I would ring him, on and off during the day, to see what I was doing,' she said, but on this particular day, 'he didn't ring me at all until later on, I didn't see him past lunch time'.

Bellfield had left Christine's house in the late morning, Emma explained, and she hadn't heard from him again until 5.38 that evening when he'd phoned her. She'd then asked him where he'd been and what time he'd be back, but he hadn't explained, and she didn't actually speak to him again until 8.51, when she'd rung him to ask him when he'd be back. He'd then phoned her back at 9.45, but still hadn't returned.

Bellfield finally got back to Christine's between 10 and 11 that evening, but when he'd arrived Emma Mills told the jury: 'He was wearing different clothes from those he had on in the morning. They would have been from the flat in Walton.'

'Did you question him?' Altman asked.

'I did, but I would never get a straight answer, and even if he did tell me something I would never know if it was the truth,' Emma replied.

The prosecution barrister then asked about the other

events of that night, and Emma told him that Bellfield had got up between 3 and 4 a.m. in the morning and told her that he was 'going back to the flat to have a lie-in' and had taken his bull terrier with him.

Then, when Emma Mills had spoken to Bellfield just before 8.30 a.m. that morning, he had suddenly announced to her that he wanted to move back to their house in Little Benty straight away. He told he wanted her to pack up – he was all 'happy and jokey', she said, admitting that sometimes it was easier 'just to say "yes" with him'.

But when she finally got back to the flat at Collingwood Place – Bellfield dropped her off there and didn't go inside with her – Emma had discovered that their double bed in the main bedroom had 'no sheets or pillow cases' and 'no duvet cover'.

She had immediately rung Bellfield to ask what had happened to them.

'He said the dog had had an accident on the bed,' Emma explained to the jury. 'I didn't believe him for a second. He said he put the sheets in the rubbish because they couldn't be washed.'

But when Emma had gone to look for the soiled sheets in the rubbish area outside the flat at 24, Collingwood Place there'd been no sign of them whatever.

Nevertheless, the couple and their children had spent that Friday night at the flat, but the following morning had packed up and set off for 11, Little Benty – even though the redecoration was far from complete.

It was a damning sequence of evidence against Bellfield from the young woman cowering behind the curtains.

Then – just after she'd described the sudden departure

from the flat in Walton-on-Thames – Bellfield suddenly coughed ostentatiously in the dock, the cough of a man making a point. It wasn't lost on his former partner. Emma immediately broke down in tears.

Asked if she wanted a break from giving evidence, Emma Mills nodded, her eyes now red and swollen, and the jury were sent out for a fifteen-minute break.

Once again, Bellfield had demonstrated his ability to manipulate the court, just as he had manipulated the women in his life for so many years.

Back in the witness box after the break, Emma Mills went on to tell the jury that when she'd got back to the flat in Walton-on-Thames on Friday, 22 March she had seen the police vans around the station and she had been aware of the hunt for Milly Dowler, but that no officers had arrived at her front door while she was there.

The following night at Little Benty Emma and Bellfield had had to sleep on sofa cushions on the floor, but while she was redecorating the children's bedroom about a week later she had asked him about the Thursday he had gone missing, 'because I thought he was with another woman'.

It was to provoke one of the trial's most dramatic moments.

'Why do you keep going on?' Bellfield had asked her. 'What do you think, I done Milly?'

Emma Mills was horrified, but didn't pursue it any further.

'I didn't ask him about it,' she told the jury. 'It was so awful. I was used to him making horrible remarks. I thought it's disgusting. It's not even funny.'

It was the remark that was to make headlines the

following morning, repeated endlessly on the television news channels, and it came just as Emma's evidence as a witness for the prosecution was coming to its end.

The only other thing of significance that Emma told the jury was that Bellfield had rung her on the Tuesday after they'd moved back into Little Benty to tell her that her red Daewoo had been stolen from outside his uncle Charlie Brazil's house in Hounslow. The car was never to be seen again. Unlike the remains of Milly Dowler, it disappeared without trace – for ever.

And so it was on the following morning, Thursday, 26 May 2011, that Emma Mills was confronted by the cross examination of Jeffrey Samuels in defence of her former partner, who had arrived in the dock that morning wearing a purple polo shirt. By contrast, the mother of three of his children was dressed all in black, with her face even whiter than it had been the day before.

Samuels began by pointing out to Emma Mills that, in spite of her horrified reaction to the disappearance of Milly Dowler, and Bellfield's remark about having 'done Milly', she'd nevertheless remained with him for the next two years and had even had a further child with him in the summer of 2004, a daughter named Georgina. Indeed, Samuels pointed out to the court Emma Mills did not even mention Milly to the police until after Bellfield's arrest on the suspicion of the murder of Amélie Delagrange in November 2004.

'You never contacted the police about Milly,' Samuels put to her directly.

'No,' she confessed.

'You didn't then harbour any suspicions?'

'I didn't think he'd done it,' Emma told him. 'But when he made that comment it made me think, "Why did he make that comment?" But I didn't think he had done it.'

Samuels then asked her what her response was to the remark about Milly.

'I asked how he could make a joke like that,' she said. 'I didn't say much' – and she paused, before adding quietly that she thought it was 'disgusting'.

'You didn't tell anyone about that remark he made, not even your mother?' Samuels asked.

'No,' Emma Mills confessed.

The defence barrister then pointed out to her that in fact she'd only tried to ring Bellfield four times on the afternoon that Milly disappeared – rather then trying to contact him 'repeatedly'.

Crouching in the witness box, clutching at the curtain, Emma Mills looked horrified.

'You say it was unusual for him to have his phone off,' Samuels said. 'I say it wasn't.'

Emma Mills's ashen face crumpled, her right hand twisting her hair into a strand.

But she firmly denied Samuels's suggestions that the true reason that she'd left the flat in Walton-on-Thames so suddenly was that it was very 'damp' or that she had discovered that Bellfield had been running a credit card fraud from the flat using the name and details of a former tenant and wanted to escape the interests of the police.

The defence cross-examination went on all day, with Samuels repeatedly questioning Emma Mills about the details of her phone conversations with Bellfield, about who had actually reported the red Daewoo car stolen, and about exactly when they had moved back to Little Benty. Throughout she twisted her hair and looked genuinely afraid, but she did not back down once in the face of Samuels's bombardment.

Then, on the following morning, Friday, 27 May, she resumed her place behind the black curtains for the final time – to face the prosecution's re-examination. Still clearly distressed, again she didn't falter, although she did become visibly distressed when she was asked to look at pictures of the former family home in Little Benty.

At last, just before 11.20 on that Friday morning, Emma Mills was released from the witness box. She had spent almost eleven hours giving evidence, and she walked slowly out of the court as though she still carried the weight of the world on her shoulders.

The exact nature of Emma Mills's relationship with Bellfield was then thrown into high relief by her mother Gillian, whose statement was read to the court. Gillian Mills insisted that her daughter had been 'well-behaved' before she'd met Bellfield when he was a bouncer at Rocky's nightclub when she was seventeen. When Emma met Levi, her statement read, 'her personality changed. She was besotted by him.'

'I didn't like the look of him,' Mrs Mills insisted. 'I would describe Levi as a big, fat lump with a high voice. He had no neck.'

Gillian Mills also explained that she had been disappointed when the couple had got back together again and had a third child.

'I think she let him back into her life because she was lonely,' she said, but it was only after Bellfield had been arrested on suspicion of murder that Emma had felt 'free and able' to talk to the police about him.

For once Bellfield may have been relieved that the witness had not come to court to give her evidence in person. The tone of Mrs Mills's statement suggested she would not have cowered behind a curtain to make her opinion of her daughter's former partner abundantly clear. She loathed him.

One other partner of Levi Bellfield's was to make an appearance in court. Johanna Collings, the woman he'd lived with in Strawberry Hill, also came to give evidence in Court 8 on the afternoon of 6 June , after a week's break in the trial. She'd been called to give evidence about her experiences of visiting Yateley Heath Woods with Bellfield in the 1990s – where the skeletal remains of Milly's body were discovered in September 2002. Now thirty-eight, Jo Collings walked into court wearing a pair of tight white trousers, a broad-shouldered, heavy-breasted woman considerably larger now than she'd been when they'd been together at the end of the 1990s. Her red hair was tied back in a ponytail, and she sported long white fake plastic fingernails as she took her seat in the witness box. To the outsider she resembled nothing so much as a rather stern barmaid on the brink of serving Malibu to a teenage patron, who may well have been under age.

Jo Collings certainly looked confident and she'd demanded no 'special measures' to prevent her making eye-contact with the defendant – although she took particular care not to look across the court at him.

In a firm voice she told Brian Altman for the prosecution that Bellfield had accompanied her to horse shows at

Yateley more than five times – and the jury were then shown two photographs of the pair there, one which showed Bellfield holding the horse's head while a rather slimmer Jo Collings was sitting in the saddle. Twisting a strand of her hair, Jo Collings also told the court that she and Bellfield had also taken their two whippet puppies to the area when he was trying to train them for coursing for rabbits, and that they'd also visited the local Blackbushe car auctions. Cross-examined by Jeffrey Samuels, she also explained that she'd told the police that he 'disappears all the time at five or six o'clock in the morning', telling her that he was 'going to the market'. When she asked which one, he would say 'Blackbushe'.

Jo Collings then told him that her former partner went through a lot of cars, although he 'didn't do legal cars, MOTs, tax or anything like that'. If one ever broke down 'he just got a new one'. One of her cars had been stolen when they were together. When a member of the jury passed a note to the judge asking if any trace of it had ever been found, she told them it had been discovered 'burned out' three or four months later.

There was none of the high drama of her predecessor Emma Mills's evidence, however, although Bellfield did start swearing under his breath when Jo Collings was asked about media interviews she had given in the past, and whether she had been paid for them.

Yet not everything was as it appeared to be in Jo Collings evidence, for the jury were to hear just a few days later that her eldest child, a daughter, was not Bellfield's at all. Bellfield had known that since the start of his first trial in 2007, and it could have been one reason why her evidence so enraged him, that and a fierce resentment that she had been making a profit out of their relationship, and he wanted her to admit it in open court. But all that she would admit was that she had been paid twice – 'less than £10,000' – on each occasion, and that she'd used the money for her children.

As Jo Collings walked back across the courtroom, still studiously refusing to look at him, Bellfield was still fuming under his breath, still intent on taking every ounce of revenge he could on anyone who questioned his right to do exactly what he pleased, whenever he pleased.

In the days that followed the jury heard detailed evidence from a CCTV expert to help to establish whether there had been any sighting of Milly Dowler on the closed-ciruit cameras on the Bird's Eye factory building on Station Avenue on that Thursday afternoon – there had not. Nor was there any sign on the cameras that a man and a girl had crossed Station Avenue that day, although there was a window of some forty-two seconds at the time Milly was starting to walk along the road which was not covered by the cameras. If the CCTV cameras on Walton-on-Thames station had been working that day there seems little doubt that they would have spotted Milly – but, tragically, they weren't, not as a result of sabotage but the simple fact that a decorator had moved the CCTV unit and inadvertently disconnected it.

The jury also heard evidence from a mobile phone expert on the whereabouts of Bellfield's mobile phone, which ended in the numbers 104, on the days in late March 2002, and in particular on the day Milly disappeared and later that night.

They learned that his phone had been 'unavailable' between 3.28 in the afternoon of Thursday, 21 March and 4.48 that afternoon, when he'd telephoned his mother Jean from somewhere near her home in Hounslow. The jury also learned that his mobile phone had fallen entirely silent during the seven hours between 1 o'clock in the morning of Friday, 22 March – in spite of his sudden trip back to Collingwood Place from Christine Hawgood's house in Harmondsworth, and that it hadn't been used again until after 8 o'clock that morning.

Then, in one of the last moments of the prosecution's case, Sally and Gemma Dowler came back to Court 8 in the late morning of Monday, 13 June to hear the official pathologist, Dr Hugh White, explain that he had conducted the examination of Milly's remains and confirmed that they were indeed hers, and point out that he could give no firm indication of a cause of death because all that he had to examine was her bones. A sombre hush fell as the white-haired pathologist explained that Milly had been left naked. No clothing whatever had been found near her remains in spite of a police search that went on for almost three weeks. Dr White also confirmed that she had been dead 'for months, not weeks' when she'd been found. Asked by Brian Altman for the prosecution how the teenager might have died, he could not rule out her having been suffocated or strangled, but he was certain she had been murdered, even though the official cause of death was formally 'unascertained'.

'This is a girl of thirteen years old found in an environment where she could not have got to by herself – and she was without any clothes,' Dr White said quietly.

In the dock Bellfield sat quite still, while beside him in court, though protected from his gaze by a large flat television screen, Sally and Gemma Dowler's faces were a study in abject misery.

It was a misery that was compounded the following day when the court heard from Detective Sergeant Tim Barrett of Surrey Police, a bluff, stocky man who had worked on the Dowler case since the day Milly had first disappeared, that Bob Dowler was one of 'fifty-four suspects' investigated by the police. It hadn't been the finest hour for Surrey Police, as DS Barrett also revealed that, although all the other occupants of all the fifty-two flats in Collingwood Place, as well as others in the area, had been interviewed, 'The occupants of Flat 24 were neither seen nor identified during eleven separate visits,' later adding: 'No inquiries were made with estate agents in order to trace those occupants.'

That admission came after the jury had been read the full details of Bellfield's murders of Amélie Delagrange and Marsha McDonnell, as well as the attempted murder of Kate Sheedy – but one person who had not been there to hear them repeated was Levi Bellfield. He had retired to the cells with a 'migraine'.

Perhaps even Bellfield could not face the jury, knowing the stark reality of what he was capable of. Whatever the truth, shortly before 4 o'clock on the afternoon of Tuesday, 14 June, Brian Altman announced to the court: 'That is the case for the prosecution.'

It was now time for Bellfield to prove his innocence – or not – to the remaining eleven jurors, the twelfth having been discharged as the result of a sudden illness.

19. End Game

'To deny all is to confess all.'

Spanish proverb

Throughout his second trial at the Old Bailey Levi Bell-field continued to play the roles of Dr Jekyll and Mr Hyde. When the jury were in court, he took great pains to present himself as the innocent defendant, taking endless notes to assist his defence, a man unfairly wronged by the judicial system. Like a malign toad Bellfield sat there impassively on the lily-pad of the dock with poison oozing from every pore, pretending that he could do no wrong, and that the outrageous allegations the prosecution were making against him were a mockery of the truth. It was only when the jury were not there that he allowed the bile within him to surface, and the dark, violent rage that his victims and his female partners had seen crept into the light of day. Only then did the true Bellfield reveal himself, with his anger bubbling to the surface in the blink of an eye – an anger directed at those who had chosen to give evidence against him, and at his counsel for not pointing that out strongly enough in his defence.

When the jury left the court for a break, Bellfield would launch into coruscating whispered attacks on the world – littered with expletives – through the gaps in the glass fronted dock at his defence team. Indeed, as the final stages of the prosecution's case drew to a close, Bellfield grew steadily more agitated – not least about his former partner Johanna Collings contacts with the media. At one point he even shouted at his counsel during a break while the jury were out that he wasn't going to bother to come up and sit in the dock that afternoon if something wasn't done to put his point of view across.

In the end Bellfield did indeed refuse to appear – although he made sure to suggest to the jury that he hadn't been receiving the correct medication from the prison service to cope with his 'headaches', which meant that he now had a migraine. It was an excuse, but one that served to make sure that he was not in the dock when the prosecution read the details of his previous murders to the jury. It is hard, after all, to present yourself as an innocent while the jury hears the details of your two convictions for murder and one for attempted murder.

But there was another, less obvious, reason for Bellfield's belligerence – beyond, of course, his desire to manipulate the court to his will at every opportunity – and that was the decision about whether he was to take the witness stand in his own defence. He knew only too well that his defence team would argue forcefully that the prosecution had not proved there was a case against him, but the temptation for him to go into the witness box himself, to convince them, was all but overwhelming. In Bellfield's supremely arrogant mind, he thought that he knew better than his defence team, and that he alone could convince the jury that he could not possibly have abducted and killed Milly Dowler. But, and it was a large but, Bellfield also knew that he had taken the witness stand in his own defence in the first trial, spending almost seven full days being examined and cross-examined, and it had done him no good whatever. He had still been convicted.

Should he risk making the same mistake again, and once again see his tortuous lies revealed to the jury by Brian Altman QC for the prosecution, or should he remain silent, allowing the defence barrister to make his case for him? It was a dilemma that only contrived to increase his headache in the Category A holding cells beneath the Old Bailey. Indeed it wasn't until after the prosecution had closed its case that Bellfield finally came to a decision that he would not give evidence on his own behalf. It was a risk, for failing to do so might suggest to the jury that he had something to hide and wasn't prepared to be cross-examined by the prosecution, but he came to the conclusion that the risk of his silence was outweighed by the fact that he might just weaken his own case by going into the witness box.

So it was that on the morning of Thursday, 16 June that Jeffrey Samuels stood up before Mr Justice Wilkie and announced that his client, Levi Bellfield, would not be giving evidence, and that the defence would not be calling any other witnesses. Mr Justice Wilkie then asked the defence counsel if he had advised his client that 'the jury may draw such inferences as it sees proper', and Samuels confirmed that he had. Meanwhile Bellfield sat expressionless in the dock.

And so, shortly after 10.40 that morning, Brian Altman got to his feet to give his closing speech to the jury, and he started, inevitably, by seizing on Bellfield's decision not to take the witness stand.

'There is a wealth of evidence in this case,' he began, 'regarding the defendant's conduct, his actions and his words around the time of Milly's disappearance that you would have wanted to hear the defendant explain and have tested on oath from the witness box. He has deprived you of that opportunity. How, for instance, would he have explained – when tested – his behaviour on the day of and night following Milly's disappearance? We don't know, because he has declined to give us his account, tested and examined from the witness box. He ducked the opportunity. You might reasonably have thought that a man accused of murdering thirteen-year-old Milly Dowler and of seeking to abduct Rachel Cowles the day before would want to grasp the opportunity of explaining and protesting his innocence to a jury. But he has not done so.'

Altman paused, then added: 'The reason you may think he has not done so is that he does not have an innocent account to give – an account that will stand the test of critical scrutiny, and he knows it. The prosecution say he has a clear case to answer, yet he declines to do so. It is his failure to give evidence about these matters that you are entitled to hold against him, if you think it fair to do so.'

Asking the jury to examine the whole of the evidence, he then explained that the Crown's case against him relied on 'many strands of circumstantial evidence'.

'No one saw Milly snatched from Station Avenue,' Altman admitted. 'As we have seen, the road was relatively quiet at that time, and no one saw it or, as I have said before, no one saw it for what it really was – such was the skill, brazenness and resourcefulness of her abductor and killer.' Bellfield must have managed to 'lure or force her' into the ground-floor flat at 24, Collingwood Place 'from which she was never to emerge alive . . . and so, as was her killer's intention, no one witnessed the fatal event either'.

'Circumstantial evidence,' he went on, 'is by no means a poor substitute for direct eyewitness evidence. It can, depending on your view . . . provide the most telling evidence of a defendant's involvement. It does not involve a leap of faith by you. Indeed, it was upon almost entirely circumstantial evidencethat the jury in 2008 convicted the defendant of the murders of Marsha McDonnell and Amélie Delagrange in 2003 and 2004, and the attempted murder of Kate Sheedy in 2004.'

But then Brian Altman turned to the brutal questioning of both Bob and Sally Dowler in the witness box by Jeffrey Samuels – on his client's direct instructions. It was impossible to ignore the disgust in the barrister's voice as he described the Dowlers' treatment. If Bellfield had planned his revenge on the Dowlers by subjecting them to an ordeal in the witness box, then Altman was returning the favour. He made it abundantly clear that the suggestions were no more than a smokescreen to conceal the truth – that Bellfield wanted to convince the jury that he was innocent.

'As we understand it,' Altman said fiercely, 'it is going to be suggested that Milly was a runaway who did not want to be alone in her father's company that day, and so she hung around in or about Station Avenue only to slip away without being noticed into the hands of another killer at another time, and at another place, so that Levi Bellfield cannot have been her abductor and killer. What underpins that theory? As we understand it, it was the father's lifestyle, as well as aspects of Milly's character.

Turning to the 'extreme' magazines that Milly had found in her parents' bedroom, Altman told the jury they could be forgiven for thinking they'd been discovered on the very day that she'd disappeared, when, in fact, they'd been found nine months earlier. 'There is no avoiding it,' Brian Altman continued, 'this evidence is now being used to suggest that he contributed to his daughter's disappearance and eventual death.'

His words hung in a stunned silence in the court. Bob Dowler and his wife, as well as their daughter Gemma, were sitting barely seven paces from the prosecuting counsel, a Surrey police liaison officer at their side.

Altman paused. 'But more than that,' he went on, 'there was the implication in cross-examination of Sally Dowler that she hadn't dealt with the matter properly, so that somehow her inadequate response to it as a mother had also contributed to her daughter's disappearance.'

Once again the contempt in Altman's voice was unmistakable.

'So the theory goes something like this,' he said firmly. 'Milly did not walk home, but must have hung back, and diverted – not to be captured by the Bird's Eye CCTV cameras – only to meet her killer at some other time, at some other location, anywhere else, of course, so long as it is not on Levi Bellfield's doorstep.'

There was a hush as he spoke.

'No one, absolutely no one in this court room,' he went on, 'other than Mr and Mrs Dowler and Gemma, their surviving daughter, can possibly know or understand what it is like to have lost a child or a sister in the dreadful circumstances they did on that March afternoon, not knowing for month after month what had become of her, only then years later to have their lives laid bare in the full glare of the national media in this courtroom.

'But the grieving parents are not the ones on trial here. That fact might have been forgotten . . . when the Dowlers came to give their evidence. There is only one person on trial in this courtroom – and that person is Levi Bellfield. Yet he has not had the courage to give you his account tested in the witness box.'

Turning to the so-called 'goodbye note' that Milly had written, found by the police among a jumble of other childhood memorabilia at the bottom of a toy box at the foot of her bed, Altman dismissed the suggestion that Milly was anything other than an 'intelligent girl, top set at school, interested in all the topics a thirteen-year-old girl would and should be.'

'Girls of her age go through developmental processes,' he explained, 'which any parent of girls that age will know can sometimes be challenging. I daresay Milly was no different.'

Witness after witness, Altman said, had told the court that Milly was 'very close to her family' and a girl with a 'very happy life', who was absolutely adored by her mother and father, and that she was 'looking forward to the rest of the week' on the day she disappeared, 'just as she was looking forward to the rest of her life'.

Did the video of Milly ironing her jeans, he asked the jury, really look, and sound, like a girl about to run away from home? Ramming the point home, he reminded them that the one thing missing from all the writings produced by the defence was 'any threat to run away'. Indeed all her friends had paid tribute in their evidence to how 'happy' she'd been on the day of her disappearance and how she'd told all of them that she would 'see them tomorrow'.

'As I've already commented,' Altman added, 'if she had truly wanted to run off – to make a stand about something, a protest – why not lodge with a friend for a time? Call Dad or Mum and seek to tell them why she was not coming home until the issue had been sorted out – whatever it was. Give Dad the cold shoulder, have a family conference, but at thirteen to run off like that with not a penny or a purpose or a plan?' Altman paused again, before adding fiercely: 'Utter nonsense.'

'So if she didn't run away' he asked the jury, 'and had been heading home along Station Avenue, but didn't make it, then she was abducted – but not abducted anywhere – but in the very place where Bellfield was that very afternoon – a conclusion the defence is trying so very hard to avoid.'

There was barely the sound of a breath in the court room as the words hung in the air.

Over the course of that Thursday Altman painstakingly took each and every aspect of the defence's apparent suggestion that she may have run away out of 'disgust' with her father and demolished them one by one.

The horrifying truth, he explained was that 'whoever abducted Milly achieved what he did without it being captured' on the CCTV cameras, which was probably the result of 'pure luck', as it just happened to take place in the critical forty seconds or so that the camera 'swept away counter-clockwise from the visible part of the roadway'.

Altman then gave the jury an explanation for why Milly might have crossed over to the north side of Station Avenue as she walked along. 'Is it too fantastic a suggestion to make that Milly did cross to the north side, almost directly opposite Collingwood Place, hoping perhaps to see and flag down her mother for a lift home – because it would be that side of the road on which Sally would be driving home?'

If she did so then she could have been quickly snatched and dragged behind the hedges of Collingwood Place, which would have made it impossible for the CCTV cameras to see her.

'It was then a short step and a simple thing,' Altman explained 'for a big man to get or drag a slight thirteen-year-old to the front access door into 24, Collingwood Place – through the door marked "No entry", which was always open and unlocked . . . then into number 24, where at some stage and somehow he killed her. You've seen for yourself how small it all is inside the area at the front of the flats,' he concluded, 'and you can see it would take seconds for a big man to have manhandled a small girl inside without screaming.'

As the court day drew to its close, Altman again rammed home the point that Bellfield was prepared to tell any lie necessary to divert their attention from the truth, and that included implicating his partner Emma Mills.

'Stooping so low,' he concluded, 'to divert police attention from him, he was quite prepared to incriminate his own partner and the mother of his children, so he could avoid his just desserts for what he had done . . . That provides you with a fine example of the dishonesty of the man you are dealing with.'

Shortly after 4 on that Thursday afternoon in June the jury filed silently out of the courtroom clearly affected by what they'd heard, a forensic, clinical representation of the prosecution case and what Altman felt was likely to be the defence's response.

As the jury were ushered back into court the following morning the air was filled with expectation, and Altman did not disappoint them. He began by describing what may have happened to the now notorious Red Daewoo Nexia that belonged to Emma Mills but which Bellfield had taken to driving himself – and in particular where it was on Thursday, 21 March 2002.

'If the theft story was a true one,' he said, 'and someone had stolen the car not for its resale value – it was a bog standard car worth £800 – but to joy-ride it, where is the evidence that it was joy-ridden, or dumped, and abandoned? Why has there not even been a simple parking ticket?' Then, as he'd done before, Altman answered his own question. 'Just like the Ford Courier van in 2004,' he told the jury, 'in poor condition and of low value, yet inexplicably it too disappeared never to be found by the Metropolitan Police.' The implication was abundantly clear – the defendant had a habit of making cars disappear, especially cars that might contain forensic evidence that might help to convict him.

As for inside the flat at 24, Collingwood Place, he went on, Bellfield had lied to Emma Mills about what had happened to the bedding as well as the theft of the Daewoo 'not in panic, and not because there was some other "truth" he didn't want to tell her . . . he lied to her on two significant matters at two different times for one reason and one reason only, and that was because he could not afford to tell her the truth about why the bedding had to go – never to be recovered – and then why the car had to go – never to be recovered'.

The reason, he said firmly, was obvious. 'Both were linked to the disappearance and – as was to be discovered 6 months later – the murder of Milly Dowler.'

Altman then took the jury to the site where Milly's body was discovered in Yateley Heath Wood, a place that Johanna Collings had told the jury that she and Bellfield had visited 'more than five times' to walk his whippets and train them to catch rabbits.

'So Milly disappeared from an area where the defendant lived,' he said, 'and at a time when he was actually present, and her remains were found in an area with which he was familiar.' Then Altman paused again before asking: 'What are the chances of that being a matter of pure coincidence?'

By now it was well into the afternoon of Friday, 17 June, and Altman was reaching the end of his closing speech. But before he did so he turned to the attempted abduction of the then eleven-year-old Rachel Cowles the day before Milly went missing. The prosecuting counsel told them that they were quite 'entitled' to use the evidence of Milly's disappearance to 'inform' their views about Rachel, and 'vice versa'. If there were similarities between the two events they could conclude they were the work of one man – Levi Bellfield.

'One important question for you,' he explained, 'is what are the chances of there being two large, big-built men, with round, chubby faces, linked with untidy red hatchbacks, with child seats in the back, appearing in the same area over two consecutive days, at the same time of day, targeting females to attack?

'Rachel, at the time looking in stature remarkably similar to Milly, wearing a ponytail, and also dressed in school uniform, shared with Milly another identical feature,' Altman went on. 'Both were walking home alone from school, and vulnerable, as indeed was each of the women the defendant chose to target in 2003 and 2004.'

Bringing his speech to its end, Altman finished by listing the links and similarities between the offences he had been describing. There were the geographical links in that all the offences – including those in his previous trial – had taken place in west London. There was the targeting of vulnerable young women. 'All of the defendant's victims,' Altman said, 'were vulnerable young women or lone girls' whom he'd either targeted on buses or spotted walking home alone quite by chance. There was the use of vehicles to flee the scene of his crimes, or in Milly's case, to dispose of the body, as well as the fact that the Ford Courier van in Amélie's case and the Daewoo Nexia had both disappeared entirely without trace. 'Speed of action and decisiveness' was another link. 'Milly disappeared from the street very suddenly, and without any opportunity to scream or call for help. In that respect, the speed of her abduction chimes with the speed and decisiveness with which the defendant later attacked his other young victims.' Then there was Bellfield's behaviour – the fact that he always turned his mobile phones off, and his 'forensic awareness' that led to the clean-up of 24, Collingwood Place. Finally, there was his decision to leave the flat in a hurry, similar to his decisions to take the family on holiday after the killing of Marsha McDonnell and after the killing of Amélie Delagrange.

'So those are similar features which we say point to these offences being the work of one man, that man being this defendant, Levi Bellfield.' They demonstrated 'a pattern of serial attacks upon girls and young women within a period of just over two years.'

But then he made his critical point.

'It would be contrary to common sense,' he went on, 'to say that there must have been two men with such capabilities appearing by chance in the same locality at the same time. You may wish to consider how likely it is that there were two such men, capable of committing murder, behaving in exactly the same way, in the same place, at the very same time.'

Pointing directly at the defendant in the dock, Altman concluded: 'The prosecution say that you can be quite sure that this defendant and no one else is responsible for these dreadful acts, and we invite you to find him guilty.'

And so, shortly before 4 o'clock on that Friday afternoon, Brian Altman sat down after addressing the jury for two days. It had been a virtuoso performance, and silenced the court room repeatedly, but it was not the end of the case.

To his left, Jeffrey Samuels, for the defence, remained seated. The jury would have to wait until the following Monday morning to hear his reply.

Bellfield, who had been writing pages of notes to his counsel throughout Altman's speech, was clearly upset that Samuels hadn't got to his feet immediately to begin the counter-attack. He left the court grumbling under his breath that he would be having a 'terrible weekend'.

The jury, of course, were not in court to hear it.

But they were certainly in court when Samuels got to his feet on behalf of the defence at 10.45 on the morning of Monday, 20 June.

Within minutes the contrast between the styles of the two barristers was clear for the jury to see. Unlike the meticulous, confident Altman, with each page of his speech typed out in front of him, there was the conversational, confidential Samuels with his hand-written notes all too clear for the jury to see.

But Samuels began with a touch of drama.

'Courage,' he said loudly, and suddenly. That is what the defence asks of the jury, 'courage to try the defendant according to the evidence'.

'This is trial by jury, not trial by media, or trial by Facebook,' he went on, the slight tone of Lancashire in his voice, then immediately defended his client's decision not to give evidence himself. 'The defendant has chosen not to give evidence, not refused . . . there is no obligation on him to prove anything, still less his innocence. People do not give evidence for all sorts of reasons. It does not alter the burden of proof one bit.'

It was for the prosecution to prove that Bellfield was guilty, Samuels said, and insisted that they were only criticizing his client's silence in an effort 'to mask the fundamental weakness' at the core of their case.

Samuels dismissed the prosecution theory about Milly's disappearance as 'pure fantasy', adding that they would not be 'doing a service to the Dowler family, still less to

Milly's memory, by convicting this man, however unattractive he may be'. And he looked at the jury steadily.

'The truth is the truth,' he told the jury, 'and its hall-mark is consistency.'

Rachel Cowles had failed to pick out Bellfield at an identification parade three years after she'd been approached by the man in the red car, and Milly Dowler was not entirely the girl in the ironing video, but a much more complex one.

Turning to Bob Dowler's evidence, he defended his questions. 'This not a court of morals,' he explained. 'No judgement should be made of a man's sexual preferences. But this is a murder trial, part of which looks at the time and place of Milly's disappearance. The subject cannot be avoided.'

She may have been 'uncomfortable' to go home to her father alone, he suggested. There was only one witness that put her in Station Avenue, and it was possible that she had turned the other way and walked away from her home. There were no other eyewitnesses who had seen her. There was no CCTV of her. There was not even any forensic evidence to put her in the flat at Collingwood Place.

'But for his convictions,' Samuels went on, 'you may think he [the defendant] would not be here,' for the prosecution had 'marshalled and tailored' evidence against him to fit their 'ludicrous theory'. Bellfield was now being 'paraded' in front of the jury as 'the local serial killer'.

'There has been an undue reliance on these convictions,' he added. 'There has been an artificial attempt to suggest similarities. The sad truth is that the police are no nearer to solving her disappearance now than in 2002.'

The prosecution's case, Samuels said quietly, 'was pure fantasy', and as he said it he looked directly across the court at each and every member of the jury.

Then, bringing his speech to a close shortly before 3 in the afternoon of Monday, 20 June, he reminded them that the 'burden of proof remains on the prosecution from first to last' and quietly resumed his seat after addressing them for just three hours.

It was the passionate speech of a man who believed in his argument, a speech for the common man, and his client should have thanked him profusely. But Bellfield remained impassive in the dock, though he did allow a smile to flicker across his face.

Later that afternoon Mr Justice Wilkie began his summing up of the case to the jury, instructing them in his light Scots voice that they must reach their verdicts 'coolly and dispassionately'. He was to spend the following day, and the morning of Wednesday, 22 June, reminding them in scrupulous detail of all the evidence they had heard. And at 12.41 that morning he sent them out to consider their verdict.

As they filed out of Court 8 the remaining four women and seven men – one young woman having been lost to illness during the trial – looked a little overawed by the task ahead of them, but the judge had complimented them on their concentration, and there was a determination about them as they left the court. For his part Bellfield sat staring at their backs. His fate now lay firmly in their hands.

The jury did not reach a verdict that Wednesday afternoon, and so the judge sent them home for the evening, so that they could reconvene the following morning to further consider their verdict. At that point it felt in court as though the trial was quietly coming to a close, without the drama that had been predicted by some. There had been no histrionics from the defendant, and the memory of the Dowlers' interrogation had dimmed. No one could have expected the high drama that was to unfold suddenly when, shortly after lunch on Thursday, 23 June, the jury asked to be brought back into court.

Amélie Delagrange's parents and Kate Sheedy were in the packed courtroom as well as the Dowlers; no one knew if the jury had even reached a verdict – perhaps they were there to ask a question of the judge.

The clerk to the court proceeded to ask them if they had reached a verdict on Count One – the attempted abduction of Rachel Cowles. The newly elected foreman simply replied: 'No.' The silence in Court 8 became almost suffocating. The clerk then asked whether they had reached a verdict on Counts Two and Three of the Indictment – the abduction and murder of Amanda Dowler. There was a slight pause, and at 2.32 on the afternoon of Thursday 23 June, the foreman announced in his soft voice that they found the defendant guilty on both counts.

Asked to stand while the jury's verdicts were read out, Bellfield remained studiously impassive. Then, as he was being led out of the dock to the cells, he yawned casually. But in the court beside him Sally Dowler and her surviving daughter Gemma let out a series of piercing screams and both collapsed to the green-carpeted floor with tears flooding down both their cheeks in what one newspaper later described as 'one of the most heart-rending scenes ever witnessed in the historic court building'. Bob Dowler and the Old Bailey's matron went to the aid of both women, but it was to be several minutes before either were able to climb back to their feet, to be helped out of the court while clinging to one another for support.

But the case against Levi Bellfield was not over. Mr Justice Wilkie instructed the jury to withdraw to continue its consideration of the case of Rachel Cowles. Indeed, later that afternoon, he was to send them home for a second night, as they had failed to reach a verdict – although he had by then instructed them that they could return with a majority verdict of ten to one.

The case might still be alive for the judge and jury, but it was over as far the media and the defendant were concerned. Bellfield refused to return to the dock from his cells at the end of the day. The reality was clear enough as far as he was concerned – he would be taking no further part in the trial, not even when it came to sentencing.

Outside the court it was also only too clear that the trial was over. No sooner had the guilty verdicts been announced in Milly Dowler's case than a tsunami of publicity swept across the media, completely drowning the court's scrupulously careful consideration of the case. Every television and radio news bulletin carried the details of the verdict within moments of the jury's decision, and within an hour the networks were playing their carefully prepared background pieces on the worst aspects of Bellfield's truly appalling character.

Two witnesses from the case even went into graphic detail about their time with the man in the dock. Emma

Mills told Sky News: 'He had been raping me for a few years. There was this particular night it was so bad that I thought he was going to kill me.' Johanna Collings, meanwhile, told ITV news: 'Once I ironed his trousers wrong for work and he went absolutely off his head. He beat me. He was biting, kicking, punching – everything.' Their statements went far further than anything they had been allowed to say in open court – had they done so there it would have unduly influenced the jury.

By the following morning the Bellfield case covered every newspaper in the land. There was relentless coverage of the blackness of Bellfield's character, and the fact that he had eleven children by five women – though without detailing their names or exactly whose children they were. His white, flat-faced police mug shot stared out from every single front page.

It was the prelude to the last act of the drama of Regina v Bellfield, a trial that had transfixed the nation for seven weeks in the early summer. Shortly before 10.45 on the morning of Friday, 24 June the trial, which had cost at least £2 million, came to a sudden and unexpected end. On an application from Jeffrey Samuels the judge ruled that he had no alternative but to 'discharge' the jury from making its decision on the Rachel Cowles case because of what he called 'an avalanche of adverse publicity' which was 'most unfortunate and deplorable'. The 'trigger had been pulled too soon' by the media, he said. Indeed, Mr Justice Wilkie then announced that he would refer the case to the Attorney General with a view to his taking out contempt of court proceedings against some of the media organizations involved.

'The one person who suffers most is Rachel Cowles,' he said, the despair clear in his quiet voice, for she was 'undoubtedly the victim of an attempted crime'. But she was to be denied 'knowing whether a jury had decided it was Levi Bellfield or someone else'. In the end her case was to be allowed to 'lie on the file', just as Anna-Maria Rennie's and Irma Dragoshi's had in the first trial, when Brian Altman announced for the Crown that they would not be seeking a retrial.

Finally, Mr Justice Wilkie turned to his sentence, though without the defendant in the dock to hear him. Bellfield had not even deigned to come to court from his temporary cell at Belmarsh prison. That fact was not lost on the judge.

'He is marked out as a cruel and pitiless killer,' he told the court. 'To this is added the fact that . . . he has not had the courage to come into court to face his victims and receive his sentence. He subjected Milly Dowler, a thirteen-year-old schoolgirl, to what must have been a terrifying ordeal for no other reason than she was at the wrong place at the wrong time . . . He robbed her of her promising life, he robbed her family and friends of the joy of seeing her grow up. He treated her in death with total disrespect, depositing her naked body without even semblance of a burial, in a wood, far away from home, vulnerable to all the forces of nature, thereby, as he clearly intended, causing her family the appalling anguish for many months of not knowing what had become of her.'

Mr Justice Wilkie then turned to the defence and pointed out firmly that it was Bellfield who had instructed his lawyers to expose to the world her 'most private, adolescent thoughts, secrets and worries' and to 'increase the anguish of her family, particularly her mother, Sally Dowler, in ways which were made dramatically clear to all in court'.

'But he has failed in what he intended. Milly's memory will survive and be cherished long after he is forgotten.'

The judge then announced that Bellfield would serve a term of life imprisonment without the chance of parole – a 'whole life' term – for the crimes.

The wheel-clamper and nightclub bouncer from a travelling family in west London thereby became the first man in modern legal history be given not one but two 'whole life' terms at two different murder trials. It is a distinction that Bellfield will take back with him to prison – and it sets him apart from his fellow murderers in infamy.

But this time there will be no chance for him to resume his place as a flash 'Jack the Lad' – one of the boys – in Wakefield, or anywhere else. Now he is the murderer of a child – a 'nonce' – and will suffer the brutal criticism, and the justice, of his fellow prisoners, a justice far less constrained than that he had faced at the Old Bailey. No matter how arrogant he may have cared to appear in court, no matter how affable before the jury, Bellfield will now forever be forced to look over his shoulder in prison for fear that his fellow prisoners might exercise their own private justice.

Yet not once has this brutal, devious, poisonous toad of a man offered as much as a single word of remorse for any of his appalling crimes; nor has he ever described what had really happened to Milly Dowler. That ushers him into a select pantheon of evil men, a pantheon that includes the Moors Murderer Ian Brady, whose victims included the twelve-year-old schoolboy Keith Bennett, whose smiling, bespectacled face has haunted the world since his disappearance in 1964 and whose body has never been found.

Like Brady, from this day forth there can be no escape for Levi Bellfield from the condemnation of the world, and yet that can do nothing to bring back to life the smiling, warm-hearted Milly Dowler, the girl whose little dance at the ironing board sent a shiver down the spine of every single person at his trial.

Epilogue: Milly's Memory

'A belief in a supernatural source of evil is not
necessary; men alone are quite capable of every
wickedness.'
Joseph Conrad, *Under Western Eyes*

Levi Bellfield's trial for the murder of Milly Dowler ended
on the day before what would have been the teenager's
twenty-third birthday – had she but lived to celebrate it.
Instead the life of this 'funny, sparky, enthusiastic teenager', as Mr Justice Wilkie described her, was brutally
snuffed out, robbing her of the chance to grow into what
the judge called a 'self-confident articulate and admirable
young woman'.

Yet in all the weeping and wailing that followed the dramatic finale of the trial of her murderer it was somehow
almost too easy to forget that Milly was the true victim of
Bellfield's crime, and that Bellfield was the true villain.
That grim reality – that this delightful, smiling schoolgirl
had had her life taken from her by a monster – seemed to
be overwhelmed in the avalanche of publicity. Outside
the Old Bailey, on the very afternoon that the case ended,
the world watched hypnotized as the Dowler family condemned the 'torture' they had suffered at the hands of
Bellfield's defence team, and how they had been forced to

pay 'too high a price' for the nightclub bouncer's conviction for their daughter's murder.

'For us,' Sally Dowler said, 'the trial has been an awful experience. We have felt that our family, who have already suffered so much, has been on trial as much as Bellfield. We have heard Milly's name defamed in court.'

'We despair of a justice system that is so loaded in favour of the perpetrator of the crime,' her husband Bob went on. 'It has often appeared almost incidental that this is a trial concerning the murder of our daughter.'

While their daughter Gemma insisted: 'In my eyes justice is "an eye for an eye". You brutally murder someone then you pay the ultimate price: a life for a life. So in my eyes no justice has been done. He took away my beautiful sister and he will now spend the rest of his life living off taxpayers' money.'

The last word was left to Sally Dowler, who said simply: 'I hope whilst he is in prison he is treated with the same brutality he dealt out to his victims and that his life is a living hell.'

It was an unprecedented outpouring of grief from the Dowlers about their treatment in court, and yet somehow the memory of the cheery schoolgirl dancing behind the ironing board while preparing to go to a Pop Idol concert seemed to get lost. The following morning, on the very anniversary of her birthday, the Chief Constable of Surrey police seemed to forget her too.

'The family's experience was so exceptionally traumatic that they now regret supporting the prosecution of Bellfield,' Mark Rowley wrote in *The Times*. 'While it is, of course, in the public interest to draw a line under an unsolved murder, I understand why they feel that way.'

It was a quite extraordinary remark from the senior officer in a force which had just convicted a man who would spend the rest of his life behind bars. The distinguished legal commentator Joshua Rozenberg was to write shortly afterwards: 'If chief constables are going to condone the refusal of witnesses to give evidence, dangerous criminals will escape conviction, and the public will be put at risk.' Turning to the Dowlers treatment, Rozenberg went on: 'Bellfield was entitled to put forward evidence that might suggest to a credulous jury that Dowler bore some responsibility for his daughter's murder. The jury had little trouble in dismissing this preposterous notion, though the same cannot be said for Surrey Police. After apparently concentrating their initial efforts on trying to implicate Dowler, they have apologized for missed opportunities that might have led to Bellfield being caught before he committed other murders.'

Surrey Police had, after all, knocked on the door of the fateful flat, 24, Collingwood Place, no fewer than eleven times before getting an answer, and they had never attempted to contact the local estate agents to see who might have been living there at the time of Milly's disappearance – even though the flat was barely 50 yards from the bus stop in Station Avenue. They had knocked on the door and talked to the residents of every single one of the other fifty-two flats in the block – but not number 24.

In the largest investigation in the force's history – costing £6 million – Surrey Police had also identified 256 people of potential interest, taken 5,000 statements, launched 15,000 separate investigative actions, used 100 officers in 3,500 house-to-house inquiries, but they had not linked the attempted abduction of schoolgirl Rachel Cowles on Wednesday, 20 March by a man in a red car with the disappearance of another schoolgirl, Milly Dowler, the following day at almost exactly the same time in the afternoon just three miles away. Had they done so, the lives of Marsha McDonnell and Amélie Delagrange might, just conceivably, have been saved, and Kate Sheedy's life prevented from being turned upside down on the very day she left her school as its head girl.

And what about the 'torture' of the Dowlers? In his article for the *Guardian* Rozenberg was equally clear. Bellfield's counsel, Jeffrey Samuels QC, he explained, was 'required to follow his client's instructions to the extent permitted by the experienced judge. Even so, those close to the case say that Samuels did not go as far as his client had wanted him to.'

Anyone who sat through their cross-examination, as I did, would agree that their cross-examination was a hideous experience for both Bob and Sally Dowler, but it is also one that they should have been better prepared for. The Crown Prosecution Service later insisted that they had explained the possibilities to Mr and Mrs Dowler, but their message clearly did not get through, or perhaps the CPS were too polite to tell them the truth about what might happen in court. Either way it is no fault of the defence, or the prosecution. This was, after all, a murder trial. In the first half of the twentieth century Bellfield's very life would have been at stake. Were the Dowlers seriously suggesting that a defendant should not explore every avenue if he were innocent of murder? The trouble, of course, was that Bellfield was a convicted murderer, which meant that to some – including perhaps the Dowlers – he did not warrant a serious defence. That is a misunderstanding of British justice. Any man, no matter how bad his character, is entitled to be treated as innocent until he is proven guilty and allowed therefore to use any arguments he may choose to in his defence.

As I explained to Rozenberg when he asked me about the case shortly after the end of the trial, 'The Dowlers were naive to think that Bellfield would not do everything in his power to make their lives a misery, and took great pleasure in it. But the villain here is not Jeffrey Samuels but Levi Bellfield.' But in the vast wave of publicity about the Dowlers' feelings, and Bellfield's sexual past – including eight women who told the *Sun* about their rapes at his hands after being given a date-rape drug, more than one of whom had been dressed up as a schoolgirl while they were in his power – the fate of Milly Dowler was overlooked.

For me that is no small tragedy, for she deserved so much more, as she had suffered so much and so brutally. Like Marsha McDonnell and Amélie Delagrange, Milly lost her life to that rarest of all murderers, a blitz attacker who kills complete strangers at random and for no apparent reason other than a delight in doing so.

She also demands to be remembered because of the implication that she may have been sexually attacked by Bellfield before her death. Thankfully, in spite of Bellfield's sexual attraction towards schoolgirls – who were all 'slags' and 'asking for it' – there is no evidence whatever that Milly Dowler was, in fact, sexually abused. Bellfield wanted pliant schoolgirls, rendered so by his date-rape drugs, not a spirited teenager who would have fought back, and by doing so enraged him still further. He would not have bothered with discussion, or waiting for a drug to take effect; death would have been his first and only response. Indeed, if the prosecution's case at her killer's trail is to be trusted, and there is no reason to suggest that it is not, there would have been very little time for a date-rape drug to take effect on the teenager or for there to have been rape followed by her suffocation and strangulation. In my view, the most likely reality is that she died as suddenly and decisively as Marsha and Amélie.

To see what I mean let us retrace Milly Dowler's last steps along Station Avenue on that sunny Thursday afternoon as she walked home from the station.

There had already been a string of terrible coincidences that delivered her there – she'd decided not to get a lift home with her mother, she'd decided to accept Danielle Sykes' sudden invitation to have some chips, she'd decided not to take the train back to Hersham but to walk instead – each and every chance decision putting her life at risk, without her knowing it.

If the prosecution's timing is correct, and the jury certainly accepted that it was, then Milly was at the start of Station Avenue beside Walton station's car park at 4.08 in the afternoon on Thursday, 21 March 2002, where she was seen by Katherine Laynes from the bus stop on the opposite side of the road. She was to disappear within the next forty seconds or so: CCTV camera two on the Bird's Eye building did not see any sign of her during its next forty-two-second rotation, when she should have been there. It did not see her on the south side of the road, nor on the north side, near the bus stop, though if she had been at the entrance to Collingwood Place she would have been hidden from the camera by the hedges.

So why did Milly cross Station Avenue, as she clearly did, and fall into the hands of Bellfield just yards from the front door of his flat? Did she cross the road in the hope that she might get a lift with her mother and sister, who would be driving back home at about that time, as the prosecution suggested? Or was she lured across the road by a trick? No one can be sure. But I believe that Bellfield may have enticed her across with an excuse. He may have waved at her, silently, appearing to need her to help him do something – say by tending to a sick animal he happened to appear to have in his arms. A trick would be typical of him.

The words of Sally Dowler during the trial stick in my mind: Milly was a 'polite' girl, she said in her evidence, and she was clearly one who would not have seen the danger in going across the road to help an apparently rather unthreatening man. Walking back from the station on a sunny afternoon, after chatting with her friends in the Travellers' café, her mind would certainly not have been set to red alert for danger. Milly was probably thinking about her school report, and the boys she was going to meet at the gig she was looking forward to the following evening.

Milly crossing Station Avenue at the very moment when the CCTV cameras couldn't see her was pure ill luck. Had her fellow Heathside pupil Katherine Laynes been on the other side of the bus stop, who is to say that she might not have fallen victim to Bellfield's subterfuge in place of Milly? Or what about April Kent, the Rydens' schoolgirl who had walked down Station Avenue in search of her brother and then set off back up the road again away from the bus stop? Had she been there moments earlier, is there not a chance that she might have replaced Milly as Bellfield's victim?

The tragic reality – in the words of Mr Justice Wilkie – is that Milly 'was at the wrong place at the wrong time and became a target of the unreasoning hatred' of a man whose loathing for women – and sexual abuse of them – had grown like an evil canker in his soul throughout the previous thirty-three years of his life.

I do not wish to speculate on the terrible fate that befell Milly once Bellfield had clapped his hand over her mouth and dragged her behind the hedges in Collingwood Place. Suffice to say she was bitterly unlucky that not a single soul saw the abduction.

Only one person can tell us how Milly came to meet her death – and that man is Levi Bellfield, and I am as certain as I can possibly be that he will never reveal the details, just as the Moors Murderer Ian Brady has never revealed the whereabouts of the body of Keith Bennett. Like Brady, Bellfield will take his secret to his grave.

If there is the slightest scrap of comfort in the story of Milly's abduction and murder it is that she did not suffer for long. She was not kept prisoner in a rat-infested sewer drain for weeks, for example, as seventeen-year-old Lesley Whittle was in 1975 by Donald Neilson, the man later to be called the Black Panther. Thankfully, if one can be thankful about such a tragedy, Milly was almost certainly dead by the time the Bird's Eye CCTV cameras spotted Bellfield's red Daewoo Nexia pulling out of Copenhagen Way at 4.32 that afternoon, barely twenty-two minutes or so after she disappeared. What happened during those minutes does not bear thinking about. On the evidence of the pathologist, it seems certain that Bellfield either strangled or suffocated the poor, terrified girl in the most despicable circumstance.

What did Bellfield do next? He almost certainly drove over to see his mother Jean, for his mobile phone was certainly in her vicinity at 4.48, and where else could possibly represent a better 'place of safety' than the home of the woman who had indulged his every whim, including wiping his bottom as a twelve-year-old?

If the prosecution's mobile phone expert was right, he then stayed at his mother's house for at least fifty minutes – but we have never heard a word from either Bellfield or his mother about what they might have talked about. Perhaps the travellers' code of 'Omerta' – preserving their secrets from outsiders – prevents it. This is, after all, man who signed himself 'Fat Gypsy Boy' in letters from Wakefield Prison and boasted that he hated the police, whom he called by the gypsy name of the 'gavvers' – though that didn't prevent him from sometimes acting as a police informant when it suited him.

What is not in doubt is that, later that evening, Bellfield went back to stay with his partner, Emma Mills, and their two children, before getting up at 'between three and four' the following morning to go back to Collingwood Place. The only logical explanation for that decision is that he went there to dispose of Milly's body – and he did so after disposing of her clothes and her possessions.

But even then his brazen, psychopathic brutality knew no bounds, for Bellfield left her naked body to rot in the open air in Yateley Heath Wood, 25 miles away from her home with nothing whatever to protect her from the elements, or the animals that roamed the woods. It was an act of unimaginable cruelty. Amidst all the brouhaha surrounding Levi Bellfield's crimes, and his trial for the abduction and murder of Milly Dowler, no one should forget for one moment that she was the only one of his victims who was humiliated and degraded in this desperate, ugly way.

It is her memory that we should never forget – an innocent, cheerful schoolgirl whose life was destroyed without a moment's hesitation and whose body was disposed of without a trace of humanity by a man who thoroughly deserves to be called a monster. As Mr Justice Wilkie put it: 'Milly's memory will survive and be cherished long after he is forgotten.' Let us pray that is the case.

Afterword

No one embarks on the biography of a serial killer without a lump in their throat and a sinking feeling in their heart, and I certainly had both when I began this book. Perhaps I should have known better, having been the official biographer of Frederick West in 1996, but that was a long time ago, and I had forgotten how much pain a work like this involves. But I was determined to capture in print the true nature of a most unusual serial killer – a man who may be sexually depraved, but has never been convicted of a sexual offence, and yet is also a man who kills totally at random with no apparent sexual motive, beyond a generalized rage at women. It is a psychological complexity that makes Bellfield very rare indeed, as does his ability to conceal the evil in his soul by charming woman after woman to have sex with him and bear his children. Monster though he undoubtedly is, his charm is not to be ignored – how else can you explain his eleven children by five partners, three of whom stayed with him in spite of the most dreadful sexual humiliation? I hope I have managed to convey that very particular, and sinister, quality.

This book could not have been written without the help and encouragement of a very large number of people, many of whom I prefer to thank privately rather than in public, though I must say at once that it would have been all but impossible without the support of the now retired Detective Chief Inspector Colin Sutton, who led the hunt for the murderer of Amélie Delagrange, and other senior officers at the Metropolitan Police. I would also like to pay tribute to the Crown Prosecution Service and the officers of Surrey Police for their politeness. They left me alone to work, but I did not rely on their help.

I would particularly like to thank my editor, Daniel Bunyard of Michael Joseph, who believed in this project as much as I did and without whom I could not have finished it, as well as his team, including Tamsin English, the copy editor David Watson and the editorial manager Samantha Mackintosh. I should also pay tribute to the many men, and women, who shared the press benches with me during Bellfield's trial, especially John McShane and Paddy Cooper. I also owe a great debt to my friends – including barrister William Clegg QC and Joshua Rozenberg – for their advice, although they should certainly not be held responsible for my conclusions, as those are mine alone.

Finally, and most importantly, I would like to thank Brian Altman QC and Jeffrey Samuels QC – and both their prosecution and defence teams – for their forbearance. I could not be more grateful. It is an unenviable task to prosecute or defend a murderer, but to criticize them for doing it to the best of their ability is grossly unfair. In our adversarial system of justice we are lucky to have such talented practitioners of their craft. Both men conducted themselves with immense restraint and dignity – in spite of what has been said about them in the press afterwards – during the most difficult days of the trial of Levi Bellfield, a man whose name is now destined, quite rightly, to live for ever in the annals of criminal infamy.

JACK HIGGINS

DIE
MORDBEICHTE

Roman

Aus dem Amerikanischen
von Dietlind Bindheim

PAVILLON VERLAG
MÜNCHEN

PAVILLON TASCHENBUCH
Nr. 02/0044

Titel der Originalausgabe
A PRAYER FOR THE DYING

Deutsche Erstausgabe 11/99
Copyright © 1973 by Jack Higgins
Copyright © der deutschsprachigen Ausgabe 1975 by
Wilhelm Heyne Verlag GmbH & Co. KG, München
Der Pavillon Verlag ist ein Unternehmen der
Wilhelm Heyne Verlag GmbH & Co. KG, München
http://www.heyne.de
Printed in Germany 1999
Umschlagillustration: H+Z Bildagentur/
Walter Allgöwer, Hannover
Umschlaggestaltung: Nele Schütz Design, München
Satz: Pinkuin Satz und Datentechnik, Berlin
Druck und Bindung: Elsnerdruck, Berlin

ISBN 3-453-16446-6

1

Als das Polizeiauto am Ende der Straße um die Ecke bog, trat Fallon instinktiv in den nächsten Hauseingang, wartete, bis der Wagen vorbeigefahren war, gab noch ein paar Minuten drauf und setzte dann seinen Weg zu den Docks fort. Es hatte zu regnen begonnen. Fallon stellte den Mantelkragen auf und hielt sich im Schatten, die Hände tief in den Taschen seines dunkelblauen Trenchcoats vergraben; ein kleiner, dunkler Mann, der mehr zu treiben als zu gehen schien.

Ein Schiff näherte sich aus dem Londoner Hafenbecken. Geisterhaft heulte das Nebelhorn.

Am Ende der Straße stand ein Lagerhaus, mit der Frontseite dem Fluß zugekehrt. *Janos Kristou – Importeur* war auf dem Schild zu lesen.

Fallon öffnete die kleine Judaspforte im Haupteingang und trat ein.

Der Raum war vollgestopft mit Ballen und Kisten verschiedenster Art. Es war sehr dunkel, aber am anderen Ende brannte ein Licht, auf das er zuging.

Ein Mann saß an einem Tischbock unter einer nackten Glühbirne und schrieb eifrig in ein großes altmodisches Hauptbuch. Der Mann war fast kahl, bis auf einen Kranz schmutzig-weißer Haare. Er trug eine alte Schaffelljacke und wollene Fausthandschuhe.

Fallon kam vorsichtig näher, und der alte Mann sagte, ohne sich umzudrehen: »Martin, bist du das?«

Fallon trat in den Lichtkegel und blieb neben dem Tisch stehen. »Hallo, Kristou!«

Auf dem Boden neben ihm stand eine Holzkiste. Der

Deckel lag lose obenauf. Fallon hob ihn hoch und nahm eine Sterling-Maschinenpistole heraus, die fett eingeölt war.

»Immer noch dabei, wie ich sehe. Für wen ist die da? Die Israelis oder die Araber – oder hast du inzwischen Partei ergriffen?«

Kristou lehnte sich vor, nahm ihm die Sterling ab und legte sie in die Schachtel zurück.

»Ich hab' die Welt nicht zu dem gemacht, was sie ist.«

»Vielleicht nicht, aber du hast höchstwahrscheinlich deinen Teil dazu beigetragen.« Fallon zündete sich eine Zigarette an. »Ich hab' gehört, du willst mich sehen.«

Kristou legte den Federhalter aus der Hand und blickte nachdenklich zu ihm auf. Er sah sehr alt aus. Seine Haut war ledern wie Pergament, faltig und zerfurcht, aber die blauen Augen hatten einen wachsamen, intelligenten Ausdruck.

»Du schaust nicht besonders gut aus, Martin«, sagte er.

»Ich habe mich niemals besser gefühlt«, erklärte Fallon. »Nun, was ist mit meinem Paß?«

Kristou lächelte gewinnend. »Du siehst mir so aus, als ob du einen Drink vertragen könntest.« Er holte eine Flasche und zwei Pappbecher aus einer Schublade. »Irischer Whisky. Damit du dich wie zu Hause fühlst.«

Fallon zögerte und ergriff dann einen der Becher.

Kristou hob den anderen hoch. »Mögest du in Irland sterben! So sagt man doch?«

Fallon spülte den Whisky hinunter und zerquetschte den Papierbecher mit der rechten Hand.

»Meinen Paß«, sagte er leise.

»Gewissermaßen steht es nicht mehr in meiner Macht, Martin. Ich will sagen – du bist in bestimmten Kreisen derartig gefragt …«

Fallon ging um den Tisch herum, stand einen Moment stumm da, den Kopf geneigt, die Hände in den Taschen des blauen Trenchcoats. Dann hob er langsam den Blick. Dunkle, leere Augen brannten in dem weißen Gesicht. »Wenn du versuchst, mich unter Druck zu setzen, alter Mann – gib's auf. Ich gab dir alles, was ich besaß.«

Kristous Herz setzte einen Schlag lang aus, und seine Eingeweide verkrampften sich. »Bei Gott, Martin – mit einer Kapuze würdest du wie der Tod persönlich aussehen.«

Fallon stand da, die Augen wie schwarzes Glas, blickte durch ihn hindurch und über ihn hinweg – und plötzlich wandte er sich um, als ob er gehen wollte.

Kristou sagte rasch: »Es gäbe einen Weg.«

Fallon zögerte. »Und der wäre?«

»Einen Paß, eine Schlafkoje auf einem Frachter, der Sonntag nacht von Hull nach Australien ausläuft« – er machte eine Pause –, »und zweitausend Pfund für einen neuen Start.«

»Was habe ich zu tun? Soll ich jemanden umbringen?«

»Erraten«, sagte der alte Mann.

Fallon lachte verhalten. »Du wirst immer besser, Kristou.«

Er griff nach der Whiskyflasche, kippte Kristous Becher aus und füllte ihn erneut. Der alte Mann beobachtete ihn abwartend. Der Regen trommelte gegen die Scheiben, als würde jemand Einlaß begehren.

Fallon trat ans Fenster und starrte auf die leere Straße. Ein Wagen parkte links von ihm an der Ecke einer Gasse. Das Nebelhorn tutete erneut – diesmal weiter flußabwärts.

»Eine häßliche Nacht.« Er wandte sich um. »Aber passend.«

»Wozu, Martin?«

»Für Menschen wie dich und mich.«

Er leerte den Becher mit einem Zug, ging zurück an den Tisch und stellte ihn sehr behutsam vor Kristou hin. »Gut. Ich höre.«

Kristou lächelte. »Nun wirst du vernünftig.«

Er klappte einen Manila-Aktendeckel auf, entnahm ihm ein Foto und schob es über den Tisch. »Sieh dir das an!«

Fallon nahm das Foto hoch und hielt es ins Licht. Es war ganz offensichtlich auf einem Friedhof aufgenommen worden. Im Vordergrund stand ein ziemlich seltsames Grabmal: eine weibliche Bronzefigur, die sich von einem Stuhl erhob, als wollte sie durch die Tür gehen, die zwischen den Marmorsäulen hinter ihr einen Spalt offenstand. Ein Mann in einem dunklen Mantel und barhäuptig kniete vor ihr auf einem Bein.

»Nun dieses.« Kristou schob ihm ein anderes Foto zu.

Es war die gleiche Szene – mit einer Ausnahme: Der Mann in dem dunklen Mantel stand nun und blickte in die Linse, den Hut in der Hand. Er war kräftig gebaut, mindestens einen Meter neunzig groß und hatte ein strenges slawisches Gesicht mit hohen, flachen Backenknochen und schmalen Augen.

»Sieht wie ein Mann aus, dem man aus dem Weg gehen sollte«, bemerkte Fallon.

»Eine Menge Leute würden dir da recht geben.«

»Wer ist es?«

»Sein Name ist Krasko – Jan Krasko.«

»Pole?«

»Ursprünglich. Er ist seit vor dem Krieg hier.«

»Und wo ist *hier*?«

»Oben im Norden. Man wird dir rechtzeitig sagen, wo.«

»Und die Frau auf dem Stuhl?«

»Seine Mutter.« Kristou griff nach dem Foto und starrte drauf. »Jeden Donnerstagmorgen erscheint er mit einem Blumenstrauß – egal, ob es regnet oder die Sonne scheint. Sie standen sich sehr nahe.«

Er legte die Fotos in den Aktendeckel zurück und sah wieder zu Fallon auf. »Nun?«

»Was hat er getan, daß er mich verdient?«

»Ist 'ne Geschäftssache. Man könnte es einen Interessenkonflikt nennen. Mein Klient hat versucht, vernünftig zu sein, aber Krasko wollte nicht mitspielen. Also muß er verschwinden. Und so spektakulär wie möglich.«

»Um die anderen zu ermutigen?«

»In etwa.«

Fallon kehrte ans Fenster zurück. Der Wagen stand immer noch in der Gasse. Er sprach, ohne sich umzudrehen, »Und was genau ist Kraskos Branche?«

»Was immer du willst – Klubs, Spielhöllen, Wettbüros ...«

»... Huren und Drogen.« Fallon wandte sich um. »Und dein Klient?«

Kristou hob verteidigend eine Hand. »Jetzt gehst du zu weit, Martin. Jetzt bist du unvernünftig.«

»Gute Nacht, Kristou.« Fallon schickte sich zum Gehen an.

»Schon gut, schon gut.« In Kristous Stimme schwang so etwas wie Panik mit. »Du gewinnst.«

Als Fallon zum Tisch zurückkehrte, öffnete Kristou eine Schublade und wühlte darin herum. Er holte einen anderen Aktendeckel hervor, klappte ihn auf und brachte einen Packen Zeitungsausschnitte zum Vorschein. Er blätterte darin herum, fand schließlich, was er suchte, und gab es Fallon.

Der Ausschnitt war an den Rändern bereits vergilbt und datierte achtzehn Monate zurück. Der Artikel trug die Überschrift: *Der englische Al Capone.* Das Foto zeigte einen großen, kräftig gebauten Mann, der eine Treppe herunterkam. Er hatte ein fleischiges, arrogantes Gesicht, einen Homburg auf und einen dunkelblauen, doppelreihigen Mantel an. Ein Taschentuch steckte in der Brusttasche. Der Jüngling an seiner Seite war vielleicht siebzehn oder achtzehn Jahre alt. Er trug einen ähnlichen Mantel, aber keinen Hut, und war ein Albino mit weißem, schulterlangem Haar, das ihm das Aussehen eines dekadenten Engels gab. Unter dem Foto stand: *Jack Meehan und sein Bruder Billy verlassen das Polizeihauptquartier in Manchester nach einer Vernehmung im Mordfall Agnes Drew.*

»Und wer war diese Agnes Drew?« fragte Fallon.

»Eine Nutte, die in einer Gasse abgemurkst wurde.«

Fallon blickte wieder auf das Foto. »Sie sehen wie zwei miese Leichenbestatter aus.«

Kristou lachte, bis ihm Tränen in die Augen traten. »Das ist wirklich zu komisch. Genau das ist Mr. Meehan. Ihm gehört eines der größten Bestattungsunternehmen im Norden Englands.«

»Wie – keine Klubs, keine Spielhöllen? Keine Huren, keine Drogen?« Fallon legte den Ausschnitt auf den Tisch. »Hier steht was anderes.«

Kristou lehnte sich zurück, nahm seine Brille ab und putzte sie mit einem fleckigen Taschentuch »Was würdest du sagen, wenn ich dir erzählte, daß Mr. Meehan zur Zeit vollkommen gesetzestreu lebt? Aber Typen wie Krasko setzen ihn unter Druck, sehr sogar – und das Gesetz will nicht helfen.«

»Oh, jetzt begreife ich. Üble Nachrede also.«

»So ist es.« Kristou schlug mit der Faust auf den Tisch. »Genau das.« Er setzte seine Brille wieder auf und sah gespannt Fallon an. »Also – abgemacht?«

»Zum Teufel damit! Ich würde weder Krasko noch deinen Freund Meehan auch nur mit der Zange anfassen.«

»Um Himmels willen, Martin, was bedeutet für dich schon einer mehr auf der Liste?« schrie Kristou, da Fallon sich erneut zum Gehen umwandte. »Wie viele hast du dort drüben getötet? Zweiunddreißig? Vierunddreißig? Allein vier Soldaten in Londonderry.«

Er sprang rasch auf. Der Stuhl kippte hintenüber. Er stürmte um den Tisch herum und packte Fallon am Arm.

Fallon stieß ihn zurück. »Alles, was ich tat, hatte einen Sinn. Ich hielt es für notwendig.«

»Sehr nobel. Und die Kinder in dem Schulbus, aus denen du Hackfleisch gemacht hast – hatte das auch einen Sinn?«

Er flog rücklings über den Tisch, eine eiserne Hand an der Kehle, und starrte in die Mündung einer Browning Automatic und in das weiße Teufelsgesicht Fallons dahinter. Es klickte, als der Hahn gespannt wurde.

Kristou wurde beinahe ohnmächtig. Er machte sich in die Hosen und verpestete die kalte, scharfe Luft im Lagerhaus. Fallon stieß ihn voll Ekel von sich.

»Nie mehr, Kristou«, flüsterte er. »Niemals mehr.«

Die Browning verschwand in der rechten Tasche seines Trenchcoats. Er wandte sich um. Seine Schritte hallten auf dem Betonboden. Die Pforte knallte zu.

Kristou rappelte sich kläglich auf, Tränen in den Augen – sowohl aus Wut als auch vor Scham.

Jemand lachte, und eine rauhe, aggressive Yorkshire-Stimme sagte aus der Dunkelheit heraus: »Damit sitzt du im wahrsten Sinne des Wortes in der Scheiße, Kristou.«

Jack Meehan trat ins Licht, seinen Bruder Billy auf den

Fersen. Sie waren beide so angezogen wie auf dem Zeitungsfoto.

Meehan hob den Zeitungsausschnitt auf. »Weshalb zum Teufel hast du ihm das hier gezeigt? Ich habe den Bastard, der diesen Artikel geschrieben hat, verklagt – und habe gewonnen.«

»Stimmt.« Billy Meehan kicherte. »Der Richter hätte auf einen Viertel Penny Schadenersatz geklagt, wenn die Münzen noch im Umlauf wären.«

Seine Stimme war schrill und widerlich.

Meehan schlug ihm mit dem Handrücken über den Mund und sagte zu Kristou, die Nase angeekelt rümpfend. »Geh und wisch dir um Himmels willen deinen Arsch ab! Dann reden wir.«

Als Kristou zurückkehrte, saß Meehan am Tisch und goß Whisky in einen sauberen Pappbecher. Sein Bruder stand hinter ihm.

Meehan kostete den Whisky, spuckte ihn aus und verzog das Gesicht. »Nun, ich weiß ja, daß die Iren immer noch mit einem Fuß im Sumpf stecken, aber wie können sie diesen Dreck trinken?«

»Tut mir leid, Mr. Meehan«, sagte Kristou.

»Es wird dir verdammt noch mehr leid tun, wenn ich erst mit dir fertig bin. Hast es ganz schön vermasselt, wie?«

Kristou befeuchtete seine Lippen und fummelte an der Brille herum. »Ich hatte nicht gedacht, daß er so reagieren würde.«

»Was zum Teufel hast du erwartet? Er ist ein Irrer – wie alle dort drüben. Schießen Frauen über den Haufen und sprengen Kinder in die Luft. Das gehört zum guten Ton.«

Kristou wußte nicht, was er sagen sollte.

Billy bemerkte naiv: »Er kam mir nicht sehr toll vor.

Ein kleiner Pinscher. Ohne das Schießeisen in der Hand wäre er ein Nichts.«

Meehan seufzte schwer. »Es gibt Tage, Billy, da bringst du mich zur Verzweiflung. Du hast soeben dem Teufel persönlich gegenübergestanden und es nicht mitbekommen.« Er lachte wieder rauh. »Das war verdammt knapp, Kristou. Er war rasend vor Wut – du alter Bastard. Wütend genug, um zu töten. Und das Schießeisen lag verdammt ruhig in seiner Hand.«

Kristou zuckte zusammen. »Ich weiß, Mr. Meehan. Ich hatte mich verrechnet. Ich hätte diese Kinder nicht erwähnen sollen.«

»Nun, was hast du also vor?«

Kristou sah zu Billy und dann wieder mit leicht gerunzelter Stirn zu seinem Bruder. »Sie wollen ihn immer noch haben?«

»Will das nicht jeder?«

»Das stimmt schon.«

Er lachte nervös, und Meehan stand auf und tätschelte seine eine Wange. »Du bringst es in Ordnung, Kristou, wie ein guter Junge. Du weißt, wo ich zu finden bin. Wenn ich bis Mitternacht nichts gehört habe, werde ich dir Fat Albert schicken – und das würde dir doch nicht gefallen, oder?«

Er verschwand in der Dunkelheit. Sein Bruder folgte ihm. Kristou lauschte verängstigt ihren Schritten.

Die Pforte wurde geöffnet, und Meehan rief: »Kristou?«

»Ja, Mr. Meehan?«

»Vergiß nicht zu baden, wenn du nach Hause kommst. Du stinkst wie der Misthaufen meiner Tante Mary.«

Die Pforte krachte zu. Kristou sank auf den Stuhl, nervös mit den Fingern auf die Tischplatte trommelnd.

Gottverdammter Fallon. Es geschähe ihm recht, wenn er ihn ins Kittchen brächte.

Und dann kam ihm die Erleuchtung. Die perfekte Lösung – und sie war so herrlich einfach.

Er hob den Telefonhörer ab, wählte die Nummer von Scotland Yard und ließ sich mit dem Sonderdezernat verbinden.

Es regnete jetzt ziemlich stark. Jack Meehan stellte seinen Mantelkragen auf, ehe er die Straße überquerte.

Billy sagte: »Ich hab's noch immer nicht kapiert. Warum ist Fallon so wichtig für dich?«

»Erstens gibt es niemanden, der so gut mit einer Kanone umzugehen weiß wie er – und zweitens ist alle Welt scharf auf ihn. Das Sonderdezernat, der militärische Geheimdienst – selbst seine alten Kumpels aus der IRA. Woraus drittens folgt, daß er ausgezeichnet verwendbar ist.«

»Was soll das heißen?«

Sie bogen in die Gasse ein und steuerten auf den Wagen zu.

»Warum um Himmels willen versuchst du nicht mal ein paar Bücher zu lesen? Du scheinst nichts wie Weiber im Kopf zu haben.«

Sie standen jetzt vor dem Wagen, einem Bentley Continental. Meehan packte Billy am Arm und riß ihn zurück. »Was zum Teufel geht hier vor? Wo ist Fred?«

»Eine leichte Gehirnerschütterung, Mr. Meehan. Nichts weiter. Er schläft sich auf dem Rücksitz des Wagens aus.«

Ein Streichholz flammte in einem nahen Hauseingang auf und entriß Fallons Gesicht der Dunkelheit. Eine Zigarette hing zwischen seinen Lippen. Er zündete sie an und warf das Streichholz in den Rinnstein.

14

Meehan öffnete die Tür des Bentley und schaltete die Scheinwerfer ein. Ruhig fragte er: »Was wollen Sie?«

»Ich wollte Sie sozusagen nur leibhaftig vor mir sehen – das ist alles«, sagte Fallon. »Gute Nacht!«

Er wollte gehen.

Meehan packte ihn am Arm. »Sie wissen, ich mag Sie, Fallon. Ich glaube, wir haben eine Menge gemein.«

»Das bezweifle ich.«

Meehan ignorierte die Bemerkung. »Ich habe vor kurzem diesen deutschen Philosophen gelesen. Sie werden ihn nicht kennen. Er behauptet, für ein verbürgtes Dasein sei die entschlossene Konfrontation mit dem Tod unerläßlich. Würden Sie dem zustimmen?«

»Heidegger«, sagte Fallon. »Himmlers Bibel.«

Er wandte sich abermals um, und Meehan baute sich rasch vor ihm auf.

»Heidegger?« wiederholte er. »Sie haben Heidegger gelesen?« Echte Überraschung schwang in seiner Stimme mit. »Ich verdopple das ursprüngliche Angebot und beschaffe Ihnen reguläre Arbeit. Fairer kann ich wohl nicht sein?«

»Gute Nacht, Mr. Meehan.«

Fallon verschmolz mit der Dunkelheit.

»Was für ein Mann!« sagte Meehan. »Was für ein hartgesottener Bastard! Aber er ist wunderbar, Billy, auch wenn er ein dreckiger Ire ist.« Er wandte sich um. »Komm, gehen wir ins Savoy zurück. Du fährst. Und wenn du dem Wagen auch nur einen Kratzer beibringst, zertrete ich dir die Eier.«

Fallon hatte ein Zimmer in einer Pension in der Hartgar Street in Stepney, auf der Höhe der Commercial Road; ein paar Meilen weit weg, nicht mehr. Deshalb ging er zu Fuß, trotz des Regens. Er hatte nicht die leiseste Ahnung, was er jetzt machen sollte. Kristou war seine einzige Hoffnung gewesen. Er war am Ende. Er konnte laufen, ja, aber wie weit?

Als er sich seinem Ziel näherte, zog er seine Brieftasche heraus und überprüfte den Inhalt. Vier Pfund und ein bißchen Silber. Und er war schon zwei Wochen mit der Miete im Rückstand.

Er ging in einen billigen Weinladen, um Zigaretten zu kaufen, dann überquerte er die Straße. Der Zeitungsverkäufer an der Ecke hatte seinen Stand verlassen und Schutz vor dem Regen in einem Hauseingang gesucht. Er war kaum mehr als ein Bündel Lumpen, ein alter Londoner Ire, auf einem Auge total blind, auf dem anderen auch nur beschränkt sehfähig.

Fallon ließ eine Münze in seine Hand fallen und nahm sich eine Zeitung. »Gute Nacht, Michael.«

Der alte Mann rollte ein milchig-weißes Auge in seine Richtung und wühlte mit einer Hand in dem Beutel, der um seinen Hals hing, herum. »Sie sind das, Mr. Fallon.«

»Wer sonst? Behalten Sie den Rest.«

Der alte Mann faßte nach seiner Hand und zählte mühselig das Wechselgeld hinein. »Da kam vor etwa zwanzig Minuten Besuch in Nummer 13.«

»Das Gesetz?« fragte Fallon leise.

»Niemand in Uniform. Sie gingen hinein und kamen nicht wieder heraus. Zwei Autos warten am Ende der Straße, ein weiteres dort auf der anderen Straßenseite.« Er zählte den letzten Penny in Fallons Hand.

Fallon ging zur Telefonzelle an der Ecke. Er wählte die Nummer der Pension. Die alte Frau, die die Pension leitete, hob augenblicklich ab.

»Mrs. Keegan? Hier ist Daly. Würden Sie mir einen Gefallen tun?«

Ihr kurzes Zögern und die Anspannung in ihrer Stim-

16

me verrieten ihm sofort, daß Michaels Vermutung richtig war.

»O ja, Mr. Daly.«

»Folgendes: Ich erwarte um neun Uhr einen Anruf. Notieren Sie die Telefonnummer und sagen Sie, ich würde zurückrufen, sobald ich heimkomme. Mir sind ein paar alte Freunde über den Weg gelaufen, und wir heben ein paar zusammen. Verstehen Sie?«

Wieder ein kurzes Zögern, ehe sie sagte: »Hört sich nett an. Wo sind Sie?«

»In einem Pub. Nennt sich *The Grenadier Guard*. In der Kensington High Street. Ich muß jetzt aufhören. Bis später!«

Er verließ die Telefonzelle und trat in einen Hauseingang, von wo aus er die Nummer 13 gut im Blickfeld hatte. Einen Moment später flog die Haustür auf. Es waren acht. Sonderdezernat, dem Aussehen nach. Der erste winkte wild, und zwei Autos tauchten vom Ende der Straße her auf. Die ganze Mannschaft stieg ein, und die Wagen rasten davon. Ein dritter, der auf der anderen Seite der Hauptstraße geparkt hatte, folgte ihnen.

Fallon kehrte zu dem alten Zeitungsverkäufer zurück, zog seine Brieftasche heraus, entnahm ihr die vier Pfundnoten und drückte sie ihm in die Hand.

»Gott segne Sie, Mr. Fallon!« sagte Michael.

Aber Fallon war schon über die Straße. Er marschierte zum Fluß zurück.

Diesmal hatte Kristou absolut nichts gehört, obgleich er etwa eine Stunde mit angespannten Nerven gewartet hatte. Er saß am Tisch, das Hauptbuch aufgeschlagen, den Fausthandschuh um den Federhalter gekrallt. Und plötzlich dieses häßliche Klicken, als der Hahn des Browning gespannt wurde.

Kristou atmete tief durch. »Weshalb, Martin? Was würde es dir einbringen?«

Fallon ging um den Tisch herum. Kristou stand auf, stützte sich, um sein Zittern unter Kontrolle zu bringen. »Ich bin der einzige Freund, der dir noch geblieben ist, Martin.«

»Bastard!« zischte Fallon. »Du hast mir das Sonderdezernat auf den Hals gehetzt.«

»Ich mußte es tun. Es war die einzige Möglichkeit, dich zurückzuholen. Es geschah zu deinem Besten, Martin. Du warst bereits ein wandelnder Toter. Ich kann dich wieder dem Leben zuführen. Kampf und Leidenschaft – das willst du doch, brauchst du doch.«

Fallons Augen waren zwei schwarze Löcher in dem weißen Gesicht. Er hob den Browning und drückte die Mündung zwischen Kristous Augen.

Der alte Mann schloß sie. »Also schön. Wenn du es nicht anders willst – bring es hinter dich. Ist das vielleicht ein Leben, dieses Leben, das ich führe? Nur vergiß eines nicht: Wenn du mich umbringst, tötest du dich selbst. Dann hast du niemanden mehr. Man wird dich einlochen oder dir eine Kugel verpassen.«

Es folgte lange Zeit nichts. Er öffnete die Augen. Fallon senkte langsam den Browning, preßte ihn gegen seinen rechten Oberschenkel und starrte ins Leere.

Kristou sagte vorsichtig: »Was bedeutet dir dieser Krasko schon? Er ist ein Gangster, ein Mörder – der Typ, der von jungen Mädchen lebt.« Er spuckte aus. »Ein Schwein.«

Fallon warnte: »Versuch nicht, die Sache zu beschönigen! Wie ist der nächste Zug?«

»Es bedarf nur eines Anrufs – das ist alles. In einer halben Stunde wird ein Auto hier sein. Du wirst zu einer Farm in der Nähe von Doncaster gebracht. Ein abgeschiedenes Plätzchen. Dort wirst du in Sicherheit sein. Zuschlagen wirst du am Donnerstag morgen auf dem Friedhof, den ich dir auf dem Foto gezeigt habe. Krasko läßt seine Schläger immer an der Pforte zurück. Er mag sie nicht um sich haben, wenn er gefühlsduselig wird.«

»Also gut«, brummte Fallon. »Aber ich mach's auf meine Weise, verstanden?«

»Ganz wie du willst.« Kristou öffnete die Schublade, holte einen Umschlag heraus und schob ihn über den Tisch. »Hier sind fünfhundert Pfund in Fünfern, als Anzahlung.«

Fallon wog kurz den Umschlag in seiner Hand, dann stopfte er ihn in die Tasche. »Wann bekomme ich den Rest? Und den Paß?«

»Mr. Meehan sorgt für den zufriedenstellenden Abschluß.«

Fallon nickte bedächtig. »Gut. Ruf an!«

Kristou lächelte, ein wenig triumphierend, ein bißchen erleichtert. »Du handelst klug, Martin. Glaub mir.« Er zögerte. »Da ist nur noch etwas …«

»Und was?«

»Der Browning. Er ist nichts für einen Job wie diesen. Du brauchst irgendwas Hübsches, Leises.«

»Mag sein. Was hast du anzubieten?«

»Was hättest du gern?«

Fallon schüttelte den Kopf. »Ich habe nie irgendein Fabrikat besonders bevorzugt. Damit können sie einen festnageln.«

Kristou öffnete einen kleinen Safe in der Ecke und holte ein Stoffbündel heraus, das er auf dem Tisch auswickelte. Es enthielt eine ziemlich häßlich aussehende Automatic, vielleicht fünfzehn Zentimeter lang, mit einem merkwürdigen Lauf von nochmals fünf Zentimetern.

19

Daneben lagen ein Schalldämpfer von siebeneinhalb Zentimetern und zwei Kartons Munition.

»Und was zum Teufel ist das?« fragte Fallon und nahm die Waffe in die Hand.

»Eine tschechische Ceska«, erklärte Kristou. »7,5 mm. Modell 27. Die Deutschen haben während des Krieges die Fabrik übernommen. Diese stammt aus der Zeit.«

»Taugt sie was?«

»Die SS hat sie eingesetzt. Aber urteile selbst.«

Er verschwand in der Dunkelheit, und wenige Augenblicke später ging am anderen Ende der Halle ein Licht an. Fallon sah eine Schießscheibe, wie die Armee sie benutzte.

Als er den Schalldämpfer auf den Lauf schraubte, gesellte sich Kristou wieder zu ihm. Fallon zielte mit beiden Händen. Er schoß noch zweimal, bis er genau ins Herz der lebensgroßen Soldatenattrappe traf.

Kristou sagte. »Hab' ich's nicht gesagt?«

Fallon nickte. »Häßlich, aber tödlich – wie du und ich.«

Sein Arm flog hoch. Ohne offensichtlich zu zielen, feuerte er zweimal und schoß der Attrappe die Augen aus.

2

Pater Michael da Costa sprach laut und unerschrocken weiter, doch seine Worte wurden vom prasselnden Platzregen fast ertränkt. Es hatte die ganze Nacht geregnet, und es goß immer heftiger. Pater da Costa war elend zumute. Es war nur eine kleine Prozession, die er zum Grab führte. Zwei Männer trugen den armseligen Sarg. Taumelnd folgte die Mutter, von ihrem Mann und ihrem Bruder gestützt. Es waren arme Leute, die mit ihrem Schmerz ganz allein waren.

Mr. O'Brien, der Friedhofsverwalter, wartete mit aufgespanntem Schirm am Rande des Grabes. Neben ihm stand ein Totengräber, der jetzt das Segeltuch vom offenen Grab zog. Es hatte nicht viel abgehalten. Das Wasser stand mindestens zwei Fuß hoch in der Kuhle. O'Brien versuchte den Schirm über den Priester zu halten, aber Pater da Costa winkte ab und reichte ihm statt dessen noch seinen Mantel. Er besprenkelte den Sarg mit Weihwasser, und während er betete, bemerkte er den wilden Blick des Vaters. Er war ein großer Mann, fast so groß wie da Costa; Vorarbeiter auf einem Baugelände. Da Costa wandte rasch den Blick ab und betete, gen Himmel blickend, für das Kind. Der Regen perlte in seinem zottigen, grauen Bart.

Es war nicht das erstemal, daß ihm die Banalität seiner Worte bewußt wurde. Wie konnte er einer Mutter erklären, daß Gott ihre achtjährige Tochter so sehr brauchte, daß sie in dem stinkigen Kanalwasser hatte ertrinken und zehn Tage darin herumschwimmen müssen?

Der Sarg platschte ins Grab. Die Totengräber zogen rasch wieder das Segeltuch über die Grube. Pater da Costa sprach ein letztes Gebet und wandte sich der Frau zu, die jetzt bitterlich weinte.

Er legte ihr eine Hand auf die Schulter. »Mrs. Dalton – kann ich irgend etwas für Sie tun?«

Der Vater fegte wütend da Costas Hand weg. »Lassen Sie sie in Frieden! Sie hat genug gelitten. Sie mit Ihren erbärmlichen Gebeten! Wozu sollen die gut sein? Ich mußte sie identifizieren – einen Klumpen verwesten Fleisches, der mal meine Tochter gewesen war. Was für ein Gott ist das, der so etwas einem Kind antun kann?«

O'Brien trat rasch dazwischen, aber da Costa hielt ihn zurück.

»Lassen Sie!« sagte er ruhig.

Daltons Gesicht bekam einen seltsam gehetzten Ausdruck. Er legte einen Arm um die Schultern seiner Frau und führte sie zusammen mit ihrem Bruder rasch weg. Die beiden Sargträger folgten ihnen.

O'Brien half da Costa in den Mantel. »Tut mir leid, Pater. Ein übles Geschäft.«

»Er hat nicht unrecht, der arme Teufel«, sagte da Costa.

Der Totengräber schien schockiert, während O'Brien langsam nickte. »Das Leben ist manchmal seltsam. Ich bringe Sie mit dem Schirm zurück zur Kapelle, Pater.«

Da Costa schüttelte den Kopf. »Ich kann noch ein bißchen Bewegung brauchen. Aber ich borge mir gern den Schirm.«

»Natürlich, Pater.«

O'Brien gab ihm den Schirm, und da Costa entschwand zwischen den Marmordenkmälern und Grabsteinen.

Der Totengräber sagte: »Ein verdammtes Eingeständnis für einen Priester.«

O'Brien zündete sich ein Zigarette an. »Nun, dieser da Costa ist kein gewöhnlicher Priester. Joe Devlin, der Küster von *St. Anna,* hat mir von ihm erzählt. Er hat während des Krieges mit Tito und den jugoslawischen Partisanen gekämpft. Später ging er auf das englische College in Rom. Er hatte eine blendende Karriere vor sich, doch nach seiner Priesterweihe beschloß er, in die Missionsarbeit zu gehen.«

»Wo wurde er hingeschickt?«

»Korea. Die Chinesen hielten ihn fast fünf Jahre gefangen. Danach gab man ihm einen Verwaltungsjob in Rom, damit er sich erholte, aber die Arbeit gefiel ihm nicht. Er ließ sich nach Moçambique schicken. Ich glaube, sein Großvater war Portugiese.«

»Was passierte dort?«

»Oh – er wurde deportiert. Die portugiesischen Behörden beschuldigten ihn, er würde zu sehr mit den Rebellen sympathisieren.«

»Und was macht er hier?«

»Gemeindepfarrer an *Holy Name.*«

»Diesem Trümmerhaufen?« fragte der Totengräber ungläubig. »Nur das Gerüst hält die Mauern noch zusammen. Wenn ein Dutzend am Sonntag zur Messe kommen, kann er glücklich sein.«

»So ist es. Dabei ist er ein guter Mann. Zu gut, um am falschen Platz zu stehen.«

Plötzlich war er der Unterhaltung überdrüssig.

»Schaufeln Sie lieber das Grab zu!« schnaubte er.

»Was – jetzt bei diesem Regen? Das hat doch noch Zeit.«

»Verdammt noch mal – nein.«

Gewöhnlich ging Pater da Costa gern im Regen spazieren. Heute nicht. Die Szene am Grab hatte ihn zu sehr aufgewühlt. Er blieb stehen und brach einen persönlichen Eid, indem er sich eine Zigarette anzündete. Langsam wanderte er weiter. Er kam in den ältesten Teil des Friedhofs, einen Abschnitt, den er erst vor ein oder zwei Monaten voll Entzücken entdeckt hatte. Zwischen Pinien und Zypressen standen prächtige viktorianische Gotik-Grabmäler. Bisher war er keiner Menschenseele begegnet, doch als er um einen Rhododendronbusch bog, blieb er abrupt stehen.

Etwa zehn Meter vor ihm gabelte sich der Weg, und am Schnittpunkt stand ein äußerst interessantes Grabmal: eine Tür zwischen Marmorsäulen, halb offen, davor die Bronzefigur einer Frau, die sich gerade von einem Stuhl erhob. Ein Mann in einem dunklen Mantel, barhäuptig, kniete vor ihr auf einem Bein. Es war sehr still – bis auf das Rauschen des Regens. Pater da Costa zögerte einen Moment – und da passierte etwas Außergewöhnliches.

Ein Priester trat durch das offenstehende Tor zur Ewigkeit, ein junger Mann in einem dunklen klerikalen Regenmantel über der Soutane und mit einem schwarzen Hut.

Was folgte, hätte einem Alptraum entstammen können.

Als der Mann in dem dunklen Mantel aufblickte, brachte der Priester eine Automatic mit einem langen schwarzen Schalldämpfer zum Vorschein. Es entstand ein dumpfes Geräusch, als er abdrückte. Knochensplitter und Gehirnmasse spritzten aus dem Hinterkopf des Opfers, das auf dem Kiesboden aufschlug.

Pater da Costa krächzte – Sekunden zu spät: »In Gottes Namen – nein!«

Der junge Priester, der eben auf sein Opfer zugehen wollte, blickte auf. Sein Arm flog automatisch hoch. Da Costa sah in das weiße teuflische Gesicht mit den unglaublich dunklen Augen. Und plötzlich, während seine Lippen ein Gebet sprachen, senkte sich die Waffe aus unerfindlichen Gründen. Der Priester bückte sich, um etwas aufzuheben. Die dunklen Augen fixierten noch eine weitere Sekunde die seinen, dann schlüpfte der Schütze wieder durch die Tür und verschwand.

Pater da Costa ließ den Regenschirm fallen und kniete neben dem Erschossenen nieder. Blut sickerte aus den Nasenlöchern, die Augen waren halb geschlossen, doch der Mann atmete noch.

Da Costa begann mit fester Stimme zu beten. Das Atmen endete abrupt in einem Röcheln.

Fallon ging über den nördlichen Teil des Friedhofes, rasch, aber nicht zu rasch; obgleich das keine Rolle spielte. Er war gut geschützt durch die Rhododendronbüsche, und es war ziemlich unwahrscheinlich, daß sich bei diesem Wetter irgend jemand hier herumtrieb. Das mit dem Priester war Pech gewesen. Wie gut man auch immer eine Sache plante, fast jedesmal trat etwas Unvorhergesehenes ein.

Er kam in ein kleines Gehölz. Der Caravan stand – gut verborgen – dort, wo er ihn zurückgelassen hatte. Der Fahrersitz war leer. Er runzelte die Stirn.

»Varley, wo sind Sie?« rief er leise.

Ein kleiner Mann in einem Regenmantel und mit einer Tuchmütze stolperte zwischen den Bäumen hindurch, keuchend, in einer Hand ein Fernglas. Er lehnte sich an die Seite des Caravans und rang nach Atem.

Fallon rüttelte ihn unsanft an den Schultern. »Wo zum Teufel haben Sie gesteckt?«

»Ich habe aufgepaßt«, japste Varley und hob das Fernglas hoch. »Mr. Meehans Befehl. Dieser Priester – er hat Sie gesehen. Warum haben Sie ihn nicht umgelegt?«

Fallon öffnete die Tür des Fahrersitzes und schubste ihn hinter das Lenkrad. »Halt die Klappe und fahr los!«

Er stieg hinten ein. Der Motor heulte auf. Der Wagen schlingerte über den zerfurchten Boden. Er öffnete das kleine Fenster zur Fahrerkabine.

»Sachte! Immer mit der Ruhe! Je langsamer, desto besser. Man erwartet, daß du nach einem Mord wie der Teufel rast – also verhältst du dich genau umgekehrt.«

Er zog den Regenmantel und die Soutane aus. Darunter trug er einen dunklen Pullover und graue Hosen. Sein Trenchcoat lag auf dem Sitz. Er zog ihn an und streifte dann die Gummigaloschen ab.

Varley schwitzte.

»O Gott!« stöhnte er, als er in die doppelspurige Straße einbog. »Mr. Meehan wird uns die Eier massieren.«

»Laß Meehan meine Sorge sein.« Fallon stopfte die Priesterkleidung in eine Segeltuchtasche und zog den Reißverschluß zu.

»Sie kennen ihn nicht, Mr. Fallon. Er ist der Teufel persönlich, wenn er wütend ist. Vor ein, zwei Monaten tauchte so 'n Kerl auf. Gregson nannte er sich. Professioneller Spieler. Hat einen von Mr. Meehans Klubs um fünftausend Dollar beschissen. Als die Jungens ihn anschleppten, hat Mr. Meehan seine Hände an eine Tischplatte genagelt. Und so hat er ihn fünf Stunden sitzen lassen – damit er über seinen Irrtum nachdenken konnte.«

»Und was hat er anschließend mit ihm gemacht?«

»Ich war dabei, als sie die Nägel herauszogen. Gregson war in einer fürchterlichen Verfassung. Mr. Meehan tätschelte ihn und riet ihm, in Zukunft ein guter Junge zu sein. Dann gab er ihm eine Zehnpfundnote und schickte ihn zum Arzt.« Varley schüttelte sich. »Ich sag' Ihnen, Mr. Fallon, er ist kein Mann, mit dem man sich anlegen sollte.«

»Er scheint offensichtlich auf seine spezielle Weise Freunde zu gewinnen und Leute zu beeinflussen«, sagte Fallon. »Diesen Priester – kannten Sie ihn?«

»Pater da Costa?« Varley nickte. »Hat in der Nähe des Zentrums eine zerfallene Kirche. *Holy Name.* In der Krypta hat er so eine Art Obdachlosenasyl für Gestrauchelte aufgezogen. Wahrscheinlich die einzige Gemeinde, die er gewinnen kann. Ist eine dieser Gegenden, wo sie alle Häuser abgerissen haben.«

»Klingt interessant. Bringen Sie mich hin!«

Varley hatte vor Überraschung das Lenkrad losgelassen. Der Wagen schleuderte heftig, und er hatte Mühe, ihn wieder unter Kontrolle zu bekommen. »Seien Sie vernünftig! Mein Auftrag lautet, Sie sofort zurück zur Farm zu bringen.«

»Ich ändere ihn«, erwiderte Fallon schlicht und zündete sich eine Zigarette an.

Die Kirche *Holy Name* lag in der Rockingham Street, eingequetscht zwischen glänzenden neuen Büroblocks aus Beton und Glas auf der einen Seite und schäbigen heruntergekommenen Lagerhäusern auf der anderen. Weiter oben an der Straße hoben Bagger bereits das Fundament für neue Betonklötze aus.

Varley parkte gegenüber von der Kirche, und Fallon stieg aus.

Holy Name war eine viktorianische Gotik-Monstrosität mit einem gedrungenen häßlichen Turm in der Mitte. Sie war mit einem Gerüst verkleidet, obgleich niemand hier zu arbeiten schien.

»Sieht nicht gerade nach Bienenfleiß aus«, bemerkte Fallon.

»Ihnen ist das Geld ausgegangen. Wie ich gehört habe, kracht das elende Ding demnächst zusammen.« Varley wischte sich nervös den Schweiß aus den Brauen. »Lassen Sie uns verduften. Bitte!«

»Gleich.«

Fallon überquerte die Straße und ging auf den Haupteingang zu. Auf dem Anschlagebrett standen da Costas Name und die Zeiten der Messen. Beichte war an Wochentagen um eins und um fünf. Er starrte einen Moment auf das Brett und lächelte dann.

Langsam wandte er sich um und kehrte zum Caravan zurück. Er lehnte sich ins Fenster der Fahrerkabine. »Dieses Bestattungsunternehmen von Meehan – wo ist es?«

»Paul's Square«, sagte Varley. »Nur zehn Minuten von hier, auf der Seite des Rathauses.«

»Ich hab' noch was zu erledigen«, sagte Fallon. »Sagen Sie Meehan, daß ich ihn dort um zwei Uhr treffen werde.«

»Um Himmels willen, Mr. Fallon! Das können Sie doch nicht machen!« rief Varley außer sich.

Aber Fallon war schon halb über die Straße.

»Bastard!« knurrte Varley und fuhr los.

Fallon ging nicht in die Kirche, sondern die Seitenstraße hoch, an einer hohen, grauen Steinmauer entlang. Sie umschloß einen alten Friedhof. Er trat durch eine seitliche Pforte. Flache Grabsteine hauptsächlich, und in einer Ecke stand ein Haus, vermutlich das Pfarrhaus. Es schien sich in etwa dem gleichen Zustand wie die Kirche zu befinden. Ein trauriger, düsterer Platz. Auf den blattlosen Bäumen lagen dicke, schwarze Rußschichten, jahrhundertealter Stadtdreck, den nicht einmal der Regen abwaschen konnte. Fallon wurde seltsam melancholisch. Das war also das Ende von allem: Worte auf verwitterten Steinen.

Eine Tür schnappte zu. Er wandte sich blitzschnell um. Eine junge Frau kam aus dem Pfarrhaus den Weg entlang, einen alten Trenchcoat um die Schultern gelegt. Sie hatte einen Spazierstock aus Ebenholz in der einen Hand und einen Packen Notenblätter unter dem anderen Arm. Fallon schätzte sie auf Ende Zwanzig. Sie hatte ein ernstes, offenes Gesicht und schwarzes, schulterlanges Haar.

Er schickte sich gerade an, eine Erklärung abzugeben, aber sie sah durch ihn hindurch, als ob er nicht vorhanden wäre. Und dann, als sie an ihm vorbeiging, bemerkte er, wie sie gelegentlich mit dem Stock gegen die Kanten eines Grabsteines klopfte.

Plötzlich blieb sie stehen, wandte sich um, leicht unsicher die Stirn runzelnd.

»Ist da jemand?« fragte sie mit einer sanften, angenehmen Stimme.

Fallon bewegte keinen Muskel. Sie verharrte noch einen Moment in der Stellung und setzte dann ihren Weg fort. Als sie eine kleine Tür an einem Ende der Kirche erreicht hatte, holte sie einen Schlüssel heraus, öffnete die Tür und trat ein.

Fallon ging wieder durch das Seitentor und um die Kirche herum zum Haupteingang. Er stieß die Tür auf, betrat die Kirche und registrierte mit einem schiefen Lächeln den typischen Geruch.

»Weihwasser, Weihrauch und Kerzen«, murmelte er leise und in einer Art Reflexhandlung tauchte er die Finger in die Weihwasserschale.

Das Kircheninnere verriet, daß in irgendwelchen grauen Vorzeiten jemand offensichtlich einmal sehr viel Geld dafür ausgegeben hatte. Ein Gerüst erhob sich aus einem Spinnwebennetz, stützte das Schiff am Altarende. Es war sehr dunkel. Nur die Ewige Lampe brannte, und vor der Jungfrau Maria flackerten Kerzen.

Das Mädchen saß an der Orgel hinter dem Chorgestühl. Sie schlug behutsam ein paar Akkorde an, und während Fallon das Mittelschiff hinunterschritt, begann sie Bachs ›Präludium und Fuge in D-Dur‹ zu spielen. Und sie war gut.

Er stand am Fuße der Stufen, lauschte und stieg dann hoch.

Sie hörte abrupt zu spielen auf und wirbelte herum. »Ist da jemand?«

»Es tut mir leid, wenn ich Sie gestört habe«, sagte er. »Ich habe Ihnen begeistert zugehört.«

Sie lächelte zaghaft und schien zu warten,

»Darf ich einen Vorschlag machen?« fragte er.

»Sie spielen Orgel?«

»Früher einmal.«

Er riet ihr, das Trompetenregister drinzulassen, und sie bedankte sich und wandte sich wieder der Orgel zu.

Fallon stieg die Stufen hinunter und setzte sich in die dunkelste Ecke, die er finden konnte. Sie spielte, und er saß mit geschlossenen Augen und verschränkten Armen da. Ja, sie war gut – war es ganz gewiß wert, daß man ihr zuhörte.

Nach etwa einer halben Stunde hörte sie zu spielen auf, packte ihre Sachen zusammen und kam die Stufen herunter. Am Fuß der Treppe blieb sie stehen, wartete, wahrscheinlich spürend, daß er noch da war, aber er rührte sich nicht, und so ging sie nach einem Moment in die Sakristei.

Fallon saß in der Dunkelheit und wartete.

3

Pater da Costa hatte soeben eine zweite Tasse Tee im Büro des Friedhofverwalters getrunken, als es an die Tür klopfte und ein junger Polizist eintrat.

»Tut mir leid, Sie noch mal belästigen zu müssen, Pater, aber Mr. Miller würde gern mit Ihnen sprechen.«

Pater da Costa stand auf. »Mr. Miller?«

»Kriminal-Superintendent Miller, Sir. Er ist der Chef des CID.«

Es regnete noch immer stark, als sie nach draußen kamen. Der Vorhof war vollgestopft mit Polizeiwagen. Sie schritten den schmalen Pfad entlang. Zwischen den Rhododendronbüschen wimmelte es von Polizisten.

Der Leichnam lag noch an der gleichen Stelle. Er war jetzt nur teilweise mit einer Plane zugedeckt. Ein Mann in einem Mantel kniete auf einem Bein daneben und nahm eine Art Voruntersuchung vor. Er sprach leise in ein tragbares Diktafon. Neben ihm auf dem Boden stand eine offene Arzttasche. Auch hier überall Polizeibeamte, in Uniform und Zivil. Einige stellten sorgfältige Messungen an, andere suchten den Boden ab.

Der junge Kriminalinspektor, der da Costas Aussage hatte, wurde Fitzgerald genannt. Er sprach mit einem großen, dünnen, ziemlich gelehrt aussehenden Mann in einem Regenmantel. Als er da Costa erblickte, kam er sofort auf ihn zu.

»Da sind Sie ja, Pater! Dies ist Kriminal-Superintendent Miller.«

Miller schüttelte da Costas Hand. Er hatte ein schmales Gesicht und sanfte braune Augen. Im Moment sah er sehr müde aus.

»Ein schlechtes Gewerbe, Pater«, sagte er.

»In der Tat«, erwiderte da Costa.

»Wie Sie sehen, sind wir bei der üblichen Routinearbeit. Professor Lawlor hier gibt eben seinen ersten Bericht durch. Heute nachmittag wird er eine Autopsie vornehmen. Im übrigen scheinen Sie offensichtlich der Schlüssel zu der ganzen Affäre zu sein. Wenn ich Ihnen noch ein paar Fragen stellen dürfte ...«

»Ich stehe natürlich zu Ihrer Verfügung, aber ich kann Ihnen versichern, daß Inspektor Fitzgerald sehr tüchtig war. Ich glaube nicht, daß er irgend etwas übersehen hat.«

Fitzgerald machte ein gebührend bescheidenes Gesicht, und Miller lächelte.

»Pater, ich bin seit nahezu fünfundzwanzig Jahren Polizist, und wenn ich eines gelernt habe, so, daß es immer etwas gibt – und gewöhnlich ist es dieses Etwas, womit man den Fall löst.«

Professor Lawlor stand auf.

»Ich bin fertig, Nick«, sagte er. »Du kannst ihn fortschaffen lassen.« Er wandte sich an da Costa. »Sie haben gesagt – falls ich Fitzgerald richtig verstanden habe –, daß er auf seinem rechten Bein am Rande des Grabes kniete.« Er ging zu der Stelle. »Etwa hier?«

»Genau.«

Lawlor wandte sich an Miller. »Es paßt. Die Einschußwunde ist etwa zweieinhalb Zentimeter oberhalb des äußeren linken Augenwinkels.«

»Sonst noch etwas Interessantes?« fragte Miller.

»Nicht wirklich. Die Einschußwunde beträgt 0,6 Zentimeter im Durchmesser. Sehr geringe Blutung. Keine Pulverrückstände. Keine Verfärbung. Austrittswunde fünf Zentimeter im Durchmesser. Explosivtyp. Splitterungen der Schädeldecke, Risse im rechten hinteren Gehirnlappen. Die Wunde …«

Er erging sich noch in weiteren medizinischen Termini, und Miller dankte ihm für seine Ausführungen.

Professor Lawlor wandte sich lächelnd Pater da Costa zu. »Sie sehen, Pater, die Medizin hat auch ihren Jargon – genauso wie die Kirche. Was ich eigentlich sagen wollte, ist, daß man ihm aus großer Nähe durch den Schädel schoß, aber nicht aus zu großer.« Er nahm seine Tasche auf. »Die Kugel – oder was davon übriggeblieben ist – dürfte nicht zu weit entfernt sein«, sagte er im Weggehen.

»Danke, daß du mich daran erinnerst«, bemerkte Miller sarkastisch.

Fitzgerald war zu dem Ewigkeitstor hinübergegangen und kam kopfschüttelnd zurück. »Sie machen einen Gipsabdruck der Fußspuren, aber wir vergeuden nur unsere Zeit. Er trug Galoschen. Und noch etwas: Wir haben das in Frage kommende Gebiet mit einem Staubkamm durchgekämmt, aber die Patronenhülse nicht gefunden.«

Miller runzelte die Stirn und wandte sich an Costa. »Sind Sie sicher, daß er einen Schalldämpfer benutzt hat?«

»Absolut.«

»Sie scheinen sehr überzeugt.«

»Als junger Mann war ich Leutnant bei einer Spezial-einheit der Luftwaffe. Jugoslawien. Mehr als einmal habe ich Angst gehabt, so ein Ding eines Tages selber benützen zu müssen.«

Miller und Fitzgerald warfen sich überraschte Blicke zu.

Pater da Costa ging jetzt seinerseits zu dem Tor hin-über. »Warten Sie – er hatte die Pistole in der rechten Hand, also sollte die Hülse irgendwo hier liegen.«

»Genau«, bestätigte Miller. »Nur können wir sie nicht finden.«

Und dann erinnerte sich da Costa. »Er kniete nieder und hob etwas auf, ehe er verschwand.«

Miller wandte sich Fitzgerald zu, der ein bekümmer-tes Gesicht machte. »Was nicht in Ihrem Bericht stand.«

»Mein Fehler, Superintendent«, sagte da Costa. »Ich hatte es ihm nicht gesagt. Es war mir entfallen.«

»Wie ich schon sagte, Pater – es gibt immer etwas.« Miller holte eine Pfeife hervor und begann sie aus einem abgewetzten ledernen Tabaksbeutel zu stopfen. »Dieser Mann ist kein dahergelaufener Strolch. Er ist ein Profes-sioneller vom Scheitel bis zur Sohle – und das ist gut.«

»Ich verstehe nicht«, sagte Pater da Costa.

»Es laufen recht viele von dieser Sorte herum, Pater. Vor etwa sechs Monaten raubte jemand fast eine Viertel-million aus einer hiesigen Bank. Er brauchte ein ganzes Wochenende, um in die Stahlkammer zu gelangen. Es stand sofort fest, daß für dieses handwerkliche Können nur fünf oder sechs Männer im Lande in Frage kamen –

und drei von ihnen saßen im Gefängnis. Der Rest war ein rein mathematisches Rechenexempel.«

»Verstehe«, sagte da Costa.

»Und nun zu unserem unbekannten Freund. Ich weiß bereits ungeheuer viel über ihn. Er ist ein außergewöhnlich cleverer Mann, denn diese Priesterverkleidung war ein genialer Einfall. Die meisten Menschen denken in Schablonen. Wenn ich sie frage, ob sie jemanden gesehen haben, sagen sie erst nein. Setze ich sie unter Druck, erinnern sie sich an einen Postbeamten – in diesem Fall an einen Priester. Und wenn ich sie frage, wie er aussah, dann sind wir schon am Ende. Denn alles, woran sie sich erinnern können, ist, daß er wie irgendein Priester ausgesehen hat.«

»Ich sah sein Gesicht«, sagte Pater da Costa. »Ziemlich gut.«

»Ich hoffe nur, daß Sie noch so sicher sind, wenn Sie ein Foto von ihm vor sich haben, auf dem er anders gekleidet ist.« Miller runzelte die Stirn. »O ja, er war clever. Gummigaloschen, wahrscheinlich ein paar Nummern zu groß – und dazu noch ein Meisterschütze.«

»Und er muß beachtenswerte Nerven haben«, bemerkte da Costa. »Er hat diese Patronenhülse noch aufgehoben, obwohl ich auf der Bildfläche erschienen war.«

»Wir sollten Sie zum Präsidium mitnehmen, Pater.« Miller wandte sich an Fitzgerald. »Sie machen hier weiter. Ich fahre Pater da Costa in die Innenstadt.«

Da Costa sah auf seine Uhr. Es war zwölf Uhr fünfzehn.

»Tut mir leid, Superintendent«, sagte er rasch, »aber das ist nicht möglich. Ich nehme um ein Uhr die Beichten ab. Und meine Nichte erwartete mich bereits um zwölf zum Lunch.«

»Und wann werden Sie frei sein?« fragte Miller ruhig.

»Offiziell um ein Uhr dreißig. Es kommt natürlich darauf an ...«

»Auf die Anzahl Ihrer Schäfchen?«

»Genau.«

Miller nickte. »Also gut, Pater. Ich hole Sie um zwei Uhr ab. Ist das recht?«

»Ich denke schon.«

»Ich bringe Sie zu Ihrem Wagen.«

Der Regen hatte etwas nachgelassen. Miller gähnte mehrere Male und rieb sich die Augen.

Pater da Costa bemerkte: »Sie sehen müde aus, Superintendent.«

»Ich bin letzte Nacht nicht viel zum Schlafen gekommen. Ein Autohändler hat seiner Frau mit einem Brotmesser die Kehle durchgeschnitten und dann die Polizei angerufen. Ein netter, einfacher Job, aber ich mußte trotzdem persönlich hin. Mord ist wichtig. Gegen neun war ich wieder im Bett, und dann riefen Sie wegen dieser Kleinigkeit hier an.«

»Sie müssen ein seltsames Leben führen«, sagte da Costa. »Was sagt Ihre Frau dazu?«

»Nichts. Sie starb letztes Jahr.«

»Das tut mir leid.«

»Mir nicht. Sie hatte Darmkrebs.« Miller runzelte leicht die Stirn. »Entschuldigen Sie – Ich weiß, Sie betrachten diese Dinge von einer anderen Seite.«

Pater da Costa erwiderte nichts, denn es wurde ihm mit plötzlicher Deutlichkeit klar, daß er an Millers Stelle wahrscheinlich genauso empfunden hätte.

Sie hatten seinen Wagen erreicht, einen alten grauen Mini-Caravan. Miller hielt ihm die Tür auf, und da Costa stieg ein und lehnte sich aus dem Fenster.

»Sie glauben, daß Sie ihn schnappen, Superintendent? Sie sind zuversichtlich?«

»Ich schnappe ihn, Pater«, sagte Miller grimmig. »Ich muß ihn schnappen, wenn ich an den Mann herankommen will, hinter dem ich eigentlich her bin – den Hintermann, den Mann, der den Auftrag gegeben hat.«

»Verstehe. Und Sie wissen bereits, wer das ist?«

»Ich würde meine Pension drauf setzen.«

Pater da Costa schaltete die Zündung ein, und der Motor heulte auf. »Etwas macht mir noch Kopfzerbrechen.«

»Was, Pater?«

»Dieser Mann, den Sie suchen, dieser Killer – wenn er wirklich so ein Professioneller ist, wie Sie sagen, weshalb hat er mich dann nicht ausgeschaltet?«

»Genau das frage ich mich auch. Bis später, Pater!«

Er trat zurück. Der Pater fuhr los.

Fitzgerald kam um die Ecke. »Das ist ein Mann, wie?«

Miller nickte. »Versuchen Sie alles über ihn herauszufinden. Alles. Haben Sie verstanden? Ich erwarte Ihren Bericht um dreiviertel zwei. Sie sind praktizierender Katholik. Es dürfte also nicht so schwer für Sie sein. Versuchen Sie es erst beim Friedhofsverwalter und dann in der Kathedrale.«

Er hielt ein Streichholz an seine Pfeife.

Fitzgerald fragte: »Aber warum, um Gottes willen?«

»Weil ich nach fünfundzwanzig Jahren Polizistendasein noch etwas gelernt habe: niemals irgend etwas oder irgend jemanden nach dem Augenschein zu beurteilen.«

Miller ging zu seinem Wagen, stieg ein, rückte dem Fahrer zu, und als sie die Hauptstraße erreichten, war er bereits eingeschlafen.

4

Anna da Costa spielte im Wohnzimmer des alten Pfarrhauses Klavier, als Pater da Costa eintrat. Sie wirbelte herum und stand auf.

»Onkel Michael, du kommst spät. Was ist passiert?«

Er küßte sie auf die Wange. »Du wirst es ohnehin bald genug erfahren, also kann ich es dir auch gleich erzählen. Ein Mann wurde heute morgen auf dem Friedhof ermordet.«

Sie sah mit leerem Blick zu ihm auf, die wunderschönen dunklen, nutzlosen Augen auf einen Punkt fixiert. »Ermordet?«

Er nahm ihre beiden Hände in seine. »Ich habe es gesehen, Anna. Ich bin der einzige Zeuge.« Er begann im Zimmer auf und ab zu schreiten und beschrieb detailliert, was geschehen war, nicht nur für sie, sondern auch für sich selbst. »Und er hat mich nicht erschossen, Anna! Das ist das Seltsamste. Ich verstehe es einfach nicht. Es ergibt keinen Sinn.«

Sie schauderte. »Oh, Onkel Michael! Es ist ein Wunder, daß du überhaupt hier bist!«

Sie hielt ihm ihre Hände hin, und er ergriff sie erneut, plötzlich von einem Gefühl der Zärtlichkeit durchflutet. Ihm wurde bewußt – und das nicht zum erstenmal –, daß sie das einzige Wesen auf dieser Welt war, das er wahrhaft liebte; was eine große Sünde war, denn schließlich sollte die Liebe eines Priesters allen gehören. Aber sie war nun mal das einzige Kind seines toten Bruders und seit ihrem fünfzehnten Lebensjahr eine Waise.

Die Uhr schlug eins, und er streichelte ihr über den Kopf. »Ich muß gehen. Ich bin schon zu spät dran.«

»Ich habe Sandwiches gemacht«, sagte sie. »Sie sind in der Küche.«

»Ich esse sie, wenn ich zurückkomme. Viel Zeit habe ich auch dann nicht. Ich werde um zwei Uhr von einem Kriminal-Superintendenten namens Miller abgeholt. Er möchte, daß ich mir ein paar Fotos anschaue, um zu sehen, ob ich den Mörder wiedererkenne. Falls er früher kommt, biete ihm eine Tasse Tee oder sonst irgend etwas an.«

Die Tür schlug zu. Es war plötzlich sehr still. Sie war noch immer ganz bestürzt und unfähig, zu begreifen, was er ihr erzählt hatte. Anna wußte wenig vom Leben. Ihre Kindheit hatte sie in Blindenschulen verbracht. Nach dem Tod ihrer Eltern war sie auf das Musik-College gekommen. Und dann war Onkel Michael zurückgekehrt, und zum erstenmal seit Jahren war wieder jemand dagewesen, um den sie sich kümmern konnte, der sich um sie kümmerte.

Wie immer suchte sie Trost in der Musik. Sie kehrte ans Klavier zurück und tastete über die Noten, suchte das Chopin-Präludium, fand es aber nicht. Und dann fiel ihr ein, daß sie am Morgen Orgel gespielt hatte. Vielleicht hatte sie die Noten liegengelassen.

Sie holte ihren Regenmantel und ihren Spazierstock und verließ das Haus.

Es regnete wieder stark, als Pater da Costa über den Kirchhof lief. Er sperrte die kleine Tür auf, die in die Sakristei führte, zog ein Chorhemd an, warf sich eine violette Stola über die Schultern und ging, um die Beichten abzunehmen. Er hatte sich verspätet, aber um diese Tageszeit kamen ohnehin nur wenige herein; an manchen Tagen wartete er die festgesetzte halbe Stunde, ohne daß überhaupt jemand erschien.

Die Kirche war feuchtkalt. Er hatte die Heizkosten nicht mehr tragen können. Eine junge Frau zündete gerade eine zweite Kerze vor der Jungfrau an, und als er an ihr vorbeiging, sah er, daß zwei weitere Personen neben dem Beichtstuhl warteten.

Er begab sich an seinen Platz und murmelte ein kurzes Gebet, aber es half ihm nichts. Die Szene auf dem Friedhof ließ ihn nicht los.

Auf der anderen Seite der Zwischenwand begann eine Frau zu sprechen. Der Stimme nach war sie mittleren Alters. Er konzentrierte sich entschlossen auf die Gegenwart und lauschte, was sie zu sagen hatte. Es war nicht sehr viel; hauptsächlich Unterlassungssünden. Als nächstes kam eine junge Frau. Sie begann zögernd mit Banalitäten und gestand schließlich eine Affäre mit ihrem Chef, einem verheirateten Mann, von dem sie nicht lassen konnte. Pater da Costa war angerührt von ihrem unerschütterlichen Glauben und erteilte ihr die Absolution, ohne ihr irgendwelche Versprechen abzunehmen.

Als sie gegangen war, fühlte er sich plötzlich ausgelaugt. Dann hörte er wieder das Klicken der Tür.

»Bitte, segnen Sie mich, Pater!« sagte eine fremde Stimme. Ein Ire. Ein gebildeter Mann zweifellos.

Pater da Costa sagte: »Möge Jesus dich segnen und dir helfen, deine Sünden zu beichten.«

Es entstand eine Pause, ehe der Mann fragte: »Pater, gibt es irgendwelche Umstände, unter denen das, was ich Ihnen jetzt sagen werde, an irgend jemand anderen weitergegeben werden könnte?«

Da Costa setzte sich auf. »Keine – was auch immer geschehen mag. Das Beichtgeheimnis ist unverletzlich.«

»Gut«, sagte der Mann. »Dann werde ich es besser hinter mich bringen. Ich habe heute morgen einen Mann getötet.«

»Einen Mann getötet?« murmelte Pater da Costa wie betäubt. »Ermordet?«

»Genau.«

Von einer schrecklichen Ahnung befallen, beugte sich da Costa vor und versuchte durch das Gitter zu sehen. Auf der anderen Seite flammte ein Streichholz auf, und zum zweitenmal sah er an jenem Tag in das Gesicht von Martin Fallon.

Es war ruhig in der Kirche, als Anna da Costa aus der Sakristei trat und auf das Chorgestühl zusteuerte. Sie fand die gesuchten Noten sofort, blieb aber noch ein paar Augenblicke vor der Orgel sitzen, an den Fremden mit der weichen Stimme und dem irischen Tonfall denkend. Er hatte recht gehabt mit dem Trompetenregister. Sie berührte es sanft, griff dann nach ihrem Stock und stand auf. Irgendwo unter ihr schlug eine Tür, und die Stimme ihres Onkels hallte zu ihr herauf. Sie erstarrte, verdeckt durch den grünen Vorhang, der neben der Orgel hing. Niemals zuvor hatte sie seine Stimme so zornig gehört.

Pater da Costa stürmte aus dem Beichtstuhl. »Kommen Sie heraus! Schauen Sie mir verdammt noch mal ins Gesicht, wenn Sie das wagen!«

Anna hörte die andere Tür des Beichtstuhls aufschlagen, leise Schritte und dann eine ruhige Stimme, die sagte: »Da stehen wir uns also wieder gegenüber, Pater.«

Fallon hatte die Hände in den Taschen seines Trenchcoats.

Pater da Costa trat näher an ihn heran und flüsterte heiser: »Sind Sie Katholik?«

»Selbstverständlich, Pater.« Ein leicht höhnischer Unterton schwang in seiner Stimme mit.

»Dann müßten Sie wissen, daß ich Ihnen unmöglich die Absolution erteilen kann. Sie haben heute morgen kaltblütig einen Mann ermordet. Ich habe Sie dabei beobachtet.« Er richtete sich auf. »Was wollen Sie von mir?«

»Ich habe bereits, was ich wollte, Pater. Sie sagten doch, das Beichtgeheimnis sei unverletzlich.«

Die Seelenpein, die aus Pater da Costas Stimme sprach, schnitt Anna ins Herz.

»Sie haben mich benutzt – in der übelsten Weise!« schrie er. »Sie haben sich dieser Kirche bedient!«

»Ich hätte Ihnen Ihren Mund auch mit einer Kugel verschließen können. Hätten Sie das bevorzugt?«

»In gewisser Hinsicht – ja.« Da Costa hatte sich wieder unter Kontrolle. Er fragte: »Wie heißen Sie?«

»Fallon – Martin Fallon.«

»Ist der echt?«

»Namen sind für mich wie Bestsellerlisten – sie wechseln ständig. Sagen wir: Als Fallon werde ich nicht gesucht.«

»Eine interessante Wahl«, sagte da Costa. »Ich kannte mal einen Priester dieses Namens. Kennen Sie die irische Bedeutung?«

»Natürlich. Fremder abseits des Lagerfeuers.«

»Und Sie finden das passend?«

»Ich kann Ihnen nicht folgen.«

»Ich meine, sehen Sie sich selbst so? Als romantischer Desperado – außerhalb der Gemeinschaft?«

Fallon zeigte keinerlei Gefühlsregung. »Ich gehe jetzt. Sie werden mich nicht wiedersehen.«

Er wandte sich um.

Pater da Costa faßte ihn am Arm. »Der Mann, der Sie für das, was Sie heute morgen getan haben, bezahlt hat, Fallon – weiß er von mir?«

Fallon musterte ihn lange, die Stirn leicht runzelnd, dann lächelte er. »Sie brauchen sich keine Sorgen zu machen. Es ist alles geregelt.«

»Für einen cleveren Mann scheinen Sie wirklich sehr dumm«, sagte da Costa.

Die Hauptpforte schlug im Wind. Eine alte Frau mit einem Kopftuch betrat die Kirche. Sie tauchte ihre Finger ins Weihwasser, machte einen Kniefall und kam das Seitenschiff hoch.

Pater da Costa faßte Fallons Arm. »Wir können hier nicht reden. Kommen Sie mit.«

Auf einer Seite des Hauptschiffes befand sich ein elektrischer Lastenaufzug, der offensichtlich von den Arbeitern als Zugang zum Turm benutzt wurde. Da Costa schob Fallon in den Förderkorb und drückte auf den Knopf. Der Korb schwebte zwischen den Gestängen des Gerüstes nach oben, passierte ein Loch im Dach und blieb schließlich stehen. Da Costa öffnete die Tür und führte Fallon auf die Laufplanken hinaus, die vom Gerüst gestützt rings um den Turm herumliefen.

»Was ist hier los?« fragte Fallon.

»Uns ist das Geld ausgegangen«, erklärte da Costa.

Keiner der beiden hörte das leise Surren des elektrischen Aufzugmotors. Der Käfig schwebte wieder in die Kirche hinunter. Als er unten angekommen war, stieg Anna da Costa ein.

Der Ausblick vom Turm dort oben auf die Stadt war fantastisch – trotz des grauen Regenschleiers. Fallon sah sich mit offensichtlichem Vergnügen um. Irgendwie hatte er sich verändert. Er lächelte kaum merklich, zitierte den Dichter Wordsworth.

Pater da Costa war irritiert. »Großer Gott, ich bringe Sie hier herauf, um ernst mit Ihnen zu reden, und Sie kommen mir poetisch. Berührt Sie eigentlich überhaupt nichts?«

»Ich wüßte nichts.« Fallon zog ein Päckchen Zigaretten hervor. »Bedienen Sie sich!«

Pater da Costa zögerte und nahm sich dann ärgerlich eine.

»So ist's recht, Pater. Genieße das Leben, solange du kannst.« Fallon gab ihm Feuer. »Schließlich gehen wir alle den gleichen Weg zur Hölle.«

»Sie glauben das tatsächlich?«

»Nach allem, was ich vom Leben gesehen habe, scheint es mir eine logische Schlußfolgerung.«

Fallon lehnte sich ans Geländer, rauchte. Pater da Costa beobachtete ihn einen Moment lang. Er kam sich seltsam hilflos vor. Dieser Mann war intelligent, gebildet, charakterstark – trotzdem schien es unmöglich, an ihn heranzukommen.

»Sie sind kein praktizierender Katholik?« fragte er schließlich.

»Nein«, erwiderte Fallon ruhig.

»Darf ich fragen, warum?«

Da Costa gab nicht auf. »Die Beichte, Fallon, ist ein Sakrament. Ein Sakrament der Versöhnung.« Er kam sich plötzlich ziemlich dumm vor, fuhr aber fort: »Wenn wir zur Beichte gehen, begegnen wir Jesus, der uns zu sich nimmt, und weil wir in ihm sind und bereuen, vergibt uns Gott.«

»Ich bitte nicht um Vergebung«, erklärte Fallon.

»Kein Mensch darf sich in dieser Weise selbst verdammen.«

»Nur für den Fall, daß Sie es nicht gehört haben sollten: Der Mann, den ich erschossen habe, hieß Krasko. Er war ein Zuhälter, ein Hurenbock und Rauschgifthändler. Und Sie wollen, daß ich bereue? Seinetwegen?«

»Das wäre Sache des Gesetzes gewesen.«

»Das Gesetz!« Fallon lachte rauh. »Männer wie er stehen über dem Gesetz. Ihn schützte seit Jahren eine dreifache Mauer, bestehend aus Geld, Korruption und Anwälten. Ich würde sagen, ich habe der Gesellschaft einen Gefallen getan.«

»Für dreißig Silberstücke?«

»Oh, für mehr als das, Pater. Sehr viel mehr. Seien Sie beruhigt, ich werde etwas in den Klingelbeutel werfen – für die Armen. Ich kann es mir leisten.« Er schnippte seine Zigarette übers Geländer. »Ich gehe jetzt.«

Er wandte sich um.

Pater da Costa faßte ihn am Ärmel und zog ihn herum. »Sie machen einen Fehler, Fallon, Gott wird Ihre Methode nicht billigen.«

»Seien Sie nicht albern, Pater.«

»Er hat bereits seine Hand im Spiel. Oder glauben Sie, es war reiner Zufall, daß ich in diesem besonderen Augenblick dort auf dem Friedhof war?« Er schüttelte den Kopf. »O nein, Fallon. Sie haben ein Menschenleben ausgelöscht, aber Gott hat Ihnen die Verantwortung für ein anderes aufgebürdet: für meines.«

Fallon sah jetzt sehr bleich aus. Er drehte sich um und steuerte wortlos auf den Aufzug zu. Ein leises Geräusch veranlaßte ihn, nach links zu schauen, und er erblickte Anna da Costa hinter einem Stützpfeiler. Er zog sie sanft hervor, aber trotzdem schrie sie vor Angst auf.

Fallon sagte sanft: »Es ist alles in Ordnung. Ich gebe Ihnen mein Wort.«

Pater da Costa eilte herbei und zog sie von ihm weg. »Lassen Sie sie in Ruhe!«

Anna begann zu weinen, und er hielt sie in seinen Armen.

Fallon betrachtete sie leicht stirnrunzelnd. »Möglicherweise hat sie mehr gehört, als gut für sie ist.«

Da Costa hielt Anna etwas von sich ab. »Stimmt das?«

Sie nickte und flüsterte: »Ich war in der Kirche.« Sie

wandte sich um, streckte die Hände aus und tastete sich zu Fallon hin. »Was für ein Mensch sind Sie?«

Eine Hand berührte sein Gesicht. Er stand wie versteinert da. Hastig zog sie ihre Hand zurück, als ob sie sich verbrannt hätte, und da Costa legte wieder schützend einen Arm um sie.

»Verlassen Sie uns«, flüsterte sie heiser. »Ich werde niemandem etwas von dem, was ich gehört habe, erzählen. Ich verspreche es. Nur gehen Sie, bitte, und kommen Sie nicht wieder. Bitte!«

Es war ein leidenschaftliches Flehen.

Pater da Costa drückte sie eng an sich.

»Ist es ihr ernst damit?« fragte Fallon.

»Sie hat es versprochen. Wir nehmen Ihre Schuld auf uns, Fallon. Und jetzt verschwinden Sie!«

Fallon wandte sich um und ging auf den Aufzug zu, Als er die Tür öffnete, rief ihm da Costa nach: »Es sind jetzt zwei, Fallon! Zwei Leben, für die Sie die Verantwortung tragen. Sind Sie dem gewachsen?«

Fallon stand lange da, eine Hand an der offenen Aufzugtür. Schließlich sagte er leise: »Es wird nichts geschehen. Ich gebe Ihnen mein Wort drauf. Mein Leben – wenn Sie wollen.«

Er trat in den Aufzug und schloß die Tür. Man hörte das leise Surren des Motors.

Anna sah auf und flüsterte: »Ist er weg?«

Pater da Costa nickte. »Ja.«

»Er war schon vorher in der Kirche gewesen«, erzählte sie. »Er hat mir gesagt, was mit der Orgel nicht stimmt. Ist das nicht seltsam?«

»Der Orgel?« Da Costa starrte verwirrt auf sie herab, seufzte dann, schüttelte den Kopf und drehte sie sanft herum. »Komm jetzt. Ich bringe dich ins Haus. Du holst dir sonst noch den Tod hier oben.«

Sie standen und warteten, daß der Aufzug wieder hochkam.

Anna fragte vorsichtig: »Was werden wir tun, Onkel Michael?«

»Mit Martin Fallon?« Er legte einen Arm um ihre Schultern. »Im Augenblick nichts. Was du mit angehört hast, war strenggenommen ein Teil der Beichte und ist nur wegen meines Zorns aus dem Beichtstuhl herausgedrungen.« Er seufzte. »Es tut mir leid, Anna. Ich weiß, daß dies eine unerträgliche Bürde für dich ist, aber ich muß dich bitten, mir zu versprechen, mit niemandem darüber zu reden.«

»Ich habe es bereits versprochen. Ihm.«

Als er wieder allein in seinem Arbeitszimmer war, tat er etwas, was selten so früh am Tage vorkam: Er goß sich ein Glas Whisky ein.

»Und was tun wir jetzt, Michael?« fragte er sich, in die Flammen des kleinen Kohlenfeuers starrend. Seit der dreijährigen Einzelhaft in einem chinesischen Gefängnis in Nordkorea hatte er die Angewohnheit, mit sich selbst zu reden. Aber dies hier war in gewisser Weise gar nicht sein Problem. Es war Fallons. Seine Hände waren gebunden.

Es klopfte an die Tür, und Anna erschien.

»Kriminal-Superintendent Miller möchte dich sprechen.«

Miller trat ins Zimmer, den Hut in der Hand.

»Ah – Superintendent!« sagte da Costa. »Sie haben meine Nichte schon kennengelernt?«

Anna war bemerkenswert beherrscht. Sie wirkte nicht ein bißchen nervös, was ihn überraschte.

»Ich lasse euch allein.« Sie blieb zögernd in der halbgeöffneten Tür stehen. »Wirst du weggehen, Onkel Michael?«

»Jetzt noch nicht.«

Miller runzelte die Stirn. »Aber das verstehe ich nicht, Pater. Ich dachte ...«

»Einen Moment, bitte, Superintendent!«

Pater da Costa warf Anna einen Blick zu, und sie schloß sanft die Tür hinter sich.

Da Costa wandte sich wieder Miller zu. »Was sagten Sie?«

»Wir hatten ausgemacht, daß Sie mich begleiten und sich ein paar Fotos ansehen«, sagte Miller.

»Ich weiß. Aber das wird jetzt nicht möglich sein.«

»Darf ich fragen, warum, Pater?«

Pater da Costa hatte sich seine Antwort genau überlegt, aber ihm war nichts weiter eingefallen, als: »Ich fürchte, daß ich nicht in der Lage sein werde, Ihnen zu helfen.«

Miller war äußerst verwirrt und ließ sich das auch anmerken. »Fangen wir also noch mal von vorn an, Pater. Vielleicht haben Sie mich nicht richtig verstanden. Ich verlange nichts weiter von Ihnen, als daß Sie sich ein paar Fotos ansehen – in der Hoffnung, Sie könnten unseren Freund von heute morgen wiedererkennen.«

»Das weiß ich«, sagte da Costa.

»Und Sie weigern sich, mitzukommen?«

»Es hätte keinen Zweck.«

»Warum nicht?«

»Weil ich Ihnen nicht helfen kann.«

Einen Moment lang glaubte Miller, den Verstand zu verlieren. Das konnte doch nicht wahr sein! Und dann kam ihm plötzlich ein schrecklicher Verdacht. »Hat Meehan Sie in irgendeiner Weise bestochen?«

»Meehan?«

Pater da Costas Verwirrung war so echt, daß Miller den Gedanken sofort wieder fallen ließ.

»Ich hätte Sie vorladen können, Pater – als Tatzeuge.«

»Sie können einen Gaul zur Tränke schleppen, aber Sie können ihn nicht zwingen, zu trinken.«

»Ich könnte es verdammt noch mal versuchen«, sagte Miller grimmig. Er steuerte auf die Tür zu und öffnete sie. »Zwingen Sie mich nicht zu einer offiziellen Vorladung, Sir!«

»Superintendent Miller, schon weitaus härtere Typen als Sie haben versucht, mich zum Sprechen zu bringen. Sie hatten keinen Erfolg, und ich versichere Ihnen, Sie werden auch keinen haben. Keine Macht der Welt wird mich dazu bringen, über diese Angelegenheit zu reden, wenn ich es nicht will.«

»Wir werden sehen, Sir. Ich lasse Ihnen etwas Zeit, darüber nachzudenken.« Er war schon auf dem Weg nach draußen, als ihm plötzlich ein verrückter Gedanke kam. Langsam wandte er sich um. »Haben Sie ihn seit heute morgen noch einmal gesehen, Sir? Sind Sie bedroht worden? Ist Ihr Leben irgendwie in Gefahr?«

»Auf Wiedersehen, Superintendent«, sagte da Costa.

Die Eingangstür schlug zu.

Da Costa trank seinen Whisky aus.

Anna schlich ins Zimmer. Sie legte eine Hand auf seinen einen Arm. »Er wird zu Monsignore Halloran gehen.«

»Der Bischof weilt zur Zeit in Rom. Ja, das wäre naheliegend.«

»Solltest du nicht lieber vorher zu ihm gehen?«

»Vermutlich.« Er leerte sein Glas und stellte es auf den Marmor-Kaminsims. »Was wirst du tun?«

»Ich werde etwas auf der Orgel üben.«

Sie drängte ihn auf den Flur hinaus und holte zielsicher seinen Mantel.

»Was würde ich nur ohne dich anfangen?« fragte er.

Sie lächelte liebevoll. »Weiß der Himmel. Komm schnell zurück!«

Er ging, und sie schloß die Tür hinter ihm. Das Lächeln auf ihrem Gesicht erstarb. Sie kehrte ins Arbeitszimmer zurück, setzte sich ans Feuer und barg ihr Gesicht in den Händen.

Nick Miller war seit fast einem Vierteljahrhundert Polizeibeamter. Fünfundzwanzig Jahre, in denen er die Abneigung der Nachbarn zu spüren bekommen hatte, in denen er von sieben nur ein Wochenende hatte zu Hause verbringen und sich mit seinem Sohn und seiner Tochter beschäftigen können. Er hatte keine großartige Ausbildung genossen, aber er war ein cleverer Mann, der bis ins Herz der Dinge zu sehen vermochte. Diese Fähigkeit und seine umfassende Kenntnis der menschlichen Natur, die er sich in tausend langen mühsamen Wochenendnächten zulegte, hatten ihn zu einem guten Polizisten gemacht. Er hatte weder die Idee noch den Wunsch, der Gesellschaft helfen zu wollen. Sein Job bestand in erster Linie darin, Diebe zu schnappen. Und letztlich waren ihm die Verbrecher lieber als die sogenannten Bürger; bei ihnen wußte man wenigstens, woran man war. Aber Dandy Jack Meehan war etwas anderes. Miller jagte ihn mit einem Haß, der fast selbstzerstörerisch war. Genaugenommen war er zehn Jahre hinter Dandy Jack her – ohne den geringsten Erfolg. Und nun hatte er zum erstenmal eine Chance. Und da stellte sich dieser Priester …

Wütend ließ er sich auf den Rücksitz des Wagens fallen. Und einem plötzlichen Impuls folgend, lehnte er sich vor und trug seinem Chauffeur auf, ihn zu Meehans Bestattungsunternehmen zu fahren.

5

Paul's Square war eine grüne Insel im Herzen der Stadt, eine Rasenfläche mit Blumenbeeten und Weiden und einem Springbrunnen in der Mitte, umgeben ringsum von gepflegten georgianischen Terrassenhäusern, in denen vor allem Rechtsanwälte und Ärzte ihre Praxen hatten. Meehans Bestattungsunternehmen paßte perfekt in diese gediegene Umgebung. Es umfaßte drei Häuser auf der Nordseite, einschließlich eines Blumenladens und einer Leichenhalle. Durch eine versteckte Toreinfahrt kam man zum Parkplatz und den Garagen. Hohe Mauern sorgten für den ruhigen und ungestörten Ablauf der Geschäfte – jederlei Art.

Der große Bentley-Leichenwagen fuhr kurz nach ein Uhr auf den Parkplatz. Meehan saß vorn mit Billy und dem Chauffeur. Er trug wie üblich seinen doppelreihigen Mantel, den Homburg und eine schwarze Krawatte, denn er hatte am Morgen persönlich einem Begräbnis beigewohnt. Der Chauffeur ging um den Wagen und öffnete die Tür. Meehan stieg aus, sein Bruder folgte.

»Danke, Donner«, sagte Meehan.

Ein kleiner grauer Whippet schlürfte aus einem Napf am Hintereingang.

Billy rief: »Hierher, Tommy!«

Der Hund flitzte über den Hof und sprang in Billys Arme. Billy kraulte ihn hinter den Ohren, und der Hund leckte aufgeregt Billys Gesicht ab.

»Na, du kleiner Bastard«, murmelte Billy zärtlich.

»Ich habe dir schon mehrmals gesagt, daß er deinen Mantel ruinieren wird«, schnauzte Meehan. »Überall diese Haare!«

Als er auf den Hintereingang zusteuerte, kam Varley aus der Garage. Er blieb abwartend stehen, die Mütze in der Hand. Ein Muskel seiner rechten Wange zuckte nervös, von seiner Stirn tropfte Schweiß. Er schien kurz vor dem Zusammenbruch.

Meehan blieb stehen, die Hände in den Taschen, und musterte ihn ruhig. »Du siehst schlecht aus, Charlie. Warst wohl ein böser Junge, hm?«

»Nicht ich, Mr. Meehan. Dieser Saukerl Fallon war es. Er …«

»Nicht hier, Charlie«, sagte Meehan sanft. »Schlechte Nachrichten höre ich immer gern privat.«

Er nickte Donner zu, der die Hintertür öffnete. Meehan ging in die Aufnahme. In der Mitte stand auf einem Rollwagen ein Sarg, sonst war das Zimmer leer.

Er steckte sich eine Zigarette zwischen die Lippen und bückte sich, um den Namen auf der Messingplatte des Sarges zu lesen.

»Für wann ist das?«

Donner trat an seine Seite, ein Feuerzeug bereithaltend. »Drei Uhr dreißig, Mr. Meehan.«

Donner sprach mit australischem Akzent. Er hatte einen leicht verzogenen Mund; die Wunde von der plastischen Operation war noch deutlich sichtbar. Die maßgeschneiderte dunkle Uniform milderte etwas sein abstoßendes Äußeres.

»Ist es eine Einäscherung?«

Donner schüttelte den Kopf. »Eine Beerdigung, Mr. Meehan.«

Meehan nickte. »Gut. Kümmere dich mit Bonati darum. Ich werde wohl beschäftigt sein.«

Er wandte sich um, einen Arm auf dem Sarg. Billy lehnte an der Wand und kraulte den Whippet. Varley stand wartend in der Mitte des Raumes, die Mütze in der Hand. Er schien zu fürchten, daß sich jeden Moment der Boden unter ihm auftun könnte.

»Alsdann, Charlie. Erzähl schon!« drängte Meehan.

Varley erzählte. Die Worte purzelten durcheinander in seinem Eifer, alles loszuwerden. Als er geendet hatte, folgte langes Schweigen. Meehan hatte keine Miene verzogen.

»Dann kommt er also um zwei Uhr her?« fragte er schließlich.

»Das hat er gesagt, Mr. Meehan.«

»Und der Caravan? Hast du ihn auf den Schrotthof gebracht, wie ich dir gesagt habe?«

»Ich sah mit eigenen Augen, wie er in die Zerkleinerungsmaschine wanderte.«

Varley wartete, das Gesicht schweißüberströmt.

Und plötzlich lächelte Meehan und tätschelte Varleys Wange. »Du hast es gut gemacht, Charlie. War nicht dein Fehler, daß die Sache anders lief. Überlaß es mir. Ich werde mich drum kümmern.«

»Danke, Mr. Meehan«, sagte Varley erleichtert. »Ich tat mein Bestes. Ehrlich. Sie kennen mich.«

»Iß was und dann marsch zurück zur Autowaschanlage! Wenn ich dich brauche, schicke ich nach dir.«

Varley ging hinaus.

Billy kicherte. »Ich hab' dir gesagt, daß es Ärger mit ihm geben wird. Wir hätten es selbst erledigen können. Aber du wolltest ja nicht hören.«

Meehan packte ihn an den langen, weißen Haaren. Der Junge schrie auf und ließ den Hund fallen.

»Möchtest du, daß ich unangenehm werde, Billy?« fragte er sanft. »Möchtest du das?«

»Ich habe es nicht böse gemeint, Jack«, winselte der Junge.

Meehan schubste ihn von sich. »Dann sei ein guter Junge. Sag Bonati, daß ich ihn sehen möchte, und dann schnapp dir eines der Autos und hol Fat Albert!«

Billys Zunge zuckte nervös zwischen seinen Lippen. »Fat Albert? Um Himmels willen, Jack, du weißt, daß ich es nicht aushalte, auch nur in der Nähe dieses Monsters zu sein. Er jagt mir Todesängste ein.«

»Das ist gut. Daran werde ich mich erinnern, wenn du wieder aus der Reihe tanzt.« Er lachte mißtönend.

Billys Augen weiteten sich. »Nein – bitte – Jack! Nicht Albert!«

»Dann sei ein guter Junge.« Meehan tätschelte ihn und öffnete die Tür. »Also los!«

Billy ging hinaus, und Meehan wandte sich mit einem Seufzer an Donner. »Ich weiß nicht, was ich mit ihm machen soll, Frank.«

»Er ist jung, Mr. Meehan.«

»Hat nichts weiter als Flittchen im Kopf. Schmutzige kleine Nutten in Miniröcken, die alles herzeigen, was sie zu bieten haben.« Er schüttelte sich angewidert. »Ich hab' ihn eines Nachmittags sogar mit der Putzfrau erwischt. Mindestens fünfundfünfzig war sie. Und auf meinem Bett!«

Donner schwieg diplomatisch, und Meehan öffnete eine Tür und ging voraus in die Leichenhalle. Es war kühl und frisch dort drin, dank der Klimaanlage, und es duftete nach Blumen. Orgelmusik auf Tonband sorgte für die passende feierliche Atmosphäre. Sechs Nischen befanden sich auf beiden Seiten.

Meehan nahm seinen Hut ab und betrat die erste. Ein Eichensarg stand auf einem verhangenen Rollwagen, ringsum mit Blumen geschmückt.

»Wer ist das?«

»Das junge Mädchen. Die Studentin, die durch die Windschutzscheibe des Sportwagens flog«, erklärte Donner.

»Ach ja. Ich habe sie selbst hergerichtet.«

Er hob das Tuch vom Gesicht. Das Mädchen war vielleicht achtzehn oder neunzehn. Man hätte glauben können, sie schliefe, so geschickt war sie zurechtgemacht worden.

»Da haben Sie toll was geleistet, Mr. Meehan«, sagte Donner.

Meehan nickte selbstzufrieden. »Als man sie mir brachte, war von ihrer linken Wange kein Fleischfetzen mehr übrig. Hackfleisch war ihr Gesicht, glaub es mir.«

»Sie sind ein Künstler, Mr. Meehan.« Echte Bewunderung schwang in seiner Stimme mit. »Ein wirklicher Künstler.«

»Nett, daß du das sagst, Frank. Ich weiß das zu schätzen.« Meehan drehte das Licht aus und ging wieder hinaus. »Ich versuche natürlich immer mein Bestes, aber bei so einem jungen Mädchen … Man muß an die Eltern denken.«

»Sehr wahr, Mr. Meehan.«

Sie kamen in die Eingangshalle. Hier waren die georgianischen Stilelemente noch wundervoll erhalten. Rechts kam man durch eine Glastür in das Empfangsbüro. Stimmen drangen zu ihnen heraus, und irgend jemand schien zu weinen. Dann öffnete sich die Tür, und eine sehr alte Frau erschien, heftig schluchzend. Sie hatte ein Kopftuch um und einen abgetragenen Wollmantel an. Über einem Arm hing ein Tragebeutel, und ihre linke Hand umklammerte eine abgewetzte lederne Geldbörse. Ihr Gesicht war vom Weinen geschwollen.

Henry Ainsley, der Empfangssekretär, kam ihr nach. Er war ein großer, dünner Mann mit eingefallenen Wangen und einem verschlagenen, hinterhältigen Blick. Er trug einen adretten grauen Anzug und eine unauffällige Krawatte, und seine Hände waren weich.

»Es tut mir leid, Madam, aber so ist es nun mal«, sagte

er spitz. »Dafür können Sie von nun an alles uns überlassen.«

»*Was* ist nun mal so?« fragte Meehan und legte seine Hände auf die Schultern der alten Frau. »Was ist los, meine Liebe?«

»Es ist alles in Ordnung, Mr. Meehan«, sagte Ainsley. »Die alte Dame ist nur ein bißchen niedergeschlagen. Sie hat ihren Mann soeben verloren.«

Meehan ignorierte ihn. Er zog die alte Dame ins Büro und plazierte sie in einen Stuhl neben dem Schreibtisch. »Nun erzählen Sie mir mal alles, meine Liebe.«

Er faßte nach ihrer Hand, und sie hielt sie fest.

»Neunzig war er, mein Billy. Ich hatte geglaubt, er würde ewig leben, und dann fand ich ihn am Fuß der Treppe, als ich Sonntag abend aus der Kirche zurückkam.« Tränen strömten über ihr Gesicht. »Er war so kräftig trotz seines Alters. Ich konnte es nicht glauben.«

»Ich verstehe, meine Liebe. Und nun wollen Sie ihn durch uns beerdigen lassen.«

Sie nickte. »Ich besitze nicht viel, aber ich wollte kein Armenbegräbnis für Bill. Ich dachte, daß ich mit dem Geld von der Versicherung etwas Hübsches arrangieren könnte. Und nun hat dieser Gentleman hier gesagt, daß ich siebzig Pfund brauche.«

Die kleine tapfere Frau rührte Meehans Herz. Er ging auf sie ein, ignorierte die Einwürfe seines Angestellten Ainsley, ließ sich die Unterlagen geben und erfand schließlich einen Sondertarif für betagte Rentner. Meehan gab ihr zwanzig Pfund des bereits eingezahlten Geldes zurück, führte sie dann in das angrenzende Blumengeschäft, wo sie sich auf Kosten der Firma die schönsten Blumen und einen Kranz aussuchen durfte, und sorgte obendrein dafür, daß einer seiner Leute sie nach Hause fuhr.

Die alte Dame war so glücklich, daß sie Meehan auf die Wange küßte. »Sie sind ein guter Mensch. Ein wundervoller Mensch! Gott segne Sie!«

»Er tut es, meine Liebe«, teilte ihr Dandy Jack mit. »Jeden einzelnen Tag meines Lebens.«

»Der Tod ist etwas, wovor man Respekt haben muß«, sagte Meehan.

Er saß in dem Schaukelstuhl vor dem Schreibtisch, Henry Ainsley stand vor ihm, Donner an der Tür.

Ainsley zwang sich zu einem Lächeln. »Ja, ich verstehe, was Sie meinen, Mr. Meehan.«

»Wirklich, Henry? Das wundert mich.«

Es klopfte an die Tür, und ein kleiner, elegant gekleideter Mann trat ein. Er sah wie ein Süditaliener aus, sprach aber mit South-Yorkshire-Akzent.

»Sie haben nach mir verlangt, Mr. Meehan?«

»So ist es, Bonati. Komm herein!« Meehan wandte sich wieder Ainsley zu. »Ja, ich wundere mich wirklich über dich, Henry. Es war ein Versicherungsfall. Sie gehört zur Arbeiterklasse. Die Versicherung zahlt fünfzig, und du hast den Preis auf siebzig hochgetrieben. Und die liebe Alte hat klein beigegeben, weil sie den Gedanken, daß ihr Bill ein Armenbegräbnis bekommt, nicht ertragen konnte.« Er schüttelte den Kopf. »Du hast ihr indessen eine Quittung über fünfzig gegeben – was sie in ihrem Zustand nicht bemerkt hat – und auch nur fünfzig in das Kassabuch eingetragen.«

Ainsley zitterte wie Espenlaub. »Bitte, Mr. Meehan, bitte, hören Sie! Ich hatte in letzter Zeit gewisse Schwierigkeiten …«

Meehan stand auf. »Ist er hier – ihr Mann?«

Ainsley nickte. »Er liegt in Nummer drei. Er ist noch nicht präpariert.«

»Nimm ihn mit!« forderte Meehan Donner auf und ging hinüber in die Leichenhalle.

Die anderen folgten ihm. Der alte Mann lag in einem offenen Sarg, mit einem Laken zugedeckt. Meehan zog es weg. Der Tote war ganz nackt und offensichtlich ein bemerkenswert kräftiger Mann gewesen.

Meehan betrachtete ihn ehrfurchtsvoll. »Er war ein Bulle. Kein Makel.« Er wandte sich Ainsley zu. »Schau dir seinen Schwanz an! Denk an die Frauen, die er beglückt hat! Denk an die alte Lady! Bei Gott, ich begreife, warum sie ihn geliebt hat. Er war ein Mann, dieser alte Knabe.«

Sein Knie schoß brutal in die Höhe, Henry Ainsley schützte seine Geschlechtsteile zu spät. Er taumelte mit einem erstickten Aufschrei vorwärts.

»Bring ihn hoch ins Sargzimmer«, trug Meehan Donner auf. »Ich komme in fünf Minuten nach.«

Als Henry Ainsley wieder zu sich kam, lag er flach auf dem Rücken, die Arme ausgebreitet. Donner stand auf seiner einen, Bonati auf der anderen Hand. Die Tür ging auf, und Meehan trat ein. Er sah einen Moment auf Ainsley herab und nickte dann.

»Gut. Hebt ihn auf!«

Der Raum wurde als Sarglager benutzt. Obgleich sie eigentlich nicht hier gezimmert wurden, standen ein paar Werkbänke herum, und auf einem Gestell an der Wand lag eine Auswahl Tischlerwerkzeuge.

»Bitte, Mr. Meehan!« bettelte Ainsley.

Meehan nickte Donner zu, und Bonati zerrte Ainsley über eine Werkbank, die Arme ausgebreitet, die Handflächen nach oben.

Meehan stand über ihm. »Ich werde dir jetzt eine Lektion erteilen, Henry. Nicht, weil du versucht hast, mich um zwanzig Pfund zu bescheißen. Das ist nicht das

Schlimmste. Ich denke an dieses alte Mädchen. Sie hat nie etwas in ihrem Leben gehabt. Alles, was sie überhaupt je besaß, wird verscharrt.« Sein Blick war verschleiert, und seine Stimme hatte einen leicht verträumten Klang. »Sie erinnerte mich an meine alte Dame – ich weiß nicht, warum. Nur eines weiß ich: Sie hat etwas Respekt verdient – so wie ihrem alten Knaben etwas Besseres als ein Armenbegräbnis zusteht.«

»Sie haben es falsch verstanden, Mr. Meehan«, plapperte Ainsley rasch.

»Nein, Henry, du hast es falsch verstanden.«

Meehan wählte zwei lange Drahtstifte, prüfte mit einem Daumen die Spitze des einen und trieb ihn durch die Mitte der rechten Handfläche Ainsleys, seine Hand damit an die Bank festnagelnd. Als er das gleiche mit der anderen Hand vornahm, fiel Ainsley in Ohnmacht.

Meehan wandte sich Donner zu. »Fünf Minuten, dann erlöse ihn und sag ihm, wenn er am Morgen nicht rechtzeitig im Büro erscheint, werde ich ihm seine Eier massieren.«

»In Ordnung, Mr. Meehan«, sagte Donner. »Was ist mit Fallon?«

»Ich bin im Behandlungszimmer. Muß ein paar Einbalsamierungen vornehmen. Wenn Fallon kommt, halt ihn so lange im Büro auf, bis ich in die Wohnung hochgehe. Dann führ ihn rauf. Und Albert soll sich sofort oben einfinden.«

»Glacéhandschuhbehandlung, Mr. Meehan?«

»Was sonst, Frank.«

Meehan lächelte, tätschelte eine Wange des bewußtlosen Ainsley und ging hinaus.

Das Behandlungszimmer befand sich auf der anderen Seite von der Leichenhalle. Meehan schloß die Tür hinter sich. Er war gern allein bei solchen Gelegenheiten. Die Arbeit erforderte Konzentration; außerdem bekam das Ganze eine persönliche Note dadurch.

Auf dem Tisch in der Mitte des Zimmers wartete ein Leichnam auf ihn. Er war zugedeckt. Daneben lag auf einem Wagen, sauber auf einem weißen Tuch ausgebreitet, sein Handwerkszeug.

Er zog das Laken weg. Es war der Leichnam einer vierzigjährigen Frau – dunkelhaarig, gutaussehend. Sie war mitten im Satz gestorben, während sie mit ihrem Mann das Weihnachtsprogramm besprochen hatte. Herzversagen. Noch immer spiegelte sich ein leicht erstaunter Ausdruck in ihrem Gesicht – wie bei vielen Toten.

Meehan nahm eine lange gebogene Nadel und hob mit geschickten Stichen die Kinnlade an. Unter die Lider stopfte er Wattebällchen, ehe er sie schloß, ebenso zwischen die Lippen und das Zahnfleisch und die Wangen, um so dem Gesicht ein volleres, natürlicheres Aussehen zu geben.

Er war völlig in seine Arbeit vertieft, pfiff leise durch die Zähne, hatte die Stirn gerunzelt. Seine Wut auf Ainsley war restlos verflogen. Selbst Fallon hatte zu existieren aufgehört. Er schmierte mit dem Finger etwas Creme auf die kalten Lippen, trat zurück und nickte zufrieden. Nun konnte er mit der Einbalsamierung beginnen.

Ungefähr eine Stunde später – er machte gerade die letzten Stiche – entstand ein Tumult draußen vor der Tür. Laute, wütende Stimmen waren zu hören, dann flog die Tür auf.

Meehan blickte über die Schulter. Miller stand in der Tür. Billy versuchte sich an ihm vorbeizuzwängen.

»Ich versuchte ihn aufzuhalten, Jack.«

»Mach etwas Tee!« befahl ihm Meehan. »Ich bin durstig. Und schließ die Tür! Denk doch an die Temperatur hier drin. Wie oft habe ich dir das schon gesagt!«

Billy zog sich zurück. Die Tür schloß sich leise hinter ihm.

Meehan wandte sich wieder dem Leichnam zu. Unendlich zart rieb er das Gesicht der toten Frau mit einer Creme ein, die als Unterlage für das Make-up diente. Miller ignorierte er restlos.

Miller zündete sich eine Zigarette an. Das Streichholz kratzte über die Reibfläche.

Meehan sagte, ohne sich umzudrehen: »Nicht hier. Hier drinnen zeigen wir ein bißchen Respekt.«

»Wirklich?« höhnte Miller, trat aber die Zigarette auf dem Fußboden aus.

Er näherte sich dem Tisch. Meehan trug Rouge auf die Wangen der Frau auf. Seine Finger brachten sie mit jeder Minute mehr dem Leben zurück.

Miller beobachtete ihn einen Moment schaudernd und zugleich fasziniert. »Sie lieben Ihre Arbeit, nicht wahr, Jack?«

»Was wollen Sie?« fragte Jack ruhig.

»Sie.«

»Nichts Neues also. Irgend jemand in der Stadt fällt hin und bricht sich ein Bein – und Sie kommen zu mir.«

»Na schön«, sagte Miller. »Also gehen wir es durch. Jan Krasko kam heute morgen auf den Friedhof, um Blumen auf das Grab seiner Mutter zu legen. Er macht das jetzt schon über ein Jahr lang – jeden Donnerstag, ohne Ausnahme.«

»Dann hat der Bastard trotz allem ein Herz. Warum erzählen Sie mir das?«

»Etwa um zehn nach elf hat ihm jemand eine Kugel durch den Schädel gejagt. Ein echter Profi-Job. Hübsch und öffentlich, damit jeder die Botschaft erhält.«

»Und was für eine Botschaft sollte das sein?«

»Unterwirf dich der Meehan-Linie oder …«

Meehan puderte das Gesicht. »Ich hatte heute morgen eine Beerdigung. Der alte Marcus – der Tuchhändler. Um zehn nach elf saß ich in *St. Saviour's* und lauschte dem Sermon des Vikars. Fragen Sie Billy! Er war dabei – zusammen mit ein paar Hundert anderen Trauergästen, einschließlich dem Bürgermeister. Er hatte eine Menge Freunde – der alte Marcus. War ein Gentleman. Gibt heute nicht mehr viele von seinem Schlag.«

Er brachte die Brauen und Wimpern mit Vaseline zum Glänzen und malte die Lippen an. Der Effekt war wirklich bemerkenswert. Die Frau schien nur zu schlafen.

Miller sagte: »Es ist mir egal, wo Sie gewesen sind. Es war Ihr Mord.«

Meehan wandte sich ihm zu, die Hände an einem Handtuch abwischend.

»Beweisen Sie es!« sagte er ungerührt.

Die jahrelang aufgestaute Wut und das Gefühl der Ohnmacht drohten Miller zu ersticken. Er zog an seiner Krawatte und riß sich den Hemdkragen auf.

»Ich krieg Sie dran, Meehan«, schrie er. »Ich häng's Ihnen an – und wenn es das letzte ist, was ich tue. Diesmal sind Sie zu weit gegangen.«

Meehans Augen begannen zu leuchten. Seine Macht war geradezu körperlich spürbar.

»Sie – an mich rankommen?« Er lachte rauh, wandte sich um und deutete auf die Frau. »Schauen Sie sie sich an, Miller! Sie war tot. Ich habe sie wieder zum Leben erweckt. Und Sie glauben, Sie können mir was anhaben?«

Miller trat unwillkürlich einen Schritt zurück.

Meehan schrie: »Raus! Verduften Sie verdammt noch mal!«

Miller lief, als ob alle Teufel der Hölle ihm auf den Fersen wären.

Es war plötzlich sehr ruhig im Präparierzimmer. Meehans Brust hob und senkte sich. Dann griff er nach einem Tiegel Creme und begann sie intensiv in den Körper einzumassieren.

6

Es regnete noch immer, als Fallon den Paul's Square überquerte und die Stufen zum Haupteingang emporstieg. Das Büro war leer, aber Rupert, der ihn durch die Glastür des Blumenladens hatte kommen sehen, erschien augenblicklich. Rupert war ein großer, schlanker junger Mann mit schulterlangem, dunklem Haar und einem wunderschönen Mund. Er lispelte leicht.

»Kann ich Ihnen behilflich sein, Sir?«

»Fallon ist mein Name. Meehan erwartet mich schon.«

»O ja, Sir.« Rupert war außerordentlich höflich. »Wenn Sie solange im Büro warten möchten – ich werde gleich nachsehen, wo er steckt.«

Er ging hinaus, und Fallon zündete sich eine Zigarette an. Gute zehn Minuten vergingen, ehe Rupert zurückkehrte.

»Ich bringe Sie jetzt nach oben, Sir«, sagte er und führte ihn mit einem strahlenden Lächeln in die Halle hinaus.

»Und wo ist dieses Oben?« fragte Fallon.

»Mr. Meehan hat die Mansarden der drei Häuser zu einer großen Dachterrassenwohnung ausgebaut. Klasse!«

Sie kamen zu einem kleinen Lift, und als Rupert die Tür öffnete, fragte Fallon: »Ist dies der einzige Weg nach oben?«

»Es gibt noch eine Hintertreppe.«

»Dann nehmen wir die Hintertreppe.«

Ruperts Lächeln erstarrte ein bißchen. »Schätzchen, lassen Sie die Spielchen! Das könnte Mr. Meehan nur verärgern. Was bedeuten würde, daß mir eine höllische Nacht bevorsteht – und um ganz offen zu sein, ich bin nicht in Stimmung dazu.«

»Oh, ich hatte geglaubt, Sie würden jeden wundervollen Augenblick genießen«, sagte Fallon und versetzte ihm einen heftigen Tritt gegen das rechte Schienbein.

Rupert schrie auf und fiel auf ein Knie. Fallon zog aus seiner rechten Tasche die Ceska. Er hatte den Schalldämpfer entfernt.

Rupert wurde weiß, gab sich aber mutig. »Er wird Sie kreuzigen dafür. Keiner kämpft mit Jack Meehan und geht als erster durchs Ziel.«

Fallon steckte die Ceska in die Tasche zurück.

»Die Treppe«, sagte er sanft.

»Na schön.« Rupert rieb sich sein Schienbein. »Es ist ja Ihre Beerdigung, Schätzchen.«

Die Treppe führte neben dem Eingang zur Leichenhalle nach oben. Rupert ging voraus. Sie stiegen drei Etagen hoch und kamen zu einer mit grünem Fries überzogenen Tür. Rupert blieb ein paar Stufen weiter unten stehen.

»Die führt direkt in die Küche.«

Fallon nickte. »Sie kehren besser wieder in den Laden zurück, meinen Sie nicht auch?«

Rupert brauchte keine zweite Aufforderung.

Fallon öffnete die Tür. Wie Rupert angekündigt hatte, befand sich eine Küche auf der anderen Seite. Eine Tür am anderen Ende stand halb offen, und er konnte Stimmen hören. Er näherte sich auf Zehenspitzen und blickte in eine prächtig möblierte Wohndiele mit breiten Mansardenfenstern zu beiden Seiten. Meehan saß in einem ledernen Klubsessel, ein Buch in der einen Hand, ein Whiskyglas in der anderen. Billy, den Whippet auf dem Arm, stand vor einem Kamin, in dem ein Holzfeuer lustig prasselte. Donner und Bonati warteten zu beiden Seiten des Lifts.

»Was hält ihn auf, in Christi Namen?« fragte Billy.

Der Hund sprang aus seinen Armen und fegte auf die Küchentür zu. Dort blieb er bellend stehen, und Fallon trat in die Diele, ging in die Hocke und kraulte den Hund hinter den Ohren, die rechte Hand in der Manteltasche.

Meehan ließ das Buch auf den Tisch fallen und schlug sich mit einer Hand auf den Oberschenkel.

»Hab' ich dir nicht gesagt, daß er ein hartgesottener Bastard ist?« rief er seinem Bruder Billy zu.

Das Telefon klingelte. Meehan hob den Hörer ab, lauschte einen Moment und lächelte.

»In Ordnung, Schätzchen. Geh an die Arbeit zurück!« Er legte den Hörer wieder auf. »Das war Rupert. Er macht sich Sorgen meinetwegen.«

»Das ist nett«, sagte Fallon.

Er lehnte sich gegen die Wand neben der Küchentür, die Hände in den Taschen. Donner und Bonati stellten sich hinter die große Ledercouch und starrten ihn an. Meehan nippte an seinem Whisky und hielt das Buch hoch.

»Haben Sie das gelesen, Fallon?«

»Vor langer Zeit.« Fallon angelte sich mit der linken Hand eine Zigarette.

»Ein gutes Thema«, sagte Meehan. »Gott und der Teufel – das Gute und das Böse. Und Sex.« Er leerte sein Glas und rülpste. »Er hat die richtigen Ansichten. Ich finde, Frauen saugen einen Mann nur aus – was ich auch immer wieder meinem kleinen Bruder zu predigen versuche. Nur, er will nicht hören. Jedem Rock läuft er nach. Schon mal 'nen Hund beobachtet, der hinter 'ner läufigen Hündin her ist? So führt sich unser Billy auf – vierundzwanzig Stunden am Tag.«

Er goß sich noch einen Whisky ein, und Fallon wartete. Sie warteten alle.

Meehan starrte vor sich hin. »Nein, diese schmutzigen kleinen Nutten sind für niemand gut. Und die Jungens sind nicht besser. Ich frage Sie, was ist aus all den hübschen wohlgeformten Sechzehn- und Siebzehnjährigen von früher geworden? Heutzutage sehen fast alle wie Strichjungen aus.«

Fallon sagte nichts, Meehan griff wieder nach der Whiskyflasche.

»Albert!« rief er plötzlich. »Warum kommst du nicht zu uns?«

Die Tür zum Schlafzimmer öffnete sich. Erst sah man niemand, dann kam ein Mann ins Zimmer, so groß, daß er den Kopf einziehen mußte, um unter dem Türstock hindurchzukommen. Ein Neandertaler in einem ausgebeulten, grauen Anzug. Er mußte an die drei Zentner wiegen. Sein Kopf war vollständig kahl, seine Arme baumelten fast bis zu den Knien herab. Er watschelte ins Zimmer, die kleinen Schweinsaugen auf Fallon fixiert. Billy ging ihm nervös aus dem Weg, und Albert sank in einen Stuhl neben dem Feuer, auf der anderen Seite von Meehan.

Meehan sagte: »Nun, Fallon, Sie haben's vermasselt.«

»Sie wollten Krasko tot. Und er liegt in diesem Moment auf einer Bahre in der Leichenhalle«, sagte Fallon.

»Und der Priester? Dieser Pater da Costa?«

»Kein Problem.«

»Er kann Sie identifizieren, oder? Varley sagt, er stand so nahe, daß er die Falten unter Ihren Augen hätte zählen können.«

»Stimmt. Aber das spielt keine Rolle. Ich habe ihm den Mund verschlossen.«

»Wollen Sie damit sagen, Sie haben ihn ins Jenseits befördert?« fragte Billy.

»Nicht nötig.« Fallon wandte sich an Meehan. »Sind Sie Katholik?«

Meehan nickte. »Was soll die Frage?«

»Wann gingen Sie das letztemal zur Beichte?«

»Zum Teufel noch mal, woher soll ich das wissen?«

»Ich war heute«, sagte Fallon. »Dort bin ich bis jetzt gewesen. Ich wartete auf da Costas Ein-Uhr-Beichte. Ich habe ihm erzählt, daß ich Krasko erschoß.«

»Aber das ist doch verrückt!« rief Billy aus. »Er hat ja mit eigenen Augen gesehen, wie Sie ihn umlegten!«

»Aber er wußte nicht, daß ich in dem Beichtstuhl saß – nicht, bevor er durch das Gitter schielte und mich erkannte – und das war, nachdem ich den Mord gebeichtet hatte.«

»Na und?« knurrte Billy.

Aber sein Bruder brachte ihn zum Schweigen.

»Habe kapiert«, sagte er mit ernstem Gesicht. »Alles, was man einem Priester in der Beichte erzählt, bleibt ein Geheimnis. Ich meine, das garantieren sie doch, nicht wahr?«

»Genau«, bestätigte Fallon.

»Das ist der größte Quatsch, den ich je gehört habe«, sagte Billy. »Er ist am Leben, oder? Und er weiß es. Was für eine Garantie haben Sie, daß er sich nicht plötzlich entschließt, das Maul aufzureißen?«

»Sagen wir: Es ist nicht wahrscheinlich«, entgegnete Fallon ruhig. »Und selbst wenn. Ich werde Sonntag nacht von Hull aus in See stechen. Oder haben Sie das vergessen?«

Meehan sagte: »Ich weiß nicht. Vielleicht hat Billy recht.«

»Billy würde nicht mal ins Männerklosett allein finden, wenn Sie ihn nicht bei der Hand nähmen«, behauptete Fallen flach.

Tödliche Stille folgte. Meehan musterte Fallon gelassen, und Albert holte einen Stahl-Schürhaken aus dem Kamin und verbog ihn zwischen seinen großen Händen zu einem Hufeisen, den Blick nicht eine Sekunde von Fallon abwendend.

Meehan lachte leise vor sich hin. »Das ist gut. Sehr gut. Das gefällt mir.«

Er stand auf, ging zu einem Schreibtisch in der Ecke, sperrte ihn auf und holte einen großen Briefumschlag heraus. Dann kehrte er zu seinem Sessel zurück und ließ den Umschlag auf den Rauchtisch fallen. »Das sind fünfzehnhundert Pfund. Sonntag nacht an Bord des Schiffes bekommen Sie noch zweitausend Dollar und einen Paß. Damit ist die Rechnung beglichen.«

»Sehr nobel von Ihnen«, sagte Fallon.

»Nur etwas noch: Der Priester verschwindet.«

Fallon schüttelte den Kopf. »Kommt nicht in Frage.«

»Was ist denn los mit Ihnen? Angst, der Allmächtige könnte Sie niederstrecken?« höhnte Meehan. »Man hat mir erzählt, daß Sie ein großes As dort drüben gewesen sind – in Belfast. Haben Soldaten erschossen und Kinder in die Luft gesprengt. Aber ein Priester ist wohl was anderes, wie?«

Fallon flüsterte fast. »Dem Priester passiert nichts. So will ich es haben – und so wird es sein.«

»So wollen *Sie* es?« Meehan konnte seine Wut nicht länger verbergen.

Albert schleuderte den Feuerhaken in den Kahn und stand auf. Er hatte eine rauhe, krächzende Stimme. »Welchen Arm soll ich ihm zuerst brechen, Mr. Meehan? Den linken oder den rechten?«

Fallon zog die Ceska und schoß augenblicklich. Die Kugel zersplitterte Alberts rechte Kniescheibe. Er fiel rückwärts in den Stuhl. Fluchend umklammerte er sein Knie mit beiden Händen. Blut quoll zwischen seinen Fingern hervor.

Einen Moment lang rührte sich niemand, dann lachte Meehan schallend.

»Hab' ich dir nicht gesagt, daß er wundervoll ist?« rief er Billy zu.

Fallon nahm den Umschlag auf und stopfte ihn in seinen Regenmantel. Wortlos zog er sich rückwärtsgehend in die Küche zurück. Meehan schrie ihm noch etwas nach, während Fallon die Tür zuschlug und die Treppe herunterstürmte.

Meehan grapschte nach seinem Mantel und rannte auf den Lift zu. »Komm, Billy!«

Als er die Tür aufriß, fragte Donner: »Was ist mit Albert?«

»Ruf den Pakistan-Doktor! Er wird ihn schon wieder zusammenflicken.«

Als der Lift nach unten fuhr, fragte Billy: »Was sollen wir machen?«

»Verflixt, folge mir und tu gefälligst, was man dir sagt!« Meehan flog regelrecht durch die Halle und den Haupteingang.

Fallon hatte die andere Straßenseite erreicht und steuerte auf einen der Wege zu, die über den grünen Platz führten.

Meehan schrie hinter ihm her und lief über die Straße, den Verkehr ignorierend.

Der Ire blickte über die Schulter zurück, ging aber weiter. Er hatte den Brunnen erreicht, als Meehan und Billy ihn einholten. Er wandte sich ihnen zu, die rechte Hand in der Tasche.

Meehan hob verteidigend eine Hand. »Ich will mich nur unterhalten.«

Er ließ sich auf eine Bank fallen, leicht außer Atem, zog ein Taschentuch heraus, um sein Gesicht abzuwischen. Der Nieselregen wurde plötzlich zum Wolkenbruch.

Billy sagte: »Das ist doch verrückt! Mein Anzug ist im Nu hin.«

Sein Bruder ignorierte ihn und betrachtete mit entwaffnendem Grinsen Fallon. »Sie haben den Teufel im Leib, Fallon. In der ganzen Stadt läuft kein verdammter Strolch herum, der nicht vor Fat Albert Reißaus nehmen würde.« Er lachte schallend. »Und Sie haben ihn für sechs Monate außer Gefecht gesetzt.«

»Er hätte sich nicht einmischen sollen«, sagte Fallon.

»Nur zu wahr. Aber zur Hölle mit Fat! Sie hatten recht, Fallon – mit dem Priester, meine ich.«

Fallon stand nur einfach da und sah ihn an.

Meehan lachte. »Bei der Ehre der Pfadfinder: Ich werde ihm nicht ein Härchen krümmen.«

»Ein Gesinnungswechsel?« fragte Fallon.

»Genau. Aber es bleibt uns trotzdem noch ein Problem. Was machen wir mit Ihnen, bis der Kahn am Sonntag ausläuft? Ich denke, Sie sollten vielleicht zurück auf die Farm.«

»Auf keinen Fall.«

»Hatte ich mir schon irgendwie gedacht, daß Sie das sagen würden.« Meehan lächelte gutgelaunt. »Doch wir müssen etwas finden.« Er wandte sich an Billy. »Wie wär's mit Jenny? Jenny Fox? Könnte sie ihn nicht aufnehmen?«

»Ich nehme an«, brummte Billy mürrisch.

»Ein nettes Mädchen«, erzählte Meehan Fallon. »Sie hat früher für mich gearbeitet. Ich habe ihr geholfen, als sie ein Kind bekam. Sie schuldet mir eine Gefälligkeit.«

»Sie ist eine Hure«, sagte Billy.

»Na und?« Meehan hob die Schultern. »Ein hübsches, sicheres Plätzchen und nicht zu weit weg. Billy kann Sie hinbringen.«

Er lächelte jovial – selbst seine Augen lachten –, aber Fallon fiel nicht einen Moment auf ihn herein. Andererseits war es die bittere Wahrheit, daß er irgendwo Unterschlupf finden mußte.

»In Ordnung«, sagte er daher.

Meehan legte einen Arm um seine Schultern. »Sie könnten keine bessere Wahl treffen. Sie kocht wie ein Engel, dieses Mädchen, und wenn sie ihr Höschen runterläßt, ist sie ein kleines Feuerwerk, kann ich Ihnen sagen.«

Sie gingen zurück und zum Parkplatz an der Rückfront. Der Whippet lag zusammengerollt am Eingang, zitternd vor Kälte. Er sprang an Billys Seite, folgte ihm in die Garage, und als Billy in einem scharlachroten Scimitar herausfuhr, kauerte der Hund auf dem Rücksitz.

Fallon schlüpfte auf den Beifahrersitz, und Meehan schloß die Tür.

»An Ihrer Stelle würde ich schön brav zu Hause bleiben. Es wäre unklug, irgendwelche unnützen Risiken einzugehen.«

Fallon sagte nichts, und Billy fuhr los.

Donner trat aus dem Haus. »Ich habe diesen Quacksalber angerufen, Mr. Meehan. Was ist mit Fallon?«

»Billy bringt ihn zu Jenny Fox«, sagte Meehan. »Ich möchte, daß du zur Autowaschanlage rübergehst und dir Varley schnappst. Er soll binnen einer halben Stunde Posten vor Jennys Haus beziehen. Wenn Fallon das Haus verläßt, soll er ihm folgen und hier anrufen, wann immer er kann.«

»Ich verstehe nicht ganz, Mr. Meehan.« Donner war offensichtlich verwirrt.

»Nur bis wir alles in Ordnung gebracht haben, Frank. Dann befreien wir uns von beiden. Von ihm und dem Priester.«

Donner grinste. »Das hört sich schon besser an.«

»Ich dachte mir, daß du das sagen würdest.«

Jenny Fox war ein kleines, ziemlich breithüftiges Mädchen von neunzehn Jahren mit einem guten Busen, hohen Backenknochen und mandelförmigen Augen. Ihre glatten, schwarzen Haare hingen wie ein dunkler Vorhang bis auf ihre Schultern herab. Das einzig Störende an ihr war ihr zu dick aufgetragenes Make-up.

Als sie die Treppe herunterkam, trug sie eine einfache weiße Bluse, einen schwarzen Mini-Faltenrock und hochhackige Schuhe. Wenn sie ging, war ihr ganzer Körper in Bewegung, was wohl die meisten Männer äußerst beunruhigte.

Billy Meehan wartete am Fuß der Treppe, und als sie nahe genug herangekommen war, faßte er ihr unter den Rock. Sie versteifte sich leicht, und er schüttelte den Kopf, ein verschlagenes, fieses Lächeln im Gesicht.

»Wieder Strumpfhosen, Jenny. Ich habe dir doch gesagt, ich möchte, daß du Strümpfe trägst.«

»Entschuldige, Billy.« In ihren Augen spiegelte sich Furcht. »Ich wußte nicht, daß du heute kommen würdest.«

»Du solltest besser achtgeben oder du bekommst eine meiner Spezialitäten zu spüren.«

Sie zitterte leicht, und er nahm seine Hand weg.

»Was ist mit Fallon? Hat er was gesagt?«

»Er hat mich gefragt, ob ich ihm ein Rasiermesser besorgen könnte. Wer ist er?«

»Geht dich nichts an. Er sollte nicht das Haus verlassen. Wenn er es aber doch tut, ruf sofort Jack an! Und versuch herauszufinden, wo er hingeht!«

»Gut, Billy.«

Sie öffnete die Eingangstür für ihn. Er trat dicht hinter sie, die Arme um ihre Taille legend. Sie spürte sein steifes Glied an ihren Gesäßbacken, und Haß und Abscheu schnürten ihr die Kehle zu.

Leise sagte er: »Und noch etwas: Zieh ihn ins Bett! Ich möchte gern wissen, was ihn erregt.«

»Und wenn er nicht mitmacht?« fragte sie.

»Strümpfe und Strumpfhalter – darauf stehen Kerle seines Alters. Du wirst's schon hinkriegen.«

Er gab ihr einen Klaps auf den Popo und ging.

Sie schloß die Tür und lehnte sich, nach Atem ringend, einen Moment dagegen. Seltsam, daß sie bei ihm immer das Gefühl hatte, zu ersticken.

Sie ging nach oben und klopfte leise an Fallons Tür. Als sie eintrat, stand er vor dem Waschbecken in der Ecke beim Fenster und trocknete sich die Hände ab.

»Ich werde Ihnen jetzt ein Rasiermesser besorgen«, sagte sie.

Er hängte das Handtuch ordentlich über die Stange und schüttelte den Kopf. »Es eilt nicht. Ich gehe eine Weile weg.«

Panik überfiel sie. »Ist das klug? Wo gehen Sie denn hin?«

Fallon lächelte, während er seinen Trenchcoat anzog. In einer seltsam intimen Geste strich er ihr über den Nasenrücken. Ein Kloß saß ihr in der Kehle.

»Mädchen, Liebes, tu, was du tun mußt. Ruf Jack Meehan an und sag ihm, daß ich spazierengegangen bin. Aber verrückt müßte ich sein, wenn ich dir sagen würde, wohin.«

»Werden Sie zum Abendessen zurück sein?«

»Um nichts in der Welt würde ich es versäumen.«

Er lächelte und verschwand.

Seltsam, daß sie plötzlich das Bedürfnis hatte, zu weinen.

Miller traf Fitzgerald bei dem Ballistik-Spezialisten im Labor. Fitzgerald sah erregt aus, und Johnson schien ziemlich mit sich zufrieden.

Miller sagte: »Ich habe gehört, Sie haben etwas für mich?«

Johnson war ein langsamer, vorsichtiger Schotte. »Es könnte etwas sein, Superintendent.« Er nahm mit einer Pinzette ein reichlich mißgestaltetes Stück Blei auf. »Das hier hat den ganzen Schaden verursacht. Die Jungens fanden es im Kies, ungefähr drei Meter von der Leiche entfernt.«

»Eine halbe Stunde nachdem Sie weg waren, Sir«, warf Fitzgerald ein.

»Besteht irgendeine Hoffnung, die Waffe zu identifizieren?« fragte Miller.

»Oh, ich glaube schon.« Johnson hatte neben sich die Abhandlung ›Kleinwaffen der Welt‹ liegen. Er durchblätterte den Band rasch, fand die gesuchte Seite und hielt sie Miller hin. »Da!«

Es war ein Foto der Ceska.

»Ich habe noch nie von dem verdammten Ding gehört«, sagte Miller. »Wie können Sie so sicher sein?«

»Nun, ich muß noch ein paar weitere Tests anstellen, aber es steht bereits ziemlich fest.«

Johnson hielt ihm einen kurzen ballistischen Vortrag.

Miller wandte sich Fitzgerald zu. »Geben Sie diese Information an den CRO von Scotland Yard weiter. Diese Ceska ist eine ausgefallene Waffe. Wenn sie den Computer damit füttern, spuckt er vielleicht einen Namen aus. Ich erwarte Sie in meinem Büro.«

Fitzgerald ging rasch raus, und Miller wandte sich an Johnson. »Falls es etwas Neues gibt, lassen Sie es mich sofort wissen.«

Er kehrte in sein Büro zurück. Auf seinem Schreibtisch lag eine Akte über Pater da Costas Karriere. Angesichts der knappen Zeit, die Fitzgerald zur Verfügung gehabt hatte, war sie wirklich sehr umfangreich.

Fitzgerald trat ins Zimmer, als Miller gerade die Akte durchgelesen hatte.

»Sie wissen noch nicht alles«, sagte Miller und erzählte ihm von dem Vorfall im Pfarrhaus.

Fitzgerald war fassungslos. »Aber das ergibt doch gar keinen Sinn!«

»Sie glauben nicht, daß er bestochen wurde?«

»Von Meehan?« Fitzgerald lachte schallend. »Pater da Costa ist kein Typ, den auch nur irgend jemand bestechen könnte. Er sagt, was er denkt und fühlt, selbst wenn er sich damit schadet. Er war ein glänzender Wissenschaftler. Hat zwei Doktortitel. Und was haben sie ihm eingebracht? Eine sterbende Gemeinde im Herzen einer ziemlich unfreundlichen Industriestadt, und eine Kirche, die buchstäblich zusammenkracht.«

Miller schlug die Akte nochmals auf. »Und wie es scheint, kann er auch physisch einiges einstecken. Wie hier steht, ist er während des Krieges dreimal in Jugoslawien und zweimal in Albanien mit dem Fallschirm abgesprungen. Zweimal wurde er verwundet.« Er hob ungeduldig die Schultern. »Aber es muß doch eine Erklärung geben. Es muß! Weshalb weigert er sich sonst, ins Präsidium zu kommen?«

»Hat er sich denn tatsächlich geweigert?«

Miller runzelte die Stirn und versuchte, sich genau an die Worte des Priesters zu erinnern. »Nein, nicht direkt. Er sagte, es hätte keinen Sinn, da er nicht in der Lage wäre, zu helfen.«

»Das ist wirklich eine seltsame Formulierung.«

»Und als ich ihm sagte, daß ich ihn jederzeit vorführen lassen könnte, entgegnete er, daß ihn keine Macht der Welt dazu bringen könnte, über diese Angelegenheit zu sprechen.«

Fitzgerald war bleich geworden. Er stand auf und beugte sich über den Schreibtisch. »Das hat er gesagt? Sind Sie sicher?«

»Ganz sicher.« Miller runzelte die Stirn. »Warum?«

Fitzgerald ging ans Fenster. »Ich kann mir nur eine Situation denken, in der ein Priester so sprechen würde.«

»Und welche?«

»Wenn die Information, die er zur Verfügung hat, Teil einer Beichte ist.«

Miller starrte ihn an. »Aber das ist nicht möglich! Ich meine, er hat diesen Typ doch tatsächlich auf dem Friedhof gesehen.«

»Und wenn der Mann einfach zur Beichte gegangen ist? Da Costa könnte sein Gesicht im Beichtstuhl nicht sehen.«

»Und Sie wollen mir erzählen, daß da Costa, sobald der Kerl sich ausgekotzt hat, die Hände gebunden sind?«

»Ganz sicher.«

»Aber das ist verrückt!«

»Nicht für einen Katholiken. Was zwischen dem Priester und dem Sünder während der Beichte ausgetauscht wird – wie schändlich es auch immer sein mag –, ist höchst vertraulich.« Er hob die Schultern. »Genauso wirksam wie eine Kugel, Sir. Hat Pater da Costa Ihnen nicht auf dem Friedhof gesagt, daß er es eilig hätte, weil er um ein Uhr die Beichten abnehmen müßte?«

Miller schoß hoch und schnappte mit der gleichen Bewegung seinen Regenmantel. »Sie können mitkommen. Vielleicht hört er auf Sie.«

»Und was ist mit der Autopsie?« fragte Fitzgerald. »Sie wollten doch persönlich anwesend sein.«

Miller sah auf seine Uhr. »Wir haben noch eine Stunde Zeit.«

Alle Lifte waren in Betrieb. Er stürmte die Treppe runter, immer zwei Stufen auf einmal nehmend. Sein Herz klopfte wild.

Als Fallon in die schmale Straße zu *Holy Name* einbog, war Varley nicht mehr als dreißig Meter hinter ihm. Fallon hatte ihn, kaum daß er Jennys Wohnung verlassen hatte, bemerkt – aber Varley störte ihn nicht. Er betrat die Kirche, und Varley steuerte auf die Telefonzelle an der Ecke zu und rief Meehan an.

»Mr. Meehan, ich bin's. Er ist in die Kirche in der Rokkingham Street gegangen. *Holy Name.*«

»Ich bin in fünf Minuten da.«

Sie kamen mit dem scharlachroten Scimitar. Billy saß am Steuer.

Varley stand bibbernd an der Straßenecke. Er kam auf sie zu, während sie ausstiegen. »Er ist noch drin, Mr. Meehan.«

»Guter Junge.« Meehan betrachtete die Kirche. »Sieht so aus, als ob sie jeden Moment einstürzen könnte.«

»Sie schenken gute Suppe aus«, sagte Varley. »An

Penner. In der Krypta. Ich bin mal drin gewesen. Der Priester und seine Nichte schmeißen den Laden. Sie ist blind. Spielt die Orgel hier.«

Meehan nickte. »Gut. Du wartest in einem Hauseingang. Wenn er rauskommt, folge ihm wieder! Komm, Billy!«

Er öffnete leise das Portal. Sie schlüpften schnell hinein, und Meehan schloß das Tor rasch wieder.

Das Mädchen spielte Orgel. Er konnte ihren Hinterkopf sehen. Der Priester kniete vor den Chorschranken, im Gebet. Fallon saß in der Mitte des Seitenschiffes, am Ende einer Bankreihe. Auf der rechten Seite entdeckte Meehan eine kleine Kapelle für St. Martin de Porres. Nicht eine einzige Kerze flackerte vor dem Bildnis. Meehan zog Billy hinter sich her in die schützenden Schatten und setzte sich in eine Ecke.

»Was zum Teufel wollen wir hier?« flüsterte Billy.

»Halt den Mund und paß auf!«

In diesem Moment erhob sich Pater da Costa und bekreuzigte sich. Als er sich umwandte, sah er Fallon.

»Sie haben hier nichts verloren. Das wissen Sie«, sagte er finster.

Anna hörte zu spielen auf. Sie schwang ihre Beine herum, während Fallon das Seitenschiff entlang nach vorn schritt.

Billy pfiff leise durch die Zähne. »Beim Himmel, hast du diese Beine gesehen?«

»Halt's Maul!« zischte Jack.

»Ich habe Ihnen gesagt, daß ich mich um die Sache kümmern würde, und ich habe es getan«, sagte Fallon, als er die Chorschranken erreicht hatte. »Ich wollte nur, daß Sie das wissen.«

»Was erwarten Sie von mir? Daß ich danke sage?« fragte da Costa.

Das Portal schlug zu. Kerzen flackerten im Wind, als es wieder geschlossen wurde. Zu Jack Meehans großem Erstaunen marschierten Miller und Fitzgerald das Seitenschiff vor zum Altar.

»Ah – da sind Sie ja, Pater!« rief Miller aus. »Ich würde gern mit Ihnen sprechen.«

»Mein Gott«, flüsterte Billy. »Wir müssen verschwinden.«

»Den Teufel werden wir tun!« Meehans Hand umschloß Billys rechtes Knie wie ein Schraubstock. »Sitz still und hör zu!«

7

Fallon erkannte in Miller sofort den Bullen und wartete, die Schultern eingezogen, die Hände in den Taschen seines Trenchcoats, die Beine gespreizt, sprungbereit. Eine elementare Kraft war in diesem Mann. Pater da Costa spürte sie körperlich. Voll Schrecken dachte er an das, was passieren konnte, und trat rasch zwischen Fallon und die beiden Polizisten, die sich näherten. Anna wartete unsicher auf der anderen Seite der Chorschranken.

Miller blieb stehen, den Hut in der Hand. Fitzgerald war ein oder zwei Schritte hinter ihm.

Da Costa sagte in die beklemmende Stille hinein: »Sie haben meine Nichte ja schon kennengelernt, Superintendent. Inspektor Fitzgerald ist bei ihm, meine Liebe.«

»Miß da Costa«, sagte Miller höflich und wandte sich dann zu Fallon um.

»Und das ist Mr. Fallon«, erklärte da Costa rasch.

»Superintendent«, sagte Fallon zwanglos.

Er wartete, ein leicht starres Lächeln um den Mund.

Miller sah in das weiße, angespannte Gesicht, in diese

dunklen Augen. Ihn fröstelte, und plötzlich kam ihm ein verrückter Gedanke, und er ging unwillkürlich einen Schritt rückwärts.

Jeder wartete. Der Regen trommelte gegen ein Fenster. Anna brach schließlich das Schweigen. Sie tastete sich einen Schritt vor und stolperte.

Fallon sprang zu ihr und fing sie auf. »Alles in Ordnung, Miß da Costa?«

»Danke, Mr. Fallon. Wie dumm von mir!« Ihr leises Lachen wirkte sehr überzeugend. Sie blickte in Millers Richtung. »Ich hatte Schwierigkeiten mit der Orgel. Ich fürchte, sie hat – wie die Kirche – die besten Zeiten hinter sich. Mr. Fallon hat sich freundlicherweise bereit erklärt, uns fachkundig zu beraten.«

»Ach ja?« sagte Miller.

Sie wandte sich an da Costa. »Macht es dir etwas aus, wenn wir schon anfangen, Onkel? Ich weiß, daß Mr. Fallon nicht viel Zeit hat.«

»Wenn es Ihnen recht ist, gehen wir in die Sakristei, Superintendent«, sagte da Costa. »Wenn Sie möchten, auch ins Haus.«

»Eigentlich würde ich gern noch ein paar Minuten hierbleiben«, erklärte Miller. »Ich spiele selbst Klavier und hatte stets eine besondere Vorliebe für Orgelmusik. Wenn Mr. Fallon nichts dagegen hat …«

Fallon lächelte verbindlich. »Es gab noch nie einen größeren Anreiz als ein Auditorium, Superintendent.«

Er nahm Annas Arm und führte sie zur Orgel hinauf.

Meehan beobachtete aus seiner dunklen Ecke heraus fasziniert die Szene.

Billy flüsterte: »Hab' ich nicht gesagt, daß er ein Verrückter ist? Wie zum Teufel will er sich hier herauswinden?«

»Mit seinen Fingern, Billy, mit seinen Fingern«, sagte

Meehan. Und mit echter Bewunderung fügte er hinzu: »Ich genieße jede einzelne Minute. Es ist immer wundervoll, einen richtigen Profi in Aktion zu sehen.« Er seufzte. »Es gibt nicht mehr viele von unserer Sorte.«

Fallon zog seinen Trenchcoat aus und legte ihn über die Rückenlehne des Chorgestühls. Dann setzte er sich und rückte den Stuhl zurecht, daß er an die Pedale herankam. Anna stand zu seiner Rechten.

»Haben Sie versucht, das Trompetenregister drinzulassen, wie ich vorgeschlagen hatte?« fragte er.

Sie nickte. »Es macht wirklich einen großen Unterschied.«

»Gut. Sehen wir weiter. Ich werde Bachs ›Präludium und Fuge in D-Dur‹ spielen, ja?«

»Ich habe es nur in Blindenschrift.«

»Das macht nichts. Ich kann es auswendig.« Er wandte sich um und blickte zu Pater da Costa und den beiden Polizisten hinunter. »Falls es Sie interessiert – es soll Albert Schweitzers Lieblingsstück gewesen sein.«

Niemand sagte etwas. Sie warteten, und Fallon wandte sich wieder der Orgel zu. Es war schon verdammt lange her, seit er gespielt hatte – und trotzdem schien es ganz plötzlich erst gestern gewesen zu sein. Er zog die Register, blickte ernst zu Anna auf und gab diese und jene Erklärungen ab. Sie konnte nicht das leicht sardonische Lächeln in seinen Mundwinkeln sehen, aber etwas von diesem Lächeln vibrierte in seiner Stimme mit.

Sie legte eine Hand auf seine Schulter und sagte: »Sehr interessant.«

Zu ihrem Entsetzen fuhr er leise fort: »Warum haben Sie sich eingemischt?«

»Ist das nicht offensichtlich? Superintendent Millers und des Inspektors wegen. Nun spielen Sie!«

»Gott vergebe Ihnen! Sie sind eine miserable Lügnerin.«

Fallon begann zu spielen. Und er spielte mit so erstaunlicher Kraft und Meisterschaft, daß sich Millers wilde Vermutungen augenblicklich in Nichts auflösten. Pater da Costa stand wie versteinert an den Chorschranken, ergriffen von Fallons brillantem Spiel.

Miller tippte dem Pater auf die Schulter und flüsterte ihm ins Ohr: »Exzellent! Aber meine Zeit wird knapp. Können wir uns jetzt unterhalten?«

Pater da Costa nickte zögernd und führte ihn in die Sakristei. Fitzgerald folgte. Die Tür knallte hinter ihm in einer plötzlichen Windbö zu.

Fallon hörte zu spielen auf. »Sind sie gegangen?«

Ehrfurcht spiegelte sich in Anna da Costas Gesicht. Sie berührte seine eine Wange. »Wer sind Sie? Was sind Sie?«

»Eine höllische Frage.«

Er wandte sich wieder der Orgel zu und begann nochmals von vorn.

Pater da Costa saß auf der Tischkante.

»Zigarette, Sir?« Fitzgerald brachte ein altes Silberetui zum Vorschein, und Pater da Costa nahm sich eine, ließ sie sich anzünden.

Miller beobachtete ihn scharf. Die massiven Schultern, das wettergegerbte Gesicht, den zerzausten Bart – und plötzlich wurde ihm fast ärgerlich bewußt, daß er diesen Mann eigentlich mochte. Und aus genau diesem Grund beschloß er, so formell wie möglich zu sein.

»Nun, Superintendent?«

»Haben Sie seit unserem letzten Gespräch Ihre Meinung geändert, Sir?«

»Nicht im mindesten.«

Miller hatte Mühe, seine Wut zu unterdrücken.

Fitzgerald fragte sanft: »Sind Sie seit heute morgen in irgendeiner Form genötigt oder bedroht worden, Sir?«

»Überhaupt nicht, Inspektor«, versicherte ihm Pater da Costa aufrichtig.

»Sagt der Name Meehan Ihnen irgend etwas, Sir?«

Pater da Costa schüttelte den Kopf, die Stirn leicht runzelnd. »Nein, ich denke nicht. Sollte er?«

Miller nickte Fitzgerald zu, der die Aktentasche, die er bei sich hatte, öffnete. Er holte ein Foto heraus, das er dem Priester überreichte.

»Jack Meehan«, sagte er. »Für seine Freunde Dandy Jack. Das Foto wurde in London aufgenommen, auf den Stufen des Polizeipräsidiums im West End, letztes Jahr. Es ging um eine Schießerei im East End. Man hatte ihn mangels Beweisen freigelassen.«

Meehan – er trug wie üblich seinen doppelreihigen Mantel – lächelte der Welt breit ins Gesicht, mit dem Hut in der rechten Hand winkend, den linken Arm um die Schultern eines wohlbekannten Mannequins gelegt.

»Das Mädchen dient nur Publicity-Zwecken«, sagte Fitzgerald. »In sexueller Hinsicht geht sein Geschmack in anderer Richtung. Was auf dem Blatt steht, das an die Rückseite des Fotos geheftet wurde, ist alles, was wir offiziell von ihm haben.«

Pater da Costa las interessiert. Jack Meehan war fünfzig. Er hatte sich 1943, mit achtzehn, der Royal Navy angeschlossen, bis 1945 auf einem Minenräumboot gedient, wurde dann zu einem Jahr Haft verurteilt, weil er einem Maat bei einer Schlägerei den Kiefer gebrochen hatte, mit Schande entlassen. 1948 hatte er sechs Monate wegen einer unbedeutenden Schmuggelaffäre gesessen, 1954 war die Anklage wegen einer Postraubverschwörung mangels Beweisen fallengelassen worden. Seitdem war er über vierzigmal mit Straftaten in Verbindung gebracht und von der Polizei verhört worden.

»Sie scheinen nicht viel Erfolg zu haben«, sagte Pater da Costa mit einem feinen Lächeln.

»An Jack Meehan ist nichts erheiternd«, sagte Miller. »Er ist das fieseste Subjekt, das mir je in meinen fünfundzwanzig Dienstjahren über den Weg gelaufen ist. Er hat ein Bestattungsunternehmen hier in der Stadt, aber hinter der Fassade der Wohlanständigkeit leitet er eine Organisation, die den Rauschgifthandel, die Prostitution, die Spielhöllen und Bestechungsaffären der meisten großen Städte im Norden Englands unter sich hat.«

»Und Sie können ihm nicht Einhalt gebieten? Ich finde das überraschend.«

»Herrschaft durch Terror, Pater. Er hat bei vielen Gelegenheiten auf Männer geschossen – gewöhnlich in die Beine, das tötet nicht, sondern schafft nur Krüppel. Er hat sie gern um sich – als Aushängeschild.«

»Ist das eine Tatsache?«

»Die ich nicht beweisen kann. Genauso wie ich nicht beweisen kann, daß er hinter der übelsten organisierten Kinderprostitution steckte oder daß er einem Mann Disziplin beibrachte, indem er ihn mit fünfzehn Zentimeter langen Nägeln kreuzigte oder einen anderen seine Exkremente essen ließ.«

Einen winzigen Augenblick lang sah sich da Costa in jenes Lager in Nord-Korea zurückversetzt – halbtot in einer Latrine liegend, während der Stiefel eines Chinesen sein Gesicht in einen Haufen menschlichen Kots stieß. Der Aufseher hatte ihn zwingen wollen, den Kot zu essen, aber er hatte sich geweigert, hauptsächlich, weil er geglaubt hatte, daß er ohnehin sterben müßte.

Er holte sich wieder in die Gegenwart zurück. »Und

Sie glauben, daß Meehan hinter der Ermordung Kraskos steckt?«

»Er muß dahinterstecken«, sagte Miller. »Krasko war sozusagen ein Geschäftsrivale in jeder Hinsicht. Meehan versuchte ihn unter seine Fittiche zu bekommen, aber Krasko widersetzte sich. In Meehans Jargon: Er wollte nicht vernünftig sein.«

»Und so mußte ihn ein Killer in aller Öffentlichkeit hinrichten.«

»In gewisser Weise beweist die Tatsache, daß Meehan so etwas zu tun wagt, seinen Größenwahn. Er weiß, daß ich sicher bin, daß er hinter der Geschichte steckt, aber er will, daß ich es weiß – will, daß es alle wissen. Er glaubt, daß ihm nichts und niemand etwas anhaben kann.«

Da Costa sah stirnrunzelnd auf das Foto, und Fitzgerald sagte: »Mit Ihrer Hilfe könnten wir ihn dieses Mal schnappen, Pater.«

Pater da Costa schüttelte den Kopf. »Tut mir leid, Inspektor.«

Miller sagte barsch: »Pater da Costa, den einzigen Schluß, den wir aus Ihrem seltsamen Benehmen schließen können, ist, daß Sie den Mann, den wir suchen, kennen. Ja, daß Sie ihn schützen. Inspektor Fitzgerald hier ist Katholik. Er vermutet, daß Ihr Wissen irgendwie mit dem Beichtgeheimnis verknüpft ist. Trifft diese Vermutung zu?«

»Glauben Sie mir, Superintendent, wenn ich helfen könnte, würde ich es tun.«

»Sie weigern sich weiterhin?«

»Ich fürchte, so ist es.«

Miller sah auf seine Uhr. »Also gut, Pater. Ich habe in zwanzig Minuten eine Verabredung. Ich möchte, daß Sie mich begleiten. Keine Drohung – kein Zwang. Nur eine simple Bitte.«

»Darf ich fragen, wohin wir gehen?«

»Zur Autopsie von Janos Krasko in die städtische Leichenhalle.«

»Soll das eine Herausforderung sein?«

»Das überlasse ich Ihnen, Pater.«

Da Costa stand auf. Er war plötzlich müde und der ganzen elenden Geschichte überdrüssig. Seltsamerweise war das einzige, was er wirklich in sich aufnahm, die Orgelmusik.

»Ich habe Abendmesse, Superintendent, und anschließend Abendessen für die Obdachlosen. Es darf nicht lange dauern.«

»Höchstens eine Stunde, Sir. Ich werde Sie zurückfahren. Aber wir müssen jetzt wirklich aufbrechen.«

Da Costa öffnete die Sakristeitür, ging in die Kirche und blieb an den Chorschranken stehen. »Anna?«

Fallon hörte zu spielen auf, und das Mädchen wandte ihrem Onkel das Gesicht zu.

»Ich gehe eben weg, Liebes, mit Superintendent Miller.«

»Was ist mit der Messe?« fragte sie.

»Ich werde nicht lange ausbleiben. Vielleicht kann Mr. Fallon nach der Messe wiederkommen? Dann können wir uns über die Orgel unterhalten.«

»Sehr gern, Pater«, rief Fallon freundlich.

Pater da Costa, Miller und Fitzgerald gingen das Seitenschiff entlang, kamen an Jack Meehan und seinem Bruder, die immer noch in den dunklen Schatten saßen, vorbei und verließen die Kirche durch das Hauptportal. Der Wind schlug es zu.

Fallon sagte leise: »Nun, Sie haben soeben sozusagen meinen Hals gerettet. Ich glaube, er vermutete etwas, der gute Miller.«

»Aber jetzt nicht mehr«, sagte sie. »Nicht nach diesem Spiel. Sie waren einzigartig.«

Er lachte leise. »Das mag einst so gewesen sein – wie ich mit geziemender Bescheidenheit zugestehen will –, aber jetzt nicht mehr. Meine Hände sind nicht mehr das, was sie früher waren.«

»Einzigartig«, wiederholte sie.

Sie war so bewegt, daß sie einen Moment lang die andere dunkle Seite seines Wesens vergessen zu haben schien. Lächelnd griff sie nach seinen Händen. »Ihre Hände – was für ein Unsinn.« Und plötzlich erstarb ihr Lächeln. »Ihre Finger«, flüsterte sie und tastete sie ab. »Was ist passiert?«

»Ach das.« Er entzog ihr seine Hände und betrachtete die vernarbten Fingerkuppen. »Ein paar Feinde von mir haben mir die Nägel ausgezogen. Eine kleine Meinungsverschiedenheit.«

Er stand auf und zog seinen Mantel an. Entsetzen malte sich auf ihrem Gesicht. Sie streckte eine Hand aus, wie um ihn zu berühren, und faßte ins Leere. Er half ihr auf und legte ihr den Mantel um die Schultern.

»Ich verstehe es nicht«, murmelte sie.

»Und bitten Sie Gott, daß es so bleibt«, sagte er sanft. »Kommen Sie, ich bringe Sie ins Haus.«

Sie stiegen die Stufen hinunter und gingen durch die Sakristei hinaus.

Nach einem kurzen Moment stand Billy Meehan auf. »Gott sei Dank! Können wir jetzt verdammt noch mal gefälligst von hier verduften?«

»Du kannst. Ich nicht«, sagte Meehan. »Bleib Fallon auf den Fersen!«

»Ich dachte, das wäre Varleys Job?«

»Jetzt ist es deiner. Sag Varley, er soll draußen warten.«

»Und was ist mit dir?« fragte Billy mürrisch.

»Ich warte hier auf die Rückkehr des Priesters. Es

wird Zeit, daß wir uns unterhalten.« Er seufzte und reckte sich. »Es ist so angenehm und friedlich hier im Dunkeln – mit all den flackernden Kerzen ringsum. Gibt einem Muße zum Nachdenken.« Und da Billy noch zögerte, gereizt: »Hau ab! Verdufte endlich, um Himmels willen! Wir sehen uns später.«

Er lehnte sich zurück, verschränkte die Arme und schloß die Augen.

Es regnete heftig, als sie den Pfad entlang dem Pfarrhaus zustrebten. Fallon schob ihren Arm durch seinen.

»Manchmal glaube ich, es hört nie mehr zu regnen auf«, sagte sie.

Sie erreichten die Eingangstür. Anna öffnete sie und blieb unter dem Vordach stehen.

»Ich begreife überhaupt nichts mehr. Ich verstehe weder Sie, noch was heute passiert ist – nachdem ich Sie spielen gehört habe. Es paßt alles nicht zusammen.«

Er lächelte sanft. »Gehen Sie jetzt hinein, mein liebes Mädchen. Und bleiben Sie in Ihrer kleinen sicheren Welt.«

»Wie kann ich das? Sie haben mich zu einer Hehlerin gemacht. Ich hätte sprechen können, aber ich habe geschwiegen.«

»Und warum haben Sie das getan?« fragte er rauh.

»Ich habe meinem Onkel mein Wort gegeben, haben Sie das vergessen? Und ich würde ihm um nichts in der Welt weh tun.«

Fallon trat zurück, lautlos.

»Mr. Fallon, sind Sie noch da?« rief sie von der Schwelle.

Er antwortete nicht. Sie wartete noch einen Moment. Unsicherheit spiegelte sich in ihrem Gesicht. Schließlich trat sie ins Haus und schloß die Tür.

Fallon wandte sich um und ging den Pfad entlang.

Billy hatte die beiden im Schutz eines großen viktorianischen Grabmales beobachtet – das heißt, er hatte Anna angestarrt. Sie war ganz anders als die Mädchen, die er kannte, ruhig, damenhaft – und trotzdem hatte sie eine exzellente Figur. Die Tatsache, daß sie blind war, brachte irgendwelche perversen Saiten in ihm zum Klingen. Er hatte fast augenblicklich eine Erektion gehabt.

Fallon blieb stehen, zündete sich eine Zigarette an, die Flamme mit der hohlen Hand schützend. Billy zog sich zurück.

Fallon sagte: »Alsdann, Billy! Ich bin jetzt fertig und bereit, heimzugehen. Da du hier bist, kannst du mich ja zu Jennys Wohnung zurückfahren.«

Billy zögerte. »Hältst dich wohl für verflixt smart, wie?«

»Um smarter als du zu sein, da gehört nicht viel zu, Sonnyboy«, sagte Fallon. »Aber merk dir: Wenn ich dich hier noch einmal herumhängen sehe, werde ich sehr ärgerlich.«

»Kümmere dich doch um deinen eigenen Schwanz!« zischte Billy wütend und rannte auf das Seitentor zu.

Fallon folgte ihm lächelnd.

Die städtische Leichenhalle war wie eine Festung gebaut und von einer sechs Meter hohen, roten Backsteinmauer umgeben. Millers Chauffeur stieg vor dem Haupteingang aus, sagte etwas in die Sprechanlage, setzte sich dann wieder hinters Lenkrad, und einen Moment später schwang das große Stahltor auf, und sie fuhren in den Innenhof.

»Da sind wir, Pater«, sagte Miller. »Die modernste Leichenhalle Europas – sagt man.«

Pater da Costa folgte den beiden Polizeibeamten. Das

Gebäude bestand aus Beton und Glas. Sie gingen über eine Rampe zum Hintereingang, und ein Assistent in einem weißen Kittel öffnete die Tür für sie.

»Guten Morgen, Superintendent«, sagte er. »Professor Lawlor erwartet Sie im Ankleidezimmer. Er möchte gern anfangen.«

Sie folgten dem Mann im weißen Kittel durch enge Korridore. Das leise Summen der Klimaanlage war zu hören.

Miller blickte über die Schulter zu da Costa und sagte beiläufig: »Sie prahlen damit, hier die reinste Luft der Stadt zu haben.«

Der Assistent führte sie durch eine Tür und verschwand.

In dem Raum befanden sich mehrere Waschbecken, eine Dusche in der Ecke, und an einem Kleiderhaken an der Wand hingen weiße Kittel. Darunter stand eine Reihe weißer Gummistiefel verschiedenster Größen.

Miller und Fitzgerald zogen ihre Regenmäntel aus, und der Superintendent nahm zwei weiße Kittel vom Haken und reichte einen da Costa.

Die Tür öffnete sich, und Professor Lawlor trat ein. »Komm, Nick! Du hältst mich auf.« Dann sah er den Priester, und seine Augen weiteten sich. »Hallo, Pater!«

»Ich möchte gern Pater da Costa dabeihaben, wenn es dir nichts ausmacht«, sagte Miller.

Professor Lawlor trug einen weißen Kittel, weiße Stiefel und lange, hellgrüne Gummihandschuhe, an denen er ungeduldig herumzupfte. »Solange er nicht im Weg herumsteht … Aber laß uns endlich anfangen. Ich habe um fünf eine Vorlesung.«

Sie folgten ihm über einen kurzen Gang und durch eine Gummi-Drehtür in das Autopsiezimmer. Das fluoreszierende Licht tat in den Augen weh. Ein halbes Dutzend rostfreier Stahl-Operationstische standen herum. Janos Krasko lag auf dem der Tür am nächsten stehenden, auf dem Rücken, den Kopf auf einem Holzklotz. Er war nackt. Zwei Assistenten standen neben einem Wagen, auf dem eine Auswahl chirurgischer Instrumente lag. Am meisten überraschten Pater da Costa die Fernsehkameras.

»Wie Sie sehen, Pater, die Wissenschaft schreitet voran«, sagte Miller.

»Ist das notwendig?« fragte da Costa.

»Ganz sicher. Besonders, wenn man sich gegen die Gutachten anderer berühmter Pathologen der Gegenpartei verteidigen will.«

Einer der Assistenten legte ein Mikrophon um Lawlors Hals.

»Haben Sie schon mal einer Autopsie beigewohnt, Pater?« fragte Lawlor.

»Nicht in dieser Form, Professor.«

»Wenn Sie sich nicht gut fühlen sollten – Sie wissen, wo der Ankleideraum ist. Und bitte treten Sie zurück! Das gilt für alle.« Er wandte sich den Kameramännern und Assistenten zu. »Alsdann, meine Herren, fangen wir an!«

Es war wohl Lawlors Verdienst, daß die Autopsie nicht zu einer Alptraumszene wurde. Er war wirklich brillant. Ein Künstler mit dem Messer. Er arbeitete flink und gründlich, und während der ganzen Prozedur kommentierte er jeden Handgriff nüchtern und präzise.

Pater da Costa beobachtete ihn fasziniert. Ventilatoren an der Decke über dem Tisch saugten alle Gerüche ab.

Die Schädeldecke war zuerst abgehoben worden, aber die genaue Untersuchung des Gehirns sollte erst nach der Autopsie erfolgen. Da Costa wunderte sich, daß auch der Körper geöffnet wurde, da es sich doch eindeutig um eine Kopfwunde handelte. Miller erklärte ihm, daß der Untersuchungsrichter einen detaillierten Bericht erwarte. Gleichzeitig unterbreitete er dem Pater seine Lebensphilosophie. Für seine Begriffe urteilte das Gesetz zu milde.

»Liberale Prinzipien sind schön und gut, solange es etwas gibt, woran man Prinzipien erproben kann.«

Pater da Costa fand es schwer, darüber zu argumentieren, und wandte sich wieder der Sezierung zu.

Schließlich war Professor Lawlor fertig.

»Das wär's also«, sagte er zu Miller. »Nichts, das erwähnenswert wäre. Das Gehirn werde ich mir vornehmen, wenn ich eine Zigarette geraucht habe.« Er lächelte da Costa an. »Nun, wie fanden Sie es?«

»Eine außergewöhnliche Erfahrung«, bekannte der Pater. »Und mehr als sonst irgend etwas beunruhigend.«

»Zu erkennen, daß der Mensch nichts weiter als rohes Fleisch ist?« fragte der Professor.

»Sind Sie der Ansicht?«

»Sehen Sie doch selbst!«

Lawlor trat an den Operationstisch, und Pater da Costa folgte ihm. Der Leichnam war geöffnet und ganz leer. Ausgeweidet. Nichts als gähnende Leere. Eine dicke Schicht gelben Fettes, darunter rotes Fleisch, praktisch kein Blut.

»Und Sie glauben, daß das alles ist?« fragte da Costa.

»Sie nicht?« konterte Lawlor.

»Der menschliche Körper ist ein technisches Meisterwerk. Unendlich zweckmäßig. Es scheint keine Aufgabe zu geben, die ein Mensch, wenn er will, nicht bewältigen könnte. Würden Sie dem zustimmen, Professor?«

»Vermutlich.«

»Und das soll alles sein, was letzten Endes von einem

Einstein oder Picasso übrigbleibt? Ein ausgeweideter Körper und ein paar zerhackte Innereien, die in einem Plastikeimer herumschwimmen?«

»O nein!« Lawlor grinste müde. »Bitte keine Metaphysik, Pater! Ich habe noch mehr zu tun.« Er wandte sich Miller zu. »Hast du genug gesehen?«

»Ich denke schon«, erwiderte Miller.

»Gut. Dann schaff diesen Advokaten des Teufels hier raus und laß mich in Ruhe zum Ende kommen. Morgen wirst du den vollständigen Bericht erhalten.« Er grinste wieder den Pater an. »Aus ersichtlichen Gründen kann ich Ihnen nicht die Hand schütteln. Aber schauen Sie herein, wann immer Sie vorbeikommen. Es ist stets jemand hier.«

Er lachte über seinen Witz, lachte noch immer, als sie ins Umkleidezimmer zurückgingen. Einer der Assistenten begleitete sie, um sicherzugehen, daß die Kittel, die sie getragen hatten, direkt in den Wäschekorb wanderten.

Miller war müde und deprimiert. Er hatte verloren. Und er wußte nicht, wie er weiter vorgehen sollte.

Es regnete immer noch. Als sie zum Wagen kamen, hielt Fitzgerald dem Pater die Tür auf, und da Costa stieg ein. Miller folgte ihm. Fitzgerald saß vorn neben dem Chauffeur.

Während sie sich in den Verkehr einreihten, sagte Miller: »Ich wollte Sie mit der Realität konfrontieren, aber es hat nichts geändert, nicht wahr?«

Pater da Costa erzählte eine Geschichte. »Als ich zwanzig war, sprang ich in den Bergen von Kreta mit einem Fallschirm ab, als Bauer verkleidet. Im Dorfgasthof angekommen, wurde ich augenblicklich von einem deutschen Geheimagenten mit vorgehaltenem Gewehr festgenommen. Einem Mitglied der Feldgendarmerie.«

Miller war interessiert. »Sind Sie verraten worden?«

»So ähnlich. Er war nicht schlecht. Sagte mir, daß es ihm leid täte, daß er mich aber festhalten müßte, bis die Gestapo käme. Wir tranken etwas zusammen. Mir gelang es, ihm mit einer Weinflasche über den Schädel zu schlagen.«

»Was passierte?«

»Er schoß mir in die linke Lunge, und ich erwürgte ihn mit meinen Händen.« Pater da Costa hielt sie hoch. »Seitdem habe ich jeden Tag für ihn gebetet.«

Sie bogen in die Straße, die an der Kirche entlangführte, ein, und Miller sagte: »Na schön. Ich habe kapiert.« Der Wagen hielt. Millers Stimme klang wieder sehr formell. »Gesetzlich machen Sie sich durch Ihre Haltung zum Mitschuldigen. Ist Ihnen das klar?«

»Vollkommen.«

»Gut. Ich habe vor, mich an Ihren Vorgesetzten zu wenden. Ein letzter Versuch, Sie zur Vernunft zu bringen.«

»Monsignore O'Halloran ist der Mann, den Sie suchen. Ich wollte ihn bereits selbst aufsuchen, aber er ist nicht in der Stadt. Er wird morgen früh zurück sein. Doch er wird Ihnen nichts nützen.«

»Dann wende ich mich an den Staatsanwalt und beantrage einen Haftbefehl.«

Pater da Costa nickte. »Sie müssen tun, was Sie für richtig halten.« Er stieg aus. »Ich bete für Sie.«

»Für mich beten!«

Miller biß die Zähne zusammen, während der Wagen sich in Bewegung setzte.

Es war feuchtkalt in der Kirche. Pater da Costa war müde – erbärmlich müde. Es war ein schrecklicher Tag gewesen – der schlimmste seit Jahren – seit dem chinesischen

Straflager in Chong Sam. Wenn Fallon und Miller sich doch einfach in Luft auflösen würden!

Er tauchte seine Finger in Weihwasser, und zu seiner Rechten flammte ein Streichholz in der Dunkelheit auf. Jemand zündete eine Kerze in der kleinen Seitenkapelle für St. Martin de Porres an und erhellte ein vertrautes Gesicht. Nach einer kleinen Pause kam der Teufel auf ihn zu. Pater da Costa wappnete sich, ihm entgegenzutreten.

8

»Was wollen Sie hier, Meehan?« fragte da Costa.

»Sie wissen, wer ich bin?«

»O ja! Man hat mich schon in jungen Jahren gelehrt, den Teufel zu erkennen.«

Meehan starrte ihn einen Moment überrascht an, dann lachte er schrill, den Kopf zurückgeworfen. Das Gelächter hallte von den Dachsparren wider. »Das ist gut! Das gefällt mir!«

Pater da Costa schwieg, und Meehan wandte sich schulterzuckend dem Altar zu. »Als Kind pflegte ich hierherzukommen. Ich war Ministrant.« Er wandte sich um und fragte herausfordernd: »Sie glauben mir nicht?«

»Sollte ich nicht?«

Meehan nickte in Richtung des Altars. »Ich habe dort viele Male gestanden. Meine alte Dame hat jede Woche mein Meßgewand gewaschen und gebügelt. Sie liebte mich in dieser Rolle. Pater O'Malley war in jenen Tagen Priester.«

»Ich habe von ihm gehört«, sagte da Costa.

Meehan erwärmte sich an seinem Thema. Er erzählte Anekdoten aus jenen Tagen, erinnerte sich glucksend des knallharten Priesters, der ihm mit einem Stock für vierzehn Tage Ehrlichkeit eingebläut hatte.

Pater da Costa wiederholte ruhig: »Was wollen Sie hier?«

Meehan machte eine Geste, die die ganze Kirche einschloß. »Nicht mehr das, was sie mal war. Einst war sie wunderschön, aber jetzt ...« Er hob die Schultern. »Kann jede Sekunde einstürzen. Habe gehört, die Restaurationsgelder haben nicht sehr weit gereicht.«

Pater da Costa begann zu verstehen. »Und Sie möchten gern helfen, ist es so?«

»Ja, genau, Pater.«

Die Tür öffnete sich hinter ihnen. Beide wandten sich um. Eine alte Dame mit einer Einkaufstasche trat ein.

»Wir können hier nicht sprechen. Kommen Sie mit«, sagte da Costa.

Sie fuhren mit dem Aufzug auf die Turmspitze. Der Nebel hatte sich gehoben. Die Sicht war ungewöhnlich gut.

Meehan war entzückt. »Ich war als Kind mal hier oben. Im Glockenturm.« Er deutete über das Geländer auf die Bagger. „Dort wohnten wir. Khyber Street 13.« Er wandte sich da Costa zu und sagte leise: »Das Arrangement zwischen Ihnen und Fallon – Sie werden dabei bleiben?«

Da Costa fragte: „Was für ein Arrangement soll das sein?«

»Tun Sie nicht so!« erwiderte Meehan, ungeduldig. »Diese Beichtgeschichte. Ich weiß Bescheid. Er hat es mir erzählt.«

»Dann wissen Sie ja als Katholik auch, daß das Beichtgeheimnis unantastbar ist.«

Meehan lachte rauh. »Er hat Grips, dieser Fallon. Er hat Ihnen ganz schön den Mund gestopft, wie?«

95

Da Costa atmete tief ein, um seinen Zorn zu unterdrücken.

Meehan gluckste. »Macht nichts, Pater. Ich zahle immer meine Schulden. Wieviel« – er machte wieder eine umfassende Geste –, »um all das richten zu lassen?«

»Fünfzehntausend Pfund«, teilte ihm der Pater mit. »Für die wichtigsten Vorarbeiten. Später wird mehr gebraucht.«

»Kein Problem«, sagte Meehan. »Mit meiner Hilfe könnten Sie das innerhalb von zwei oder drei Monaten auftreiben.«

»Darf ich fragen, wie?«

Meehan zündete sich eine Zigarette an. »Da sind zuerst einmal die Klubs. Dutzende über den ganzen Norden verteilt. Sie alle würden den abgewetzten Klingelbeutel herumwandern lassen, wenn ich es ihnen auftrage.«

»Und Sie bilden sich tatsächlich ein, daß ich das annehmen könnte?«

Meehan schien verwirrt. »Es ist nur Geld. Papier. Ein Zahlungsmittel. Ist es nicht das, was Sie brauchen?«

»Für den Fall, daß Sie es vergessen haben, Mr. Meehan: Christus hat die Geldverleiher aus dem Tempel getrieben.«

Meehan runzelte die Stirn. »Das verstehe ich nicht.«

»Meine Religion lehrt mich, daß eine Versöhnung mit Gott immer möglich ist, daß kein menschliches Wesen – wie schlecht es auch immer sein mag – nicht Gottes Gnade teilhaftig werden kann. Und bis jetzt habe ich immer daran geglaubt.«

Meehans Gesicht war bleich vor Wut. Er packte da Costas Arm, stieß ihn gegen das Geländer und deutete nach unten. »Khyber Street 13. Ein Reihen-Kaninchenstall. Ein Raum unten, zwei oben. Eine stinkende Toilette für alle vier Häuser. Mein alter Herr verduftete, als ich noch ein Kind war. Er hatte Verstand. Meine alte Dame hat uns mit Putzen durchgebracht – sofern sie Arbeit fand. Wenn nicht, standen Sonnabendnacht immer noch die Zehn-Shilling-Bumser hinter der Kneipe. Eine dreckige Hure – das war sie.«

»… die Zeit fand, jede Woche Ihr Ministrantengewand zu reinigen«, sagte da Costa. »Die Sie gefüttert und gewaschen und in diese Kirche geschickt hat.«

»Zum Teufel damit!« schrie Meehan wütend. »Alles, was sie je bekam – was jemals jemand aus der Khyber Street bekommen hat – war eine Kuhle in der Erde. Aber nicht ich. Nicht Jack Meehan. Ich stehe auf dem Gipfel, wo mir niemand etwas anhaben kann.«

Pater da Costa empfand kein Mitleid, nur Ekel. Er sagte ruhig: »Ich glaube, daß Sie die böseste und verdorbenste Kreatur sind, der ich jemals begegnet bin. Wenn ich könnte, würde ich Sie freudig den zuständigen Behörden übergeben, aber leider ist das unmöglich.«

Meehan schien sich wieder mehr unter Kontrolle zu haben. Er höhnte: »Das ist gut – wirklich. Mich würden Sie nicht mit einer drei Meter langen Stange berühren, aber Fallon – der ist etwas anderes, nicht wahr? Ich meine, er ermordet nur Frauen und Kinder.«

Einen Moment lang rang da Costa nach Luft. Nur mühsam brachte er heraus: »Wovon sprechen Sie?«

»Sagen Sie bloß nicht, daß er es Ihnen nicht erzählt hat«, spottete Meehan. »Nichts über Belfast oder Londonderry oder den Bus mit den Schulkindern, den er in die Luft gesprengt hat?« Er lehnte sich vor, da Costa seltsam gespannt anstarrend, und dann lächelte er. »Gefällt Ihnen wohl nicht, wie? Auf seinen irischen Charme hereingefallen, was? Mochten ihn wohl? Ich habe gehört, einige von euch Priestern …«

Eine Hand war an seiner Kehle, eine eiserne Hand, und die Augen des Priesters sprühten Feuer. Meehan versuchte, ein Knie hochschießen zu lassen, traf aber nur auf einen Oberschenkel, der seinen Stoß abblockte. Pater da Costa schüttelte ihn durch, öffnete dann die Tür und warf ihn in den Aufzug.

Meehan rappelte sich auf, während die Aufzugtür zuschlug.

»Das werden Sie mir büßen!« krächzte er. »Sie sind bereits ein toter Mann.«

»Mein Gott, Mr. Meehan«, rief da Costa durch die Stäbe des Käfigs, »ist ein Gott der Liebe. Aber er ist auch ein Gott des Zorns. Ich übergebe Sie in seine Hände.«

Er drückte auf den Knopf.

Als Meehan unter dem Kirchenportal auftauchte, blies ihm eine Windbö Regen ins Gesicht. Er stellte seinen Mantelkragen auf und zündete sich eine Zigarette an. Es begann dunkel zu werden. Als er die Stufen hinunterstieg, sah er eine Anzahl Menschen an einem Seitentor warten. Sie drückten sich gegen die Mauer, Schutz vor dem Regen suchend. Menschliche Wracks in zerlumpten Mänteln und zerschlissenen Stiefeln. Er überquerte die Straße, und Varley trat aus dem Hauseingang des alten Lagerhauses an der Ecke.

»Ich habe gewartet, Mr. Meehan, wie Billy es gesagt hat.«

»Was ist mit Fallon?«

»Fuhr mit Billy im Wagen weg.«

Meehan wandte seine Aufmerksamkeit wieder der kleinen Schlange zu. »Worauf warten die alle? Daß diese verflixte Suppen-Küche aufmacht?«

»So ist es, Mr. Meehan. In der Krypta wird ausgeschenkt.«

Meehan starrte die Leute eine Weile an und lächelte dann plötzlich. Er holte seine Brieftasche hervor und entnahm ihr ein Bündel Ein-Pfund-Noten. »Ich zähle zweiundzwanzig, Charlie. Gib jedem ein Pfund mit meinen Empfehlungen und sag ihnen, daß der Pub an der Ecke eben aufgemacht hat.«

Varley überquerte verwirrt die Straße, um die großzügige Spende zu verteilen, und innerhalb von Sekunden löste sich die Schlange auf. Einige der Männer tippten sich an die Mützen, zu Meehan hinüberblickend, der ihnen freundlich zunickte.

»Es wird heute abend eine Menge von dieser verdammten Suppe übrigbleiben«, sagte Meehan grinsend, als Varley wieder zu ihm trat.

»Ich weiß nicht, Mr. Meehan. Sie werden zurückkommen, wenn sie das Geld verpulvert haben.«

»Aber dann werden sie schwer geladen haben, so daß sie ihm ein bißchen Ärger machen könnten. Das heißt – ich glaube, wir sollten sichergehen. Schnapp dir diesen Rausschmeißer vom *Kit-Kat-Klub* – diesen Iren O'Hara.«

»Den dicken Mick, Mr. Meehan? Das gefällt mir nicht sehr. Er wird schrecklich, wenn er in Fahrt kommt.«

Meehan schlug ihm die Mütze vom Kopf und packte ihn bei den Haaren. »Du sagst ihm, daß er mit einem seiner Kumpel zur Öffnungszeit draußen vor der Tür sein soll. In der ersten Stunde geht niemand rein. Niemand! Er soll warten, bis ihm mindestens ein Dutzend Betrunkene den Rücken stärken, und dann die Bude auseinandernehmen. Wenn er es gut macht, ist es fünfundzwanzig Pfund wert. Wenn er dem Priester – so nebenbei – den Arm bricht, ist es fünfzig wert.«

Varley kroch auf dem Boden, um seine Mütze aus dem Rinnstein zu fischen. »Ist das alles, Mr. Meehan?«

»Für den Anfang – ja.« Glucksend entfernte er sich.

Pater da Costa hatte nur drei Ministranten für die Abendmesse. Es war eine aussterbende Gemeinde. Er hatte es gewußt, als sie ihn hierherschickten. Seine Vorgesetzten hatten es gewußt. Eine hoffnungslose Aufgabe, um ihm Demut beizubringen, wie der Bischof gesagt hatte. Ein bißchen Demut einem Mann, der so arrogant gewesen war, zu glauben, er könnte die Welt ändern.

Zwei der Jungens waren Westinder, der dritte hatte ungarische Eltern. Alle ein Produkt der wenigen verbliebenen Slum-Straßen. Sie standen wartend in einer Ecke, flüsternd, gelegentlich lachend, frisch gewaschen und gekämmt. Hatte Jack Meehan auch so ausgesehen?

Bei der Erinnerung an Meehan fuhr ihm ein Schwert durchs Herz. Gewalt war so oft schon sein Verderben gewesen. Er dachte an den chinesischen Soldaten in Korea, der eine Flüchtlingskolonne mit dem Maschinengewehr niedermähen wollte. Er hatte dem Mann aus hundert Metern Entfernung eine Kugel durch den Kopf geschossen. Hatte er falsch gehandelt? Obgleich er so viele Menschenleben hatte retten können? Und dann dieser portugiesische Captain in Moçambique, der Partisanen an den Beinen aufgeknüpft hatte. Er hatte den Mann halbtot geschlagen. Der Vorfall hatte ihn endgültig in die Heimat zurückgebracht.

Gewalt gegen Gewalt, das war Meehans Parole. Deprimiert und angewidert zog sich da Costa für die Messe um. Als er den alten rosa Priestermantel umlegte, öffnete sich die Tür, und Anna trat ein, in einer Hand den Stock, den Regenmantel umgelegt.

Er nahm ihr den Mantel ab. »Alles in Ordnung?«

Sorge spiegelte sich auf ihrem Gesicht. »Was ist los? Du bist deprimiert? Ist etwas geschehen?«

»Ich hatte ein sehr unerfreuliches Gespräch mit Mr. Meehan«, erwiderte er leise. »Er sagte einiges Fallon betreffend – Dinge, die eine Menge erklären könnten. Ich erzähle es dir später.«

Er führte sie in die Kirche hinaus, wartete ein paar Minuten und nickte dann den Jungen zu. Als die Orgel zu spielen begann, prozessierten sie in die Kirche.

Ungefähr fünfzehn Leute hatten sich eingefunden. Seit Korea hatte sich da Costa nicht mehr so entmutigt gefühlt. In dieser Messe flehte er seinen Gott an, ihm gnädig zu sein, ihm zu helfen und zu zeigen, was er tun sollte, und Tränen kullerten über seine Wangen, die ersten seit vielen Jahren.

9

Der Wind heulte durch die Stadt – wie ein lebendes Wesen, Regen vor sich hertreibend, die Straßen säubernd, an alten Fensterrahmen rüttelnd, an die Scheiben klopfend.

Als Billy Meehan in Jenny Fox' Schlafzimmer trat, stand sie vor dem Spiegel und kämmte sich. Sie trug den schwarzen Mini-Faltenrock, dunkle Strümpfe, hochhackige, glänzende Lackschuhe und eine weiße Bluse.

Billy schloß die Tür und sagte weich: »Hübsch. Sehr hübsch. Er ist immer noch in seinem Zimmer, ja?«

Sie wandte sich um. »Er sagte, er würde wieder ausgehen.«

»Dann werden wir seine Meinung ändern müssen, nicht wahr?« Billy setzte sich auf ihr Bett. »Komm her!«

Sie versuchte gegen die Panik anzukämpfen, die sie zu ersticken drohte, gegen den Ekel, der ihren Körper mit einer Gänsehaut überzog, während sie sich ihm näherte.

Er fuhr ihr unter den Rock und tätschelte das warme Fleisch oberhalb des Strumpfansatzes. »Das ist gut, Mädchen. Das wird ihm gefallen.« Er sah zu ihr auf, diesen seltsamen verträumten Ausdruck in den Augen. »Wenn du die Sache versaust, wirst du Schwierigkeiten bekommen. Ich müßte dich dann bestrafen. Und das würde dir doch nicht gefallen, oder?«

Ihr Herz klopfte wild. »Billy, bitte!«

»Dann mach es richtig. Ich möchte sehen, was diesen Kerl geil macht.«

Er stieß sie von sich, stand auf und ging zu einem Bild an der Wand, das er abnahm. Darunter befand sich ein winziges Guckloch, durch das er spähte. Nach wenigen Augenblicken wandte er sich um und nickte. »Zieht gerade sein Hemd aus. Geh jetzt zu ihm und vergiß nicht, daß ich zuschaue!«

Sein Mund war weich und konturlos, seine Hände zitterten leicht. Sie schluckte den Ekel hinunter, öffnete die Tür und schlüpfte hinaus.

Fallon stand am Waschbecken, als sie eintrat, den Oberkörper entblößt, Seifenschaum im Gesicht. Er drehte sich grüßend um, in der einen Hand ein geradezu mörderisches Rasiermesser.

Sie lehnte sich gegen die Tür. »Tut mir leid – das mit dem Rasiermesser. Ich konnte kein anderes auftreiben.«

»Macht nichts.« Er lächelte. »Mein Vater hatte so eins. Hätte kein anderes benutzt.«

Eine Linie häßlicher krumpliger Narben zog sich quer über seinen Bauch bis zur linken Hüfte hin.

Ihre Augen weiteten sich. »Was ist da passiert?«

Er sah nach unten. »Oh – eine Maschinengewehrsalve. Eines der wenigen Male, wo ich mich schneller hätte bewegen sollen.«

»Waren Sie in der Armee?«

»Sozusagen.«

Er wandte sich wieder dem Spiegel zu, um seine Rasur zu beenden. Sie trat zu ihm. Er lächelte schief, seinen Mund anspannend und den Rasiermesserbewegungen anpassend.

»Du siehst zum Anbeißen aus. Willst du ausgehen?«

Da war wieder dieses Prickeln, und plötzlich stellte sie überrascht fest, wie sehr sie diesen seltsamen kleinen Mann liebgewonnen hatte. Und im gleichen Moment erinnerte sie sich an Billy, der auf der anderen Seite der Wand lauerte.

Sie lächelte schelmisch, strich mit einem Finger über seinen nackten Arm. »Ich wollte heute abend zu Hause bleiben. Was ist mit Ihnen?«

Fallons Blick huschte zu ihr hin. In seinen Augen spiegelte sich fast so etwas wie Amüsement. »Liebes Mädchen, du weißt nicht, in was du da hineingeraten würdest. Außerdem bin ich zweimal so alt wie du.«

»Ich habe eine Flasche irischen Whisky da.«

»Gott bewahre! Reicht das nicht aus, um den Teufel höchstpersönlich in Versuchung zu führen?«

Er rasierte sich weiter, und sie ging zum Bett und setzte sich. Es lief nicht gut. Es lief überhaupt nicht gut, und bei dem Gedanken an Billys Wut fröstelte sie.

»Darf ich eine Zigarette haben?« fragte sie scheu.

Auf dem Nachttischchen lag eine Packung, daneben eine Schachtel Streichhölzer. Sie nahm sich eine Zigarette, zündete sie an und lehnte sich aufs Bett zurück, ein Kissen im Nacken. »Müssen Sie wirklich ausgehen?«

Sie zog ein Knie an, so daß der Rock hochrutschte, provozierend das nackte Fleisch über den dunklen

Strümpfen und den durchsichtigen, schwarzen Nylonslip zur Schau stellend.

Fallon seufzte tief, legte das Rasiermesser weg und griff nach einem Handtuch. Er wischte den Schaum aus dem Gesicht, ging zum Bett hinüber und sah auf sie hinab. »Du wirst dich erkälten« – er lächelte sanft und zog ihren Rock herunter –, »wenn du nicht aufpaßt. Und ich gehe immer noch aus. Aber ich werde vorher ein Glas mit dir trinken. Los, öffne die Flasche!«

Er zog sie hoch und schubste sie energisch durchs Zimmer.

An der Tür wandte sie sich um. Furcht spiegelte sich in ihren Augen.

»Bitte!« flehte sie ungestüm. »Bitte!«

Fallon runzelte leicht die Stirn, und dann umspielte kurz ein trauriges Lächeln seinen Mund. Er küßte sie zart und schüttelte den Kopf. »Nicht ich, mein liebes Mädchen, nicht gerade ich auf dieser großen, weiten Welt. Du brauchst einen Mann. Ich bin nur ein wandelnder Leichnam.«

Die Bemerkung war so schrecklich, daß sie einen Moment lang alle anderen Gedanken verscheuchte. Sie starrte ihn mit großen Augen an, und er öffnete die Tür und stieß sie hinaus.

Niemals im Leben hatte sie solche Angst gekannt. Wenn sie nur nach unten … Aber als sie auf Zehenspitzen an ihrer Schlafzimmertür vorbeischleichen wollte, öffnete sie sich. Billy zog sie so brutal ins Zimmer, daß sie stolperte. Sie verlor einen Schuh und landete quer über dem Bett.

Ängstlich drehte sie sich um. Er schnallte bereits seinen Gürtel auf.

»Du hast es vermasselt«, zischte er leise. »Und das nach allem, was ich für dich getan habe.«

»Billy, bitte! Bitte nicht! Ich werde alles machen!«

»Du wirst jetzt meine Spezialität zu spüren bekommen, damit du auf der rechten Fährte bleibst. Und vielleicht wirst du dann das nächstemal, wenn ich dir was auftrage, verdammt dafür sorgen, daß es klappt.« Er begann seine Hosen aufzumachen. »Los! Dreh dich um!«

Sie erstickte fast. Benommen schüttelte sie den Kopf. Wahnsinn leuchtete ihr aus den blassen Augen entgegen. Er schlug ihr heftig ins Gesicht.

»Du tust, was dir verdammt noch mal gesagt wird, du Hure!«

Er packte sie an den Haaren und drehte sie gewaltsam herum, bis sie mit dem Gesicht nach unten auf der Bettkante lag. Seine andere Hand zog ihren Schlüpfer runter. Und als sie sein steifes Glied spürte, als er sich wie ein Tier zwischen ihre Popobacken zwängte, schrie sie gellend auf, den Kopf in höchster Pein zurückgebogen.

Die Tür wurde so heftig aufgerissen, daß sie gegen die Wand knallte, splitterte. Fallon stand im Türrahmen, das mörderische Rasiermesser in der rechten Hand.

Billy ließ von dem Mädchen ab, brabbelte unzusammenhängendes Zeug, grapschte nach seinen Hosen. Als er sich aufrichtete, machte Fallon rasch zwei Schritte ins Zimmer hinein und trat Billy in die Geschlechtsteile. Billy fiel wie ein Stein um, die Knie hoch an die Brust gezogen, in der Stellung eines Fötus.

Das Mädchen brachte ihre Kleidung in Ordnung und stand auf. Tränen strömten über ihr Gesicht.

Fallons Augen waren sehr dunkel.

Sie konnte vor Schluchzen kaum sprechen. »Er hat – mich gezwungen – in Ihr Zimmer zu gehen. Er hat – zugeschaut.«

Sie deutete auf die Wand. Fallon ging auf das Guckloch zu.

Langsam wandte er sich um. »Ist so etwas oft passiert?«

»Er sah gern zu.«

»Und du? Was ist mit dir?«

»Ich bin eine Hure«, sagte sie. Und plötzlich brach es aus ihr heraus – all der Ekel, all die Selbstverachtung, aus jahrelanger Erniedrigung geboren. »Haben Sie auch nur irgendeine Ahnung, was das bedeutet? Er hat mich früh dazu gemacht – sein Bruder.«

»Jack Meehan?«

»Wer sonst? Ich war dreizehn. Gerade recht für eine gewisse Art von Kunden. Und von da an ist's bergab gegangen.«

»Du könntest gehen.«

»Wo sollte ich hingehen?« Sie hatte ein bißchen ihre Fassung wiedergewonnen. »Dazu braucht man Geld. Und ich habe eine drei Jahre alte Tochter, an die ich denken muß.«

»Hier?«

Sie schüttelte den Kopf. »Ich habe sie bei einer Frau untergebracht. Einer netten Frau, in einem anständigen Stadtviertel. Aber Billy weiß, wo sie ist.«

In diesem Augenblick bewegte Billy sich und richtete sich auf. Tränen schimmerten in seinen Augen, und Schaum stand vor seinem Mund.

»Sie sind erledigt«, hauchte er schwach. »Wenn mein Bruder hiervon hört, sind Sie eine Leiche.«

Er begann den Reißverschluß seiner Hose zuzuziehen. Fallon kauerte sich neben ihn.

»Mein Großvater«, begann er im Konversationston, »hatte eine Farm zu Hause in Irland. Schafe hauptsächlich. Jedes Jahr hat er ein paar Hammel kastriert, um den

Geschmack des Fleisches zu verbessern – oder damit die Wolle dichter wächst. Weißt du, was *kastrieren* ist, Billy, mein Junge?«

»Zum Teufel noch mal – Sie sind total verrückt – wie alle verdammten Iren«, krächzte Billy.

»Er hat ihre Hoden mit einer Schafschere abgeschnitten.«

Grauen malte sich auf dem Gesicht des Jungen.

Fallon sagte sanft: »Wenn du das Mädchen noch einmal anrührst« – er hielt das mörderische Rasiermesser hoch –, »werde ich mich persönlich um dich kümmern. Mein Wort drauf.«

Der Junge kroch von ihm weg und schob sich an der Wand hoch.

»Sie sind verrückt«, flüsterte er. »Total übergeschnappt.«

»So ist es, Billy. Zu allem fähig. Vergiß das nicht!«

Der Junge haute ab. Seine Stiefel polterten die Treppe hinunter. Die Haustür schlug zu.

Fallon wandte sich zu Jenny um. »Kann ich jetzt gehen?«

Sie hielt ihn an beiden Armen fest. »Bitte, gehen Sie nicht weg! Bitte, lassen Sie mich nicht allein!«

»Ich muß«, sagte er. »Er wird nicht wiederkommen – nicht, solange ich hier wohne.«

»Und danach?«

»Werden wir uns was einfallen lassen.«

Sie wandte sich ab, und er faßte rasch nach ihrer Hand. »Ich bin nur eine Stunde weg, nicht mehr. Ich verspreche es. Und dann können wir unseren Whisky trinken. Was hältst du davon?«

Sie wandte sich um. Tränen hatten ihr Make-up gemasert. Sie sah jetzt irgendwie sehr jung aus. »Meinen Sie das wirklich?«

»Das Wort eines irischen Gentleman.«

Sie schlang glücklich ihre Arme um seinen Hals. »Ich werde gut zu Ihnen sein. Bestimmt.«

Er verschloß ihren Mund mit einem Finger. »Das ist nicht nötig, ganz und gar nicht nötig.« Er streichelte ihre eine Wange. »Nur etwas kannst du für mich tun.«

»Was?«

»Wasch dir um Himmels willen dein Gesicht!«

Er schloß sanft die Tür hinter sich, und sie trat ans Waschbecken und blickte in den Spiegel. Er hatte recht. Sie sah schrecklich aus, und trotzdem lächelten ihre Augen zum erstenmal seit Jahren.

Pater da Costa konnte es nicht verstehen. Die Krypta war seit über einer Stunde geöffnet, und niemand war gekommen. Es war kein großartiger Platz, aber die Mauern waren weiß getüncht. Im Ofen brannte ein Koksfeuer, und Bänke und Tischböcke standen herum. Anna saß hinter einem und strickte einen Pullover. Vor ihr stand in einem wärmespeichernden Behälter die Suppe, daneben stapelten sich Teller und mehrere Brotlaibe vom gestrigen Tag, die eine Bäckerei kostenlos zur Verfügung stellte.

Pater da Costa schüttete Koks in den Ofen und stocherte ungeduldig mit dem Feuerhaken herum.

Anna hörte zu stricken auf. »Wie erklärst du dir das?«

»Weiß der Himmel, was passiert ist!«

Er ging nach draußen. Die Straße wirkte verlassen. Es nieselte im Moment nur. Er ging wieder rein.

Der Ire O'Hara trat aus der Toreinfahrt eines kleinen Hofes, etwas weiter die Straße unten, und stellte sich unter eine Laterne. Er war ein breitschultriger Mann, mindestens einen Meter neunzig groß, mit gekräuseltem, schwarzem Haar und einem stereotypen Lächeln. Der

Mann, der aus dem Schatten auftauchte, um sich ihm anzuschließen, war sechs bis acht Zentimeter kleiner und hatte ein gebrochenes Nasenbein.

In diesem Augenblick bog Fallon am Ende der Straße um die Ecke. Er näherte sich lautlos, und als er O'Hara und seinen Freund sah, blieb er kurz stehen, trat dann in einen Hauseingang und lauschte.

»Na, ich glaube, der Pfaffe ist jetzt soweit, Daniel«, sagte O'Hara. »Wie viele haben wir hier versammelt?«

Daniel schnalzte mit den Fingern, und einige Gestalten tauchten aus der Dunkelheit auf. Er zählte rasch. »Acht. Das sind zehn mit uns.«

»Neun«, sagte O'Hara. »Du bleibst draußen und behältst die Tür im Auge – nur für den Fall. Sie wissen, was sie zu tun haben?«

»Dafür hab' ich gesorgt«, versicherte Daniel. »Für ein Pfund pro Mann werden sie den Schuppen auseinandernehmen.«

O'Hara wandte sich den Gestalten zu. »Vergeßt eines nicht: Da Costa gehört mir!«

Daniel fragte: »Macht dir das nichts aus, Kumpel? Ich meine, du bist doch ein Ire und so. Schließlich ist er ein Priester.«

»Ich muß dir ein schreckliches Geständnis machen, Daniel, O'Hara legte eine Hand auf Daniels eine Schulter. »Einige Iren sind Protestanten – und ich bin einer von ihnen.« Er wandte sich den anderen zu. »Kommt, Jungens!«

Sie überquerten die Straße und verschwanden durch die Tür der Krypta. Daniel wartete am Geländer, die Ohren spitzend.

Hinter ihm hustete jemand leise, und als er sich umwandte, stand Fallon keine zwei Meter von ihm entfernt, die Hände in den Taschen.

»Wo zum Teufel kommen Sie denn her?« fragte Daniel.

»Das spielt keine Rolle. Was geht da drinnen vor?«

Daniel schätzte den Mann restlos falsch ein. Verächtlich zischte er: »Du kleiner Wichtigtuer, verschwinde, verdammt noch mal!«

Er machte eine schnelle Bewegung, die Arme zum Angriff abgewinkelt, aber sie konnten sich nur an der dünnen Luft festhalten, als seine Beine geschickt unter ihm weggeschlagen wurden. Er knallte auf das nasse Pflaster und rappelte sich, Obszönitäten von sich gebend, mühsam wieder auf. Fallon packte sein rechtes Handgelenk mit beiden Händen und drehte es hoch und anschließend herum. Daniel stieß einen Schmerzensschrei aus. Ihn weiter im Griff haltend, rammte Fallon ihn mit dem Kopf gegen das Geländer.

Daniel zog sich hoch, eine Hand demütig bittend vorgestreckt. Blut strömte über sein Gesicht. »Um Himmels willen, hören Sie auf!«

»Gut. Dann antworte! Worum geht es?«

»Sie sollen den Schuppen auseinandernehmen.«

»Für wen?«

Daniel zögerte, und Fallon schlug ihm wieder die Beine unter dem Leib weg. »Für wen?«

»Jack Meehan«, plapperte Daniel rasch.

Fallon zog ihn in die Höhe und trat zurück. »Das nächste Mal bekommst du eine Kugel in die Kniescheibe. Das ist ein Versprechen. Und jetzt verschwinde!«

Daniel taumelte davon.

Pater da Costa begriff sofort, daß es Ärger geben würde. Er machte ein paar Schritte vorwärts. Eine Bank flog um, dann eine zweite. Hände grapschten nach ihm. Jemand zog an seiner Soutane. Anna schrie ängstlich auf, und er

wirbelte herum und sah, wie O'Hara sie von hinten umfaßte, die Arme um ihre Taille gelegt.

»Nun, Liebling, wie wär's mit einem kleinen Kuß?«
fragte er.

Sie riß sich in panischem Schrecken los, streckte die
Hände vor, prallte gegen den Tisch und stieß ihn um.
Die Suppe ergoß sich über den Boden, Teller klapperten.

Pater da Costa kämpfte sich zu ihr durch.

O'Hara lachte schallend. »Na sieh mal, was du ange-
stellt hast!«

Eine leise, ruhige Stimme rief von der Tür her: »Mik-
keen O'Hara, bist du das?«

Es wurde still im Raum. Alle warteten. O'Hara wandte sich um. Ungläubiges Staunen spiegelte sich in seinem
Gesicht, ein Ausdruck, der rasch durch eine Mischung
aus Ehrfurcht und Angst ersetzt wurde.

»Gott im Himmel«, murmelte er. »Bist du das, Martin?«

Fallon ging auf ihn zu, die Hände in den Taschen. Alle
warteten.

»Sag ihnen, daß sie aufräumen sollen, Mick! Und
dann warte draußen auf mich!«

O'Hara gehorchte, ohne zu zögern, und steuerte auf
die Tür zu. Die anderen begannen die Tische und Bänke
wieder aufzustellen. Einer schnappte sich einen Eimer
und einen Schrubber und wischte den Boden auf.

Pater da Costa versuchte Anna zu beruhigen.

Fallon trat zu ihnen. »Tut mir leid, Pater. Es wird nicht
wieder vorkommen.«

»Meehan?« fragte da Costa.

Fallon nickte. »Haben Sie etwas Ähnliches erwartet?«

»Er besuchte mich etwas früher am Abend. Man
könnte sagen, daß wir nicht besonders gut miteinander
auskamen.« Er zögerte. »Der große Ire – er kannte Sie?«

111

»Ich bin bekannt wie ein bunter Hund.« Fallon lächelte und wandte sich der Tür zu. »Gute Nacht!«

Pater da Costa lief ihm nach und hielt ihn am Arm zurück. »Wir müssen uns unterhalten, Fallon. Das schulden Sie mir.«

»Gut. Wann?«

»Den Morgen über bin ich beschäftigt, aber die Beichte mittags fällt aus. Wäre Ihnen ein Uhr recht? Im Pfarrhaus?«

»Ich werde kommen.«

Fallon ging hinaus, schloß die Tür hinter sich und überquerte die Straße. O'Hara wartete nervös unter der Laterne.

»Bei Gott, wenn ich gewußt hätte, daß du in die Sache verwickelt bist, Martin, hätte ich mich nicht mal bis auf eine Meile herangewagt. Ich dachte, du wärst schon tot. Alle dachten das.«

»Wieviel hat dir Meehan gezahlt?« fragte Fallon.

»Fünfundzwanzig Pfund, fünfzig, wenn ich dem Priester einen Arm breche.«

»Wieviel im voraus?«

»Nichts.«

Fallon zog zwei Zehn-Pfund-Noten aus seiner Brieftasche und reichte sie ihm. »Reisegeld – eingedenk alter Zeiten. Ich glaube kaum, daß die Luft jetzt sehr gesund für dich hier sein wird, wenn Jack Meehan erst herausgefunden hat, daß du ihn hast hochgehen lassen.«

»Gott segne dich, Martin! Ich werde noch diese Nacht verduften.« Er wollte sich abwenden, zögerte dann aber. »Quält es dich immer noch, Martin – das, was damals passiert ist?«

»Jede einzelne Minute meines Lebens.«

Pater da Costa trat aus der schützenden Dunkelheit des Portals und sah, wie O'Hara die Straße überquerte und auf das Pub in der Ecke zusteuerte. Er betrat die Saloon-Bar. Der Pater folgte ihm.

Es war ruhig im Saloon. O'Hara war immer noch ziemlich durcheinander. Er bestellte einen großen Whisky, den er auf einmal hinuntergoß. Als er nach dem zweiten verlangte, öffnete sich die Tür, und Pater da Costa trat ein.

O'Hara versuchte, frech aufzutreten. »Oh, da sind Sie ja, Pater! Wollen Sie einen mit mir heben?«

»Ich würde noch eher mit dem Teufel trinken.« Da Costa zog ihn in eine Nische und setzte sich ihm gegenüber. »Woher kennen Sie Fallon?«

O'Hara starrte ihn erstaunt an, das Glas halb erhoben. »Fallon? Ich kenne niemanden, der Fallon heißt.«

»Martin Fallon, Sie Dummkopf«, sagte da Costa ungeduldig. »Ich habe Sie doch eben vor der Kirche mit ihm sprechen sehen.«

»Oh, Sie meinen Martin! Nennt er sich jetzt Fallon?«

»Was können Sie mir über ihn erzählen?«

»Weshalb sollte ich Ihnen etwas erzählen?«

»Weil ich sonst die Polizei anrufe und Sie wegen des Überfalls verhaften lasse. Kriminal-Superintendent Miller wird sich sicherlich sehr freuen.«

»Also gut, Pater, pfeifen Sie Ihre Hunde zurück.« O'Hara, durch die zwei großen Whisky enthemmt, ging zur Bar, um sich einen dritten zu holen. »Weshalb fragen Sie?« wollte er wissen, als er zurückkehrte.

»Spielt das eine Rolle?«

»Für mich – ja. Martin Fallon – wie Sie ihn nennen – ist wahrscheinlich der beste Mensch, dem ich je in meinem Leben begegnet bin. Ein Held.«

»Für wen?«

»Für das irische Volk.«

»Ich kann Ihnen versichern, daß ich ihm nichts Böses will.«

»Geben Sie mir Ihr Wort?«

»Natürlich.«

»Also gut. Ich werde Ihnen nicht seinen richtigen Namen sagen. Der spielt keine Rolle. Er war Leutnant in der Provisional IRA. Man nannte ihn in Derry den Henker. Ich habe niemals jemanden gekannt, der so mit der Waffe umzugehen wußte. Und er hätte auch den Papst getötet, wenn er überzeugt gewesen wäre, daß es der Sache dienlich ist. Und Köpfchen hat er! Ein Akademiker, Pater. Würden Sie das glauben? Trinity College. An manchen Tagen floß alles aus ihm heraus – Gedichte, Romane und so. Und er spielte Klavier wie ein Engel.« O'Hara zögerte, angelte sich nachdenklich eine Zigarette. »Und dann kamen andere Zeiten.«

»Was meinen Sie damit?« fragte der Pater.

»Er veränderte sich vollständig. Ging ganz in sich. Keine Gefühlsregung, kein Echo mehr. Nichts. Kalt und dunkel.« O'Hara schüttelte sich, steckte sich die Zigarette in einen Mundwinkel. »Er hat alle das Fürchten gelehrt – einschließlich mich.«

»Sie waren lange mit ihm zusammen?«

»Nur kurze Zeit. Man hat mir nie wirklich vertraut. Ich bin ein Tramp. Also stieg ich aus.«

»Und Fallon?«

»Er baute den Hinterhalt für den sarazenischen Panzerwagen, irgendwo in Armagh. Verminte die Straße. Jemand hatte die falsche Zeit erfahren, und ein Schulbus mit einem Dutzend Kindern wurde statt dessen in die Luft gejagt. Fünf wurden getötet, der Rest ist verkrüppelt. Es hat Martin fertiggemacht. Ich glaube, er hatte schon eine Weile über das Töten und all das nach-gedacht. Das mit dem Bus war sozusagen das letzte Tüpfelchen auf dem i. Ich dachte, er wäre tot. Als letztes hörte ich, daß die IRA ein Hinrichtungskommando nach ihm ausgeschickt hat. *Ich* – ich zähle nicht. Aber Martin – das ist etwas anderes. Er weiß zuviel. Jemand wie er kann nur auf einem Weg die Bewegung verlassen: im Sarg.« Er stand auf, das Gesicht gerötet. »Alsdann, Pater. Ich gehe jetzt. Diese Stadt und ich – wir trennen uns.«

Er steuerte auf die Tür zu, und da Costa begleitete ihn. Draußen knöpfte O'Hara seinen Mantel zu und sagte freundlich: »Haben Sie sich jemals über den Sinn des Lebens Gedanken gemacht?«

»Laufend«, erwiderte der Pater.

»Alsdann in der Hölle, Pater!«

Er entfernte sich pfeifend.

Pater da Costa überquerte die Straße. In der Krypta war inzwischen alles wieder aufgeräumt. Die Männer waren weg. Anna wartete geduldig.

»Tut mir leid, daß ich dich allein lassen mußte«, sagte da Costa, »aber ich wollte mit dem Mann sprechen, der Fallon kannte. Er ging in das Pub an der Ecke.«

»Was hast du herausgefunden?«

Er zögerte und erzählte ihr dann alles. Als er geendet hatte, sagte sie langsam: »Dann ist er also gar nicht das, wofür wir ihn anfangs gehalten hatten.«

»Er tötete Krasko«, erinnerte sie da Costa. »Kaltblütig.«

»Du hast recht – natürlich.« Sie griff nach ihrem Mantel und stand auf. »Was hast du jetzt vor?«

»Was erwartest du denn von mir? Daß ich seine Seele rette?«

»Das wäre eine Idee.«

Sie hakte sich bei ihm ein, und gemeinsam verließen sie die Krypta.

Auf der Rückseite von Meehans Grundstück stand ein altes Lagerhaus. Über eine Feuerleiter kam man bequem auf das alte Dach. Fallon duckte sich hinter einen niedrigen Wall, während er den Schalldämpfer auf den Lauf der Ceska schraubte. Die beiden Mansardenfenster auf der Rückseite von Meehans Dachterrassenwohnung waren keine zwanzig Meter von ihm entfernt. Die Vorhänge waren nicht zugezogen, Er hatte Meehan bereits mit einem Glas in der Hand auf und ab schreiten sehen. Einmal war Rupert zu ihm getreten und hatte einen Arm um ihn gelegt, aber Meehan hatte ihn weggeschoben – ärgerlich, nach seiner Miene zu urteilen.

Es war schwierig, auf diese Entfernung mit einer Handfeuerwaffe zu treffen, aber nicht unmöglich. Fallon hielt die Ceska mit beiden Händen und zielte auf das linke Fenster. Meehan tauchte kurz auf. Fallon schoß.

In der Dachwohnung zersplitterte ein Spiegel an der Wand, und Meehan ging zu Boden. Rupert, der auf der Couch liegend ferngesehen hatte, wandte sich blitzschnell um. Seine Augen weiteten sich.

»Mein Gott, das Fenster! Jemand hat auf dich geschossen!«

Meehan sah zu dem Loch im Fenster, dann zum Spiegel. Er erhob sich langsam.

Rupert ging zu ihm. »Soll ich dir was sagen, Schätzchen? Dich zu kennen, wird langsam verdammt gefährlich.«

Meehan stieß ihn ärgerlich beiseite. »Hol mir was zu trinken, verflucht noch mal! Ich muß nachdenken.«

Wenige Minuten später läutete das Telefon. Er hob den Hörer ab.

»Sind Sie das, Meehan?« fragte Fallon. »Sie wissen, wer hier spricht?«

»Sie Bastard!« zischte Meehan. »Was haben Sie vor?«

»Diesmal habe ich absichtlich danebengezielt«, sagte Fallon. »Vergessen Sie das nicht! Und sagen Sie Ihren Schlägern, sie sollen sich nicht mehr in der Nähe von *Holy Name* blicken lassen! Das gilt auch für *Sie*.«

Die Verbindung riß ab.

Meehans Gesicht war weiß vor Wut.

Rupert reichte ihm den Drink. »Du siehst nicht besonders gut aus, Schätzchen. Schlechte Nachrichten?«

»Fallon«, stieß Meehan zwischen den Zähnen hervor. »Es war dieser Bastard Fallon. Und er hat nicht getroffen, weil er nicht treffen wollte.«

»Mach dir nichts draus, Schätzchen. Schließlich hast du immer noch mich.«

»Das stimmt«, sagte Meehan. »Das hatte ich ganz vergessen.«

Und er boxte ihm die Faust in den Magen.

Es war schon spät, als Fallon heimkehrte. Er schlüpfte aus den Schuhen und schlich lautlos die Treppe hoch und in sein Zimmer. Dort zog er sich aus, stieg ins Bett und zündete sich eine Zigarette an. Er war müde. Es war ein höllischer Tag gewesen.

Jemand klopfte schüchtern an die Tür. Dann öffnete sie sich und Jenny kam herein. Sie trug ein dunkelblaues Nylon-Nachthemd. Ihr Haar war zurückgebunden, ihr Gesicht blank geschrubbt.

Sie sagte: »Jack Meehan hat vor einer halben Stunde angerufen. Er möchte Sie morgen früh sehen.«

»Sagte er, wo?«

»Nein. Ich soll Ihnen nur ausrichten, daß es nicht öffentlicher sein könnte, so daß Sie nichts zu befürchten

117

haben. Er schickt um sieben Uhr dreißig einen Wagen vorbei.«

Fallon runzelte die Stirn. »Ein bißchen früh für ihn, hm?«

»Keine Ahnung.« Sie zögerte. »Ich wartete. Sie sagten – eine Stunde. Sie sind nicht gekommen.«

»Tut mir leid. Ich konnte nicht, glaub mir.«

»Ich glaube es. Sie sind seit Jahren der erste Mann, der mich nicht wie Dreck, den er von den Schuhsohlen abgekratzt hat, behandelt.«

Sie begann zu weinen. Wortlos schlug er die Decke zurück und streckte eine Hand aus. Sie stolperte durchs Zimmer und legte sich neben ihn. Er knipste die Lampe aus. Sie lag in seinen Armen, preßte ihr Gesicht gegen seine Brust und schluchzte. Er drückte sie fest an sich, strich ihr übers Haar, und nach einer Weile schlief sie ein.

10

Der Wagen, der Fallon am nächsten Morgen um sieben Uhr dreißig abholte, war eine schwarze Leichen-Limousine. Varley saß am Steuer. Er hatte einen adretten blauen Anzug an und eine Schirmmütze auf.

Fallon kletterte hinten rein, schloß die Tür und schob das Glasfenster zur Fahrerkabine auf.

»Wo fahren wir hin?« fragte er.

Varley startete. »Zum katholischen Friedhof.«

Fallon, der sich gerade seine erste Morgenzigarette anzündete, wollte losbrausen, aber Varley sagte besänftigend: »Kein Grund zur Aufregung, Mr. Fallon. Ehrlich. Mr. Meehan muß heute morgen nur als erstes zu einer Exhumierung.«

»Einer Exhumierung?« echote Fallon.

»Ganz recht. So etwas kommt nicht sehr häufig vor, und Mr. Meehan ist immer gern persönlich zugegen. Er nimmt seine Arbeit sehr genau.«

»Das glaube ich gern. Was ist Besonderes an diesem Fall?«

»Nichts im Grunde. Ich vermute, er glaubte, Sie könnten sich dafür interessieren.«

Sie waren in zehn Minuten am Friedhof. Varley fuhr durch das Tor, an der Kapelle und dem Büro des Friedhofsverwalters vorbei einen schmalen Weg entlang.

Um das Grab scharten sich mindestens ein Dutzend Leute, ein Lastwagen und zwei Autos standen daneben. Meehan sprach mit einem grauhaarigen Mann in Gummistiefeln und einem Gummimantel. Er selbst trug einen Homburg und seinen doppelreihigen Mantel. Donner hielt einen Schirm über ihn.

Als Fallon ausstieg und durch den Regen platschte, wandte sich Meehan lächelnd um. »Ah, da sind Sie ja! Dies ist Mr. Adams, der Inspektor der Gesundheitsbehörde. Mr. Fallon ist ein Kollege von mir.«

Adams schüttelte Fallon die Hand und wandte sich wieder Meehan zu. »Ich will mal sehen, wie sie vorankommen, Mr. Meehan.«

Er ging, und Fallon sagte: »Welches Spiel ist nun dran?«

»Kein Spiel«, sagte Meehan. »Das hier ist Geschäft. Und danach habe ich eine Beerdigung. Aber wir müssen miteinander reden. Und dazu haben wir nachher im Auto Zeit. Bleiben Sie im Augenblick nur in meiner Nähe und tun Sie so, als gehörten Sie zur Firma.«

Er näherte sich dem Grab, Donner mit dem Regenschirm im Schlepptau. Fallon folgte. Es stank entsetzlich.

»Das Wasser steht etwa sechzig Zentimeter hoch,

Mr. Meehan«, sagte Inspektor Adams. »Zu viel Lehm. Das bedeutet, daß der Sarg in einem schlechten Zustand sein wird. Wahrscheinlich fällt er auseinander.«

»Auch dafür ist vorgesorgt«, sagte Meehan. »Vielleicht sollten wir den anderen gleich parat haben.«

Er nickte, und zwei der Totengräber hoben einen großen Eichensarg vom Lastwagen und stellten ihn neben das Grab. Als sie ihn öffneten, sah Fallon, daß er innen mit Zink ausgekleidet war.

Plötzlich kam Bewegung in die Gruppe. Die sechs Männer, die sich um das Grab geschart hatten, hievten den Sarg hoch, der gewissermaßen von den Tragegurten zusammengehalten wurde.

Und als der Sarg oben auftauchte, brach ein Ende ab, und zwei verweste Füße kamen zum Vorschein.

Der Gestank war noch unerträglicher geworden. Die bedauernswerten Totengräber taumelten auf den neuen Sarg zu. Nur Meehan schien riesigen Spaß zu haben, trat nahe heran und bellte Befehle.

Als der Deckel des neuen Sargs geschlossen wurde, wandte er sich strahlend an Fallon: »Alsdann – gehen wir. Ich habe um neun Uhr dreißig eine Einäscherung.«

Donner fuhr, und Meehan und Fallon saßen hinten.

Meehan öffnete einen Schrank an der unteren Hälfte der Trennwand, holte eine Thermosflasche und eine halbe Flasche Cognac heraus, goß eine Tasse halb voll Kaffee, halb voll Cognac und lehnte sich zurück. »Letzte Nacht – das war sehr dumm. Nicht gerade das, was ich eine freundschaftliche Geste nennen würde. Weshalb mußten Sie so etwas tun?«

»Sie haben versprochen, daß man den Priester in Ruhe lassen würde, und dann haben Sie O'Hara in die Krypta geschickt. Ein Glück, daß ich noch rechtzeitig auftauchte. O'Hara und ich sind übrigens sozusagen alte Kameraden. Er hat sich verkrümelt – zu Ihrer Orientierung.«

»Sie sind rührig gewesen.« Meehan goß Cognac nach. »Ich gebe zu, daß ich ein bißchen ärgerlich auf Pater da Costa war. Aber er war auch nicht sehr nett, als ich gestern abend mit ihm sprach. Und dabei habe ich ihm nur helfen wollen, Geld aufzutreiben für die Instandsetzung seiner Kirche.«

»Und Sie haben gedacht, er würde akzeptieren?« Fallon lachte schallend. »Sie müssen scherzen.«

Meehan hob die Schultern. »Auf jeden Fall war diese Kugel ein unfreundlicher Akt.«

»Genauso wie Billys Voyeurspielchen bei Jenny Fox«, entgegnete Fallon. »Wann werden Sie übrigens endlich etwas wegen dieses Wurms unternehmen? Ohne Aufseher kann er nicht das Haus verlassen.«

Meehans Miene verdüsterte sich. »Er ist mein Bruder. Er hat seine Fehler, aber die haben wir alle. Jeder, der ihn verletzt, verletzt auch mich.«

Fallon zündete sich eine Zigarette an, und Meehan lächelte breit. »Sie kennen mich nicht, nicht wahr, Fallon? Ich meine mein anderes Gesicht – den Leichenbestatter.«

»Sie nehmen das Geschäft ernst.«

Meehan nickte. »Man muß etwas Respekt vor dem Tod haben. Es ist ein ernstzunehmendes Gewerbe. Viele Kollegen gehen heutzutage zu lässig an die Dinge heran. Ich möchte, daß alles seine Ordnung hat.«

»Das kann ich mir vorstellen.«

Meehan lächelte. »Deshalb hielt ich es auch für eine gute Idee, daß wir uns dort heute morgen trafen. Wer weiß, vielleicht sehen Sie sogar irgendeine Zukunft in dem Geschäft.«

Er legte eine Hand auf Fallons Knie. Fallon rutschte beiseite.

»Nun, wie auch immer, wir werden Ihre Karriere mit einer Einäscherung beginnen«, schloß er und goß sich eine zweite Tasse ein, diesmal mehr Cognac nehmend. Zufrieden aufseufzend lehnte er sich zurück.

Als der Wagen durch das Tor des Krematoriums *Pine Trees* fuhr, stellte Fallon überrascht fest, daß Meehans Name in goldenen Lettern auf der Tafel stand. Er gehörte zu den sechs Direktoren.

»Ich bin mit einundfünfzig Prozent an dem Laden beteiligt«, erklärte Meehan. »Ist das modernste Krematorium in ganz Nordengland. Kostet uns eine Stange Geld, aber es lohnt sich. Die Leute kommen von überallher.«

Sie fuhren am Haus und Büro des Krematoriumverwalters vorbei und kamen zu einem prächtigen Gebäude mit Kolonnaden. Meehan klopfte an die Glasscheibe, und Donner hielt an.

Meehan kurbelte das Fenster herunter. »Das ist die Urnenhalle. In den Wänden befinden sich Nischen. Die meisten sind voll. Wir versuchen die Leute von diesem Aufbewahrungssystem abzubringen.«

»Und was würden Sie empfehlen?« fragte Fallon.

»Die Asche über den Rasen zu streuen«, erwiderte er ernst.

Die Kapelle und das Krematorium lagen ungefähr in der Mitte des Grundstücks. Neben einigen anderen Autos parkte ein Leichenwagen mit einem Sarg hinten drin. Bonati saß am Steuer, Meehan erklärte, daß Trauerprozessionen bei dem heutigen Verkehr nicht mehr üblich seien und der Leichenwagen daher – falls die Anverwandten einverstanden waren – vorausfahren würde.

Einen Moment später rollte eine Limousine an, der

drei weitere folgten. Billy saß in der ersten vorn neben dem Chauffeur.

Meehan stieg aus, um die Trauergäste zu begrüßen, den Hut in der Hand. Es war eine richtige Theatervorstellung, und Fallon beobachtete fasziniert Meehans Mienenspiel. Besonders gut konnte er es mit den älteren Damen. Er folgte dem Sarg und den Trauernden in die Kapelle und zog Fallon am Ärmel hinter sich her. Dieser war erleichtert, als die kurze unpersönliche Feier beendet war und der Sarg hinter einem Vorhang verschwand. Meehan machte noch eine Runde bei den Angehörigen, dann führte er Fallon zur Rückseite des Gebäudes. Er öffnete eine Tür, und sie betraten einen Raum, in dem vier riesige zylindrische Hochöfen standen. Zwei waren in Betrieb, in einem harkte ein Mann in einem weißen Kittel herum, der vierte war kalt.

Meehan nickte ihm vertraulich zu und erklärte: »Außer Arthur ist niemand hier vonnöten. Alles vollautomatisiert. Über ein Förderband kommt der Sarg aus der Kapelle hierher.«

Meehan führte Fallon an dem Sarg, den er eben noch in der Kapelle gesehen hatte, stolz den reibungslosen Ablauf der Verbrennung vor.

Fallon sah durch ein Glas-Guckloch in den Ofen, beobachtete, wie der Sarg in Flammen aufging, wandte sich aber rasch wieder ab, als ein Kopf sichtbar wurde, dessen Haare Feuer fingen.

Meehan stand neben Arthur, der geschäftig harkte.

»Schauen Sie sich das an!« forderte Meehan Fallon auf. »Das ist alles, was letztlich nach einer Stunde übrigbleibt.«

Die fein säuberlich von Arthur zusammengeharkten Rückstände wurden anschließend samt der Asche, die in einem großen Zinnbehälter aufgefangen worden war, durch einen Zerstäuber gejagt, unter den bereits eine beschriftete Metallurne montiert war. Meehan war stolz auf die Perfektion seines Systems. Er holte aus der Schublade eines Schreibtisches eine schwarzumrandete weiße Karte heraus – eine sogenannte Ruhe-sanft-Karte, die dem nächsten Angehörigen überreicht wurde. Darauf wurde die Parzellennummer eingetragen.

Es regnete noch immer, als sie hinter dem Gelände einen Pfad entlang zwischen Zypressen zu einer Rasenfläche schritten, die von Buchsbaumhecken durchzogen war. Am Rande des Pfades standen numerierte Tafeln. Ein Gärtner hackte etwas abseits in einem Blumenbeet herum, einen Schubkarren neben sich. Meehan übergab ihm die Urne, und der Gärtner mußte in ein kleines, schwarzes Büchlein die Angaben, die auf der Urne standen, notieren.

»Nummer 537, Mr. Meehan«, sagte er, als er fertig war.

Dann ging er zu der Tafel mit der entsprechenden Nummer, streute die Urnenasche über das feuchte Gras und bürstete sie mit einem Reisigbesen in den Boden ein.

Meehan wandte sich an Fallon. »Das ist alles – eine Ruhe-sanft-Karte mit der korrekten Nummer drauf.«

Während sie zur Kapelle zurückgingen, erklärte Meehan, daß er lieber beerdigt werden wollte. »Es ist passender. Aber man muß den Leuten das geben, was sie haben wollen.«

Als sie die Kapelle erreichten, waren Billy und Bonati bereits gegangen. Donner wartete noch, Varley war mit der zweiten Limousine da.

Der Krematoriumsverwalter erschien und wollte mit Meehan sprechen. So war Fallon einen Moment lang allein. Er hatte immer noch den Gestank aus dem offenen Grab in der Nase. Gleich im Haupteingang der Kapelle entdeckte er eine Toilette. Er ging hinein und wusch sich Gesicht und Hände in kaltem Wasser. In dem kleinen Fenster über dem Becken fehlte ein Stück in der Glasscheibe. Es regnete durch das Loch. Niedergeschlagen stand Fallon einen Moment da und starrte vor sich hin. Das offene Grab, die verwesten Füße, die aus dem morschen Sarg herausgeragt hatten – das war schon ein höllischer Tagesanfang gewesen. Und nun noch dies.

Als er aus der Toilette trat, wartete Meehan bereits auf ihn.

»Möchten Sie noch einer Verbrennung beiwohnen?« fragte er.

»Wenn es geht – nein.«

Meehan gluckste. »Ich habe noch zwei heute morgen, aber Varley kann Sie zu Jennys Wohnung zurückbringen.« Er grinste breit. »Es lohnt sich übrigens nicht, an einem Tag wie diesem auszugehen, wenn man nicht muß. An Ihrer Stelle würde ich schön brav zu Hause bleiben. Ich glaube, es könnte interessant werden. Sie ist ein richtiges kleines Feuerwerk, wenn …«

»Ich weiß«, sagte Fallon. »Sie haben's mir schon erzählt.«

Er stieg hinten in die Limousine ein. Varley fuhr nicht durch die Haupteinfahrt zurück, sondern einen abkürzenden Schleichweg.

Als sie ins Zentrum der Stadt kamen, sagte Fallon: »Du kannst mich hier irgendwo rauslassen, Charlie.«

»Aber das können Sie nicht machen, Mr. Fallon!« brummte Varley. »Sie wissen, was Mr. Meehan gesagt hat.«

»Sagen Sie Mr. Meehan mit meinen Empfehlungen, daß er sich ja daran halten könnte.«

Sie fuhren jetzt die Rockingham Street entlang. Als sie zu *Holy Name* kamen, beugte sich Fallon plötzlich vor und drehte den Zündschlüssel herum. Der Wagen rollte aus. Fallon öffnete die Tür, sprang heraus und überquerte die Straße. Varley sah ihn im Seiteneingang der Kirche verschwinden.

11

Monsignore Canon O'Halloran stand am Fenster seines Arbeitszimmers, als Miller und Fitzgerald hereingeführt wurden. Er wandte sich um, grüßte und ging zu seinem Schreibtisch, sich schwer auf einen Stock stützend, das linke Bein nachziehend.

»Guten Morgen, meine Herren – falls es Morgen ist. Manchmal glaube ich, es hört nie mehr zu regnen auf.«

Er sprach mit Belfast-Akzent, und Miller mochte ihn auf Anhieb. Sein Haar war schon weiß, seine Nase schien mehrmals gebrochen zu sein; er sah so aus, als wäre er einst ein tüchtiger Schwergewichtsboxer gewesen.

Miller stellte sich vor. »Ich bin Kriminal-Superintendent Miller. Ich glaube, Inspektor Fitzgerald kennen Sie schon.«

»O ja. Einer unserer Ritter vom St.-Columba-Orden.« Er ließ sich auf dem Stuhl hinter dem Schreibtisch nieder. »Der Bischof ist in Rom. Sie werden mit mir vorliebnehmen müssen.«

»Haben Sie meinen Brief erhalten, Sir?«

»O ja. Er wurde gestern abgegeben.«

»Ich dachte, daß uns das Zeit ersparen würde.« Miller zögerte und äußerte dann vorsichtig: »Ich bat, daß Pater da Costa anwesend sein möge.«

»Er wartet nebenan.« Monsignore O'Halloran stopfte sorgfältig seine Pfeife. »Ich dachte, ich höre mir erst an, was die Anklage zu sagen hat.«

»Nun, Sie haben meinen Brief bekommen. Da steht alles drin.«

»Und was erwarten Sie von mir?«

»Daß Sie Pater da Costa zur Vernunft bringen. Er muß uns helfen. Er muß diesen Mann identifizieren.«

»Wenn Ihre Vermutung stimmt, kann der Pater Ihnen unmöglich helfen«, erklärte Monsignore O'Halloran ruhig. »Das Beichtgeheimnis ist unantastbar.«

»Auch in einem solchen Fall?« fragte Miller ärgerlich. »Das ist doch lächerlich!«

Inspektor Fitzgerald legte eine Hand auf O'Hallorans Arm, aber dieser war nicht im mindesten verstimmt.

Sanft erwiderte er: »Jedem, der nichts mit der katholischen Kirche zu tun hat, muß die Beichtidee tatsächlich absurd erscheinen. Unsere Kirche hat sie indessen immer als eine Art Therapie aufgefaßt. Die Sünde ist eine schreckliche Last. Durch die Beichte wird den Menschen ein neuer Start ermöglicht.«

Miller wurde ungeduldig, aber O'Halloran fuhr im gleichen ruhigen Tonfall fort, und er hatte etwas außerordentlich Bezwingendes.

»Aber hier geht es um Mord, Monsignore!« warf Miller schließlich aufgebracht ein. »Um Mord, Korruption und Greueltaten, die Sie erschauern ließen.«

»Das bezweifle ich.« O'Halloran lachte kurz auf und hielt ein neues Streichholz an seine Pfeife. »Die meisten Menschen glauben, daß der Priester von der wirklichen Welt irgendwie abgeschnitten sei, aber glauben Sie mir, ich werde innerhalb einer Woche mit mehr Schlechtigkeit konfrontiert als ein Durchschnittsmensch während seines ganzen Lebens. Und denken Sie, es sei leicht, diese aufgebürdete Last mit sich herumzutragen, Superintendent? Es vergeht kaum eine Woche, in der mir nicht jemand Vergehen anvertraut, für die man ihn strafrechtlich verfolgen würde.«

Miller stand auf. »Dann können Sie uns also nicht helfen.«

»Das habe ich nicht gesagt. Ich werde mit ihm sprechen. Würden Sie, bitte, draußen ein paar Minuten warten?«

»Gewiß. Aber ich würde ihn gern, bevor wir gehen, noch in Ihrem Beisein sehen.«

»Wie Sie wünschen.«

Sie gingen hinaus, und Monsignore O'Halloran ließ Pater da Costa über die Sprechanlage hereinrufen. Eine unangenehme Aufgabe stand ihm bevor. Niedergedrückt starrte er in den triefenden Garten hinaus und überlegte, was er da Costa sagen sollte.

Die Tür hinter ihm klickte. Er wandte sich langsam um. Da Costa näherte sich dem Schreibtisch.

»Michael, was soll ich nur mit Ihnen machen?«

»Es tut mir leid, Monsignore«, sagte Pater da Costa formell, »aber ich habe mir die Situation nicht ausgesucht.«

»Das tut man nie. Ist es wahr, was sie annehmen? Steht diese Geschichte in irgendeinem Zusammenhang mit dem Beichtgeheimnis?«

»Ja«, sagte Pater da Costa schlicht.

»Das dachte ich mir.« Er seufzte tief und schüttelte den Kopf. »Es ist anzunehmen, daß der Superintendent beabsichtigt, die Sache weiterzuverfolgen. Sind Sie darauf vorbereitet?«

»Natürlich«, entgegnete der Pater ruhig.

»Dann sollten wir es hinter uns bringen.« Monsignore O'Halloran drückte wieder auf den Knopf der Sprechanlage. »Schicken Sie Superintendent Miller und Inspektor Fitzgerald rein!« Er grinste leicht. »Das Ganze entbehrt nicht der Komik. Das müssen Sie doch zugeben.«

»Wirklich, Monsignore?«

»Man hat Sie nach *Holy Name* geschickt, um Ihnen ein bißchen Demut beizubringen, und nun stehen Sie wieder bis über beide Ohren in einem Skandal. Ich kann mir das Gesicht des Bischofs schon gut vorstellen.«

Die Tür ging auf, und Miller und Fitzgerald wurden wieder hereingeführt. Miller nickte da Costa zu. »Guten Morgen, Pater.«

Monsignore O'Halloran erhob sich. Er hatte das Gefühl, die Situation erforderte es.

»Ich habe das Problem mit Pater da Costa durchdiskutiert, Superintendent«, sagte er. »Um ganz ehrlich zu sein – es scheint, daß ich nicht sehr viel für Sie tun kann.«

»Verstehe, Sir.« Miller wandte sich Pater da Costa zu. »Ich frage Sie zum letztenmal, Pater: Sind Sie bereit, uns zu helfen?«

»Es tut mir leid, Superintendent.«

»Mir auch, Pater.« Miller war jetzt frostig-formell. »Ich habe den Fall mit dem Polizeipräsidenten erörtert und folgenden Entschluß gefaßt. Der Staatsanwalt wird noch heute einen Bericht über die ganze Affäre und Ihre Rolle, die Sie darin spielen, bekommen.«

»Und was glauben Sie, was Ihnen das einbringt?« fragte O'Halloran.

»Sie werden zugeben, daß die Aussichten, einen Haftbefehl für Pater da Costa zu bekommen, ausgezeichnet sind. Die Anklage lautet: Begünstigung eines Mörders.«

Monsignore O'Halloran machte ein ernstes Gesicht und schüttelte bedächtig den Kopf. »Sie vergeuden Ihre Zeit, Superintendent. So ein Haftbefehl wird niemals ausgestellt werden.«

»Wir werden sehen, Sir.«

Miller wandte sich um und verließ das Zimmer. Fitzgerald folgte ihm.

Monsignore O'Halloran seufzte und setzte sich wieder. »Nun können wir nur noch warten.«

»Es tut mir leid, Monsignore«, sagte Pater da Costa.

»Ich weiß, Michael, ich weiß.« O'Halloran sah zu ihm auf. »Kann ich irgend etwas für Sie tun?«

»Würden Sie meine Beichte anhören, Monsignore?«

»Natürlich.«

Pater da Costa ging um den Schreibtisch herum und kniete nieder.

Als Fallon in die Kirche kam, spielte Anna auf der Orgel. Er setzte sich in die erste Reihe und lauschte. Nach einer Weile hörte sie abrupt zu spielen auf. Er stieg die Stufen hoch.

Sie wirbelte herum. »Sie sind früh dran. Onkel Michael sagte ein Uhr.«

»Ich hatte nichts anderes zu tun.«

Sie stand auf. »Möchten Sie gern spielen?«

»Nicht im Moment.«

»Gut. Dann können Sie mit mir spazierengehen. Ich könnte etwas frische Luft brauchen.«

Ihr Trenchcoat hing in der Sakristei. Er half ihr hinein, und sie traten in den Kirchhof hinaus. Es regnete stark, aber das schien ihr nichts auszumachen.

»Wo wollen Sie hingehen?« fragte er.

»Oh, hier ist es schön. Ich liebe Kirchhöfe. Sie sind so erholsam.«

Anna hakte sich bei ihm ein, und sie spazierten zwischen den alten viktorianischen Grabmälern entlang. Der Wind wirbelte Blätter auf und jagte sie wie etwas Lebendiges vor ihnen her. Sie blieben neben dem alten Marmor-Mausoleum stehen, als Fallon sich eine Zigarette anzündete. Genau in diesem Moment tauchten Billy Meehan und Varley am Seitentor auf. Sie sahen Fallon und das Mädchen augenblicklich und gingen in Deckung.

»Er ist noch da«, sagte Varley. »Gott sei Dank!«

»Fahr zum Paul's Square zurück und warte auf Jack!« sagte Billy. »Erzähl ihm, wo ich bin. Ich werde hier aufpassen.«

Varley verzog sich, und Billy arbeitete sich vorsichtig zu Fallon und Anna vor, die Grabmäler als Deckung nutzend.

Anna sagte: »Ich möchte Ihnen für gestern abend danken.«

»Nicht der Rede wert.«

»Einer der Männer war ein alter Freund von Ihnen. O'Hara – so hieß er doch?«

Fallon sagte rasch: »Nein, Sie haben sich verhört.«

»Ich glaube nicht. Onkel Michael hat sich, nachdem Sie gegangen waren, mit ihm unterhalten, in dem Pub auf der anderen Straßenseite. Er hat eine Menge über Sie erzählt. Belfast, Londonderry – die IRA.«

»Dieser Bastard!« sagte Fallon verbittert. »Er hatte schon immer ein großes Mundwerk. Wenn er nicht achtgibt, wird ihm eines schönen Tages jemand die Äuglein schließen.«

»Ich glaube nicht, daß er es böse gemeint hat. Onkel Michael hatte vielmehr den Eindruck, daß er sehr viel von Ihnen hält.« Sie zögerte und fügte dann behutsam hinzu: »Im Krieg passieren manchmal Dinge, die niemand beabsichtigt hat, die ...«

Fallon unterbrach sie scharf – »Ich denke nie zurück. Es lohnt sich nicht, ist sinnlos.« Sie bogen in einen anderen Pfad ein, und er blickte zum Himmel empor. »Mein Gott, hört es nie mehr zu regnen auf? Was für eine Welt!

Selbst der verdammte Himmel kann das Weinen nicht lassen.«

»Sie haben eine verbitterte Lebenseinstellung, Mr. Fallon.«

»Ich sage, was ich empfinde. Leben – eine höllische Bezeichnung für die Welt, wie sie ist.«

»Und es gibt nichts – keine winzige Kleinigkeit, für die es sich lohnt – in Ihrer Welt?«

»Nur Sie«, sagte er.

Sie befanden sich jetzt in der Nähe des Pfarrhauses. Billy Meehan, hinter einem Grabstein versteckt, beobachtete sie durch ein Fernglas.

Anna blieb stehen. »Was haben Sie gesagt?«

»Sie gehören nicht hierher.« Er machte eine Geste, die den ganzen Friedhof einschloß. »Dieser Platz gehört den Toten – und Sie leben noch.«

»Und Sie?«

Er sagte lange nichts, dann erklärte er ruhig: »Ich bin ein wandelnder Toter. Bin es nun schon seit langem.«

Es war eines der schrecklichsten Bekenntnisse, das sie je in ihrem Leben gehört hatte. Sie sah mit ihren blinden Augen zu ihm auf, irgendeinen Punkt fixierend, und plötzlich zog sie seinen Kopf zu sich herunter und küßte ihn heftig und bewußt herausfordernd. Dann entzog sie sich ihm.

»Haben Sie das gespürt?« fragte sie hitzig. »Bin ich vorgestoßen?«

»Das kann man wohl sagen«, murmelte er verwirrt.

»Gut. Ich gehe jetzt rein. Ich möchte mich umziehen und dann muß ich den Lunch vorbereiten. Sie sollten vielleicht Orgel spielen, bis mein Onkel zurückkommt.«

»Ja«, sagte Fallon und wandte sich um.

Er hatte erst ein paar Schritte gemacht, als sie ihm nachrief: »Oh – Fallon?«

Er drehte sich um. Sie stand in der halboffenen Tür.

»Denken Sie an mich! Erinnern Sie sich an mich! Konzentrieren Sie sich auf mich! Ich existiere! Ich bin da!«

Sie ging ins Haus, schloß die Tür, und Fallon entfernte sich rasch.

Als er außer Sichtweite war, kam Billy aus seinem Versteck. Fallon und die Nichte des Priesters. Das war interessant. Billy wollte sich schon abwenden, da sah er eine Bewegung an einem der Fenster des Pfarrhauses. Er kroch in sein Versteck zurück und hob das Fernglas an die Augen. Anna stand am Fenster und begann ihre Bluse aufzuknöpfen. Sein Mund wurde trocken, und als sie den Reißverschluß ihres Rockes aufmachte und aus dem Rock herausschlüpfte, begannen seine Hände, die das Fernglas umklammerten, zu zittern. Dieses Flittchen! dachte er. Und sie gehört Fallon. Der Schmerz zwischen seinen Schenkeln war fast unerträglich. Er wandte sich ab und rannte davon.

Fallon hatte fast über eine Stunde Orgel gespielt. Es war lange her, und seine Hände taten ihm weh, aber es war wohltuend. Als er sich umdrehte, sah er Pater da Costa in der ersten Reihe sitzen.

»Wie lange sind Sie schon hier?« Fallon stand auf und kam die Stufen herunter.

»Eine halbe Stunde, vielleicht auch mehr«, erwiderte da Costa. »Sie sind brillant. Aber das wissen Sie ja.«

»Ich war es.«

»Ehe Sie zur Waffe griffen, um für die liebe alte Mutter Irland und diese ruhmreiche Sache zu kämpfen?«

Fallon war lange still, und als er sprach, war es fast nur ein Flüstern. »Das ist nicht von Interesse für Sie.«

»Sogar von großem Interesse«, erklärte ihm da Costa.

»Guter Mann, wie konnten Sie das, was Sie getan haben, tun – Sie, der Sie so viel Musik in sich haben?«

»Sir Philip Sidney soll einer der vollkommensten Ritter am Hofe Elizabeth Tudors gewesen sein. Er komponierte und schrieb Gedichte. In seinen lichteren Momenten hat er zusammen mit Sir Walter Raleigh Iren an günstigen Punkten zusammengetrieben und sie wie Vieh abgeschlachtet.«

»Also gut. Lassen wir das. Aber sehen Sie sich selbst wirklich so? Als Soldat?«

»Mein Vater war einer.« Fallon lehnte sich an die Chorschranken. »Er war Sergeant bei einem Fallschirm-jäger-Regiment. Wurde in Arnheim getötet – für England kämpfend.«

»Und was wurde aus Ihnen?«

»Mein Großvater hat mich aufgezogen. Er hatte eine Berg-Farm in den Sperrins. Hauptsächlich Schafe – ein paar Pferde. Ich wuchs ganz glücklich auf, wild und barfüßig – bis zu meinem siebten Lebensjahr. Da entdeckte der neue Schulleiter, der auch Organist in der Kirche war, daß ich ein absolutes Gehör besitze. Von da an änderte sich mein Leben.«

»Sie kamen aufs Trinity College, nicht wahr?«

Fallon runzelte leicht die Stirn. »Wer hat Ihnen das gesagt?«

»Ihr Freund O'Hara. Haben Sie promoviert?«

Plötzlich spiegelte sich so etwas wie Humor in Fallons Augen. »Pater, würden Sie mir glauben, wenn ich Ihnen erzählte, daß aus dem Bauernjungen nichts Geringeres als ein Doktor der Musik wurde?«

»Warum nicht? Beethovens Mutter war eine Köchin. Und das andere? Wie kam es dazu?«

»Die Zeit und der Zufall. Ich verbrachte ein Wochen-ende im August 1969 bei einem Cousin in Belfast. Er wohnte in der Falls Road. Erinnern Sie sich, was damals passierte?«

Pater da Costa nickte ernst. »Und Sie wurden mit hineinverwickelt?«

»Jemand gab mir ein Gewehr in die Hand, und ich entdeckte etwas Seltsames: Worauf ich zielte, traf ich.«

»Eine Naturbegabung also.«

»Genau.« Fallons Miene war düster, und plötzlich holte er die Ceska aus der Tasche. »Wenn ich das hier in der Hand halte, wenn ich den Finger am Abzug habe, geht etwas Merkwürdiges in mir vor. Es ist, als ob sich meine Persönlichkeit erweitern würde. Ergibt das irgendeinen Sinn?«

»O ja. Aber einen höchst schrecklichen. Und Sie fuhren also fort, zu töten.«

»Zu kämpfen«, berichtigte Fallon mit versteinerter Miene. Die Ceska glitt in seine Tasche zurück. »Als Soldat der republikanischen irischen Armee.«

»Und es wurde einfacher. Mit jedem Mal fiel es Ihnen leichter.«

Fallon richtete sich langsam auf. Seine Augen waren wieder sehr dunkel. Er antwortete nicht.

Pater da Costa sagte: »Ich komme gerade von einem letzten Kräftemessen mit Superintendent Miller. Würde es Sie interessieren, was er vorhat?«

»Erzählen Sie!«

»Er will die Fakten dem Staatsanwalt vorlegen und ihn um einen Haftbefehl für mich ersuchen – wegen Begünstigung eines Mörders.«

»Damit wird er niemals durchkommen.«

»Und was ist, wenn er Erfolg hat? Würde Sie das auch nur im entferntesten beunruhigen?«

»Wahrscheinlich nicht.«

»Nun, wenigstens sind Sie aufrichtig. Es gibt also

noch Hoffnung für Sie. Fallon – die Schießereien, die Bomben, die vielen Toten und Verkrüppelten – war die Sache, für die Sie gekämpft haben, all das wert?«

Fallons Gesicht war jetzt weiß, seine Augen pechschwarz, leer.

»Ich genoß jeden goldenen Augenblick«, sagte er leise.

»Und die Kinder? Hat es sich auch dafür gelohnt?«

»Das war ein Unfall«, erklärte Fallon rauh.

»Nun, wenigstens steckte hinter all dem noch so etwas wie eine Idee – wie falsch sie auch immer sein mochte. Aber Krasko – das war kaltblütiger Mord.«

Fallon lachte leise. »Also gut, Pater, Sie wollen Antworten. Ich werde versuchen, Ihnen einige zu geben.« Er trat an die Chorschranken, stellte einen Fuß drauf, stützte einen Ellenbogen aufs Knie, das Kinn in die Hand. »Es gibt ein Gedicht von Ezra Pound, das ich immer geliebt habe. Es handelt vom Glauben an die Lügen der Alten. Dafür habe ich Gott weiß wie viele Menschen getötet.«

»Schön, Sie haben sich geirrt. Gewalt führt nie zu einem Ziel. Das hätte ich Ihnen vorher sagen können. Aber Krasko« – da Costa schüttelte den Kopf –, »das verstehe ich nicht.«

»Schauen Sie, wir leben in verschiedenen Welten. Menschen wie Meehan sind Abtrünnige. Ich auch. Krasko war ein Hurenbock, ein Zuhälter, ein Rauschgifthändler …«

»Den Sie ermordeten.«

»Ich kämpfte für eine Sache, Pater, tötete dafür, selbst als ich aufhörte, daran zu glauben, daß sie auch nur ein einziges Menschenleben wert war. *Das war Mord.* Jetzt töte ich nur Schweine.«

Ekel und Selbstverachtung sprachen aus jedem Wort.

»Ich verbrachte mehrere Jahre in einem chinesischen kommunistischen Gefangenenlager in Korea«, erzählte da Costa. »Es war als Schulungszentrum bekannt.«

»Gehirnwäsche?« fragte Fallon interessiert.

»Genau das. Von ihrer Warte aus war ich ein besonderes Zielobjekt – wenn man die Haltung der katholischen Kirche dem Kommunismus gegenüber bedenkt. Man bediente sich einer ganz außerordentlich einfachen Technik, die so oft zum Erfolg führt: Man versuchte die Schuldkomplexe in jedem einzelnen anzusprechen. Mich fragte man als erstes, ob ich in meiner Missionsstation jemanden hätte, der für mich putzt und mir mein Bett macht. Als ich bejahte, zitierte man die Bibel. Ich erlaubte jemandem, dem ich zu helfen gekommen war, mir zu dienen. Erstaunlich, wie schuldig ich mich fühlte.«

Pater da Costa erzählte weiter. Sie hatten die dunklen Seiten in jedem Menschen aufzudecken versucht. Erst dann hatte die Umerziehung eingesetzt. Bei ihm hatten sie es mit Sex versucht.

Sie hatten ihn drei Monate lang in einer feuchten Zelle halb verhungern lassen und ihn dann in ein Bett zwischen zwei junge Frauen gelegt. Aber die Erektion, die er hatte, war unter den Umständen eine vollkommen verständliche chemische Reaktion, fand da Costa.

»Gott hätte die Sache nicht anders beurteilt.«

»So sind Sie also ohne alle Sünde«, bemerkte Fallon.

»Ganz und gar nicht. Ich bin ein sehr gewalttätiger Mann, Mr. Fallon. Es gab eine Zeit in meinem Leben, in der ich Freude am Töten hatte. Wahrscheinlich hätten die Umschuler Erfolg gehabt, wenn sie es damit bei mir versucht hätten. Um dieser Seite in mir zu entfliehen, trat ich der Kirche bei. Es war – und es ist noch – meine größte Schwäche, aber wenigstens weiß ich darum. Und Sie?«

»Was verlangen Sie von mir – daß ich den Becher bis

zur Neige austrinke?« Fallon stieg die Stufen zur Kanzel empor. »Mir ist niemals bewußt geworden, daß Sie so eine gute Aussicht von hier oben haben. Was wollen Sie, daß ich sage?«

»Es steht Ihnen frei.«

»Gut. Wir sind letztlich allein. Nichts ist von Dauer. Nichts hat einen Sinn.«

»Sie haben unrecht. Sie haben Gott vergessen.«

»Gott?« schrie Fallon. »Was für ein Gott ist das, der eine Welt zuläßt, in der Kinder in einer Minute glücklich singen – und in der nächsten blutig zerfetzt werden? Können Sie wirklich ehrlich behaupten, daß Sie immer noch an einen Gott glauben, nach dem was man Ihnen in Korea angetan hat? Wollen Sie mir sagen, daß Sie nie auch nur einen einzigen Moment schwankend geworden sind?«

»Kraft erwächst einem immer aus der Not«, erklärte da Costa. »Sechs Monate habe ich am Ende einer Kette im Finstern in meinem eigenen Kot gelegen, und es gab einen Moment, da wäre ich zu allem fähig gewesen. Doch dann rollte der Stein beiseite, und ich roch den Duft des Grabes und sah *ihn* heraussteigen. Und da wußte ich es, Fallon. *Wußte* es.«

»Wenn er existiert, Ihr Gott, dann wünschte ich, daß Sie ihn verdammt noch mal dazu bringen, sich für etwas zu entscheiden.«

»Haben Sie denn nichts gelernt?«

»O ja. Ich habe gelernt, mit einem Lächeln zu töten. Aber die wichtigste Lektion lernte ich zu spät.«

»Und welche war das?«

»Daß es sich für nichts auf der Welt zu sterben lohnt.«

Fallon kam die Kanzelstufen herunter und blieb neben da Costa stehen. »Und das Schlimmste ist, daß es sich auch für nichts zu leben lohnt.«

Er schritt das Seitenschiff entlang. Seine Schritte hallten durch die Kirche. Die Tür schlug zu, die Kerzen flackerten.

Pater da Costa kniete nieder und betete – mit einer Intensität wie selten.

Nach einer Weile öffnete sich eine Tür, und eine vertraute Stimme fragte: »Onkel Michael, bist du da?«

»Hier!«

Sie kam auf ihn zu, und er ging ihr entgegen, erfaßte ihre ausgestreckten Hände und führte sie zur ersten Bankreihe. Und wie immer spürte sie seine Stimmung.

»Was ist?« fragte sie besorgt. »Wo ist Mr. Fallon?«

»Weg. Wir haben uns unterhalten. Ich glaube, ich verstehe ihn jetzt besser.«

»Er ist tot – innerlich«, sagte sie. »Erstarrt.«

»Und von Selbstverachtung zerfressen. Er haßt sich selbst, und darum haßt er das ganze Leben. Ich glaube, er sucht den Tod. Ein möglicher Grund, weshalb er das Leben, das er führt, fortsetzt.«

»Das verstehe ich nicht.«

»Er hat sein ganzes Leben einer Sache gewidmet, die er für ehrenvoll hielt. Ein gefährliches Unterfangen. Denn wenn etwas schiefläuft, wenn man am Ende feststellen muß, daß diese Sache keinen Pfifferling wert ist, steht man mit leeren Händen da.«

»Er sagte, er sei ein wandelnder Toter.«

»Ja, so sieht er sich wohl.«

Sie griff nach seinem einen Arm. »Aber was kannst du tun? Was kann man überhaupt tun?«

»Ihm helfen, sich selbst zu finden. Seine Seele retten, vielleicht. Ich weiß es nicht. Aber ich *muß* etwas tun!«

12

Fallon trank mit Jenny in der Küche Tee, als es an der Tür läutete. Sie ging aufmachen und kam mit Jack Meehan und Billy zurück.

»Komm schon, Süße, mach dich dünn!« befahl ihr Meehan. »Das hier ist Geschäft.«

Sie warf Fallon einen besorgten Blick zu, zögerte und ging dann hinaus.

»Sie hat Sie ins Herz geschlossen«, kommentierte Meehan.

Er setzte sich auf die Tischkante und goß sich eine Tasse Tee ein. Billy lehnte an der Wand neben der Tür, die Hände in den Taschen, mürrisch Fallon fixierend.

»Sie ist ein nettes Mädchen«, sagte Fallon. »Aber Sie sind sicher nicht hergekommen, um über Jenny zu sprechen.«

Meehan seufzte. »Sie sind wieder ein ungezogener Junge gewesen, Fallon. Ich hatte Ihnen heute morgen aufgetragen, hierher zurückzukehren, und was taten Sie bei der erstbesten Gelegenheit? Sie entschlüpften dem armen Varley erneut. Das ist nicht nett, denn er weiß, wie ärgerlich ich werde und …«

»Kommen Sie zur Sache!«

»Also gut. Sie sind wieder zu diesem verdammten Priester gegangen.«

»Er war mit dieser da Costa-Biene im Kirchhof«, warf Billy ein.

»Dem blinden Mädchen?« fragte Meehan.

»Ganz recht. Sie hat ihn geküßt.«

Meehan schüttelte bedauernd den Kopf. »Das arme Mädchen so zu verführen – und übermorgen verlassen Sie das Land.«

»Sie ist ein richtiges Flittchen«, geiferte Billy. »Hat sich an dem verdammten Fenster ausgezogen. Jeder hätte sie sehen können.«

»Was kaum wahrscheinlich ist«, sagte Fallon. »Nicht bei einer sechs Meter hohen Mauer. Ich dachte übrigens, ich hätte dir gesagt, du sollst dich dort nicht mehr blikken lassen?«

»Was ist? Angst, ich könnte Ihnen Ihr Konzept verderben?« spottete Billy. »Möchten wohl alles für sich behalten, wie?«

Fallon erhob sich langsam. »Wenn du noch einmal in die Nähe des Mädchens kommst, ihr auch nur irgend etwas zuleide tust, bringe ich dich um.«

Er hatte gefährlich leise gesprochen.

Jack Meehan klatschte seinem Bruder den Handrücken ins Gesicht. »Du unersättliches kleines Ferkel! Sex ist alles, was du im Kopf hast. Als ob ich nicht schon genug Ärger hätte. Verschwinde! Raus hier!«

Billy öffnete die Tür und starrte Fallon an. Sein Gesicht war weiß. »Warte nur, du Bastard! Ich geb's dir schon noch. Verlaß dich drauf! Dir und deiner pikfeinen Biene.«

»Raus!« brüllte Meehan.

Billy schlug die Tür hinter sich zu.

Meehan wandte sich zu Fallon um. »Ich werde dafür sorgen, daß er nicht mehr aus der Reihe tanzt.«

Fallon steckte sich eine Zigarette zwischen die Lippen. »Und Sie? Wer paßt auf, daß Sie nicht aus der Reihe tanzen?«

Meehan lachte amüsiert. »Nichts bringt Sie aus der Ruhe, wie? Als Miller gestern in die Kirche hereinspazierte und Sie mit dem Priester reden sah, war ich beunruhigt, das kann ich Ihnen flüstern. Aber als Sie sich an die Orgel setzten …« Er schüttelte grinsend den Kopf. »Das war wirklich Klasse.«

Fallon runzelte die Stirn. »Sie waren da?«

»O ja!« Meehan zündete sich eine Zigarette an. »Nur etwas verstehe ich nicht.«

»Und was?«

»Sie hätten mir gestern abend eine Kugel verpassen können. Warum haben Sie es nicht getan? Ich meine, wenn da Costa so wichtig für Sie ist und Sie glauben, daß ich so etwas wie eine Bedrohung für ihn bin, dann wäre es doch das Logischste gewesen, was Sie hätten tun können.«

»Und was wäre aus meinem Paß und meiner Schiffs-passage geworden?«

Meehan gluckste. »Sie denken an alles, was? Wir sind uns ziemlich ähnlich, Fallon – wir beide.«

»Ich würde lieber der Teufel höchstpersönlich sein.«

Meehans Miene verdüsterte sich. »Wohl wieder so 'n Gefasel von was Höherem, hm? Mein Leben für Irland. Der galante Rebell mit der Waffe in der Hand. Machen Sie mir doch nichts vor, Fallon! Es macht Ihnen Spaß, in einem Trenchcoat und mit einer Kanone in der Tasche herumzulaufen – wie jemand aus einem alten Stumm-film. Das Töten hat Ihnen Spaß gemacht. Und soll ich Ihnen sagen, weshalb ich das weiß? Weil Sie zu ver-dammt gut darin sind, als daß Sie es hätten sein lassen können.«

Fallon saß da und starrte ihn an. Sein Gesicht war schneeweiß. Und plötzlich war die Ceska in seiner Hand.

Meehan lachte rauh. »Sie brauchen mich, Fallon. Er-innern Sie sich? Also stecken Sie das Ding weg wie ein guter Junge.«

Er ging zur Tür, öffnete sie.

Fallon peilte sein Ziel neu an.

Meehan wandte sich ihm zu. »Na, dann drücken Sie schon ab!«

142

Die Waffe lag ruhig in Fallons Hand. Meehan wartete, die Hände in den Taschen seines Mantels. Nach einer Weile drehte er sich langsam um und ging hinaus.

Fallon hielt noch einen Moment die Ceska vor sich, ins Leere starrend, dann senkte er sie sehr langsam, die Hand auf dem Tisch aufstützend, den Finger immer noch am Abzug. So saß er auch noch, als Jenny hereinkam.

»Sie sind weg«, sagte sie.

Fallon antwortete nicht.

Sie blickte auf die Waffe. »Wozu brauchst du das Ding da? Was ist passiert?«

»Nicht viel. Er hat mir einen Spiegel vorgehalten – das ist alles. Aber da war nichts, was ich nicht schon vorher gesehen hätte.« Er stand auf. »Ich glaube, ich werde ein paar Stunden schlafen.«

Er ging zur Tür, und sie fragte schüchtern: »Möchtest du, daß ich hochkomme?«

Es war, als ob er sie nicht gehört hätte. Er ging, und sie setzte sich an den Tisch und barg ihr Gesicht in den Händen.

Als Fitzgerald in Millers Büro kam, stand der Superintendent am Fenster und las den Durchschlag eines Briefes.

Er reichte ihn Fitzgerald. »Das haben wir dem Staatsanwalt geschickt.«

Fitzgerald überflog das Schreiben. »Wann können wir eine Entscheidung erwarten?«

»Das ist das Ärgerliche. Wahrscheinlich wird es ein paar Tage dauern. Inoffiziell habe ich mit dem Mann, der die Sache bearbeitet, bereits am Telefon gesprochen.«

»Und was meint er, Sir?«

»Er hegt keine allzu großen Hoffnungen. Sie wissen

ja, wie die Leute reagieren, wenn es etwas mit Religion zu tun hat.«

Erst jetzt bemerkte Miller, daß der Inspektor auch einen Durchschlag in der rechten Hand hielt. »Was haben Sie da?«

»Schlechte Nachrichten, fürchte ich, Sir. Vom CRO über die Ceska.«

Miller setzte sich müde. »Na, erzählen Sie schon!«

»Dem Computer zufolge wurde in diesem Land zum letztenmal im Juni 1952 jemand mit einer Ceska getötet, Sir. Ein ehemaliger polnischer Soldat erschoß seine Frau und ihren Liebhaber. Man hat ihn drei Monate später aufgehängt.«

»Hervorragend!«

»Natürlich werden die Waffenhändler im Londoner Raum abgeklappert«, fuhr Fitzgerald fort. »Das wird Zeit beanspruchen, aber es könnte was dabei herauskommen.«

»Schweine könnten auch fliegen«, sagte Miller verdrossen. Er zog seinen Regenmantel an. »Wissen Sie, was das Besondere an diesem Fall ist?«

»Ich glaube nicht, Sir.«

»Dann werde ich es Ihnen sagen. Es gibt nichts zu lösen. Wir wissen bereits, wer hinter dem Mord steckt: Jack Meehan. Und wenn der verdammte Priester seinen Mund aufmachen würde, könnte ich seinen Kopf auf einem Tablett servieren.«

Miller schlug die Tür so heftig hinter sich zu, daß die Glasscheibe einen Sprung bekam.

Fallon hatte nur seine Schuhe und sein Jackett ausgezogen und sich oben aufs Bett gelegt. Als er aufwachte, war es dunkel im Zimmer. Er war mit einer Daunendecke zugedeckt, was bedeutete, daß Jenny dagewesen war. Es war kurz nach acht. Er zog rasch seine Schuhe an, grapschte nach der Jacke und ging nach unten.

Jenny bügelte, als er in die Küche kam. Sie sah auf. »Ich habe vor drei Stunden bei dir reingeschaut.«

»Du hättest mich wecken sollen«, sagte er und griff nach seinem Mantel hinter der Tür.

»Jack Meehan hat gesagt, du sollst nicht ausgehen.«

»Ich weiß.« Er steckte die Ceska in die Tasche des Mantels.

»Es ist das Mädchen, nicht wahr? Du machst dir Sorgen um sie.«

Er runzelte die Stirn, und sie setzte das Bügeleisen ab.

»Ich habe draußen an der Tür gehorcht. Wie ist sie?«

»Sie ist blind. Und das bedeutet, daß sie verletzbar ist.«

»Du hast Angst, Billy könnte sich für gestern abend rächen und sich an sie heranmachen?«

»So etwas Ähnliches.«

»Ich kann es dir nicht verübeln.« Sie begann eine weiße Bluse zu bügeln. »Laß dir von ihm erzählen, damit du weißt, mit wem du es zu tun hast. Mit zwölf sind die meisten Jungen glücklich, wenn sie zu onanieren verstehen. Billy trieb es in diesem Alter bereits mit Frauen. Huren meistens, die für Jack Meehan arbeiteten. Billy war Jacks Bruder, also trauten sie sich nicht, nein zu sagen. Mit fünfzehn war er ein dreckiger perverser Sadist. Danach ging es nur noch bergab. An deiner Stelle würde ich mir also auch Sorgen machen.«

»Danke«, sagte er. »Warte nicht auf mich.«

Die Tür schlug zu.

Anna da Costa wollte gerade ins Bad gehen, als sie das Telefon läuten hörte. Sie zog einen Morgenrock über und ging nach unten. Ihr Onkel legte eben den Hörer wieder auf.

»Wer war es?« fragte sie.

»Das Krankenhaus. Die alte italienische Dame, die ich neulich besucht habe. Sie hat einen Rückfall gehabt. Man erwartet, daß sie irgendwann heute nacht stirbt. Ich muß hin.«

Sie holte seinen Mantel und hielt ihn bereit für ihn. Er zog ihn an und öffnete die Eingangstür. Es goß in Strömen.

»Ich werde zu Fuß gehen«, sagte er. »Geht's dir gut?«

»Mach dir keine Sorgen meinetwegen. Wie lange wirst du ausbleiben?«

»Wahrscheinlich einige Stunden. Warte nicht auf mich.«

Er eilte den Pfad entlang. Billy Meehan flüchtete rasch in die Schatten eines viktorianischen Mausoleums, doch als der Priester weg war, steuerte er weiter aufs Haus zu. Er hatte den Wortwechsel an der Tür mitbekommen, und sein Unterleib hatte sich vor Erregung verkrampft. Billy hatte an diesem Abend schon zweimal mit einer Prostituierten Geschlechtsverkehr gehabt, aber er schien nicht mehr fähig zu sein, irgendwelche Befriedigung dabei zu empfinden. Eigentlich hatte er nach Hause gehen wollen, doch dann hatte er sich an Anna erinnert – Anna, wie sie sich am Fenster stehend ausgezogen hatte. Und Fallon fiel ihm ein und die Erniedrigung vom Abend zuvor.

»Dieser Bastard«, murmelte er. »Dieser kleine fiese Bastard. Ich werde es ihm zeigen.«

Er hatte erst zehn Minuten da draußen herumgelungert, aber ihm war schon bitterkalt. Er zog eine halbe Flasche Scotch aus der Tasche und nahm einen großen Schluck.

Pater da Costa eilte in die Kirche, um eine Hostie und Salbungsöl für die Sterbende zu holen. Etwa fünf Minuten nach seinem Weggang knarrte das Portal gespenstisch, und Fallon trat ein. Er blickte sich kurz um, ging rasch das Seitenschiff hinunter, trat in den Lastenaufzug und drückte auf den Knopf. Fallon fuhr nicht bis zum Turm hoch, sondern hielt auf der anderen Seite der Zeltleinwand, die das Loch im Dach des Hauptschiffes abdeckte. Er tastete sich bis zu der niedrigen Stützmauer vor und verbarg sich im Schatten eines Strebepfeilers. Von dort aus konnte er das Pfarrhaus ausgezeichnet sehen. Zwei hohe Laternen in der Straße zur Linken warfen einen Lichtkegel über die Vorderfront des Hauses. In einem der Schlafzimmerfenster brannte Licht. Fallon konnte direkt ins Zimmer sehen.

Plötzlich erschien Anna, in ein großes, weißes Handtuch gehüllt. Offensichtlich war sie eben aus dem Bad gestiegen. Sie dachte nicht daran, die Vorhänge zuzuziehen, fühlte sich wahrscheinlich durch die sechs Meter hohe Friedhofsmauer vor fremden Blicken geschützt. Fallon beobachtete, wie sie sich abtrocknete, bewunderte ihre Erscheinung, das schwarze Haar, das fast bis zu den Brustwarzen herabreichte, die schmale Taille, die üppigen Hüften. Sie zog Strümpfe, einen schwarzen Büstenhalter, schwarzen Slip und ein grünes Seidenkleid an; dann begann sie ihr Haar zu bürsten.

Fallon war seltsam traurig. Er begehrte sie nicht physisch; es war vielmehr die plötzliche schreckliche Erkenntnis, wie unerreichbar sie für ihn war. Sie band ihr Haar zurück, trat aus seinem Blickfeld, und eine Sekunde später wurde das Licht gelöscht.

Fallon fröstelte, als der Wind ihm den Regen ins Gesicht klatschte. Er stellte den Mantelkragen auf. Es war sehr still. Und dann hörte er auf einmal ganz deutlich Schritte auf dem Kiesweg unten. Als er hinunterblickte, trat eine Gestalt in den Lichtkegel. Das weiße, schulterlange Haar verriet ihn augenblicklich. *Billy Meehan!* Er stieg jetzt die Stufen zur Haustür hoch und faßte nach dem Türgriff. Die Tür öffnete sich, und er schlüpfte ins Haus.

Fallon kroch über das Dach zurück und sprang in den Käfig.

Der Anblick Annas am Fenster hatte Billy so erregt, daß er sich nicht länger zurückhalten konnte. Die Schmerzen zwischen seinen Schenkeln waren unerträglich geworden, und die halbe Flasche Whisky hatte den letzten Rest an Selbstdisziplin weggeschwemmt. Als die Klinke tatsächlich nachgab, erstickte er fast vor Aufregung. Er schlich auf Zehenspitzen ins Haus, schloß die Tür und schob den Riegel vor. In einem Zimmer am Ende des Ganges hörte er jemanden leise singen. Er näherte sich lautlos und spähte durch die angelehnte Tür.

Anna saß in einer Ecke des viktorianischen Sofas, einen kleinen Tisch, auf dem ein großer Nähkasten stand, zur Seite. Sie nähte einen Knopf an ein Hemd, griff dann in den Nähkasten, suchte nach der Schere und schnitt den Faden ab.

Billy zog seinen Mantel aus, ließ ihn auf den Boden fallen und steuerte auf sie los.

Stirnrunzelnd wandte sie ihm ihr Gesicht zu. »Wer ist da? Ist da jemand?«

Er hielt kurz inne. Sie stand auf. Billy schlich weiter, und während sie sich halb umwandte, das Hemd an sich pressend, eine Nadel in der anderen Hand, umkreiste er sie.

»Wer ist da?« Angst schwang in ihrer Stimme mit.

Er faßte von hinten unter ihren Rock, zwischen ihre Schenkel und kicherte. »Das ist hübsch. Du magst das, hm? Die meisten Mädchen mögen, was ich mit ihnen mache.«

Sie schrie auf, entzog sich ihm, drehte sich herum, und im selben Moment fuhr eine Hand in ihren Ausschnitt und grapschte nach ihrer einen Brust.

Anna schrie. Ihr Gesicht war eine Maske des Grauens. »Nein – bitte! Im Namen Gottes – wer ist es?«

»Fallon«, sagte Billy. »Ich bin es, Fallon.«

»Lügner!« schrie sie. »Lügner!« Und schlug ihm mitten ins Gesicht.

Billy verpaßte ihr eine Ohrfeige mit dem Handrücken. »Du Hure! Ich werde dich schon noch kriechen lehren!«

Er warf sie rücklings übers Sofa, zerrte an ihrem Höschen, riß brutal ihre Schenkel auseinander und preßte seinen Mund auf den ihren. Sie spürte, wie seine Hand zwischen ihren Beinen am Reißverschluß seiner Hose herumfummelte, und dann stieß das steife Glied zu. Sie kreischte. Er schlug sie abermals und bog ihren Kopf zurück. Sie versuchte sich mit der rechten Hand am Tisch festzuhalten, und ihre Finger umklammerten die Schere. Zu diesem Zeitpunkt war sie schon fast bewußtlos. Sie merkte nicht mehr, wie ihre Hand durch die Luft zuckte und wie sie mit aller Kraft die Schere in seinen Leib rammte, sein Herz durchbohrte und ihn auf der Stelle tötete.

Nachdem die Eingangstür verriegelt war, mußte Fallon ein Küchenfenster einschlagen. Er fand Billy Meehan über dem bewußtlosen Mädchen hingestreckt und stürzte sich auf ihn. Erst als er ihn wegzerrte, sah er den Griff der Schere unterhalb der Rippen herausragen.

Er hob Anna auf die Arme und trug sie nach oben, legte sie auf ihr Bett und deckte sie mit einer Daunendecke zu. Dann setzte er sich zu ihr und hielt ihre eine Hand.

Nach einer Weile zuckten ihre Lider. Sie bäumte sich auf, versuchte, ihm ihre Hand zu entziehen.

Fallon sagte besänftigend: »Ist ja gut. Ich bin's – Martin Fallon. Sie brauchen keine Angst zu haben.«

Sie seufzte. »Gott sei Dank! Was ist passiert?«

»Können Sie sich nicht erinnern?«

»Nur an diesen grauenvollen Mann. Er sagte, er wäre Sie – und dann versuchte er – versuchte er …« Sie schüttelte sich. »O Gott, seine Hände! Es war so schrecklich! Grauenhaft! Ich glaube, ich fiel in Ohnmacht.«

»Das stimmt«, sagte Fallon ruhig. »Dann kam ich, und er rannte davon.«

Sie wandte ihm ihr Gesicht zu. »Haben Sie gesehen, wer es war?«

»Ich fürchte – nein.«

»War es …« Sie zögerte. »Glauben Sie, daß Meehan dahintersteckt?«

»Das glaube ich allerdings.«

Sie schloß die Augen, und als Fallon sanft ihre Hand ergriff, zuckte sie zurück; als ob sie im Moment die Berührung eines Mannes nicht ertragen könnte.

Er riß sich zusammen und stellte die naheliegende Frage: »Hat er seinen Willen durchgesetzt?«

»Nein – ich glaube nicht.«

»Möchten Sie, daß ich einen Arzt rufe?«

»Um Himmels willen, nein! Nur das nicht! Allein schon der Gedanke, irgend jemand könnte etwas erfahren, erfüllt mich mit Entsetzen.«

»Und Ihr Onkel?«

»Er ist bei einer sterbenden Frau im Krankenhaus. Es kann Stunden dauern, bis er zurückkommt.«

Fallon stand auf. »Gut. Ruhen Sie sich aus! Ich werde Ihnen einen Brandy holen.«

Sie schloß wieder die Augen. Die Lider waren durchscheinend. Sie sah sehr verwundbar aus.

Fallon ging nach unten. Er kniete neben Billy nieder,

holte ein Taschentuch hervor, wickelte es um den Griff der Schere und zog sie heraus. Sie war nur sehr wenig blutig. Er reinigte die Schere und hob dann den Mantel des Jungen auf. Autoschlüssel fielen zu Boden. Er nahm sie automatisch an sich und breitete den Mantel über den Leichnam. Ekel und Abscheu erfüllten ihn. Die Menschheit konnte gut ohne Billy Meehan auskommen. Er hatte sein Ende redlich verdient. Aber konnte Anna da Costa mit dem Wissen leben, ihn getötet zu haben? Selbst wenn das Gericht sie freisprechen sollte – die ganze Welt würde es wissen. Und bei dem Gedanken an die Erniedrigung dieses zarten Geschöpfes packte Fallon eine solche Wut, daß er dem Leichnam einen Fußtritt versetzte. Und im gleichen Augenblick kam ihm eine Idee. Was, wenn sie es überhaupt nie erfuhr – weder jetzt noch später? Was, wenn Billy vom Antlitz der Erde hinweggefegt würde, als hätte er nie existiert? Es gab eine Möglichkeit; und er schuldete es ihr auf jeden Fall, sie auszuprobieren.

Die Autoschlüssel sagten ihm, daß Billys Wagen irgendwo in der Nachbarschaft stand; und falls es der rote Scimitar war, würde es ein leichtes sein, ihn zu finden.

Fallon schlüpfte aus dem Haus und eilte über den Friedhof zur Seitenpforte. Der Scimitar stand nur wenige Meter entfernt am Straßenrand. Er sperrte die Hecktür auf, und Tommy, der graue Whippet, bellte einmal und schnüffelte dann an seiner Hand. Die Anwesenheit des Hundes war ungünstig, aber nicht zu ändern.

Fallon schloß die Hecktür wieder und eilte ins Pfarrhaus zurück. Er zog den Mantel vom Leichnam und leerte systematisch Billys Taschen, nahm ihm ein goldenes Medaillon, das an einem Kettchen um den Hals hing, einen Siegelring und eine Armbanduhr ab und steckte alles ein. Dann wickelte er den Leichnam in den Mantel, hievte ihn sich über die Schulter und ging. An der Pforte blieb er stehen und vergewisserte sich, daß die Luft rein war. Rasch steuerte er auf den Scimitar zu, öffnete die Hecktür mit einer Hand und ließ den Körper hineinplumpsen. Der Whippet fing fast augenblicklich zu winseln an. Fallon schmiß die Tür rasch wieder zu und kehrte ins Pfarrhaus zurück. Er wusch in der Küche die Schere gründlich mit heißem Wasser und legte sie wieder in den Nähkasten. Dann goß er etwas Brandy in ein Glas und ging damit nach oben.

Sie war schon fast eingeschlafen, setzte sich aber auf und trank den Brandy.

Fallon fragte: »Wollen Sie, daß Ihr Onkel erfährt, was passiert ist?«

»Ja – ja, ich glaube schon. Er sollte es wissen.«

»Gut. Schlafen Sie jetzt. Ich werde unten sein. Sie brauchen keine Angst zu haben. Ich warte, bis Ihr Onkel zurückkommt.«

»Das kann noch Stunden dauern«, murmelte sie schlaftrunken.

»Das macht nichts.« Er ging zur Tür.

»Es tut mir leid, daß ich so eine Plage bin«, flüsterte sie.

»*Ich* habe Sie in diese Lage gebracht«, erinnerte er sie.

»Für alles unter diesem Himmel gibt es einen Grund – selbst für meine Blindheit. Wir erkennen ihn bloß nicht immer, weil wir so winzig sind, aber er ist da.«

Gott weiß, warum ihn ihre Worte seltsam trösteten.

Der Whippet verhielt sich ruhig während der Fahrt. Er saß zusammengekauert neben der Leiche, winselte nur gelegentlich.

Fallon fuhr die Abkürzung, die Varley am Morgen benutzt hatte, und näherte sich dem Krematorium von hinten. Die letzten hundert Meter schaltete er den Motor aus und ließ den Wagen den sanften Abhang zwischen den Zypressen hinunterrollen, obgleich das Haus des Verwalters gut eine Viertelmeile weit ab lag. Er parkte den Scimitar seitlich von der Kapelle und verschaffte sich durch die zerbrochene Fensterscheibe in der Toilette Zutritt ins Gebäude. Die Tür der Kapelle ließ sich von innen mühelos öffnen. Er kehrte zum Scimitar zurück, fand im Handschuhfach eine Taschenlampe, die er an sich nahm, und hob dann den Leichnam aus dem Wagen. Der Whippet wollte ihm folgen, aber es gelang Fallon, ihn mit der freien Hand in den Wagen zurückzuschubsen.

Fallon ließ den Leichnam auf dem Förderband aus der Kapelle in den Raum mit den Hochöfen rollen und kroch selbst durch die Gummitüren hinterher. Die Öfen waren kalt und dunkel. Er schob den Leichnam in den ersten und inspizierte rasch im Schein der Taschenlampe die verschiedenen Gegenstände, die er aus Billys Taschen geholt hatte. Außer dem Ring, der Uhr und dem Medaillon legte er alles auf Billys Brustkorb, dann schloß er die Ofentür und drückte auf den Knopf. Höchstens eine Stunde, hatte Meehan gesagt.

Er zündete sich eine Zigarette an und trat durch die Hintertür nach draußen. Das Getöse des Hochofens war außerhalb des Gebäudes kaum hörbar. Er ging wieder hinein und stellte fest, daß das Meßgerät soeben die Tausend-Grad-Celsius-Marke erreicht hatte, und als er durch das Guckloch blinzelte, sah er, wie die Brieftasche gerade in Flammen aufging.

Er zündete sich eine neue Zigarette an und wartete an der Hintertür. Als er nach einer Stunde den Ofen ausschaltete, waren noch Teile des Skeletts deutlich sichtbar, aber sie zerfielen bei der ersten Berührung mit der

Harke. Fallon fällte den Zinnbehälter, kehrte mit einem Handfeger und einer Schaufel sorgfältig die letzten Aschenreste aus dem Ofen und ließ die Tür angelehnt, wie er sie vorgefunden hatte. Er fand eine leere Urne, schraubte sie unter den Zerstäuber, schüttete den Inhalt des Zinnbehälters hinein und setzte den Apparat in Betrieb. Aus der Schublade des Schreibtisches holte er eine leere Ruhe-sanft-Karte. Als er etwa zwei Minuten später den Zerstäuber ausschaltete und die Urne abschraubte, waren von Billy Meehan nur noch ungefähr fünf Pfund grauer Asche übrig.

Fallon blieb neben dem Schubkarren und den Gerätschaften des Gärtners stehen, merkte sich die Parzellennummer und verstreute sorgfältig die Asche, sie mit dem Besen vom Schubkarren gewissenhaft in den Rasen einbürstend. Schließlich legte er den Besen wieder zurück, wandte sich zufrieden ab und spazierte zum Scimitar zurück. Als er die Tür öffnete, schlüpfte der Whippet zwischen seinen Beinen hindurch und flitzte davon. Fallon folgte ihm. Der Hund lief um die Ecke der Kapelle, den Pfad hinunter, den Fallon soeben gekommen war, und kauerte sich dort, wo er Billys Asche verstreut hatte, leise winselnd ins nasse Gras.

Fallon hob ihn auf, kraulte ihn hinter den Ohren und redete beruhigend auf ihn ein.

Erst als er in die Hauptstraße einbog, entspannte er sich etwas. Mit zitternden Händen zündete er sich eine Zigarette an. Es hatte geklappt. Billy Meehan war vom Antlitz der Erde gefegt. Und Fallon hatte nicht die geringsten Gewissensbisse.

Am Paul's Square fuhr er vorsichtig durch die versteckte Toreinfahrt, und das Glück blieb ihm treu. Der

Hof lag verlassen da. Er fuhr den Scimitar in die Garage, ließ die Schlüssel und den Hund zurück und machte sich rasch aus dem Staub.

Pater da Costa war bei seiner Rückkehr ins Pfarrhaus noch nicht da. Fallon schlich auf Zehenspitzen nach oben und sah in Annas Schlafzimmer. Sie schlief tief. Er schloß die Tür und ging wieder nach unten. Im Wohnzimmer untersuchte er nochmals genau den Teppich, entdeckte aber keinerlei Blutspuren. Dann trat er ans Büfett und schenkte sich einen großen Whisky ein. Als er Soda dazugoß, ging die Haustür auf.

Fallon wandte sich um. Der Priester blieb überrascht in der Zimmertür stehen.

»Fallon, was machen Sie denn hier?« Und dann wurde er sehr blaß. »O Gott, Anna!«

Er wollte die Treppe hoch, aber Fallon hielt ihn zurück. »Es geht ihr gut. Sie schläft.«

Pater da Costa wandte sich langsam um. »Was ist passiert?«

»Jemand ist ins Haus eingedrungen. Ich kam rechtzeitig, um ihn davonzujagen.«

»Einer von Meehans Männern?«

»Vielleicht. Ich habe ihn nicht richtig gesehen.«

Da Costa schritt auf und ab. »O mein Gott, wann hört das nur endlich alles auf?«

»Ich verschwinde Sonntag nacht«, teilte ihm Fallon mit, »Sie haben auf einem Schiff, das von Hull ausläuft, eine Passage für mich gebucht.«

»Und Sie glauben, daß damit alles zu Ende ist?« Da Costa schüttelte den Kopf. »Sie sind ein Dummkopf, Fallon. Jack Meehan wird sich nie mehr sicher fühlen, solange ich unter den Lebenden weile. Vertrauen, Wahrhaftigkeit, Ehrenwort – das sind alles Begriffe, die für ihn nicht existieren. Weshalb sollte er glauben, daß sie für jemand anderen eine Bedeutung haben?«

»Es ist alles meine Schuld, Was wollen Sie, daß ich tue?«

»Sie können nur eines tun: Entbinden Sie mich von meiner Schweigepflicht.«

»Damit ich mein Leben in einer streng bewachten Zelle verbringe? Die Art von Held bin ich nicht.«

Er steuerte auf die Haustür zu, und da Costa fragte noch einmal: »Geht es ihr wirklich gut?«

Fallon nickte. »Eine Nacht Schlaf ist alles, was sie braucht.«

Er ging, und da Costa rief ihm nach: »Sie kamen nicht zufällig gerade in jenem Moment?«

»Nun ja – ich habe das Haus beobachtet.«

Pater da Costa schüttelte traurig den Kopf. »Sie sehen, mein Freund – trotz Ihrer Einstellung gute Taten. Sie sind ein verlorener Mann.«

»Zur Hölle mit Ihnen!« Und Fallon stürmte in den Regen hinaus.

13

Pater da Costa packte seine liturgischen Gewänder in einen kleinen Koffer, als Anna ins Arbeitszimmer trat, Es war ein grauer Morgen; immer noch prasselte der Regen gegen die Scheiben. Sie war etwas blasser als sonst.

Da Costa ergriff ihre Hände. »Wie fühlst du dich?«

»Gut. Wirklich. Willst du fortgehen?«

»Leider muß ich. Eine der Nonnen in der Klosterschule starb gestern. Man hat mich gebeten, zu amtieren.« Er zögerte. »Ich lasse dich nicht gern allein.«

»Unsinn! Mir geht es gut. Schwester Claire wird um zehn Uhr dreißig die Kinder aus der Grundschule zur Chorprobe bringen. Danach habe ich bis zwölf eine Privatstunde.«

»Fein. Bis dahin werde ich zurück sein.«

Sie nahm seinen Arm, und gemeinsam gingen sie zur Haustür. »Du wirst deinen Regenmantel brauchen.«

»Der Regenschirm genügt.« Er öffnete die Tür und zögerte. »Ich habe nachgedacht, Anna. Vielleicht solltest du weggehen – bis diese Angelegenheit in irgendeiner Form abgeschlossen ist.«

»Nein!« sagte sie entschieden.

Er setzte seinen Koffer ab und faßte sie an den Schultern. »Noch nie habe ich mich so hilflos gefühlt. Nach dem Vorfall gestern nacht wollte ich sogar schon mit Miller sprechen.«

»Aber das kannst du doch nicht machen!« sagte sie rasch – zu rasch. »Nicht, ohne Fallon mit hineinzuziehen.«

Er musterte sie. »Du magst ihn, nicht wahr?«

»Das ist nicht genau das Wort, das ich wählen würde«, erwiderte sie ruhig. »Ich habe Mitleid mit ihm. Er ist in einer unfairen Weise vom Leben benutzt worden.« Und plötzlich voller Leidenschaft: »Niemand kann so viel Musik in sich haben und ohne Seele sein. Gott kann nicht so unmenschlich sein.«

»Das größte Geschenk, das Gott dem Menschen gegeben hat, ist sein freier Wille, Liebes.«

»Ich weiß nur etwas mit Sicherheit: Als ich letzte Nacht Hilfe brauchte – war es Fallon, der mich gerettet hat.«

»Er hat das Haus beobachtet.«

Farbe schoß in ihre bleichen Wangen. »Und dir ist egal, was ihm zustößt?«

»O nein. Ich sorge mich mehr um ihn, als du vielleicht glaubst. Ich sehe einen genialen Menschen vor mir, der in der Gosse gelandet ist und aus irgendwelchen dunklen Gründen eine Art Selbstmord begeht.«

»Dann hilf ihm!«

Pater da Costa schüttelte traurig den Kopf. »Er ist ein Mann, der den Tod sucht, Anna, der ihn mit offenen Armen willkommen heißen würde. Er haßt das, was aus ihm geworden ist. O ja, ich sorge mich sehr darum, was aus ihm wird –, die Tragödie ist nur, daß es *ihm* egal ist.«

Er eilte über den Kirchhof, den Kopf gesenkt, und dachte gar nicht daran, den Schirm aufzuspannen, Als er in die Sakristei kam, sah er Fallon auf der schmalen Bank sitzen, der, Kopf auf die Brust gesunken, die Hände in den Taschen seines Trenchcoats.

Da Costa schüttelte ihn an den Schultern, und Fallon hob den Kopf und öffnete augenblicklich die Augen. Er hatte dringend eine Rasur nötig, die Haut spannte über den Backenknochen, sein Blick war leer.

»Eine lange Nacht«, sagte Pater da Costa sanft.

»Zeit zum Nachdenken«, erwiderte Fallon mit seltsam erloschener Stimme.

»Irgendwelche Entschlüsse gefaßt?«

»O ja.« Fallon stand auf und trat in den Regen hinaus. »Der richtige Platz für mich – ein Friedhof.« Er wandte sich um, ein Lächeln in den Mundwinkeln. »Ich habe endlich etwas sehr Wichtiges erkannt.«

»Und was ist das?«

»Daß ich nicht mehr mit mir leben kann.«

Er entfernte sich sehr rasch. Pater da Costa streckte eine Hand aus – als wollte er ihn zurückhalten.

»Fallon!« rief er heiser.

Ein paar Saatkrähen flogen aus einem Baum auf, ratterten wie eine Handvoll schmutzig-schwarzer Lumpen im Wind, ärgerlich krächzend.

Als Anna die Haustür des Pfarrhauses schloß, hörte sie die Orgel spielen. Sie stand ganz still da und lauschte. Ihr Herz schlug schneller, während sie mit ihrem Stock den Weg abklopfend über den Kirchhof hastete. Sie öffnete die Sakristeitür. Die Musik schien die Kirche auszufüllen.

Die letzten Töne verhallten. Einen unendlich langen Augenblick saß er mit hängenden Schultern da. Als er auf dem Stuhl herumschwang, stand sie an den Chorschranken.

»Ich habe niemals jemanden so spielen hören«, sagte sie.

Er stieg herab und blieb auf der anderen Seite der Barriere stehen. »Gute Beerdigungsmusik.«

Seine Worte griffen ihr eiskalt ans Herz. Sie zwang sich zu einem Lächeln. »So dürfen Sie nicht reden. Wollten Sie mich sehen?«

»Sagen wir, ich hoffte, Sie würden kommen.«

»Hier bin ich also.«

»Ich möchte, daß Sie Ihrem Onkel eine Botschaft überbringen. Sagen Sie ihm, daß es mir leid tut, mehr leid tut, als ich sagen kann, aber ich werde alles in Ordnung bringen. Sie brauchen keine Angst mehr zu haben. Er hat mein Wort drauf.«

»Aber wie? Ich verstehe nicht.«

»Es ist meine Affäre«, sagte er ruhig. »Ich habe sie begonnen, ich werde sie auch beenden. Leben Sie wohl, Anna da Costa! Sie werden mich nicht wiedersehen.«

»Ich habe Sie nie *gesehen*«, sagte sie traurig und legte eine Hand auf seinen Arm. »Ist das nicht schrecklich?«

Er zog sich langsam zurück, lautlos.

Ihr Gesichtsausdruck veränderte sich. Unsicher streckte sie eine Hand aus. »Mr. Fallon, sind Sie da?«

Fallon strebte rasch der Tür zu. Sie knarrte, als er sie öffnete, und als er sich umwandte, um ein letztes Mal zurückzublicken, rief sie: »Martin, komm zurück!«, und furchtbare Verzweiflung schwang in ihrer Stimme mit.

Fallon ging.

Tränen strömten über Annas Gesicht. Sie fiel auf die Knie.

Jenny Fox hatte am Abend zuvor zwei Schlaftabletten eingenommen. Es war schon nach elf, als sie aufwachte. Sie zog ihren Morgenrock an und ging nach unten in die Küche. Fallon saß am Tisch, die Flasche mit irischem Whisky vor sich, ein halbvolles Wasserglas daneben. Er hatte die Ceska auseinandergenommen und setzte sie nun gewissenhaft wieder zusammen.

»Du fängst früh an«, kommentierte sie.

»Es ist schon lange her, seit ich getrunken habe – wirklich getrunken habe. Ich mußte nachdenken.«

Er leerte sein Glas mit einem Zug, rammte das Magazin in die Ceska und schraubte den Schalldämpfer auf den Lauf.

Jenny fragte vorsichtig: »Bist du zu irgendwelchen Entschlüssen gekommen?«

»O ja. Ich glaube, das kann man sagen.« Er goß sich einen weiteren Whisky ein und schüttete ihn hinunter. »Ich habe beschlossen, eine Jack-Meehan-muß-weg-Kampagne zu starten. Eine Art Einmannfeldzug, wenn du so willst.«

»Du mußt verrückt sein. Du hast nicht die geringste Chance.«

»Er wird irgendwann heute nach mir schicken, Jenny.

Er muß – weil er mich morgen nacht von Hull aus ausschiffen will.«

Er schielte über den Lauf der Waffe, und Jenny flüsterte: »Was hast du vor?«

»Ich werde den Bastard umbringen«, sagte er schlicht. »Eine gute Tat in einer unanständigen Welt.«

Er war betrunken, aber auf seine Weise.

Sie sagte verzweifelt: »Sei kein Dummkopf! Wenn du ihn tötest, gibt es keine Schiffspassage.«

»Das könnte mir wirklich nicht gleichgültiger sein.«

Sein Arm schoß hoch, und er feuerte. Ein dumpfer Laut, und ein kleiner Porzellanhund auf dem obersten Brett über dem Kühlschrank zerschellte.

»Nun, wenn ich nach einer halben Flasche Whisky noch so gut treffe, ist kaum zu befürchten, daß ich Dandy Jack verfehle.«

Er stand auf und packte die Whiskyflasche.

»Martin, hör mir zu, um Gottes willen!« flehte sie.

Er ging an ihr vorbei auf die Tür zu. »Ich war letzte Nacht nicht im Bett, also werde ich es jetzt nachholen. Weck mich, wenn Meehan anruft, und laß mich auf keinen Fall länger als bis fünf schlafen. Ich muß was erledigen.«

Sie lauschte seinen Schritten auf der Treppe, hörte, wie er die Tür seines Schlafzimmers öffnete und schloß.

Der Bull and Bell yard war nicht weit vom Paul's Square entfernt, eine schmutzige sonnenlose gepflasterte Gasse, die nach dem Pub, das dort seit mehr als zweihundert Jahren stand, benannt worden war. Neben dem Eingang drängten sich überquellende Mülleimer, stapelten sich Pappschachteln und Packkisten.

Das *Bull and Bell* machte sein Hauptgeschäft abends, weshalb Jack Meehan es bevorzugte, nachmittags hin-zugehen. Er saß auf einem Stuhl, einen Krug Bier vor sich, auf einem Roastbeef-Sandwich kauend und die *Financial Times* lesend. Donner hockte am Fenster und legte Patience.

Meehan leerte seinen Krug und schob ihn über die Bar. »Noch einmal, Harry!«

Harry war ein großer, stämmiger junger Mann mit der Figur eines professionellen Rugbyspielers. Er hatte lange, dunkle Koteletten und sah kalt und gefährlich aus. Als er den Krug füllte, öffnete sich die Tür, und Rupert und Bonati traten ein. Rupert hatte einen knöchellangen, großkarierten Kapuzenmantel an. Er schüttelte sich heftig und knöpfte ihn auf.

Meehan trank einen Schluck Bier und rülpste. »Was, zum Teufel, willst du hier? Wer paßt auf den Laden auf?«

Rupert glitt auf den Stuhl neben ihm und legte eine Hand auf seinen einen Schenkel. »Ich muß manchmal essen, Schätzchen. Ich glaube, es ist angebracht, daß ich bei Kräften bleibe, oder?«

»Also gut, Harry«, grunzte Meehan. »Gib ihm seine Bloody Mary!«

Rupert fragte: »Weiß übrigens jemand, wo Billy steckt?«

»Ich habe ihn seit gestern abend nicht mehr gesehen«, sagte Meehan. »Wer will was von ihm?«

»Der Verwalter von *Pine Trees* hat eben angerufen.«

»Und was wollte er?«

»Es scheint, daß Billys Whippet dort herumstreunt, total aufgeweicht und wie Espenlaub zitternd. Er wollte wissen, was er mit ihm machen soll.«

Meehan runzelte die Stirn. »Was, zum Teufel, treibt das Vieh da?«

Donner sagte: »Ich sah Tommy etwa gegen halb acht Uhr heute morgen, als ich in die Garage ging. Er saß im

Scimitar. Ich glaubte, Billy hätte ihn dort letzte Nacht vergessen und ließ ihn raus. Ich meine, es ist doch schon vorgekommen, wenn er verärgert war – daß er Tommy im Wagen gelassen hat.«

»Er war heute morgen noch nicht zurück«, sagte Meehan. »Wenn er den Wagen in der Garage hat stehenlassen, dann kann er nur in einen Klub im Zentrum gegangen sein. Wahrscheinlich liegt er noch mit irgendeiner Hure im Bett. Dieser dreckige kleine Bastard.« Er wandte sich an Bonati. »Fahr nach *Pine Trees* und hol das Vieh! Und gib ihm was zu fressen!«

»In Ordnung, Mr. Meehan.« Bonati verschwand.

Meehan schüttete weiter Bier in sich hinein. »Rücksichtsloses kleines Ferkel. Ich werde ihm den Arsch versohlen.«

»Er ist jung, Mr. Meehan«, sagte Harry. »Er wird's schon noch kapieren.«

Er ergriff einen Kübel mit Schmutzwasser, kam hinter der Bar hervor, öffnete die Tür und trat hinaus. Als er das Wasser ausgoß, tauchte Pater da Costa auf. Er trug seine Soutane und hatte den Schirm aufgespannt. Harry musterte ihn leicht erstaunt.

Pater da Costa sagte höflich: »Ich suche Mr. Meehan – Mr. Jack Meehan. Man hat mir in seinem Büro gesagt, daß ich ihn hier treffen könnte.«

»Drinnen«, sagte Harry.

Er ging voran, und der Pater folgte ihm. Er blieb auf der Schwelle stehen, um seinen Schirm zuzumachen.

Rupert entdeckte ihn im Spiegel hinter der Bar.

»Allmächtiger!« rief er aus.

Meehan drehte sich sehr langsam um. »Und was, zum Teufel, machen Sie hier? Wollen Sie für Weihnachten oder dergleichen sammeln? Werde ich Sie mit einem Pfund los?«

Er zog großkotzig seine Brieftasche heraus, und Pater da Costa sagte ruhig: »Ich hoffte, Sie kurz unter vier Augen sprechen zu können.«

Er stand da, den Schirm in der Hand, der Saum der Soutane klitschnaß vom hohen Gras des Klosterfriedhofs, die Schuhe voll Morast, der graue Bart zerzaust.

Meehan lachte schallend. »Ich wünschte, Sie könnten sich sehen! Männer in Röcken! Wie lächerlich!«

Pater da Costa fragte geduldig: »Nun, können wir reden?«

Meehan wies mit einer kurzen Handbewegung auf Donner und Rupert. »Es gibt nichts, was Sie mir sagen könnten, was diese beiden nicht hören dürften.«

»Also gut. Ich möchte, daß Sie *Holy Name* fernbleiben. Und ich wünsche keine Wiederholung des Vorfalls von gestern nacht.«

Meehan runzelte die Stirn. »Wovon, verflixt noch mal, sprechen Sie?«

»Letzte Nacht, als ich weg war, ist jemand ins Pfarrhaus eingedrungen und ist über meine Nichte hergefallen. Wenn Fallon nicht im richtigen Moment aufgetaucht wäre und den Mann davongejagt hätte – weiß Gott, was passiert wäre. Aber ich vermute, Sie werden mir jetzt erzählen, Sie wüßten nichts davon.«

»Verdammt noch mal, so ist es!« schrie Meehan.

Pater da Costa versuchte sich zu beherrschen.

»Sie lügen«, sagte er schlicht.

Meehan schoß das Blut in den Kopf, seine Augen traten aus den Höhlen. »Wer, zum Teufel, glauben Sie, daß Sie sind?«

»Es ist meine letzte Warnung. Als wir uns das letztemal unterhielten, sagte ich Ihnen, daß mein Gott auch ein Gott des Zornes ist. Sie täten gut daran, es nicht zu vergessen.«

Meehans Gesicht war jetzt purpurrot. Wütend wandte er sich an den Barkeeper. »Schaff ihn raus!«

Harry kam hinter der Bar hervor. »Auf den Weg, Kamerad!«

»Ich gehe, wenn ich fertig bin«, erklärte ihm da Costa.

Harrys rechte Hand packte ihn am Kragen, die linke am Gürtel, und so stürzten sie durch die Tür, begleitet vom Gelächter Donners und Ruperts. Beide drängten hinaus, um dem Spaß beizuwohnen, und Meehan schloß sich ihnen an.

Pater da Costa kauerte auf Händen und Knien in einer Pfütze.

»Na, was ist los, Schätzchen?« höhnte Rupert. »Hast dich vollgepißt?«

Es war eine dumme Bemerkung, kindisch und vulgär, aber sie war der letzte Tropfen, der da Costas Wut zum Überkochen brachte. Als Harry ihn auf die Füße zog, einen Arm um seinen Hals, reagierte er, wie er es dreißig Jahre zuvor in der harten, brutalen Schule des Guerillakampfes gelernt hatte.

Harry grinste breit. »Wir können so aufgeblasene Angeber, die uns die Kundschaft verärgern, nicht leiden.«

Zu mehr kam er nicht. Da Costas rechter Ellbogen landete zwischen seinen Rippen. Der Pater schwenkte auf einem Fuß herum, während Harry, nach Luft schnappend, zurücktaumelte.

»Du solltest niemals jemanden so nah herankommen lassen.«

Harry sprang vorwärts, mit der Rechten zu einem fürchterlichen Faustschlag ausholend. Da Costa neigte sich zur Seite, packte mit beiden Händen Harrys Handgelenk, drehte es herum und nach oben und stieß ihn mit dem Kopf voran in die Kisten.

Als er sich umwandte, kam Donner angerannt. Er bekam einen Fußtritt unter die linke Kniescheibe und krümmte sich vor Schmerz. Da Costa rammte rasch ein Knie in Donners Gesicht, daß dieser hochschnellte und rückwärts gegen die Wand knallte.

Rupert stieß einen entsetzten Schrei aus. Er hatte es so eilig, in die Pinte zu kommen, daß er auf der obersten Stufe ausrutschte und Meehan mit sich riß. Als Meehan sich erheben wollte, versetzte ihm da Costa einen Faustschlag ins Gesicht. Knochen knirschten, und Meehans Nase wurde von da Costas Knöcheln plattgewalzt. Blut schoß aus seinen Nasenlöchern, und er fiel aufstöhnend in die Kneipe.

Rupert kroch auf Händen und Knien hinter die Bar, während da Costa über Meehan stand, die Fäuste geballt, das Gesicht in mörderischer Wut verzerrt. Und plötzlich blickte er auf seine Hände herab, sah das Blut daran, und Entsetzen malte sich in seinen Zügen. Langsam wich er zurück auf die Gasse. Harry lag mit dem Gesicht nach unten zwischen den Kisten, Donner kotzte gegen die Wand. Da Costa betrachtete noch einmal voll Grauen das Blut an seinen Händen und entfloh.

Als er sein Arbeitszimmer betrat, saß Anna strickend am Feuer. Sie wandte ihm ihr Gesicht zu. »Du kommst spät. Ich habe mir Sorgen gemacht.«

Er war immer noch äußerst erregt und hatte Mühe, ruhig zu sprechen. »Tut mir leid. Es ist etwas dazwischengekommen.«

Sie legte ihr Strickzeug beiseite und erhob sich. »Nachdem du weg warst, ging ich in die Kirche. Fallon spielte auf der Orgel.«

»Hat er irgend etwas gesagt? Hast du mit ihm gesprochen?«

»Er hat mir eine Botschaft für dich gegeben. Es wäre

alles seine Schuld gewesen, sagte er, und es täte ihm leid.«

»Sonst noch was?«

»Ja. Wir sollten von nun an keine Angst mehr haben. Er hätte es begonnen und er würde es beenden. Und wir würden ihn nicht wiedersehen. Was meint er? Glaubst du, daß er sich freiwillig stellen will?«

»Weiß der Himmel!« Er legte eine Hand auf ihre eine Schulter. »Ich gehe kurz in die Kirche. Es wird nicht lange dauern.«

Pater da Costa eilte in die Kirche um zu beten, aber im tiefsten Innern spürte er, daß er nichts bedauerte. Und was noch viel schlimmer war: Eine winzige Stimme in ihm raunte, daß er der Menschheit einen Gefallen tun würde, wenn er Jack Meehan vom Erdboden fegte.

Meehan trat aus dem Badezimmer, einen seidenen Kimono an einen Eisbeutel ans Gesicht drückend. Der Arzt war gegangen, die Blutung war gestillt, aber seine Nase war ein häßlicher geschwollener zerquetschter Fleischklumpen. Donner, Bonati und Rupert warteten ergeben an der Tür. Donners Unterlippe war zweimal so dick wie gewöhnlich.

Meehan warf den Eisbeutel durch den Raum. »Taugt überhaupt nichts, das Zeug. Jemand soll mir einen Drink bringen.«

Rupert eilte zur Getränkebar, goß einen großen Brandy ein und brachte ihn Meehan, der am Fenster stand. Plötzlich wandte sich Meehan um und war wieder ganz er selbst.

»Frank, wie hieß doch dieser Knabe, der so gut mit Sprengstoff umzugehen wußte?« fragte er Donner.

»Ellerman, Mr. Meehan. Meinen Sie den?«

»Genau. Er sitzt nicht, oder?«

»Nicht, daß ich wüßte.«

»Gut. Dann möchte ich, daß er innerhalb der nächsten Stunde hier ist. Sag ihm, daß zweihundert Dollar für ihn drin sind.«

Er trank von seinem Brandy und wandte sich Rupert zu. »Und für dich, mein Schatz, habe ich auch einen Job. Du kannst Jenny besuchen. Wir werden sie brauchen bei dem, was ich vorhabe.«

»Glaubst du, daß sie mitspielt? Sie kann ein schreckliches Weibsstück sein, wenn sie nicht mag.«

»Diesmal nicht.« Meehan gluckste. »Du wirst mit einem Angebot von mir kommen, das sie nicht ablehnen kann.«

Er lachte, und Rupert sah unsicher zu Donner hinüber.

Donner fragte vorsichtig: »Wozu das alles, Mr. Meehan?«

»Ich habe genug«, zischte Meehan. »Vom Priester, Fallon und der ganzen Geschichte. Ich werde ein für allemal reinen Tisch machen. Noch diese Nacht.«

Harvey Ellerman war fünfzig Jahre, sah aber zehn Jahre älter aus, wahrscheinlich weil er alles in allem zweiundzwanzig Jahre seines Lebens hinter Gittern verbracht hatte. Er war ein kleiner schüchterner Mann, der gewöhnlich eine Tweed-Mütze und einen braunen Regenmantel trug. Doch dieser ängstlich aussehende Mann stand in dem Ruf, der beste Sprengstoffexperte von ganz Nordengland zu sein. Seine Genialität hatte sich letztlich jedoch als sein Verderben erwiesen. Seine Einzigartigkeit hatte ihn jedesmal verraten, als hätte er seinen Namen hinterlassen, und lange Jahre hindurch verhaftete ihn die Polizei mit monotoner Regelmäßigkeit.

Er trat aus dem Lift der Dachterrassenwohnung, in

einer Hand einen billigen Vulkanfiber-Koffer, der mit einem Lederriemen zusammengehalten wurde. Meehan ging ihm mit ausgestreckter Hand entgegen, und Ellerman setzte den Koffer ab.

»Eine Freude, dich zu sehen, Harvey!« sagte Meehan. »Ich hoffe, du wirst uns helfen können. Hat dir Frank schon erklärt, um was es geht?«

»Ja, Mr. Meehan.« Ellerman zögerte. »Sie wünschen doch nicht meinen persönlichen Einsatz bei dieser Sache?«

»Natürlich nicht«, beruhigte ihn Meehan.

Ellerman sah erleichtert aus. »Ich habe mich nämlich von jeglicher aktiven Beteiligung distanziert, Mr. Meehan. Sie wissen ja, warum.«

»O ja, Harvey. Du warst zu verdammt gut für sie.« Er legte Ellermans Koffer auf den Tisch. »Na, was hast du mitgebracht?«

Ellerman öffnete den Koffer. Er enthielt ein ganzes Sortiment verpackter Sprengsätze, Zünder, Sprengkapseln, Drahtknäuel und Werkzeuge.

»Frank sagte mir, daß Sie etwas Ähnliches wollen, wie die IRA in Irland verwendet hat.«

»Nicht ähnlich, Harvey – ich möchte genau dasselbe. Wenn die Jungens von der Spurensicherung die Reste der Bombe untersuchen, möchte ich nicht, daß auch nur der leiseste Zweifel besteht, aus welcher Richtung das Ding kommt.«

»In Ordnung, Mr. Meehan«, sagte Ellerman mit seiner farblosen Stimme. »Wie Sie wünschen.«

Nachdem er Meehan kurz über sein Projekt informiert hatte, machte er sich an die Arbeit.

Meehan stellte sich ans Fenster und pfiff fröhlich vor sich hin.

14

Fallon wachte auf und merkte, daß Jenny ihn an den Schultern rüttelte.

»Wach auf! Wach auf!« sagte sie immer wieder.

Er fühlte sich seltsam benommen, und hinter seinem rechten Auge registrierte er einen leichten, hartnäckig klopfenden Schmerz. Er setzte sich auf, schwang die Beine aus dem Bett und fuhr sich mit den Händen über das stoppelige Kinn.

»Wie spät ist es?« fragte er.

»Gegen vier. Dein Freund, Pater da Costa, hat angerufen. Er möchte dich gern sehen.«

Fallon runzelte leicht verwirrt die Stirn. »Wann rief er an?«

»Etwa vor zehn Minuten. Ich wollte dich holen, aber er sagte, er könnte nicht warten.«

»Und wo will er mich sehen? In *Holy Name*?«

Sie schüttelte den Kopf. »Nein. Er sagte, er würde seine Nichte aufs Land bringen. Er glaubt, sie wäre dort sicherer. Ein kleines Nest – Grimsdyke genannt. Etwa zwanzig Meilen von hier in der Marsch. Er möchte dich dort möglichst bald treffen.«

Fallon fragte: »Weißt du, wo das ist?«

Sie nickte. »Als ich noch ein Kind war, sind wir oft zum Picknick dort hingefahren. Bei dem *Mill House* bin ich allerdings nie gewesen, aber er hat mir gesagt, wie ich es finde.«

»Und du würdest mich hinbringen?«

»Wenn du es gern möchtest. Wir könnten mit meinem Wagen fahren. Wir brauchen nicht viel mehr als eine halbe Stunde bis dorthin.«

Er starrte sie an, ausdruckslos, die Augen sehr dunkel.

Sie blickte nervös zur Seite, wurde rot. Ärgerlich sagte sie: »Hör zu, es ist nicht mein Bier. Willst du hin oder nicht?«

Er wußte, daß sie log, aber er war todsicher, daß sie ihn an das richtige Ziel bringen würde.

»Gut«, sagte er. »Ich will mich nur rasch frischmachen. Wir treffen uns unten.«

Sobald Jenny gegangen war, holte er die Ceska aus seiner Jackentasche, lud sie mit acht Patronen nach und steckte sie in die rechte Tasche seines Trenchcoats. Dann ging er zum Fenster, hob den Teppich etwas an und zog die Browning Automatic heraus. Darunter lag ein großer, dicker Briefumschlag, der das meiste der zweitausend Pfund in Zehn-Pfund-Noten enthielt. Er steckte den Umschlag in seine Brusttasche und überprüfte rasch den Browning. In dem Schränkchen über dem Waschbecken fand er eine Rolle Heftpflaster. Er schnitt mit dem Rasiermesser ein paar Lagen ab, heftete den Browning an die Innenseite seines linken Beines, direkt über dem Sprungbein, und verdeckte ihn mit dem Socken.

Während er hinunterging, knöpfte er seinen Trenchcoat zu. Jenny wartete in einem roten Gummiregenmantel. Sie lächelte verkrampft und zog Handschuhe an.

Er öffnete die Haustür und hielt sie an der Schulter zurück, als sie hinausgehen wollte. »Du hast mir nicht irgendwas zu erzählen vergessen?«

Sie wurde rot, und ihre Stimme klang wieder ärgerlich. »Wäre es denn wahrscheinlich, daß ich so etwas tue?«

Er lächelte. »Dann sollten wir jetzt fahren.«

Der Mini-Cooper parkte am Straßenrand.

Die Marsch bei Grimsdyke an der Flußmündung war eine wildromantische einsame Landschaft, die etwas Gespenstisches hatte, eine fremde Welt, hauptsächlich von Vögeln bewohnt, die den Winter über aus dem Süden Sibiriens hierherzogen.

Sie fuhren durch das Dorf. Dreißig oder vierzig Häuser, eine Tankstelle, ein Pub – dann waren sie durch. Es regnete ziemlich stark. Der Wind jagte Wolkenberge über die Marsch.

»Eine halbe Meile nach dem Dorf rechts.« Jenny sah kurz zu Fallon hinüber. »Das hat er gesagt.«

»Hier scheint's zu sein«, murmelte Fallon.

Sie bogen von der Hauptstraße ab und fuhren einen schmalen erhöhten Grasdamm entlang. Zu beiden Seiten wogten meilenweit Sumpfgras und Schilf, und der Wind trieb feine Nebelfetzen vom Meer herein.

Fallon kurbelte das Fenster an seiner Seite herunter und atmete tief die prickelnde Salzluft ein. »Ein verdammt schönes Plätzchen!«

»Als Kind liebte ich diese Gegend«, sagte sie. »Es ist eine ganz andere Welt, wenn man aus der Stadt kommt.«

Je mehr sie sich der Flußmündung näherten, um so dichter schien sie der Nebel einzuhüllen. Als sie auf eine kleine Anhöhe kamen, sahen sie etwa hundert Meter südlich aus einer Baumgruppe etwas aufragen. Das mußte die Mühle sein.

Fallon legte eine Hand auf ihren Arm, und sie hielt an.

»Wir werden von hier ab zu Fuß gehen«, sagte er.

»Ist das notwendig?«

»Wenn ich etwas im Leben gelernt habe, dann: niemals etwas unbesehen zu akzeptieren.«

Sie stieg wortlos aus, und Fallon verließ die Fährte und durchquerte mit ihr eine Tannenschonung. Schließlich kroch er hinter einen Busch, zog Jenny zu sich herunter und inspizierte die Gegend. Er sah einen dreistökkigen Stein-Turm, oben offen. An der einen Seite davon eine Art Holzscheune, die in einem besseren Zustand zu sein schien als der Rest. Ein dünner Rauchfaden wehte aus einem Eisen-Schornstein. Auf der anderen Seite drehte sich, gespenstisch knarrend und stöhnend, ein riesiges Wasserrad.

»Sein Mini-Caravan ist nirgends zu sehen«, sagte Fallon leise.

»Er wird ihn in der Scheune stehen haben«, meinte Jenny und fügte ungeduldig hinzu: »Um Himmels willen, entschließ dich endlich! Gehen wir weiter oder nicht? Ich werde klitschnaß.«

Sie schien ärgerlich, doch er bemerkte das Zittern ihrer linken Hand.

»Geh vor!« sagte er. »Und ruf mich, wenn die Luft rein ist!«

Sie musterte ihn, hob dann die Schultern, stand auf und steuerte auf die Scheune zu. Am Tor drehte sie sich einmal um, dann öffnete sie es und verschwand im Innern.

Einen Moment später erschien sie wieder und rief: »Alles in Ordnung! Komm!«

Fallon zögerte noch einen Moment und trat dann auf die Lichtung hinaus, ein leicht starres Lächeln um den Mund. Als er bis auf vier oder fünf Meter herangekommen war, sagte Jenny: »Sie sind da.«

Damit kehrte sie in die Scheune zurück, und er folgte ihr.

Es roch nach altem Heu und Mäusen. In einer Ecke stand ein klappriger Karren, und über drei Seiten lief ein großer Heuboden mit runden glaslosen Fenstern, durch die Licht hereinfiel. In einem alten Eisen-Ofen in der Ecke knisterte ein Feuer.

Pater da Costa und Anna waren nicht zu sehen, doch

Fallon hatte sie auch nicht hier vermutet. Jenny lehnte an der Wand gegenüber, neben einem schmalen eisernen Feldbett stehend, auf dem ein kleines blondhaariges Mädchen offensichtlich schlief.

»Es tut mir leid, Martin«, sagte sie unglücklich. »Ich hatte keine Wahl.«

»Hände hoch, Fallon!« rief eine Stimme.

Fallon blickte nach oben und sah Donner am Rande des Heubodens, ein Armalite-Gewehr in Händen. Rupert stand neben ihm mit einer abgesägten Schrotflinte, und der Barkeeper aus dem *Bull and Bell* tauchte auf der anderen Seite des Heubodens auf, irgendeinen Revolver in der Rechten.

Donner hob das Gewehr etwas an. »Man hat mir gesagt, daß eine Kugel aus einem solchen Ding einen Körper durchschlägt und ein beachtliches Stück Fleisch des Betreffenden mit auf den Weg nimmt. Also rate ich dir, brav stillzustehen.«

»Oh, das werde ich«, versicherte Fallon ironisch und hob die Hände hoch.

Harry stieg als erster die Leiter herunter. Er sah schrecklich aus. Sein linkes Auge war total zugeschwollen und die eine Gesichtshälfte böse zugerichtet. Er blieb ein oder zwei Meter vor Fallon stehen, während Rupert herabstieg, und als sie beide ihre Stellungen bezogen hatten, schloß sich Donner ihnen an.

»Trau niemals einem Weib, Schätzchen«, sagte Rupert mit einem mokanten Lächeln. »Unverläßliche Flittchen – die meisten von ihnen. Ich zum Beispiel…«

Donner trat nach seinen Beinen. »Halt's Maul und filz ihn! Er hat vermutlich das Schießeisen in der rechten Tasche.«

Rupert fand die Ceska auf Anhieb und auch den dicken Umschlag mit dem Geld.

Donner sah in den Umschlag, pfiff durch die Zähne und fragte: »Wieviel?«

»Zweitausend«, sagte Fallon.

Donner grinste. »Das ist wohl das, was man unter einem unerwarteten Bonus versteht.«

Er steckte den Umschlag in seine Innentasche, und Rupert begann Fallons Körper abzutasten.

»Bezaubernd«, säuselte er. »Ich könnte mich wirklich in dich verknallen, mein Schätzchen.« Und er tätschelte Fallons Wangen.

Fallon stieß ihn zurück, daß er taumelte. »Wenn du mich noch einmal anfaßt, breche ich dir das Genick!«

Ruperts Augen funkelten. Er nahm die abgesägte Schrotflinte auf und spannte den Hahn. »Du meine Güte, sind wir nicht das Weibchen, das die männliche Rolle spielen möchte? Na, das kriegen wir schon hin.«

Donner trat ihm in den Hintern. »Du verdammter dämlicher kleiner Homo! Willst du alles verderben?« Er schubste ihn wütend beiseite. »Hau ab und mach Tee! Zu was anderem taugst du ja nicht.«

Rupert trottete mürrisch zum Ofen, und Donner holte Polizeihandschellen aus einer seiner Taschen. Er ließ sie um Fallons Handgelenke zuschnappen, schloß sie ab und ließ den Schlüssel in seine Brusttasche gleiten.

»Du kannst die harte Tour haben oder die weiche. Mir ist es einerlei. Verstanden?«

»Ich bemühe mich«, sagte Fallon.

»Gut. Geh und setz dich neben das Mädchen, damit ich euch beide im Auge habe!«

Fallon ging zu dem Feldbett und setzte sich daneben, mit dem Rücken gegen die Wand gelehnt. Er betrachtete das Kind. Es atmete ruhig.

»Die Tochter – von der du mir erzählt hast? Fehlt ihr nichts?«

»Sie haben ihr nur ein Beruhigungsmittel gegeben.« Jennys Augen schwammen in Tränen. »Es tut mir so leid, Martin. Ich holte sie nach dem Lunch ab, wie jeden Sonnabend, und brachte sie zum Spielplatz im Stadtpark. Dort haben Rupert und dieser Wurm Harry uns aufgelauert.«

»Und sie haben dich bedroht?«

»Sie haben gesagt, daß sie sich an Sally halten würden. Und daß ich sie zurückhaben könnte, wenn es mir gelingt, dich hier herauszulocken. Was hätte ich tun sollen? Du kennst Jack Meehan nicht so wie ich. Er ist zu allem fähig – genau wie Billy.«

»Billy wird dich nie mehr belästigen«, sagte Fallon. »Ich habe ihn letzte Nacht umgebracht.«

Sie starrte ihn mit aufgerissenen Augen an.

»Und ebenso beabsichtige ich, Dandy Jack zu töten«, fuhr er ruhig fort. »In meiner linken Jackentasche steckt ein Päckchen Zigaretten. Bist du ein gutes Mädchen und zündest mir eine an?«

Sie schien fassungslos über das eben Gehörte, kam aber seiner Aufforderung nach und steckte ihm eine Zigarette in den Mund. Als sie ein Streichholz anriß, trat Donner zu ihnen, eine karierte Tasche in der einen Hand. Er ging vor Fallon in die Hocke und zog den Reißverschluß der Tasche auf. Nacheinander brachte er drei Flaschen irischen Whisky zum Vorschein, die er auf den Boden vor ihn stellte.

»*Jameson*«, sagte Fallon. »Meine Lieblingsmarke. Wie kamst du drauf?«

»Sind alle für dich. Alle drei Flaschen.«

»Ich muß sagen, das hört sich interessant an. Erzähl weiter!«

»Die Idee ist tatsächlich sehr gut. Ich glaube, sie wird dir gefallen. Wir haben drei Probleme: den Priester, seine Nichte ...«

»… und mich«, vollendete Fallon.

»Genau.« Donner angelte sich eine Zigarette. »Mr. Meehan hat also folgende ausgesprochen hübsche Idee. Sie ist herrlich einfach. Wir werden da Costa und seine Nichte los und schieben dir die Schuld in die Schuhe.«

»Verstehe«, sagte Fallon. »Und wie soll das vor sich gehen?«

»Du warst ein As mit der Bombe in der Hand – drüben, in Ulster, nicht wahr? Also wird es nur natürlich erscheinen, wenn du hier genauso verfährst, um jemanden loszuwerden.«

»Mein Gott!« stöhnte Jenny.

Donner ignorierte sie. Offensichtlich machte ihm das Ganze Spaß. Er fuhr fort: »Um sechs Uhr ist Abendmesse in *Holy Name*. Gleich anschließend werden Meehan und Bonati Pater da Costa und seine Nichte auf den Turm hochbringen – zusammen mit etwa zwanzig Pfund Kunststoff-Gelatine-Dynamit, verpackt in einer Waverley-Keksbüchse und mit einem chemischen Zünder versehen. Wenn die Kleinigkeit hochgeht – genau zwanzig Minuten nachdem die Zündkapsel abgebrochen ist – werden sie mitgerissen, und die Kirche stürzt ein.«

»Und was ist mit mir?« fragte Fallon.

»Bonati fährt in da Costas Mini-Caravan hier raus. Man wird drei Flaschen irischen Whisky durch deine Kehle laufen lassen, dann setzen wir dich hinter das Lenkrad und schicken dich auf die Reise. Etwa drei Meilen von hier entfernt kommst du zu einem Berg – *Cullen's Bend*. Ein gräßlich unfallträchtiger Platz.«

»Und du glaubst, dadurch werden die Zusammenhänge verschleiert?«

»Wenn man das Autowrack untersucht, wird man Material finden, das zur Bombenherstellung benutzt wurde, und ein bißchen Gelatine-Dynamit – nicht zu vergessen die Kanone, mit der Krasko erledigt wurde. Die Jungens von der Spurensicherung werden einen Paradetag haben. Und seien wir doch offen: Das Sonderdezernat und der Geheimdienst sind seit Jahren hinter dir her. Sie werden entzückt sein.«

»Miller wird das keine Sekunde lang schlucken«, sagte Fallon. »Er weiß, daß Meehan hinter dem Krasko-Mord steckt.«

»Vielleicht. Aber er wird es nicht beweisen können.«

Jenny flüsterte: »Es ist Mord. Kaltblütiger Mord.«

»Halt dein Maul!« schnauzte Donner sie an.

Sie wich ängstlich zurück. Und plötzlich bemerkte sie etwas sehr Merkwürdiges. Fallons Augen schienen leicht die Farbe verändert zu haben, leuchteten auf, und als er zu ihr hochblickte, spürte sie die Kraft, die von ihm ausging. Als hätte er geschlafen und wäre nun wieder aufgewacht. Er sah zu den beiden anderen hinüber. Harry untersuchte den alten Karren, ihnen den Rücken zukehrend, Rupert stand neben dem Ofen, an der Schrotflinte herumfummelnd.

»Dann ist also nichts mehr zu machen?« fragte Fallon leise.

Donner schüttelte mit gespieltem Bedauern den Kopf. »Du hättest zu Hause bleiben sollen, Fallon. Das hier ist nicht deine Kragenweite.«

»So könnte es aussehen«, sagte Fallon.

Donner neigte sich vor, um sich noch eine Zigarette zu angeln. Fallon griff mit beiden Händen nach dem Kolben des Browning, zog ihn heraus und schoß Donner aus allernächster Nähe ins Herz. Die Wucht des Geschosses hob Donner hoch. Er knallte rückwärts auf den Boden, und im selben Moment schoß Fallon Harry in den Rücken, ehe dieser sich umdrehen konnte. Die Kugel zerschmetterte sein Rückgrat. Er fiel kopfüber in den Karren.

Jenny schrie. Fallon stieß sie zur Seite. Er stand jetzt. Der Browning schwenkte zu Rupert herum, der sich erschrocken umwandte – aber zu spät –, die Schrotflinte mit beiden Händen umklammernd. Sein Mund öffnete sich zu einem lautlosen Schrei. Fallons dritte Kugel traf ihn direkt in die Stirn. Blut und Gehirnmasse spritzte über den grauen Steinboden. Rupert wurde rückwärts gegen die Wand geschleudert. Sein Finger verkrampfte sich im Tod um den Hahn der Schrotflinte, deren beide Läufe sich entluden.

Jenny warf sich schützend über das Kind. Es war totenstill. Sie blickte ängstlich auf und sah, daß Fallon mit gespreizten Beinen dastand, vollkommen ruhig, ausbalanciert, den Browning mit beiden Händen vor sich haltend. Sein Gesicht war schneeweiß, ausdruckslos, die Augen waren sehr dunkel. Sein rechter Ärmel war zerrissen. Blut tropfte auf den Boden.

Sie kam unsicher auf die Beine. »Du bist verletzt.«

Er schien sie nicht zu hören, ging zu dem Karren, stieß Harry mit einem Fuß an. Dann steuerte er auf Rupert zu. Jenny folgte ihm.

»Ist er tot?« flüsterte sie.

Und dann sah sie den Hinterkopf und wandte sich ab. Ihr Magen hob sich, und sie mußte sich an der Wand stützen. Als sie sich wieder umdrehte, kniete Fallon neben Donner und fummelte in der Brusttasche des Toten herum. Er fand den gesuchten Schlüssel und stand auf.

»Befrei mich hiervon!«

Sie wankte benommen auf ihn zu, stolperte und wäre fast hingefallen.

Er faßte nach ihrem einen Arm und hielt sie fest. »Ruhig, Mädchen! Mach jetzt nicht schlapp! Ich brauche dich.«

»Ich bin in Ordnung«, sagte sie. »Wirklich.«

Sie schloß die Handschellen auf. Fallon schmiß die Dinger weg, fiel auf ein Knie nieder und holte den prallen Briefumschlag aus Donners Innentasche, aus einer anderen die Ceska.

Als er sich erhob, sagte Jenny schwach: »Du solltest mich deinen Arm anschauen lassen.«

»Na schön.«

Er zog auch seine Jacke aus und setzte sich auf die Bettkante, eine Zigarette rauchend, während sie ihn, so gut sie konnte, versorgte. Der Arm war zerfetzt. Die Schrotkugeln hatten drei oder vier häßliche Wunden ins Fleisch gerissen. Sie bandagierte ihn mit einem Taschentuch aus Donners Brusttasche. Fallon packte eine der Jameson-Flaschen, zog den Korken mit den Zähnen heraus und nahm einen großen Schluck.

Als sie fertig war, setzte sie sich neben ihn aufs Bett, und ihr Blick schweifte durch die Scheune. »Wie lange hat es gedauert? Zwei – vielleicht drei Sekunden.« Sie fröstelte. »Was für ein Mensch bist du, Martin?«

Fallon zog unbeholfen seine Jacke an. »Du hast Donner ja gehört. Ein kleiner Ire, der zu Hause hätte bleiben sollen.«

»Er hatte unrecht.«

»Wo ich herkomme, hätte er nicht einen Tag überlebt. Wie spät ist es?«

Sie sah auf ihre Uhr. »Fünf Uhr dreißig.«

»Gut.« Er stand auf und griff nach seinem Trenchcoat. »Die Abendmesse in *Holy Name* beginnt um sechs und endet gegen sieben. Bring mich jetzt dorthin.«

»Das Schiff – das von Hull ausläuft – ich hörte den Namen. Donner und Rupert sprachen darüber. Du könntest immer noch hin.«

»Ohne Paß?«

»Geld spricht für sich«, sagte sie. »Und du hast eine Menge davon in dem Umschlag da.«

Sie stand sehr nahe bei ihm, seinen Gürtel zuschnallend und zu ihm aufblickend.

Fallon sagte ruhig: »Ich vermute, daß du gern mit mir mitkommen möchtest.«

Sie schüttelte den Kopf. »Es ist zu spät für mich, noch ein neues Leben zu beginnen. Ich denke an *dich*.«

Fallon starrte sie lange düster an und sagte schließlich: »Nimm das Kind und komm!«

Er schritt auf die Tür zu. Jenny hob ihre Tochter hoch, wickelte sie in die Decke, die über ihr lag, und folgte Fallon. Er stand draußen, die Hände in den Taschen, zu den Wildgänsen emporblickend.

»Sie sind frei, und ich bin es nicht, Jenny. Begreifst du das?«

Als er seine rechte Hand aus der Tasche zog, tropfte Blut von seinen Fingern.

»Du brauchst einen Arzt«, sagte sie.

»Ich brauche Dandy Jack und sonst niemanden. Los, machen wir, daß wir von hier wegkommen.«

15

Meehan war zufrieden mit sich, zufrieden und erregt. Er trug eine Segeltuchreisetasche in der Rechten, in der die Bombe war. Sie spazierten am Rathaus vorbei und überquerten die Straße.

»Ich möchte doch zu gern wissen, wo unser Billy gerade steckt«, sagte er zu Bonati. »Dafür werde ich ihm den Arsch versohlen.«

»Sie wissen doch, wie es ist, wenn diese jungen Burschen mit einer Biene zusammen sind, Mr. Meehan«, sagte Bonati besänftigend. »Er wird schon auftauchen.«

»Dreckige kleine Nutten«, brummte Meehan angewidert. »Der Junge denkt an nichts weiter als an seinen Schwanz.«

Sie bogen in die Rockingham Street ein, und er bekam seinen ersten Schock, als er die Orgel spielen und die Gemeinde ein Lied anstimmen hörte.

Rasch drückte er sich in einen Hauseingang und zischte Bonati zu. »Was, zum Teufel, hat das zu bedeuten? Die Abendmesse beginnt doch um sechs, und es ist erst zehn vor?«

»Keine Ahnung, Mr. Meehan.«

Sie überquerten die Straße, sich gegen den Regenwind stemmend, und blieben vor dem Anschlagbrett stehen.

Bonati las laut: »*Abendmesse sechs Uhr, Sonnabend fünf Uhr dreißig.*«

Meehan fluchte leise. »Verdammt gut, daß wir zu früh dran sind. Komm, laß uns reingehen!«

Es war feuchtkalt in der Kirche und roch intensiv nach Kerzen. Etwa ein Dutzend Leute hatten sich versammelt. Pater da Costa stand betend vor dem Altar, Anna da Costa spielte auf der Orgel. Sie setzten sich hinter eine Säule. Die Segeltuchtasche stellte Meehan zwischen seine Beine. Es war wirklich sehr angenehm, hier in dem flackernden Dämmerlicht zu sitzen und dem Orgelspiel zu lauschen, dachte Meehan. Wehmutsvoll gedachte er seiner Jugend. Und plötzlich stellte er überrascht fest, daß er freudig und enthusiastisch die Liturgie mitsang und für seine Seele betete.

Als der Cooper über eine bucklige Brücke fuhr, setzte sich Fallon, dessen Kopf auf die Brust herabgesunken war, ruckartig auf.

»Wie geht es dir?« fragte Jenny ängstlich.

»Gut.«

Seine Stimme klang ruhig und beherrscht. Behutsam tastete er über seinen rechten Arm. Er begann jetzt höllisch zu schmerzen. Jenny bemerkte, wie er zusammenzuckte.

»Ich glaube, ich sollte dich schnurstracks ins Krankenhaus bringen.«

Er wandte sich nach dem Kind um, das auf dem Rücksitz lag, immer noch in seinem narkotischen Schlaf befangen.

»Sie ist ein hübsches Mädchen«, sagte er.

Der starke Regen und die hereinbrechende Dunkelheit machten die Fahrerei äußerst gefährlich. Die Straße erforderte ihre ganze Aufmerksamkeit. Doch etwas in seiner Stimme veranlaßte sie, kurz zur Seite zu schauen.

Er zündete sich eine Zigarette an und lehnte sich zurück. »Diese Kinder in dem Schulbus – du hast sicher davon gehört – das war ein Unfall – ein Irrtum.«

Er schlug mit der linken Faust auf sein rechtes Knie. Tränen füllten ihre Augen.

Die Gemeinde strömte aus der Kirche. Anna spielte weiter, und Pater da Costa ging mit den Ministranten in die Sakristei, wo sie sich umzogen. Er verabschiedete die Jungen am Seitenausgang. Anna spielte immer noch. Es war wieder Bach – ›Präludium und Fuge in D-Dur‹. Plötzlich hörte sie abrupt zu spielen auf. Da Costa wollte gerade sein Chorhemd anziehen. Er wartete, daß sie fortfuhr, aber es blieb still. Stirnrunzelnd öffnete er die Sakristeitür und trat in die Kirche hinaus.

Anna stand an den Chorschranken. Jack Meehan hatte ihren einen Arm gepackt.

Pater da Costa wollte ärgerlich auf Meehan zugehen,

da trat Bonati hinter einer Säule hervor, eine Luger in der Linken. Pater da Costa erstarrte.

Meehan lächelte. »So ist's recht. Jetzt werden wir alle gemeinsam eine kleine Fahrt zum Turm hoch machen. Da immer nur zwei in den Aufzug passen, werden wir uns aufteilen müssen. Ich halte mich an das Mädchen, Sie, Pater, fahren mit Bonati. Und merken Sie sich eines: Alles, was Sie unternehmen, wird sich in der Behandlung des Mädchens niederschlagen. Also keine Gewalttätigkeiten!«

»Gut, Mr. Meehan«, sagte da Costa. »Was wünschen Sie von mir?«

»Alles zu seiner Zeit.« Meehan stieß Anna auf den Lastenaufzug zu, öffnete die Tür und folgte ihr in den Förderkorb. Noch einmal sah er zu Pater da Costa hinaus. »Vergessen Sie nicht, was ich gesagt habe! Keine krummen Touren!«

Da Costa versuchte seine mörderische Wut unter Kontrolle zu bringen. Was wollte der Mann? Was sollte das alles? Als der Förderkorb wieder nach unten schwebte, stürzte er eifrig hinein. Bonati folgte ihm und drückte auf den Knopf.

Meehan hatte oben Licht gemacht. Die regennassen Laufplanken glitzerten.

Anna hielt sich mit einer Hand am Geländer fest. Grenzenlose Unsicherheit spiegelte sich in ihrem Gesicht. Da Costa machte einen Schritt auf sie zu, und Meehan zog seinen Browning.

»Bleiben Sie, wo Sie sind!« Er nickte Bonati zu. Fessele seine Handgelenke!«

Da Costa blieb nichts anderes übrig, als seine Hände auf den Rücken zu legen. Bonati band seine Handgelenke mit einer dünnen Schnur zusammen.

»Nun das Mädchen!« befahl Meehan.

Anna ließ schweigend die Prozedur über sich ergeben.

Ihr Onkel trat zu ihr und fragte leise: »Alles in Ordnung?«

»Ich denke schon. Was passiert mit uns?«

»Ich fürchte, diese Frage mußt du an Mr. Meehan richten.«

Meehan zog den Reißverschluß der Segeltuchtasche auf, faßte hinein, brach die Zündkapsel ab, zog den Reißverschluß wieder zu und stellte die Tasche beiseite ins Dunkle.

»Alsdann, Pater. Ich werde Sie und Ihre Nichte jetzt hier oben fünfzehn Minuten allein lassen – zum Meditieren. Wenn ich zurückkehre, sind Sie hoffentlich etwas vernünftiger geworden. Wenn nicht, dann …«

»Aber ich verstehe nicht«, unterbrach ihn da Costa. »Was in aller Welt versprechen Sie sich davon?«

In diesem Moment ertönten auf der Orgel unten die ersten Töne von Bachs ›Präludium und Fuge in D-Dur‹.

Meehans erstauntes Gesicht war sehenswert.

»Es ist Fallon«, murmelte er.

»Das kann nicht sein«, widersprach Bonati.

»Wen, zum Teufel, höre ich dann? Einen Geist? Geh und hol ihn rauf!« brüllte er, und der Zorn durchraste ihn wie ein heißer Lavastrom. »Bring den Bastard her! Und sag ihm, daß das Mädchen dran glauben muß, wenn er nicht kommt!«

Bonati betrat eilig den Förderkorb, schloß die Tür und fuhr nach unten. Als er auf halber Höhe war, hörte die Orgel zu spielen auf. Es war plötzlich sehr still. Der Käfig kam ratternd zum Stehen. Er spannte den Hahn der Luger, stieß die Tür auf und trat hinaus.

Als der Cooper in die Rockingham Street einbog und gegenüber von *Holy Name* stehenblieb, lehnte Fallon in der Ecke, die Augen geschlossen. Zuerst glaubte Jenny, er sei bewußtlos – oder zumindest eingeschlafen, doch als sie ihn sanft berührte, öffnete er augenblicklich die Augen und lächelte sie an.

»Wo sind wir?«

»*Holy Name.*«

Er atmete tief durch und richtete sich auf. »Gutes Mädchen.« Er griff in die Tasche seines Mantels, holte den prallen Umschlag hervor und überreichte ihn ihr. »Das sind fast zweitausend Pfund. Ich werde sie nicht brauchen – dort, wo ich hingehe. Nimm das Kind und versuch es noch mal. Geh irgendwohin – an einen Ort, von dem du zuvor noch nie gehört hast.«

Der Umschlag war glitschig. Blut klebte daran.

»O mein Gott!« stöhnte sie und knipste die Innenbeleuchtung an. »O Martin! Du bist voll mit Blut!«

»Das macht nichts.« Er öffnete die Autotür.

Sie stieg ebenfalls aus.

»Er wird dich umbringen«, sagte sie verzweifelt. »Du kennst ihn nicht so wie ich. Du hast keine Chance. Laß mich die Polizei holen! Überlaß ihn Mr. Miller!«

»Ich habe nie in meinem Leben einen Polizisten um Hilfe gebeten.« Ein leicht ironisches Lächeln umspielte flüchtig seinen Mund. »Zu spät, jetzt damit zu beginnen.« Er streichelte zärtlich über ihr Gesicht. »Du bist ein nettes Mädchen, Jenny. Ein liebes Mädchen. Das alles geht dich nichts an. Und jetzt hau ab! Und Gott segne dich!«

Er wandte sich um und überquerte die Straße. Jenny stieg in den Cooper und ließ den Motor an. Er ging in seinen Tod. Sie mußte ihn retten. Entschlossen fuhr sie um die Ecke, hielt bei der nächsten Telefonzelle, wählte 9–9–9 und verlangte Kriminal-Superintendent Miller.

Fallon registrierte verwirrt, daß keinerlei Musik aus der Kirche drang. Er sah auf das Anschlagebrett und machte dieselbe Entdeckung wie Jack Meehan. Panik erfaßte ihn. Die Pforte krachte gegen die Wand, so heftig hatte er sie aufgestoßen.

Die Kirche war leer. Er rannte zum Lastenaufzug. Der Korb war nicht unten. Sie waren also noch oben. Er drückte auf den Knopf, um den Korb herunterzuholen, aber nichts erfolgte, was bedeutete, daß die Tür oben offenstand. Aber es mußte doch einen Weg geben, Meehan herunterzulocken? Und es gab ihn auch. Natürlich. Die Idee war so herrlich einfach, daß er laut lachte.

Er steuerte auf die Chorschranken zu, stieg die Stufen zur Orgel empor, setzte sich an die Orgel, zog fieberhaft die Register und begann Bachs ›Präludium und Fuge in D-Dur‹ zu spielen. Blut tropfte auf die Tasten, aber das machte nichts. Er ignorierte den Schmerz in seinem rechten Arm und legte alles in sein Spiel, was er zu geben vermochte.

»Komm her, du Bastard!« schrie er laut. »Laß dich fertigmachen!«

Er unterbrach sein Spiel und vernahm augenblicklich das leise surrende Geräusch des Aufzugs. Langsam stand er auf, stieg die Stufen hinunter, zog die Ceska aus der Tasche, schraubte mühevoll mit einer Hand den Schalldämpfer auf den Lauf und stand genau in dem Moment am günstigsten Punkt, als der Korb unten ankam. Er drückte sich gegen die Wand und wartete.

Die Tür des Aufzugs wurde aufgestoßen. Bonati trat heraus, die Luger umklammernd. Fallon schoß ihm durch die Hand.

Bonati ließ die Luger mit einem spitzen Aufschrei fallen und wirbelte herum.

»Meehan – ist er dort oben?« fragte Fallon.

Bonati zitterte wie Espenlaub. Er versuchte zu sprechen, war aber nur fähig, nachdrücklich mit dem Kopf zu nicken.

»Gut.« Fallon lächelte. »Geh nach Hause und ändere dein Leben!«

Bonati brauchte keine zweite Aufforderung. Das Tor schlug hinter ihm zu, die Kerzenflammen flackerten.

Fallon trat in den Förderkorb und drückte auf den Knopf.

Oben warteten Meehan, Anna und da Costa. Der Aufzug hielt an. Die Tür schwang auf. Fallon stand noch im Dunkeln.

Meehan hob seinen Browning leicht an. »Bonati?«

Fallon trat ins Licht – ein bleiches Gespenst. »Hallo, Bastard!«

Meehan zielte. Pater da Costa duckte sich, schubste ihn mit der Schulter zum Geländer und stellte ihm so geschickt ein Bein, daß Meehan hinschlug. Der Browning schlitterte über die Planken, und Fallon stieß ihn in den Abgrund. Er lehnte sich ans Geländer, plötzlich seltsam müde. Sein Arm schmerzte jetzt sehr. Er gestikulierte mit der Ceska herum.

»Marsch, binden Sie ihn los!«

Meehan folgte zögernd.

Pater da Costa befreite anschließend Anna von ihren Fesseln und wandte sich besorgt an Fallon. »Sind Sie in Ordnung?«

Fallon konzentrierte sich ganz auf Meehan. »Die Bombe? Haben Sie sie gezündet?«

»Kümmern Sie sich um Ihren eigenen Dreck!« knurrte Meehan.

»Bombe?« echote Pater da Costa.

»Ja«, sagte Fallon. »Hatte er eine Tasche bei sich?«

»Dort drüben!« Pater da Costa deutete ins Dunkle.

»Gut«, sagte Fallon. »Sie sollten Anna rasch von hier

wegbringen, hören Sie? Wenn dieses Ding da losgeht, wird die ganze Kirche wie ein Kartenhaus zusammenfallen.«

Pater da Costa zögerte keine Sekunde. Er faßte Anna am Arm und führte sie zum Aufzug, aber sie riß sich los und wandte sich Fallon zu.

»Martin!« schrie sie und klammerte sich an seinen Mantel. »Wir können nicht ohne Sie gehen!«

»Es passen nur zwei in den Korb. Seien Sie vernünftig!«

Blut von seinem Ärmel klebte an ihrer Hand. Sie hielt sie nahe vors Gesicht, als ob sie versuchen wollte, es zu sehen.

»O mein Gott«, flüsterte sie.

Pater da Costa legte einen Arm um ihre Schultern und fragte Fallon: »Sind Sie verletzt?«

»Sie verlieren Zeit«, entgegnete Fallon ungeduldig.

Pater da Costa schob Anna in den Korb und folgte ihr. Er drückte auf den Knopf und rief durch die Stäbe: »Ich komme zurück, Martin! Warten Sie auf mich!«

Fallon wandte sich Meehan zu und lächelte. »Sie und ich, Jack – am Ende aller Dinge. Ist das nicht was? Wir können gemeinsam zur Hölle fahren.«

»Sie sind verrückt«, sagte Meehan. »Ich warte hier nicht auf meinen Tod. Ich werde mich dieses Dings da entledigen.«

Er steuerte auf die Tasche zu, und Fallon hob drohend die Ceska. »Ich habe Erfahrung – erinnern Sie sich? In diesem Stadium würde die Bombe bei der leisesten Berührung hochgehen.« Er lachte vor sich hin. »Wir werden es Gott überlassen. Wenn der Aufzug rechtzeitig zurückkommt, werden wir verschwinden. Wenn nicht …«

»Sie verdammter Wahnsinniger!« brüllte Meehan.

Fallon sagte ruhig: »Übrigens, mir fällt gerade ein, daß ich etwas für Sie habe.«

Er brachte eine zerknitterte schwarzumrandete weiße Karte zum Vorschein und hielt sie ihm hin.

Meehan fragte: »Was, zum Teufel, soll das denn sein?«

»Eine Ruhe-sanft-Karte. So bezeichneten Sie sie doch? Für Billy. Nummer 582. *Pine Trees.*«

»Sie lügen!«

Fallon schüttelte den Kopf. »Ich tötete ihn letzte Nacht, weil er versuchte, Anna da Costa zu vergewaltigen. Dann brachte ich ihn ins Krematorium und ließ ihn den Prozeß durchmachen, den Sie mir am Morgen vorgeführt hatten. Als ich Ihren Bruder das letztemal sah, war er fünf Pfund graue Asche.«

Meehan schien zu explodieren.

»Billy!« schrie er und warf sich mit eingezogenem Kopf auf Fallon.

Fallon zog den Abzug der Ceska durch. Meehan schmetterte ihn gegen das Geländer. Es splitterte und gab nach. Fallon stürzte in die Tiefe. Er landete auf der Zeltplane, die über das Loch im Kirchendach gespannt war, und segelte durch.

Meehan wandte sich um und griff nach der Tasche. Als er sie hochhob und sich umdrehte, um sie in die Dunkelheit hinauszuschleudern, explodierte sie.

Pater da Costa und Anna traten auf die Straße. Zwei Polizeiwagen kamen angebraust. Miller hechtete aus dem ersten und stürmte auf sie zu. Als er den Fuß auf die erste Stufe zum Portal setzte, explodierte die Bombe. Die ganze Kirche begann in sich zusammenzufallen – fast im Zeitlupentempo.

Miller packte Annas anderen Arm, und gemeinsam mit Pater da Costa zerrte er sie über die Straße. Als sie die Autos erreichten, prallte eine Gerüststange von der Wand des Lagerhauses ab, und alle gingen zu Boden.

Pater da Costa war als erster wieder auf den Beinen. Die Hände zu Fäusten geballt, blickte er zur Kirche empor. Als sich die Staubwolke setzte, sah er, daß die Wände zum großen Teil noch standen.

Ein junger Polizist rannte aus einem der Polizeiwagen auf sie zu, eine Scheinwerferlampe in Händen haltend.

Pater da Costa nahm sie ihm ab und wandte sich Miller zu. »Ich gehe hinein.«

Miller hielt ihn am Arm zurück. »Sie müssen verrückt sein!«

»Fallon war drinnen. Er hat uns gerettet. Vielleicht ist er noch am Leben. Ich muß es wissen.«

»Fallon?« wiederholte Miller verblüfft. »Mein Gott, dann war es also Fallon die ganze Zeit!«

Pater da Costa lief die Stufen zum Portal empor und stieß die Tür auf. Das Bild, das sich ihm bot, war niederschmetternd. Am schlimmsten zerstört war der Turm. Pater da Costa schritt das Hauptschiff entlang. Vor dem Altar hatte sich ein Berg aus Backsteinen und Mörtel gebildet – die Überreste des Turms und des Daches. Das Scheinwerferlicht erfaßte etwas, das ein Gesicht sein konnte.

Da Costa sank auf Hände und Knie und kroch durch eine Art Tunnel, der entstanden war. Er fand Fallon am Ende des Tunnels. Nur sein Kopf und seine Schultern lagen frei. Das große Kreuz Christi, das neben dem Altar gestanden hatte, war auf ihn gefallen und schützte ihn für den Moment.

Pater da Costa kauerte sich neben ihn und das Kreuz senkte sich etwas unter dem auf ihm lastenden Gewicht. Mörtel rieselte herab.

»Martin? Können Sie mich hören?« fragte er.

Hinter sich vernahm er scharrende Geräusche. Miller war ihm gefolgt.

»Um Himmels willen, Pater, wir müssen hier raus! Der ganze verdammte Mist kann jeden Moment in sich zusammensacken.«

Pater da Costa ignorierte ihn. »Martin?«

Fallon öffnete die Augen. »Haben Sie Anna herausgebracht?«

»Ja, Martin.«

»Das ist gut. Es tut mir leid. Alles.«

Das Kreuz senkte sich noch ein bißchen mehr. Steine und Geröll regneten auf da Costas Rücken. Er beugte sich schützend über Fallon.

»Martin, können Sie mich hören?«

Fallon öffnete wieder die Augen.

»Ich möchte, daß Sie bereuen. Sprechen Sie mir nach: O mein Gott, der du endlich gut bist ...«

»O mein Gott«, wiederholte Fallon und starb.

Aus irgendeinem seltsamen Grund hatte Miller plötzlich das Gefühl, kein Recht zu haben, hier zu sein. Er kroch zurück.

Hinter ihm begann Pater da Costa für die Seele des Mannes zu beten, der sich Martin Fallon genannt hatte.